Studies in Jewish and Christian Literature

Messiah and the Throne, Timo Eskola
Defilement and Purgation in the Book of Hebrews, William G. Johnsson
Father, Son, and Spirit in Romans 8, Ron C. Fay
Within the Veil, Félix H. Cortez
Jude's Apocalyptic Eschatology as Theological Exclusivism, William Wilson
Intertextuality and Prophetic Exegesis in the War Scroll of Qumran, César Melgar
The Past Is Yet to Come, Barbara Isbell
At the End of All Things, Jason P. Kees
Prophetic Patterns in the Passion of Jesus, Donald Lee Schmidt

Prophetic Patterns in the Passion of Jesus:
Typological Uses of Davidic Psalms by John and Luke

Prophetic Patterns in the Passion of Jesus: Typological Uses of Davidic Psalms by John and Luke

Donald Lee Schmidt

Fontes

Prophetic Patterns in the Passion of Jesus:
Typological Uses of Davidic Psalms by John and Luke

Copyright © 2023 by Donald Lee Schmidt

ISBN-13: 978-1-948048-82-8 (paperback)
ISBN-13: 978-1-948048-83-5 (hardback)

Scripture quotations taken from the (NASB®) New American Standard Bible®, Copyright © 1960, 1971, 1977, 1995 by The Lockman Foundation. Used by permission. All rights reserved. www.lockman.org.

All rights reserved. No part of this publication may be reproduced, stored in a retrieval system, or transmitted in any form or by any means—electronic, mechanical, photocopy, recording, or any other—except for brief quotations in printed reviews, without the prior permission of the publisher.

Typeset by Monolateral.

FONTES PRESS
DALLAS, TX
www.fontespress.com

To Melody, my beautiful wife and my best friend, who always encourages and supports me. I love being your husband.
And to my precious children, Titus, Truett, and Kinsley, who fill my life with joy. I love being your dad.

Contents

Abbreviations xi

1. Introduction 1
   Thesis 2
   Survey of Literature on the Psalms in the New Testament 4
      Non-Typological Hermeneutical Conclusions 5
      Typological Hermeneutical Conclusions 8
      Methodology 12

2. Clarifying Traditional Typology 15
   Traditional Typology: Definition, Description, and Illustration 15
      Definition and Description of Traditional Typology 16
      Typology as Prospective/Predictive Prophecy 19
      Typology As Correspondence 24
      Illustration of Traditional Typology 26
   Traditional Typology: Comparison with the Modern View 28
   Traditional Typology: Principles for Exegetical Control 34
   Summary 37

3. Biblical and Historical Evidence in Support of Traditional Typology 39
   Biblical Evidence in Support of Traditional Typology 39
      Jesus' Teachings and Examples 40
      Typology in the Epistle of Hebrews 43
      Fulfillment Language 44
      Hermeneutical Τύπος Language 50
      The OT Basis of Typology 53
   Historical Evidence in Support of Traditional Typology 54
      Patristic Era 54
      Reformation Era 58
   Summary 62

4. Prophetic David Typology in John 63
   Ps 41:9 in John 13:18 63
      Correspondence in the David-Jesus Typology 64
      Prophecy in the David-Jesus Typology 70
   Ps 69:4 in John 15:25 77
      Correspondence in the David-Jesus Typology 78
      Prophecy in the David-Jesus Typology 82
   Ps 22:18 in John 19:24 84
      Correspondence in the David-Jesus Typology 85
      Prophecy in the David-Jesus Typology 92
   Ps 69:21 in John 19:28 97
      Correspondence in the David-Jesus Typology 98
      Prophecy in the David-Jesus Typology 103
   Summary 106

5. Prophetic David Typology in Acts 109
   Pss 69:25 and 109:8 in Acts 1:20 109
      The David-Jesus Typology: The Element of Correspondence 111
      The David-Jesus Typology: The Element of Prophecy 119
   Ps 16:8–11 in Acts 2:25–28 124
      The David-Jesus Typology: The Element of Correspondence 126
      The David-Jesus Typology: The Element of Prophecy 135
   Ps 110:1 in Acts 2:34–35 140
      The David-Jesus Typology: The Element of Correspondence 141
      The David-Jesus Typology: The Element of Prophecy 149
   Ps 2:1–2 in Acts 4:25–26 151
      The David-Jesus Typology: The Element of Correspondence 152
      The David-Jesus Typology: The Element of Prophecy 159
   Summary 162

6. Conclusion 165
   Review of Chapters 1 to 5 166
   Comparing John and Acts 168
   Implications of Study 170
   Suggestions for Further Research 171

Bibliography 173

Index 193

Abbreviations

AB	Anchor Bible
ACNT	Augsburg Commentary on the New Testament
AGJU	Arbeiten zur Geschichte des antiken Judentums und des Urchristentums
ANTC	Abingdon New Testament Commentaries
AUSDDS	Andrews University Seminary Doctoral Dissertation Series
BBC	Broadman Bible Commentary
BCOTWP	Baker Commentary on the Old Testament Wisdom and Psalms
BDAG	Bauer, Walter, Frederick W. Danker, William F. Arndt, and F. Wilbur Gingrich. *Greek-English Lexicon of the New Testament and Other Early Christian Literature.* 3rd ed. Chicago: University of Chicago Press, 2000. BibleWorks 9
BDB	Brown, Francis, S. R. Driver, and Charles A. Briggs. *A Hebrew and English Lexicon of the Old Testament.* Oxford: Clarendon Press, 1907. BibleWorks 9
BDF	Blass, Friedrich, Albert Debrunner, and Robert. W. Funk. *A Greek Grammar of the New Testament and Other Early Christian Literature.* Chicago: University of Chicago Press, 1961
BECNT	Baker Exegetical Commentary on the New Testament
BETL	Bibliotheca Ephemeridum Theologicarum Lovaniensium
BHS	*Biblia Hebraica Stuttgartensia.* 4th rev. ed. Edited by E. Elliger and W. Rudolph. Stuttgart: Deutsche Bibelgesellschaft, 1990. BibleWorks 9
BNTC	Black's New Testament Commentaries

BR	*Biblical Research*
BS	Biblical Series
BSac	*Bibliotheca Sacra*
BTNT	Biblical Theology of the New Testament
BZ	*Biblische Zeitschrift*
CBC	Cambridge Bible Commentary
CBET	Contributions to Biblical Exegesis and Theology
CBQ	*Catholic Biblical Quarterly*
CNTC	Calvin's New Testament Commentaries
CNTUOT	Commentary on the New Testament Use of the Old Testament
CQR	*Church Quarterly Review*
CTJ	*Calvin Theological Journal*
CTM	*Concordia Theological Monthly*
DBI	*Dictionary of Biblical Imagery*. Edited by Leland Ryken, James C. Wilhoit, Tremper Longmann III. Downers Grove: IL: InterVarsity Press, 1998
DJG	*Dictionary of Jesus and the Gospels*. Edited by Joel B. Green, Scot McKnight, I. Howard Marshall. Downers Grove: IL: InterVarsity Press, 1992
DOTP	*Dictionary of the Old Testament Prophets*. Edited by Mark J. Boda and J. Gordon McConville. Downers Grove, IL: InterVarsity Press, 2012
DOTWPW	*Dictionary of the Old Testament: Wisdom, Poetry, & Writings*. Edited by Tremper Longman III and Peter Enns. Downers Grove: IL: InterVarsity Press, 2008
DSD	*Dead Sea Discoveries*
DTIB	*Dictionary for Theological Interpretation of the Bible*. Edited by Keven J. Vanhoozer. Grand Rapids: Baker Academic, 2005
EBC	The Expositor's Bible Commentary
ECB	The Evangelical Commentary on the Bible
EDNT	*Exegetical Dictionary of the New Testament.* Edited by Horst Balz and Gerhard Schneider. ET. 3 vols. Grand Rapids: Eerdmans, 1990–1993
EJT	*European Journal of Theology*
EKKNT	Egangelisch-katholischer Kommentar zum Neuen Testament
ESV	English Standard Version

EvQ	*Evangelical Quarterly*
ExpTim	*Expository Times*
FAT	Forschungen zum Alten Testament
FG	Fourth Gospel
GKC	*Gesenius' Hebrew Grammar*. Edited by Emil Kautzsch. Translated by Arther E. Cowley. 2nd ed. Oxford: Clarendon Press, 1910; Repr. Mineola, NY: Dover Publication, 2006
GNT	Grundrisse zum Neuen Testament
GNTE	Guides to New Testament Exegesis
GTJ	*Grace Theological Journal*
HALOT	*The Hebrew and Aramaic Lexicon of the Old Testament*. L. Koehler, W. Baumgartner, and J. J. Stamm. Translated and edited under the supervision of Mervyn E. J. Richardson. 5 vols. Leiden: Brill, 1994–2000. BibleWorks 9
HCSB	Holman Christian Standard Bible
HNT	Handbuch zum Neuen Testament
IBHS	*An Introduction to Biblical Hebrew Syntax*. Bruce K. Waltke and Michael O'Connor. Winona Lake, IN: Eisenbrauns, 1990
ICC	International Critical Commentary
Int	*Interpretation*
ISBE	*International Standard Bible Encyclopedia*. Edited by Geoffrey W. Bromiley. 4 vols. Fully Revised. Grand Rapids: Eerdmans, 1979–1988
IVPNTCS	IVP New Testament Commentary Series
JBL	*Journal of Biblical Literature*
JETS	*Journal of the Evangelical Theological Society*
Joüon	Joüon, Paul and T. Muraoka. *A Grammar of Bible Hebrew: Third Reprint of Second Edition, with Corrections*. SubBi 27. Rome: Gregorian & Biblical Press, 2011
JSNT	*Journal for the Study of the New Testament*
JSNTSup	Journal for the Study of the New Testament: Supplement Series
JSOT	*Journal for the Study of the Old Testament*
JSOTSup	Journal for the Study of the Old Testament: Supplement Series
KEK	Kritisch-exegetischer Kommentar über das Neue Testament
KEL	Kregel Exegetical Library
LD	Lectio Divina

Louw-Nida	Louw, J. P. and E. A. Nida. *Greek-English Lexicon of the New Testament.* 2nd ed. New York: United Bible Societies, 1988. BibleWorks 9
LXX	*Septuaginta.* Edited by Alfred Rahlfs. Stuttgart: Württembergische Bibelanstalt/Deutsche Bibelgesellschaft, 1935. BibleWorks 9
MNTC	Moffatt New Testament Commentary
MT	Masoretic Text
NA27	*Novum Testamentum Graece.* Nestle-Aland 27th ed. Edited by Kurt Aland, Barbara Aland, Erwin Nestle, and Ebherhard Nestle. Stutgart: Deutsch Bibelgesellschaft, 1993. BibleWorks 9
NAC	New American Commentary
NASB	New American Standard Bible
NCB	New Clarendon Bible
NCCS	New Covenant Commentary Series
NCBC	New Century Bible Commentary
NDT	*New Dictionary of Theology.* Edited by Sinclair B. Ferguson, David F. Wright, and J. I. Packer. Downers Grove, IL: Intervarsity Press, 1988
NIBC	New International Biblical Commentary
NICNT	New International Commentary on the New Testament
NIDNTT	*New International Dictionary of New Testament Theology.* Edited by Colin Brown. 4 vols. Grand Rapids: Zondervan, 1975–1978
NIGTC	New International Greek Testament Commentary
NIV	New International Version
NIVAC	NIV Application Commentary
NovT	*Novum Testamentum*
NovTSup	Supplements to Novum Testamentum
NT	New Testament
NTD	Das Neue Testament Deutsch
NTS	*New Testament Studies*
OT	Old Testament
PNTC	Pillar New Testament Commentary
ResQ	*Restoration Quarterly*
RevExp	Review and Expositor
RevScRel	*Revue des sciences religieuses*

RHPR	*Revue d'histoire et de philosophie religieuses*
RSV	Revised Standard Version
RTR	*Reformed Theological Review*
SBLDS	Society of Biblical Literature Dissertation Series
SBS	Stuttgarter Biblestudien
SBT	Studies in Biblical Theology
ScEs	*Science et esprit*
SK	*Skrif en kerk*
SNT	Studien zum Neuen Testament
SP	Sacra Pagina
SPHS	Scholars Press Homage Series
SSEJC	Studies in Scripture in Early Judaism and Christianity
SubBi	Subsidia Biblica
SwJT	*Southwestern Journal of Theology*
TDNT	*Theological Dictionary of the New Testament.* Edited by Gerhard Kittel and Gerhard Friedrich. Translated by Geoffrey W. Bromiley. 10 vols. Grand Rapids: Eerdmans, 1964–1976
Thayer's	*A Greek-English Lexicon of the New Testament.* Translated, revised, and enlarged by Joseph H. Thayer. 1889. Repr., International Bible Translators, 1998–2000. BibleWorks 9
THOTC	Two Horizons Old Testament Commentary
ThTo	*Theology Today*
TJ	*Trinity Journal*
TKNT	Theologischer Kommentar zum Neuen Testament
TLNT	*Theological Lexicon of the New Testament.* C. Spicq. Translated and edited by J. D. Ernest. 3 vols. Peabody, MA: Hendrickson, 1994
TLOT	*Theological Lexicon of the Old Testament.* Edited by Ernst Jenni and Claus Westermann. Translated by Mark E. Biddle. 3 vols. Peabody, MA: Hendrickson, 1997
TLZ	*Theologische Literaturzeitung*
TNTC	Tyndale New Testament Commentaries
TOTC	Tyndale Old Testament Commentaries
TWNT	*Theologicsches Wörterbuch zum Neuen Testament.* Edited by Gerhard Kittel and Gerhard Friedrich. Stuttgart: Kohlhammer, 1932–1979

TWOT	*Theological Wordbook of the Old Testament.* Edited by R. Laird Harris, Gleason L. Archer Jr., and Bruce K. Waltke. 2 vols. Chicago: Moody Press, 1980
TynBul	*Tyndale Bulletin*
UBS4th	*The Greek New Testament.* Edited by Barbara Aland, Kurt Aland, Johannes Karavidopoulos, Carlo M. Martini, and Bruce M. Metzger. 4th rev. ed. Stuttgart: United Bible Societies, 2001
VT	*Vetus Testamentum*
WBC	Word Biblical Commentary
WTJ	*Westminster Theological Journal*
WUNT	Wissenschaftliche Untersuchungen zum Neuen Testament
WW	*Word and World*
ZNW	*Zeitschrift* für die *neutestamentliche Wissenschaft und die* Kunde der
ZPBD	*Zondervan Pictorial Bible Dictionary.* Edited by Merrill C. Tenney. Grand Rapids: Zondervan, 1963

1

Introduction

The New Testament's (NT) use of the Old Testament (OT) is a subject that has received much attention in recent years within NT scholarship.[1] Amidst all the treatments in this subject area, a lack of clarity presently surrounds the particular discussion of the typological use of the OT in the NT. This lack of clarity stems in large part from a renewed interest in typology in recent years that has introduced "newer varieties of typology," which differ from the traditional, prophetic understanding of the concept.[2] Against these newer varieties of typology, however, the traditional, prophetic understanding of typology seems to be the hermeneutical axiom that explains best the use of various Psalms quotations in John and Acts.

---

1 For example, see G. K. Beale, *Handbook on the New Testament Use of the Old Testament: Exegesis and Interpretation* (Grand Rapids: Baker Academic, 2012); G. K. Beale, ed., *The Right Doctrine from the Wrong Texts? Essays on the Use of the Old Testament in the New* (Grand Rapids: Baker Books, 1994); G. K. Beale and D. A. Carson, eds., *Commentary on the New Testament Use of the Old Testament* (Grand Rapids: Baker, 2007); Kenneth Berding and Jonathan Lunde, eds., *Three Views on the New Testament Use of the Old Testament*, Counterpoints Series, Bible & Theology (Grand Rapids: Zondervan, 2008); D. A. Carson and H. G. M. Williamson, eds., *It is Written: Scripture Citing Scripture. Essays in Honour of Barnabas Lindars* (Cambridge: Cambridge University Press, 1988); James M. Efird, ed., *The Use of the Old Testament in the New and Other Essays: Studies in Honor of William Franklin Stinespring* (Durham: Duke University Press, 1972); E. Earle Ellis, *The Old Testament in Early Christianity: Canon and Interpretation in the Light of Modern Research* (Grand Rapids: Baker Book House, 1992); Craig A. Evans and W. Richard Stegner, eds., *The Gospels and the Scriptures of Israel*, JSNTSup 104, SSEJC 3 (Sheffield, England: Sheffield Academic Press, 1994); Stanley E. Porter, ed., *Hearing the Old Testament in the New Testament* (Grand Rapids: Eerdmans, 2006).

2 G. P. Hugenberger, "Introductory Notes on Typology," in *The Right Doctrine from the Wrong Texts? Essays on the Use of the Old Testament in the New*, ed. G. K. Beale (Grand Rapids: Baker Books, 1994), 331–333. For other works noting the differing kinds of typology, see also David L. Baker, *Two Testaments, One Bible: A Study of the Theological Relationships Between the Old & New Testaments*, rev. ed. (Downers Grove: InterVarsity Press, 1991), 180–199; Paul M. Hoskins, *Jesus as the Fulfillment of the Temple in the Gospel of John* (Eugene, OR: Wipf & Stock, 2006), 18–32.

Thesis

The purpose of this work is to demonstrate that the application of Psalms quotations to Jesus and his passion in select chapters in John (i.e., 13:18; 15:25; 19:24, 28) and in Acts (i.e., 1:20; 2:25–28, 34–35; 4:25–26) can be best explained in terms of traditional typology, which is the classical view that takes seriously the element of prophecy.[3] The Psalms references in each of these passages are psalms of David, which establish clear points of connection between David and Jesus and suggest a typological relationship between them. Furthermore, prophetic language appears with each of these Psalms references, thus, suggesting that these Psalms texts were understood to be the fulfillments of prophecies. When all evidence is considered, this work argues that Davidic typology in the traditional, prophetic sense accounts most precisely for Jesus' (John 13:18; 15:25), John's (John 19:24, 28), and Peter's (Acts 1:20; 2:25–28, 34–35; 4:25–26) application of these Davidic psalms to the various events of Jesus' passion in John and Acts.

This work understands traditional typology to represent best the "appropriation technique"[4] John and Luke employ in their use of the Psalms quotations in these focal passages. According to this typological hermeneutic, the Psalms quotations indicate that David and the experiences he describes bear theological significance in connection to Jesus, which justifies the application of Davidic psalms to Jesus. That is, David and Jesus share a typological relationship. Consequently, these event-based psalms show that David and his experiences prefigure in a predictive way the similar but climactic NT realities fulfilled in Jesus' life.

---

3 Psalms references in the John passages include: (1) John 13:18/Ps 41:9, (2) John 15:25/Ps 69:4, (3) John 19:24/Ps 22:18, (4) John 19:28/Ps 69:21. Those in the Acts passages include: (1) Acts 1:20/Pss 69:25; 109:8, (2) Acts 2:25–28/Ps 16:8–11, (3) Acts 2:34–35/Ps 110:1, (4) Acts 4:25–26/Ps 2:1–2.

4 Douglas Moo designates typology as a "direct appropriation technique" common to Jewish hermeneutics. Douglas J. Moo, *The Old Testament in the Gospel Passion Narratives* (Sheffield, Eng.: The Almond Press, 1983), 30–34, 76–78. By appropriation technique, Moo means the "exegesis and application" of OT texts, which are governed by core presuppositions or hermeneutical axioms. Ibid., 8, 75–78. To be noted, Moo argues for typology as a "basic appropriation technique" in Jewish hermeneutics, and he contends that typology is the basic approach used in appropriating the lament psalms to Jesus in the Gospels. Ibid., 33, 298–300. D. A. Carson similarly states, "When we ask more narrowly what kind of hermeneutical axioms and appropriation techniques . . . John adopts when he cites the OT, the answers prove complex and the literature on each quotation legion. At the risk of oversimplification, the dominant approach is that of various forms of typology . . . . The Davidic typology that surfaces repeatedly in the NT may well stand behind some of the Psalm quotations in the FG (2:17; 15:25; 19:24, 28)." D. A. Carson, "John and the Johannine Epistles," in *It is Written: Scripture Citing Scripture. Essays in Honour of Barnabas Lindars*, ed. D. A. Carson and H. G. M. Williamson (Cambridge: Cambridge University Press, 1988), 249.

Exegesis is limited to these focal passages in John and Acts for several reasons. First, they contain clear references to identifiable psalms in the OT.[5] Second, they possess prophetic language in their immediate contexts. The use of the verbs πληρόω (cf. John 13:18; 15:25; 19:24) and τελειόω (cf. John 19:28) appear to indicate clearly that John intends the Psalm references to be understood as prophetic fulfillments.[6] Luke, likewise, uses the Psalm quotations in conjunction with language suggesting these texts bear a prophetic force.[7] Based on the terminology, therefore, it seems that both John and Luke view these Psalm quotations as OT texts reaching prophetic fulfillments. Third, all of these quotations are referenced in connection to specific events of Jesus' passion: his betrayal (John 13:18; Acts 1:20), the world's hatred of him (John 15:25), his crucifixion and the division of his clothing (John 19:24), his thirst on the cross (John 19:28), his resurrection (Acts 2:25–28), his exaltation (Acts 2:34–35), and the conspiracy of the nations and their leaders against him (Acts 4:25–26).

Researching the thesis of this work stands to contribute to NT scholarship in several ways. First, this research offers a comparative study of John's use of Psalms with Luke's use of the book.[8] Such a comparative study by its very nature provides more evidence to support the legitimacy of prophetic Davidic typology as a key way the NT writers understand the psalms of David to apply to Jesus and the realities of his gospel. Second, a typological, prophetic understanding of Psalms in John and Acts is not without representation in contemporary NT scholarship. The recent treatment by Yuzuru Miura on the use of the Psalms in Acts and the treatment by Douglas Moo on the use of Psalms in the Gospels argue that a hermeneutic of prophetic Davidic typology stands behind the application of the Psalms quotations to Jesus.[9] Yet,

---

5 These Psalms references are obvious in these NT contexts because (1) they all appear with some kind of scripture introductory formula and (2) they all constitute OT quotations, with the exception of an allusion in John 19:28. Even in the case of John 19:28, however, the immediate context suggests an obvious allusion to Ps 69:21.

6 Both terms appear in BDAG with the possible meaning of "fulfilling" in the sense of divine prophecies and promises. BDAG, s.v. "πληρόω" and "τελειόω." On πληρόω and τελειόω as likely synonyms in John, see Moo, *The Old Testament*, 383–387; C. F. D. Moule, "Fulfillment-Words in the New Testament: Use and Abuse," *NTS* 14 (1967–68): 314–315, 318.

7 For example, Luke cites Psalms with the following prophetic language: (1) he combines πληρόω and προλέγω together in Acts 1:16, 20, (2) he speaks of τῇ ὡρισμένῃ βουλῇ καὶ προγνώσει τοῦ θεοῦ ("the predetermined plan and foreknowledge of God") in Acts 2:23 (cf. 4:28), (3) he designates David as a prophet, who "foresaw" (προοράω) in Acts 2:30–31, and (4) he stresses that David spoke the words of the Psalms by the Holy Spirit (cf. Acts 1:16; 4:25).

8 At least to this writer's knowledge, no preexisting study compares John's use with Luke's use of Psalms in the focal passages being examined in this work.

9 Yuzuru Miura, *David in Luke-Acts: His Portrayal in the Light of Early Judaism*, WUNT 2, Reihe 232 (Tübingen: Mohr Siebeck, 2007); Moo, *The Old Testament*. A few commentaries un-

their studies are marked by limitations,[10] which, therefore, present an opportunity to substantiate further their initial claims. So, examining more closely the psalms quoted in John and Acts will validate and also develop more clearly the prophetic Davidic typology that both Miura and Moo see present in John's and Luke's uses of Davidic psalms.

Third, establishing prophetic Davidic typology as the way in which John and Luke apply Davidic psalms to Jesus will, in turn, bring to light the weaknesses of alternative explanations (e.g., direct verbal prophecy, pure analogical typology, etc.). Fourth, Jesus taught the disciples that the Psalms predicted things about him that had to be fulfilled (cf. Luke 24:44–47). The study of quotations of Psalms in John and Acts, therefore, will help to clarify how the psalms exactly are prophetic of him (i.e., typologically).[11] Fifth, several OT texts substantiate an expectation of a future David.[12] If prophetic Davidic typology is the way John and Luke apply Davidic psalms to Jesus, the psalms of David, then, provide a Davidic portrait of Jesus. Thus, this research will show that in fulfilling Davidic psalms, John and Luke present Jesus as the promised New David of OT expectation. Finally, this research will demonstrate that the understanding of typology in these specific NT passages bears a prophetic force. Thus, it will provide evidence that typology and prophecy coalesce, which agrees with the traditional understanding of typology that defines it as a form of biblical prophecy.

Survey of Literature on the Psalms in the New Testament

A survey of the literature on the use of Psalms in John and Acts reveals the research gap that this work aims to fill. To establish the background for this work, I summarize a sample of literature on the use of the psalms as they appear in the focal passages of John 13; 15; 19 and Acts 1; 2; 4. First, this survey discusses those works that do not advocate for traditional, prophetic typology in John's and Luke's uses of Psalms. Then, I evaluate those works that do

---

derstand Psalms in a typological, prophetic way. For the psalms in John, see e.g., D. A. Carson, *The Gospel According to John*, PNTC (Grand Rapids: Eerdmans, 1991), 470–471, 527, 611–613, 618–620. For the psalms in Acts, see e.g., Darrell L. Bock, *Acts*, BECNT (Grand Rapids: Baker Academic 2007), 81–87, 123–138.

10 The study by Douglas J. Moo is too brief to be definitive, and the study by Yuzuru Miura provides only a partial examination of the relevant texts. Neither study, however, develops at length the Davidic typology in the focal passages in John and Acts.

11 In other words, this work will show that John and Luke understood the psalms in question to be typologically prophetic of Jesus and the events of his passion.

12 Cf. 2 Sam 7:12–16; Pss 89:3–4, 20–21, 29, 35–37; 132:11, 17; Isa 9:7; 55:3–4; Jer 23:5–6; 30:9; Ezek 34:23–24; 37:24–25; Hos 3:4–5.

argue specifically for prophetic David typology but stand in need of further development.

NON-TYPOLOGICAL HERMENEUTICAL CONCLUSIONS

In 1932, Edgar McKown researched the use of Psalms in the NT to discern the extent of their influence in the NT and upon NT ideas.[13] McKown asserts that the hermeneutical method behind the appropriation of Psalms in the NT is multidimensional.[14] McKown explains the appeal to Psalms in John and Acts as proof from prophecy in their appropriation to the events of Jesus' suffering and death.[15]

Published in 1961, Barnabas Lindars's *New Testament Apologetic* suggests several possibilities for the hermeneutic behind the psalms quoted in the NT.[16] The psalms found in the Acts 2 speech (i.e., Pss 16; 68; 110) concerning Jesus' resurrection and those utilized elsewhere in the NT in connection with Jesus' passion (i.e., Pss 22; 31; 34; 41; 69; 109) apply to him because of either a messianic prophecy, eschatological, or righteous sufferer understanding.[17] Lindars clearly rejects a Davidic typological understanding of Psalms 16 and 110 in the Acts 2 speech, claiming these are instead "literal fulfillment" and not true of David.[18] Typology is not considered in his discussion of the passion Psalms, nor is a Davidic connection mentioned with those Psalms.

In the updated publication of his doctoral thesis, Darrell Bock examines Luke's use of the OT in both the Gospel of Luke and Acts in order to determine its overall implications for Luke's Christology.[19] One specific question Bock seeks to answer in his examination of the OT in Luke-Acts centers on Luke's hermeneutical method.[20] Bock's study of Luke leads him to suggest Luke's use of the OT encompasses both a prophetic and typological-prophetic hermeneutic. He does not, however, conclude that a typological-prophetic

---

13 Edgar Monroe McKown, "The Influence of the Psalms upon the Ideas of the New Testament" (PhD diss., Boston University, 1932), 12.

14 McKown attributes the diversity of the NT writers' hermeneutical uses of the Psalms to rabbinic exegetical practices, to the need to verify gospel events prophetically, and to Jesus' unique use of Psalms. Ibid., 113–122, 263.

15 Ibid., 182–191, 264.

16 Lindars concludes that the psalms were used primarily for apologetic purposes, namely for "scriptural argument" and "scriptural warrant" for Jesus' identity as the Messiah. Barnabas Lindars, *New Testament Apologetic: The Doctrinal Significance of the Old Testament Quotations* (Philadelphia: The Westminster Press, 1961), 33, 110.

17 Ibid., 32–59, 77, 88–110.

18 Ibid., 33; for comments on David, see 40–41, 45.

19 Darrell L. Bock, *Proclamation from Prophecy and Pattern: Lucan Old Testament Christology*, JSNTSup 12 (Sheffield: JSOT Press, 1987), 7, 11–12, 46–47.

20 Ibid., 46, 49–52.

hermeneutic describes the use of Psalms in Acts 2 and 4 (the Psalms quotations in Acts 1 are not included in the examination).[21] Bock maintains that Psalms 2, 16, and 110 are not typological fulfillments but direct prophecy fulfillments. Prophecy, as opposed to typology, better represents the hermeneutic behind the use of Psalms 16 and 110 primarily because David ultimately speaks as a prophet and speaks about Christ and not himself.[22]

Donald Juel provides a section in his book, *Messianic Exegesis*, which discusses the role of the Psalms in the passion tradition. In this section, Juel does not consider typology in the connection of the Psalms to Jesus and his passion.[23] Juel argues that Messianic exegesis best explains the connection of Psalms to Jesus' passion. Certain psalms could be appropriated to Jesus because "from the outset the psalms were part of a tradition that narrated the death of the King of the Jews. The psalms were read as messianic—that is, as referring to the anointed King from the line of David expected at the end of the days."[24]

Jerry Eugene Shepherd argues for a "Christo-canonical" hermeneutic as the appropriate paradigm for understanding the relationship of the Psalms to Jesus in the NT.[25] The implications a Christo-canonical hermeneutic has for Psalms, according to Shepherd, is that "the Psalter should be seen as a messianic reservoir."[26] Consequently, this means "anything in the Psalter was 'fair

---

21 Ibid., 149, 155. Darrell Bock prefers to describe Luke's use of the OT as "proclamation from prophecy and pattern," arguing the term "pattern" to be more "clearly descriptive than typology, which can have various nuances which we wish to avoid." Ibid., 49–50, 149. Bock distinguishes between a typological-prophetic (i.e., pattern) usage and direct prophecy as follows: "This [typology/pattern] is a category of prophetic classification, along with direct prophecy . . . but is distinct from the latter in that the OT text does not look exclusively to a future event or figure. Rather it looks to a pattern within events that is to culminate in a final fulfillment in light of the passage's and the OT's context of hope and deliverance." Ibid. 50; see also 49; 274–276.

22 Ibid., 177, 179–181; 186–187; 212. Though he does not explain his change in reasoning, Bock classifies the use of Psalm 16 in Acts 2 as typological-prophetic in his recent commentary on Acts. He appears to indicate that Psalm 110 functions similarly but is less clear on the issue. He also designates Psalms 69 and 109 in Acts 1 as being typological-prophetic. Bock, *Acts*, 81–87, 123–138, and 133n16.

23 He also rejects the paradigm of the righteous sufferer as sufficient because (1) Jesus is not presented in such a light in the NT and (2) this paradigm is too general to be applied to the specifics of Israel's suffering King and Christ. Donald Juel, *Messianic Exegesis: Christological Interpretation of the Old Testament in Early Christianity* (Philadelphia: Fortress Press, 1988), 102–103.

24 Ibid., 116.

25 According to this "Christo-canonical" hermeneutic, "Christ is the Canon above the canon" so that he is both its ultimate author and Lord. Jerrry Eugene Shepherd, "The Book of Psalms as the Book of Christ: A Christo-Canonical Approach to the Book of Psalms" (PhD diss., Westminster Theological Seminary, 1995), 275–276, 376–377, 384–385.

26 Ibid., 593.

game' to use in reference to the person of Christ" by the NT authors.[27] Typological exegesis may be relevant at times according to the Christo-canonical approach, but a canonical rather than a typological hermeneutic reflects the biblical paradigm for applying Psalms to Christ.[28]

In his dissertation, Mark Hoffman attempts to answer the question, "How did the early Christians find Ps 22 to be meaningful in understanding the crucifixion of Jesus?"[29] In his review of modern scholarship, Hoffman makes clear that he rejects proposals for understanding the interpretation of Psalm 22 in the NT along the lines of messianic prophecy, typological fulfillment, or the Righteous Sufferer motif.[30] Concerning typology specifically, Hoffman states, "I, however, am not convinced that any typological interpretation is sufficient to account for the early Christian application of Ps 22 to Jesus."[31] Psalm 22, according to Hoffman, was most likely read as a Messianic Psalm and applied to Jesus on this basis.[32]

David in the Fourth Gospel provides one of the most detailed analyses on the use of Psalms in the Gospel of John. In this work, Margaret Daly-Denton concentrates specifically on the psalms quoted in John to show that there is a Davidic motif applied to Jesus in this Gospel.[33] Daly-Denton concludes that the psalms of David in both citations and allusions along with other biblical material in John work together to present David functioning paradigmatically of Jesus.[34] Daly-Denton classifies the psalms in John as either functioning prophetically of Jesus' passion circumstances or in a revelatory way of His true identity.[35] Typology and corresponding language do appear throughout the book at various points in her argument for specific David/Jesus connections. One of the glaring weaknesses of this project, however, centers on Daly-Denton's failure to clarify what she understands typology really to be. In her conclusion, she states that David is "an important paradigm for the Johannine portrayal of Jesus."[36] She further concludes, "The genre of

---

27 Ibid., 593.
28 Ibid., 378–381.
29 Mark George Vitalis Hoffman, "Psalm 22 (LXX 21) and the Crucifixion of Jesus" (PhD diss., Yale University, 1996), 2.
30 Ibid., 12–28.
31 Ibid., 24.
32 Ibid., 322–323, 438–447.
33 Margaret Daly-Denton, *David in the Fourth Gospel: The Johannine Reception of the Psalms*, AGJU 47 (Leiden: Brill, 2000), 5–8.
34 Ibid., 289, 314–315, 319.
35 Ibid., 188, 241–242, 321–322.
36 Ibid., 319. Daly-Denton adds that in the FG John presents Jesus as "the fulfillment of so many different scriptural 'types' or motifs." The fact that typology is not given more attention in the conclusion raises questions on how important it is to John's underlying hermeneutic.

the psalms formally cited as fulfilled in the events of 'the hour,' Pss [68]69, [40]41, 21[22] and [33]34 . . . allows the Evangelist to present passages from them as prophetic anticipations of what would actually happen to Jesus . . ."[37] Even though Daly-Denton uses the language of "prophetic anticipations" concerning the way David's Psalms apply to Jesus' passion events, this does not appear to equate to a traditional, prophetic view of typology. Daly-Denton appears to indicate that the use of the Psalms in John is mostly a literary device because John employs them in the "re-working of Jesus," whereby the compilation produces a "purely literary construct."[38]

The key to John's use of Psalms, according to Steven Nash, rests upon the work of J. H. Eaton, who argues for a royal interpretation of Psalms.[39] That is, the NT writers understood the Psalms to be "royal" (i.e., centrally concerned with Israel's king), which allowed for an eventual messianic interpretation of the book in its application to Jesus.[40] Nash concludes, therefore, that John follows this line of messianic interpretation, quoting and alluding to Psalms in order to show the sufferings of the Messiah to be in accordance with the OT Scriptures.[41]

In sum, the above survey of literature yields a diverse group of hermeneutical conclusions on the use of Psalms in the passages relevant to this work. Notably, the possibility of a typological, prophetic hermeneutic is discussed minimally and does not factor into the hermeneutical conclusions in any determinative manner.

TYPOLOGICAL HERMENEUTICAL CONCLUSIONS

Douglas Moo gives significant consideration to the use of Psalms in the NT in his work, *The Old Testament in the Gospel Passion Narratives*.[42] He restricts his overall study to the four Gospels and is primarily concerned with answering the hermeneutical question behind OT texts that are connected to

---

37 Ibid., 321.
38 Ibid., 320. For more discussion of literary considerations, see pp. 8–9, 110–112, and 317–318. Indeed, much of Daly-Denton's background research is useful for further studies of the psalms in John and their Davidic connections to Jesus. Her final analysis, however, does not contend for a traditional typological framework in understanding the application of these psalms to Jesus.
39 Steven Boyd Nash, "Kingship and the Psalms in the Fourth Gospel" (PhD diss., Westminster Theological Seminary, 2000), 45–52.
40 Ibid., 41, 46, 52.
41 Ibid., 206–207.
42 In addition to Psalms, Moo also considers the NT's use of Isaiah, Zechariah, and other miscellaneous OT passages.

Jesus' passion.[43] His chapter on the lament psalms is approximately 76 pages in length, and the hermeneutical conclusion he reaches is beneficial for this work's interest in the use of the quotations from Psalms in John. Specifically, Moo contends that Davidic typology, rather than messianic prophecy, is the most "probable" explanation of the relationship the Gospel writers made of the lament psalms to Jesus' sufferings.[44]

He suggests that typological correspondence with David's sufferings is what "legitimizes the transfer of language" from the psalms to Jesus.[45] Most notably, Moo puts forth that this Davidic typology possesses some element of predictiveness.[46] According to Moo, the references were in some way "anticipatory of the sufferings of Christ," and in some of the texts David "looks beyond his immediate circumstances to the promised Son."[47] While Moo advocates an approach of prophetic David typology, his assertions are not without certain limitations in regards to this research project.

First, the Psalms quotations in John are not given the adequate attention they deserve. Only about 13 total pages concentrate on the quotations in John 13, 15, and 19.[48] So, before more definitive claims can be made about the use of these quotations in John, they need to be examined in more detail. Second, David typology receives minimal treatment within the overall chapter (about two pages at the most). The reader is left wondering what correlations are being made exactly in the typology between David and Jesus. These correlations can be presented more clearly to substantiate further the Davidic typology Moo sees present in these Johannine contexts. Finally, Moo does

---

43 Moo, *The Old Testament*, 3–4.

44 Ibid., 289–300.

45 Ibid., 300. Moo suggests the David/Jesus typology based on the following reasons: (1) the comparison of Jesus' life with the psalmist's life, (2) David's authorship of the psalms, (3) David's betrayal situation by Ahithophel, which corresponds to Judas' betrayal, (4) Jesus' title as "Son of David" and its Christological understanding, and (5) reoccurring Davidic motifs throughout the Gospels. Ibid., 298–300.

46 Ibid., 298–299. Just exactly how "prophetic" Moo holds typology to be is not always clear. For example, in chapter one on "The Hermeneutics of Late Judaism," Moo discusses typology in general, stating, "Typology is fundamentally retrospective; there is no attempt to assert that the original text had any forward-looking element at all." Ibid., 31; also see, 30–34. Yet, in his discussion of Psalms, Moo relates that typology "is construed with an eschatological, forward-looking time line," so that past events point forward the events of the last days. Ibid., 299. He further adds that an eschatological dimension of certain psalms leaves them "possessing semi-predictive elements." Ibid., 299. By these two statements, Moo affirms that the Davidic typology of the Psalms in the Gospels is to some degree predictive of the events of Jesus' passion. Admittedly, there appears to be some inconsistency in Moo's presentation of typology, but his argument still implies that the David/Jesus typology is prophetic in some sense.

47 Ibid., 300.

48 This brevity of treatment stems from the broader focus of Moo's study on the allusions and quotations of the Psalms as they appear not only in John but in all four Gospels.

not emphasize adequately in his discussion of the texts the role πληρόω and τελειόω play in the introductory formulas to John's psalm quotations.[49] These terms are significant because they denote the idea of prophetic fulfillment for the Davidic psalms, which describe events in their original contexts. This fulfillment terminology, thus, identifies a prophetic force to the Davidic typology. Consequently, this prophetic fulfillment language needs to be considered more closely in the assessment of how the Psalms function in John to indicate a prophetic force to the Davidic typology.

Yuzuru Miura reaches a hermeneutical conclusion similar to that of Moo in the revised version of his doctoral thesis, *David in Luke-Acts: His Portrayal in the Light of Early Judaism*. Miura maintains that the Psalms quotations in Acts are best explained in terms of prophetic Davidic typology. His analysis of the quotations in Acts 1, 2, and 4 is of most relevance to this project.

Miura recognizes a shortfall in previous studies of David in the Lukan corpus. These previous studies have centered so much on the Davidic Messiah theme that the fuller portrayal of the David and Jesus relationship has been neglected in Luke's writings.[50] Miura argues, therefore, that the relationship between David and Jesus needs to be explored not only from the genealogical aspect (as in previous studies) but also from the possibility of the typological as well. His major research objective, then, is to examine all of Luke's references to David in order to see if legitimate evidence establishes a David/Jesus typology in Luke-Acts.[51] This research effort requires two main divisions for Miura's thesis. In the first division, he studies the portraits of David in the OT and early Judaism, trying to discover if there was a first century precedent for a Messianic-Davidic typology.[52] In the second division, Miura begins his NT study of David in Acts and then transitions to the Gospel of Luke.[53] He primarily investigates the typological relationship between David and Jesus in Luke and Acts, but he also gives some attention to the genealogical relationship.

What is the fruit of Miura's labor? First, Miura discovers that Davidic messianism "is well attested in the Jewish writings in the first centuries BCE and

---

49 Moo does provide some helpful information on πληρόω in the concluding chapter of his study. Ibid., 383–387. What is lacking, however, is a more integrated understanding of what this prophetic language means for the David typology in the FG.

50 Miura, *David in Luke-Acts*, 2–6.

51 Ibid., 5–6.

52 Ibid., 6–10. This is an important first step, because his findings will allow him to compare the perception of David in first-century Jewish literature with the findings in his second division.

53 The reasoning behind this order of study is Miura's contention that the David-Jesus typology finds clearer expression in Acts. Consequently, beginning the study with Acts will illuminate better the picture of David in the Gospel. Ibid., 10–11.

CE."⁵⁴ Second, Miura establishes not only a genealogical relationship but also a clear emphasis upon the typological relationship between David and Jesus in Luke-Acts.⁵⁵ How Miura characterizes the function of the Psalms quotations in Acts 1, 2, and 4 supports the contention of this present thesis. Miura writes, "We insist that early Christian use of the psalms in Acts 1; 2; and 4 is *consistently* [emphasis original] typological-prophetic."⁵⁶ Concerning what typological-prophetic means, Miura explains, "The point is to recognize patterns in events between David and Jesus so that the former figure is prophetic of the latter in early Christian interpretation of the Psalms."⁵⁷

If Miura has already made a case that the Psalms quotations in Acts 1, 2, and 4 function in terms of prophetic Davidic typology, why examine them again in this present work? Further examination is necessary because Miura's research contains a few weaknesses. One weakness concerns his brief explanation of the typological-prophetic method of interpretation that is so central to his thesis.⁵⁸ Such brevity leaves the reader unclear on the exact nature of prophetic typology and, thus, the significance of David and Jesus' typological relationship. A second weakness is that Miura's examination of the focal passages is too partial at points. That is, he does not give a detailed explanation on the typological parallels between David and Jesus nor does he highlight adequately all the textual evidence that supports a prophetic understanding of the David typology in each NT context. By addressing these foregoing weaknesses in Miura's research, this work will clarify better the hermeneutic of prophetic David typology that stands behind Luke's use of David's psalms and, thus, strengthen Miura's initial thesis.

In sum, the works by Moo and Miura lay an invaluable foundation for this research project. Specifically, they argue that David typology in a prophetic sense is the most probable way John (Moo) and Luke (Miura) apply Davidic psalms to Jesus in John and Acts, respectively. Since their works are marked by certain limitations, however, there is warrant to reexamine the use of the Psalms quotations in John 13, 15, and 19 and Acts 1, 2, and 4 in order to present

---

54 Ibid., 137. Davidic messianism depicted both the genealogical and typological relationships between David and the future Messiah. Thus, there was the expectation that the coming Messiah would be a David-like figure, an eschatological David because the historical David was believed to be paradigmatic of a greater David to come. Ibid., 132–137. This discovery is relevant because it shows the typological relationship between David and the Messiah was already present in the NT era. Miura, therefore, sees reason to find Jesus being presented in Luke-Acts not only in genealogical but also typological relation to David.

55 Ibid., 239–241.

56 Ibid., 150; see also 154, 160, 174.

57 Ibid., 149–150.

58 Miura briefly defines the label typological-prophetic, referring his readers to Bock for a more developed definition of the concept. Ibid., 149–150, 149n40.

a clearer and stronger case that prophetic Davidic typology best explains how these originally Davidic psalms can legitimately provide the biblical rationale for specific events in Jesus' passion.

Methodology

The method of this work does not depend on the employment of a specific, critical method for the study of the NT. Rather, the method of this work basically involves several steps that will accomplish the goals for chapters 2–5. The collective aim of all the steps will be to show that traditional prophetic typology that is specifically Davidic in focus is the hermeneutic with the most explanatory power behind the use of the quotations from Psalms in John 13, 15, and 19 and Acts 1, 2, and 4.

Chapter two clarifies the understanding of the traditional view of typology by (1) defining, describing, and illustrating the concept in detail, (2) distinguishing it from the modern analogical view of typology, and (3) delineating common principles for its exegetical controls.[59]

Chapter three considers two categories of evidence to show why the traditional, prophetic view of typology seems to accord more faithfully with the biblical concept. The first kind of evidence is biblical in nature and includes (1) Jesus' teachings and examples, (2) typology in the Epistle of Hebrews, (3) NT "fulfillment" language, (4) hermeneutical τύπος language,[60] and (5) the OT basis of typology. The second kind of evidence is historical in nature. Here, the focus concerns the pre-critical understanding of typology espoused by several of the Church Fathers and by the Reformers, John Calvin and Martin Luther. Historical evidence from pre-critical times serves to demonstrate that typology was recognized in earlier eras as a form of prophecy.

Chapters four and five constitute the heart of this work, analyzing the quotations from Psalms in John and Acts, respectively. Both chapters follow a similar approach in the exegetical analysis of each psalms quotation.[61] First, a short discussion will be given to establish the proper OT reference for each psalm quotation. Second, the typological relationship each psalm quotation establishes between David and Jesus will be analyzed in detail. To analyze the

---

59 Concerning this last item, a point of clarification is necessary. This work is not attempting to delineate a typological methodology for the NT. It only identifies and summarizes core principles that scholarship has previously recognized as helpful for evaluating whether a possible typological use of the OT is present in the NT.

60 The meaning of τύπος and other relevant language for understanding NT typology will be limited and restricted to an examination of these terms as they are found only in the NT.

61 The exegetical analysis of each Psalms quotation incorporates the principles for discerning typology, which are identified in chapter 2 of this work.

Introduction

David-Jesus typology, each quotation will first be examined to demonstrate that it is a Davidic, event-based psalm (i.e., a psalm of David which describes an event specific to him in its original context).[62] Then, the textual analysis will show how each psalm quotation in its NT context juxtaposes David and Jesus to highlight a typological relationship between them and their similar life events. Third, the textual evidence indicating a prophetic force to the David typology in each context will be examined.[63]

---

[62] A full exegesis, however, of the various psalms quoted is unnecessary for the purposes of this study. Instead, exegesis will be limited specifically to the quotations, while the larger contexts of the various psalms will only be summarized as needed.

[63] Concerning specific "fulfillment" terminology (i.e., πληρόω and τελειόω) and other NT language appearing to indicate prophetic fulfillment, analysis of these terms will be restricted to the meanings as derived from the NT.

2

Clarifying Traditional Typology

This chapter aims to present a clear understanding of the traditional view of typology. Three main sections structure this chapter in this aim. In the first section, discussion focuses initially upon defining traditional typology and describing its major tenets. Then, a NT example of typology follows to help illustrate the concept. In the second section, a summary of the modern analogical view of typology is given in order to show how it diverges from the traditional view. In the last section, discussion centers on the principles commonly used for discerning instances of NT typological interpretation.

Traditional Typology: Definition, Description, and Illustration

Interest in typology has fluctuated from the Patristic to the modern era.[1] The current state of affairs evidences ongoing interest in the subject in NT scholarship, such as recent monographs by Paul M. Hoskins, Anthony Le Donne,

---

1 For a detailed survey of the historical figures and their works which shaped the understanding and direction of typological studies from the Patristic era up to the latter part of the twentieth century, see Richard M. Davidson, *Typology in Scripture: A Study of Hermeneutical Τύπος Structures*, AUSDDS 2 (Berrien Springs, MI: Andrews University Press, 1981), 15–92; Patrick Fairbairn, *Typology of Scripture: Two Volumes in One* (New York: Funk & Wagnalls, 1900; repr., Grand Rapids: Kregel, 1989), 1:1–41. No single factor is responsible for the ebb and flow of attention which has characterized typology studies in academic literature throughout the years. Lampe, however, identifies the emergence of historical critical study as the predominate factor, which led to the typological method of interpretation having "very little importance or significance for the modern reader" in comparison to the importance it held for medieval and early Christian interpreters. G. W. H. Lampe, "The Reasonableness of Typology," in *Essays on Typology*, SBT (Naperville, IL: Alec R. Allenson, 1957), 16; see 14–17. Because historical criticism undermined the conception of the unity of Scripture, Lampe says that this ultimately resulted in the "consequent discrediting of the typological and prophetical exegesis familiar to so many generations of Christians." Ibid., 17. See also G. R. Osborne, "Type; Typology," *ISBE* 4:930–932;

and Karl-Heinrich Ostmeyer.[2] However, when reading some of the more recent literature on typology, one often observes a use of the term without clear explanation and with differing meanings. The following section, therefore, attempts to circumvent any misunderstanding in this work by supplying a clear definition and description of the typology central to this thesis: traditional typology.

Definition and Description of Traditional Typology

The problems arising from varied and vague definitions of typology have not gone unnoticed in scholarship.[3] W. Edward Glenny states, "Part of the problem in coming to a unified view on the subject of typology is the lack of definition that is acceptable to all."[4] Hoskins likewise observes how an absence of a uniform definition for typology and its related terminology has "complicated" the field of study and created "ambiguity" in discussion.[5]

Various modern conceptions of typology currently exist, each of which defines the concept differently.[6] The view of typology central to this work

---

Gerhard Von Rad, "Typological Interpretation of the Old Testament," in *Essays on Old Testament Hermeneutics*, ed. Claus Westermann (Richmond: John Knox, 1963), 22.

2 Glenny briefly explains that the "revival of interest" in typology may be attributed to (1) renewed interest in both biblical theology and the NT's use of the OT; (2) OT scholarship's effort to interpret the OT in a more relevant way for Gentile believers; and (3) the recognition of the phenomenon in the OT corpus. W. Edward Glenny, "Typology: A Summary of the Present Evangelical Discussion," *JETS* 40 (1997): 627–628. See also Paul M. Hoskins, *Jesus as the Fulfillment of the Temple in the Gospel of John* (Eugene, OR: Wipf & Stock, 2006); Anthony Le Donne, *The Historiographical Jesus: Memory, Typology, and the Son of David* (Waco, TX: Baylor University Press, 2009); Karl-Heinrich Ostmeyer, *Taufe und Typos: Elemente und Theologie der Tauftypologien in 1. Korinther 10 und 1. Petrus 3*, WUNT 2, Reihe 118 (Tübingen: Mohr Siebeck, 2000); Paul M. Hoskins, *That Scripture Might Be Fulfilled: Typology and the Death of Christ* (Longwood, FL: Xulon 2009). For a recent study of typology in Revelation, see Barbara Ann Isbell, *The Past is Yet to Come: Exodus Typology in Revelation*, Studies in Jewish and Christian Literature (Fontes, 2022).

3 David L. Baker, *Two Testaments, One Bible: A Study of the Theological Relationships Between the Old & New Testaments,* rev. ed. (Downers Grove: InterVarsity Press, 1991), 180. David Baker recognizes the diversity of modern definitions of typology and classifies them into two general categories. According to Baker, typology definitions of the first part of the twentieth century focus on "prefiguration." Those definitions of the latter part of the twentieth century focus on "correspondence." Baker's category of "prefiguration" should not be misunderstood as a strictly modern category. As will be shown in chapter three of this work, the prefiguration (or prophetic) sense can be traced back to the Reformation and Patristic eras.

4 Glenny, "Typology," 628.

5 Hoskins, *Jesus as the Fulfillment*, 18.

6 Some of these modern definitions of typology categorize according to the following labels: (1) Analogical typology: This view defines typology primarily in terms of analogies (i.e., comparisons) and correspondences between the testaments in their similar historical events, which is based upon God's similar ways of acting in salvation history. Baker, *Two Testaments,*

is "traditional" typology.[7] The adjective "traditional" designates the classical conception of typology that was prevalent in pre-critical exegesis: a prophetic typology. *Traditional* typology, thus, stands distinct from the *modern* views of typology, which surfaced after the rise of modern critical scholarship.[8]

Both Richard M. Davidson and Hoskins provide clear definitions of traditional typology. Davidson defines typology as follows:

> The traditional understanding—as articulated in previous centuries and still advocated in certain conservative circles—views biblical typology as the study of specific OT realities which were divinely ordained to be prospective/predictive prefigurations of Jesus Christ and/or the Gospel realities brought about by him.[9]

Hoskins similarly explains typology, stating:

> Typology is the aspect of biblical interpretation that treats the significance of Old Testament types for prefiguring corresponding New Testament antitypes or fulfillments. . . . This definition brings together three related characteristics of the relationship between a type and its antitype. First, an Old Testament type prefigures its New Testament antitype. Sec-

---

179–199. (2) Literary typology: This view defines typology primarily as a method of writing in the NT, which means the NT authors provide "the description of an event, person or thing in the New Testament in terms borrowed from the description of its prototypal counterpart in the OT." K. J. Woollcombe, "The Biblical Origins and Patristic Development of Typology," in *Essays on Typology*, SBT (Naperville, IL: Alec R. Allenson, 1957), 39–40. See also, M. D. Goulder, *Type and History in Acts* (London: S. P. C. K., 1964), 1–13, 179–205. (3) Allegorical typology: This view defines typology as being without distinction from allegory. James Barr, *Old and New in Interpretation: A Study of the Two Testaments* (New York: Harper & Row, 1966), 103–148; especially pp. 105, 107, 111, 113, 147. (4) Cyclical typology: This view defines typology in terms of the idea of cyclical repetition in history, which is a secular view of history that stands separate from salvation history. Rudolph Bultmann, "Ursprung und Sinn Der Typologie als hermeneutische Methode," *TLZ* (1950): 205–212. (5) Mnemonical Typology: This view defines typology primarily as a "means of remembering" (i.e., a mnemonic tool) and maintains that "it is a particular manifestation of memory refraction and that it provides an apt example of how memories are propelled forward by certain patterns of interpretation that evolve over time and (re)consideration." Le Donne, *The Historiographical Jesus*, 14, 59, 77, 93.

7 The modifying adjective "traditional" follows the label Hoskins utilizes in his discussion of typology. The adjective "traditional" differentiates the view of typology that was common before more modern views arose to accommodate historical-critical principles in biblical studies. Hoskins, *Jesus as the Fulfillment*, 18–32; Davidson, *Typology in Scripture*, 111–112, 409–410.

8 Davidson, *Typology in Scripture*, 111–112; 409–410.

9 Ibid., 409; see also 111. For a similar definition, see Walther Eichrodt, "Is Typological Exegesis an Appropriate Method?," in *Essays on Old Testament Hermeneutics*, ed. Claus Westermann (Richmond: John Knox, 1963), 224–225. Cf. Gerhard F. Hasel, *New Testament Theology: Basic Issues in the Current Debate* (Grand Rapids: Eerdmans, 1978), 190.

ond, in order to prefigure its antitype, a type possesses certain significant correspondences or similarities to its antitype. Third, as the fulfillment or goal of the imperfect type, the antitype will be greater than the type that anticipated it.[10]

The foregoing definitions highlight two elements of traditional typology that need to be considered in more detail: (1) the prophetic element and (2) the correspondence element. Before discussing these two elements, an explanation of the key terms of NT typology is necessary.

Characteristic to the discussion of typology are the NT terms τύπος (Rom 5:14; 1 Cor 10:6) and ἀντίτυπος (1 Pet 3:21).[11] In typological interpretation, τύπος designates the OT "type," while ἀντίτυπος designates the NT "antitype." A "type" is an OT person, event, or institution, which prefigures and corresponds to a NT person, event, or institution that is called the "antitype."[12] As seen in the definitions above by Davidson and Hoskins, proponents of traditional typology refer to the OT "type" as the "prefiguration" and the NT "antitype" as the "fulfillment" or "goal."[13]

Some rather obvious inferences about typology come to light in view of the explanation of the terms "type" and "antitype." First, the relationship between the two terms highlights a relationship between the OT and NT.[14] Second, the OT type stands chronologically as the original event in relation to

---

10 Hoskins, *That Scripture Might Be Fulfilled*, 20.

11 The traditional view of typology understands these terms to function in a technical, hermeneutical manner in these NT passages, designating a typological interpretation of the OT. See Leonhard Goppelt, "τύπος κτλ," *TDNT* 8:246–259.

12 Milton S. Terry, *Biblical Hermeneutics: A Treatise on the Interpretation of the Old and New Testaments* (Hunt & Eaton, 1890; repr., Eugene, OR: Wipf & Stock, 1999), 246. Sometimes the general classification of events and institutions are further enumerated into OT offices, things, or actions. Cf. Ibid; Bernard Ramm, *Protestant Biblical Interpretation: A Textbook of Hermeneutics*, 3rd rev. ed. (Grand Rapids: Baker Book House, 1970), 231–232; Henry A. Virkler and Karelynne Gerber Ayayo, *Hermeneutics: Principles and Processes of Biblical Interpretation*, 2nd ed. (Grand Rapids: Baker Academic, 1981), 184–185. Throughout this chapter, "event" will be the term used most often in discussion of OT types and NT antitypes.

13 See also E. Earle Ellis, *Paul's Use of the Old Testament* (Eugene: Wipf and Stock, 1981), 126–128.

14 Typology is, thus, primarily horizontal in scope and concerned with historical realities involving both testaments. This statement deserves qualification, since NT typology is not only horizontal but also vertical in scope. Whereas horizontal typology is concerned with the historical realities between the OT and NT, vertical typology is concerned with the relationship between the earthly and heavenly realities. An example of such vertical typology can be found in Hebrews 8:1–6 and 9:23–24. For a brief discussion of vertical typology, especially as it occurs in Hebrews, see Davidson, *Typology in Scripture*, 99–100; 336–367; Peter V. Legarth, "Typology and its Theological Basis," *EuroJTh* 5 (1996): 146.

the NT antitype, the future event. Third, the type and antitype share some kind of meaningful correspondence or analogy.[15]

Typology as Prospective/Predictive Prophecy

Traditional typology values a prospective or predictive element in the understanding of the biblical concept. Accordingly, OT historical events that types serve a prophetic function, prefiguring and predicting corresponding NT fulfillments. Typology, therefore, is a kind of biblical prophecy. While typology deserves distinction from direct prophecy (i.e., verbal prophecy), the two constructs are the same in *essence* and only different in *form*. Bernard Ramm explains their relatedness, stating:

> The form of prophecy may be either verbally predictive or typically predictive. The former are those prophecies which in poetry or prose speak of the age to come . . . ; the latter are those typical persons, things, or events, which forecast the age to come. Thus a type is a species of prophecy and should be included under prophetic studies. Typological interpretation is thereby justified because it is part of prophecy, the very nature of which establishes the nexus between the two Testaments.[16]

Charles T. Fritsch supports this same understanding of relationship, explaining that prophecy and typology are only different "means" of the same act. "Prophecy predicts mainly by means of the word," according to Fritsch, "whereas typology predicts by institution, act or person."[17] Similarly, Milton S. Terry writes that "typology constitutes a specific form of prophetic revelation."[18] Likewise, G. K. Beale argues, "Both [direct prophecy and typological prophecy] ultimately prophesy about the future but do so in a different manner: one by words and the other by events."[19]

---

15 Hoskins explains, "The basic point is that *antitypon* is consistently associated with correspondence to a *typos*." Hoskins, *That Scripture Might Be Fulfilled*, 28.
16 Ramm, *Protestant Biblical Interpretation*, 216.
17 Charles T. Fritsch, "Biblical Typology," *BSac* 104 (Jan–Mar 1947): 215.
18 Terry, *Biblical Hermeneutics*, 248.
19 G. K. Beale, *Handbook on the New Testament Use of the Old Testament: Exegesis and Interpretation* (Grand Rapids: Baker Academic, 2012), 58. Typology, Beale adds, can be thought of as "event prophecy." See also Bock, who writes, "This [typology] is a category of prophetic classification, along with direct prophecy . . . but it is distinct from the latter in that the OT text does not look *exclusively* to a future event or figure. Rather it looks to a pattern within events that is to culminate in a final fulfillment in light of the passages and the OT's context of hope and deliverance." Bock, *Proclamation from Prophecy and Pattern: Lucan Old Testament Christology*, JSNTSup 12 (Sheffield: JSOT Press, 1987), 50.

A twofold basis justifies the prophetic nature of typology according to the traditional understanding. As Hoskins explains, "[T]ypology rests upon a basic understanding of God's work in history and of the inspiration of the Scriptures."[20] Put simply, typology takes into account "divine intent" in both salvation history (i.e., *Heilsgeschichte*) and the Scriptures.[21] Concerning the element of divine intent in salvation history, it is significant for a prophetic understanding of typology, because salvation history theology emphasizes the notion of "a divine economy or plan of history from the beginning to the end of all things."[22] Such a framework of salvation history highlights a unity between the Old and New Testaments that is "teleological" in orientation, progressing according to God's redemptive plan from inception towards a "single goal": Christ and his gospel.[23] The teleological character of salvation history ensures that "the gospel is determinative of the Old Testament events that make up salvation history."[24] Implications wise, as salvation history unfolds various OT events purposefully prefigure future NT realities or goals specific to Christ and his gospel.[25] Accordingly, traditional typology recognizes God's

---

20   Hoskins, *That Scripture Might Be Fulfilled*, 20–21.

21   Ellis, *Paul's Use of the Old Testament*, 27. See also Hoskins, *Jesus as the Fulfillment*, 21.

22   Charles T. Fitsch, "Biblical Typology," *BSac* 103 (Oct–Dec 1946): 420. Fritsch adds that the special significance of redemptive history is that it is "history through which God was revealing Himself to man in an ever ongoing process." Ibid., 418. Thus, salvation history is progressive, consisting of "a series of divine acts which are purposefully connected and which grow in meaning and clarity until they are fulfilled in Christ." Ibid., 421. According to Oscar Cullmann, typology "presupposes a salvation-historical background" oriented towards a consummation. Oscar Cullmann, *Salvation in History*, trans. Sidney G. Sowers (Tübingen: J. C. B. [Paul Siebeck], 1965), 133. Cullmann explains, "Scripture as such wishes to invite us to perceive a divine plan in the way events correspond with one another and develop further.... Finally, we note that in the genesis of New Testament salvation history, all events, the past, the present, and the ones expected in the future, are summed up in the one event as their high-point and mid-point: the crucifixion of Christ and the subsequent resurrection." Ibid., 86. The NT conception of salvation history, according to Cullman, acknowledges an overarching divine plan of redemption, marked by progression and correspondence that climaxes in an epochal goal, Christ and his redemptive work. Ibid., 103, 122–126, 154, 158, 166, 232.

23   Fritsch, "Biblical Typology," 420–421. J. C. K. von Hoffmann writes, "The history recorded in the Old Testament is the history of salvation as proceeding towards its full realization. Hence the things recorded therein are to be interpreted teleologically, i.e., as aiming at their final goal." J. C. K. von Hofmann, *Interpreting the Bible*, trans. Christian Preus (Minneapolis: Augsburg Publishing House, 1959), 135. See also Francis Foulkes, *The Acts of God: A Study of the Basis of Typology in the Old Testament* (London: The Tyndale Press, 1958), 32–35; John H. Stek, "Biblical Typology Yesterday and Today," *CTJ* 5 (1970): 162.

24   Graeme Goldsworthy, *Preaching the Whole Bible as Christian Scripture: The Application of Biblical Theology to Expository Preaching* (Grand Rapids: Eerdmans, 2000), 90. Goldsworthy also states that "the gospel is God's ultimate plan that all other aspects of history must serve." Ibid., 89.

25   On this, Hoffmann argues, "Since the course of the events of that history [salvation history] are determined by their goal, this goal will manifest itself in all important stages of its progress in a way which, though preliminary, prefigures it." Hofmann, *Interpreting the Bi-*

"Lordship in moulding and using history to reveal and illumine His purpose."²⁶ Hoskins summarizes this point well, explaining:

> God worked it out such that certain Old Testament events, persons, and institutions would prefigure New Testament events, persons, and institutions. As a result, one aspect of the significance of these Old Testament types is their ability to be used by God to predict their New Testament antitypes.²⁷

Traditional typology, then, understands Scripture to present God as the Lord of history.²⁸ As the Lord of history, God ultimately shaped and used various OT events within his telic-directed, redemptive plan to serve as prophetic prefigurements of climactic NT realities that would find their fulfillments in Christ.²⁹ Thus, as Fritsch maintains, "Type and antitype not only resemble each other, but are inextricably bound together by a divine purpose and plan."³⁰ There is, therefore, an economic or organic relationship between an OT type and its NT antitype in the divine economy.³¹ That organic relationship means that OT types were initially planned by God with a view towards their NT antitypes.³² Ultimately, then, OT types constitute prospective patterns, which

---

ble, 135. Similarly, as Fritsch clarifies, OT events resemble corresponding NT events in Christ "because of an underlying, teleological connection" between the testaments. Fritsch, "Biblical Typology," 420.

26 Ellis, *Paul's Use of the Old Testament*, 128.

27 Hoskins, *Jesus as the Fulfillment*, 21.

28 God's Lordship over history entails his acting through both "ordinary" events and "supernatural" events in human history. George Eldon Ladd, *A Theology of the New Testament*, ed. Donald A. Hagner, rev. ed. (Grand Rapids: Eerdmans, 1974; repr., 1993), 23–25. Admittedly, traditional typology accepts a real notion of transcendence in salvation history that is incompatible with a purely historical-critical investigation of Scripture. A purely historical investigation of Scripture that does not allow for transcendence or the theological, as Adolf Schlatter pointed out, results in an "atheistic" dogma and ethic. Adolf Schlatter, "Atheistische Methoden in der Theologie," in *Zur Theologie des Neuen Testaments und zur Dogmatik*, ed. Ulrich Luck (Munich: C. Kaiser, 1969), 139.

29 On Christ as the one who fulfills OT expectations, see Douglas J. Moo, "The Problem of *Sensus Plenior*," in *Hermeneutics, Authority, and Canon*, ed. D. A. Carson and John D. Woodbridge (Grand Rapids: Zondervan, 1986), 196. See also David E. Aune, "Early Christian Biblical Interpretation," *EvQ* 41 (1969): 92–93; Cullmann, *Salvation in History*, 86; Goldsworthy, *Preaching the Whole Bible*, 88–91; Sidney Greidanus, *Preaching Christ from the Old Testament: A Contemporary Hermeneutical Method* (Grand Rapids: Eerdmans, 1999), 48–50; H. Dale Hughes, "Salvation-History as Hermeneutic," *EvQ* 48 (1976): 89.

30 Fritsch, "Biblical Typology," 421. Cf. Ellis, *Paul's Use of the Old Testament*, 128; Fairbairn, *Typology of Scripture*, 1:46–48; Terry, *Biblical Hermeneutics*, 248.

31 Ellis, *Paul's Use of the Old Testament*, 128; Fritsch, "Biblical Typology," (1947): 214–215.

32 As Patrick Fairbairn explains, "[The relation between type and antitype] implies, first, that the realities of the Gospel, which constitute the antitypes, are the ultimate objects which were contemplated by the mind of God, when planning the economy of His successive dispen-

were pointing forward to future fulfillments God would bring about in Christ. Since the antitype is the goal to which the type was pointing, the antitype fulfills the type and, thus, stands as the greater and more important event in the scheme of God's redemptive plan.[33]

As for the element of divine intent in relation to the Scriptures, it is significant to the prophetic understanding of typology, because it takes seriously the divine inspiration of the Scripture. The same God who was shaping OT history to prefigure his redemptive plan in Christ, Hoskins explains, "was also inspiring the Scriptures to be written in a way that would preserve a record of Old Testament types and anticipate their predictive significance."[34] In other words, God providentially superintended what was written down in Scripture to the end that "the past was recorded with a view to the future."[35] Traditional typology, therefore, sees God as the ultimate author and unifier of Scripture.[36] As such, God caused the various OT events to be written down in Scripture, intending for these event-based texts to possess a typological import for his future purposes in NT salvation.[37]

In sum, the traditional view of typology defines the concept as essentially prospective in nature. The twofold framework of God superintending both salvation history and the Scriptures for his redemptive and revelatory purposes undergirds this prospective understanding. Traditional typology, therefore, highlights that "the Old Testament type prefigures and predicts its goal, the New Testament antitype."[38] To summarize, God uses OT typical events to give advance notice of future, climactic NT events that become real in Christ and

---

sations. And it implies, secondly, that to prepare the way for the introduction of these ultimate objects, He placed the Church under a course of training, which included instruction by types, or designed and fitting resemblances of what was to come." Fairbairn, *Typology of Scripture*, 1:47. Cf. Georges A. Barrois, who concludes, "Thus do the Old Testament types prepare the revelation of the New, and the Gospel illumines the mysterious events of the past. Typology, therefore, appears to be an integral part of the divine economy, essentially linked with the progression of Sacred History toward its τέλος, its ultimate goal, the kingdom that is to come." Georges A. Barrois, *The Face of Christ in the Old Testament* (Crestwood, NY: St. Vladimir's Seminary Press, 1974), 43.

33 Cf. E. Earle Ellis, *The Old Testament in Early Christianity: Canon and Interpretation in the Light of Modern Research* (Grand Rapids: Baker Book House, 1992), 106; Leonhard Goppelt, *Typos: The Typological Interpretation of the Old Testament in the New*, trans. Donald H. Madvig (Eugene, OR: Wipf and Stock, 2002), 200–201.

34 Hoskins, *That Scripture Might Be Fulfilled*, 21. Osborne similarly states that typology is "built upon the belief that God is in control and has unified His Word and the events in redemptive history." Osborne, "Type; Typology," 4:931.

35 David E. Garland, *1 Corinthians*, BECNT (Grand Rapids: Baker Academic, 2003), 464. Garland says this with reference to the record of the Exodus events in 1 Cor 10:11.

36 Hoskins, *Jesus as the Fulfillment*, 24–26.

37 Ibid., 21–26. Cf. Ellis, *Paul's Use of the Old Testament*, 127.

38 Hoskins, *Jesus as the Fulfillment*, 22.

his gospel. Ultimately, the OT type and NT antitype relate as prophecy and fulfillment, thus, delineating typology as a form of biblical prophecy.[39]

Before moving on to the next section, a point needs brief clarification. Specifically, the typical character of an OT event may not always be apparent from its original context. It is possible an OT author wrote at times with no perception of an event's typological significance. Consequently, the traditional proponent admits that, although OT types are prospectively oriented, they can be retrospective in a sense.[40] This admission refers to their *detection* rather than their *design*. That is, OT types may sometimes only be recognizable retrospectively in light of final NT revelation.[41] Retrospective recognition of an OT type follows suit with the nature of progressive revelation that climaxes in Christ and, consequently, makes clearer previous OT revelation (cf. 2 Cor 3:14–16; Heb 1:1–2).[42] Accordingly, the full meaning of the OT type naturally surfaces because the NT antitype sheds light on its typical function. The retrospective identification of an OT type does not conflict with original, authorial intent in the OT. Rather, typological import, as Hoskins explains, is compatible with original authorial intent when allowance is made for a canonical approach to interpretation.[43] A canonical approach takes seriously the divine

---

39 Goppelt, *Typos*, 199.

40 According to Moo, "It appears, then, that typology does have a 'prospective' element, but the 'prospective' nature of specific Old Testament incidents could often be recognized only retrospectively.... [A]nd the prospective element in many Old Testament types, though intended by God in a general sense, would not have been recognized at the time by the Old Testament authors or the original audience.... [I]t is nevertheless true that we would not know of some types had the New Testament not revealed them to us ...." Moo, "The Problem of *Sensus Plenior*," 197.

41 G. K. Beale, "Positive Answer to the Question: Did Jesus and His Followers Preach the Right Doctrine from the Wrong Texts? An Examination of the Presuppositions of Jesus' and the Apostles' Exegetical Method," in *The Right Doctrine from the Wrong Texts? Essays on the Use of the Old Testament in the New*, ed. G. K. Beale (Grand Rapids: Baker Books, 1994), 394; Ellis, *The Old Testament in Early Christianity*, 151; Moo, "The Problem of *Sensus Plenior*," 197.

42 Cf. Moo, who explains that "the new, climactic revelation of God in Christ" is the fulfillment of the OT revelation which was "preparatory" and "incomplete." Moo, "The Problem of *Sensus Plenior*," 191. The progressive nature of revelation, according to John H. Stek, naturally leads to the clarity of God's prior providential initiatives in OT types because, Christ who is the climax and consummation of salvation history, makes them "ever more distinct." Stek, "Biblical Typology," 162. Similarly, Fritsch avers that "the type becomes more clear and understandable as the time for its fulfillment in the antitype draws near." Fritsch, "Biblical Typology," (1947): 220.

43 Hoskins, *Jesus as the Fulfillment*, 23–26. Hoskins appeals primarily to Moo on this "canonical approach," but also lists J. I. Packer, G. K. Beale, and Vern S. Poythress as advocating a similar interpretive approach. Ibid., 25n119. The kind of canonical approach Hoskins has in mind is one that acknowledges God as the ultimate author and unifier of Scripture. Ibid., 25. On this premise, God determines various OT events to not only serve their present time but also to "anticipate" later fulfillments that find their ultimate clarification in NT revelation. Ibid., 25–26. The canonical approach Hoskins advocates has two advantages. First, it keeps one from

authorship of Scripture. Thus, it recognizes that the NT reveals that God ultimately intended for various OT texts to have a future significance within the total canon that the original author may not have fully comprehended.[44]

Typology As Correspondence

Traditional typology also emphasizes the element of correspondence.[45] Correspondence (i.e., resemblance or analogy) between the type and antitype stems from the prophetic nature of typology.[46] Put simply, the prophecy and fulfillment relationship that the type shares with its antitype determines some measure of real resemblance between the two.[47] Since God uses the type to point forward to its antitype, the type by design embodies characteristics of likeness to its NT counterpart. To better grasp the element of typological correspondence, it is helpful to frame the discussion along the following four points.

First, typological correspondence is textual. Typological correspondence fundamentally refers to correspondence between texts that describe historical events.[48] Rather than being "event" centered, typology is really "text" centered. That is, NT texts use OT texts to accentuate a relationship between the historical events they relay (i.e., type and antitype). There is still real historical

---

appealing to the controversial explanation of a fuller meaning of Scripture typically known as *sensus plenior*. Typically, *sensus plenior* meaning conceives of interpretation that cannot be textually substantiated, since it is a hidden, mystical sense. Ibid., 25n118. Hoskins explains that with a canonical approach, however, typological interpretation is "open to verification, since the texts relevant to each type and antitype are found within the canon." Ibid., 26. Second, a canonical approach places proper weight upon the doctrine of inspiration. Regardless of what the inspired human author was or was not aware of in the typological import of certain OT events, the divine inspiration of the Bible reminds the interpreter that "divine intention is also important and relevant." Ibid., 24. See also Beale's excellent discussion on the role divine authorship and canonical interpretation play in the recognition of typological meaning. Beale, *Handbook on the New Testament*, 22–25.

44 Moo, "The Problem of *Sensus Plenior*," 209–211. John Wenham adds the following insight: "But New Testament principles of interpretation do not end with a discovery of what the Old Testament writer meant. Each writer was author of a segment of Scripture, not comprehending the whole. But the inspiring Spirit who directed their pens was author of the whole and comprehended the whole.... The Holy Spirit knew beforehand the course of history with its consummation in Christ, and so in guiding the writers he intended a deeper meaning than they understood." John Wenham, *Christ and the Bible* (Eugene, OR: Wipf & Stock, 1994), 107.

45 Davidson, *Typology in Scripture*, 95–96; Ellis, *The Old Testament*, 106.

46 Terry, *Biblical Hermeneutics*, 247.

47 This point accords with Hoskins's definition of typology above, where he states that "in order to prefigure its antitype, a type possesses certain significant correspondences or similarities to its antitype." See also Fairbairn, *Typology of Scripture*, 1:46.

48 I owe this clarification to my doctoral advisor Paul Hoskins, who brought to my awareness how typology has long struggled with the "text" versus "event" in explaining correspondence.

correspondence in typology relationships, but that historical correspondence is justified through the texts that juxtapose OT and NT events.[49] The fact that typological correspondence is textual or text-centered means that typology (1) relies upon NT and OT texts for its verification,[50] (2) affirms the historicity of the events the texts describe,[51] (3) and seeks the literal interpretation (i.e., original, authorial meaning) of the biblical texts.[52]

Second, typological correspondence is Christological in focus.[53] In other words, typology concerns connections between OT events that relate to NT events specific to Jesus and the realities his redemptive work brought into being. The Christological focus of typological correspondence stems from Christ and his gospel being the teleological goal of redemptive history and typical events being construed by God to anticipate and point forward to that

---

49 Contra James D. G. Dunn, who argues that typology is not textual but historical correspondence. He states that "the correspondence with the past is not found within the written text but *within the historical event* [emphasis original]." James D. G. Dunn, *Unity and Diversity in the New Testament: An Inquiry into the Character of Earliest Christianity*, 3rd ed. (London: SCM Press, 2006), 93.

50 The textual nature of typological correspondence is important, because it means "this [typological] import is open to verification, since the texts relevant to each type and antitype are found within the canon." Hoskins, *Jesus as the Fulfillment*, 26. Thus, the biblical texts provide the evidence to substantiate typological relationships. Ibid., 26n124.

51 Traditional typology takes seriously the historical events described in the biblical texts, affirming their actual historicity. Davidson, *Typology in Scripture*, 96. So, the OT and NT texts describe real historical events, which make up typological relationships. Cf. Ellis, *Paul's Use of the Old Testament*, 127n1.

52 That is, typological interpretation involves serious exegesis of the relevant texts in their literary and historical contexts to establish original, authorial meaning or "literal" meaning. R. A. Markus, "Presuppositions to the Typological Approach to Scripture," *Church Quarterly Review* 158 (October–December 1957): 445–446. Here, the way typology approaches the "literal" sense of the text sharply contrasts it with allegorical interpretation. As F. Torm explains, "Der Unterschied zwischen der typologischen Auslegung (oder Betrachtungsweise) und der allegorischen ist m. a. W. der: Die allegorische Auslegung geht neben der buchstäblichen Erklärung ihren eignene Weg (ist von ihr unabhängig, ja kann sie sogar ausschließen), während die typologische Auslegung (Betrachtungsweise) gerade von der buchstäblichen Erklärung ausgeht" ("The difference between the typological interpretation (or approach) and the allegorical interpretation is, in my opinion, that the allegorical interpretation goes its own way in addition to the literal explanation (is independent of it, even can exclude it), while the typological interpretation (approach) proceeds precisely from the literal explanation" [my translation]). F. Torm, *Hermeneutik des Neuen Testaments* (Göttingen: Vandenhoek and Ruprecht, 1930), 223n2. Cf. Gerald Bray, "Allegory," *DTIB*, 34–36. Thus, as Goppelt avers, "The typical meaning is not really a different or higher meaning, but a different or higher use of the same meaning that is comprehended in type and antitype." Goppelt, *Typos*, 13. So also Fairbairn, *Typology of Scripture*, 1:3. Importantly, then, typological interpretation adheres to the literal, historical sense of the biblical texts to highlight meaning that "rises naturally" between the testaments. Ramm, *Protestant Biblical Interpretation*, 223.

53 Davidson, *Typology in Scripture*, 111, 417–418; Fairbairn, *Typology of Scripture*, 1:46–48; Goppelt, *Typos*, 202; Gerhard Maier, *Biblical Hermeneutics*, trans. Robert W. Yarbrough (Wheaton, IL: Crossway Books, 1994), 87.

consummation. Third, typological correspondence is always notable in form. Typology does not attend to "superficial" connections between type and antitype but to "real and substantial" connections.[54]

Lastly, typological correspondence involves escalation.[55] That is, "the antitype (the NT correspondence) is heightened in some way in relation to the OT type."[56] Because the OT type foreshadows its NT fulfillment or goal, there must always be clear progress in the movement from the shadow to the substance.[57] This progress or heightening signals that the antitype, in relation to the type, is the greater and more important event in God's redemptive plan.[58] In that the antitype fulfills the type and surpasses it in significance, such escalation highlights not only how the two compare but also ultimately how they contrast. Thus, to some degree points of contrast or dissimilarity always factor into typological relationships.[59]

ILLUSTRATION OF TRADITIONAL TYPOLOGY

The foregoing definition and description of traditional typology can be better comprehended by a biblical example. One clear case of typology appears in John 3:14–15.[60] In this passage Jesus makes reference to Moses and the bronze

---

54 Ramm, *Protestant Biblical Interpretation*, 228. See also Beale, "Positive Answer to the Question," 400; A. Berkeley Mickelsen, *Interpreting the Bible* (Grand Rapids: Eerdmans, 1963), 245–246; Terry, *Biblical Hermeneutics*, 247, 250–252.

55 Types and antitypes do not mirror each other in a "'one-to-one' equation." Instead, there is always escalation from type to antitype, so that the latter complements but transcends the former. E. Earle Ellis, foreword to *Typos: The Typological Interpretation of the Old Testament in the New* by Leonard Goppelt (Eugene, OR: Wipf and Stock Publishers, 2002), x.

56 Beale, *Handbook on the New Testament*, 14.

57 Cf. Terry, who relays that "the type from its very nature must be inferior to the antitype, for we cannot expect the shadow to equal the substance." Terry, *Biblical Hermeneutics*, 252. Cf. Fairbairn, *Typology of Scripture*, 1:51.

58 Goppelt, *Typos*, 200–201. Similarly, Torm notes, "Der neutestamentliche Verfasser findet aber im Inhalte des alttestamentlischen Textes - gerade durch die buchstäbliche Meinung des Textes - einen Hinweis auf etwas Kommendes, das gleicher Art, *aber von noch größerer Bedeutung und Tragweite* [emphasis added] ist" ("The New Testament author, however, finds in the contents of the Old Testament text - precisely through the literal view of the text - an indication of something to come that is of the same kind, *but of even greater importance and scope*" [my translation, emphasis added]). Torm, *Hermeneutik des Neuen Testaments*, 223. See also Bock, *Proclamation*, 49–50.

59 Eichrodt, "Is Typological Exegesis an Appropriate Method?," 225–226; Terry, *Biblical Hermeneutics*, 247, 250–251. Cf. Hans Walter Wolff's remarks on NT correspondence having "antithesis in some details" with the OT because "God's previous action and speaking have reached a new stage of their history—they have attained their goal." Hans Walter Wolff, "The Hermeneutics of the Old Testament," *Int* 15 (1961): 453.

60 See e.g., John Calvin, *The Four Last Books of Moses*, vol. 4 of *Calvin's Commentaries*, trans. Charles W. Bingham (Grand Rapids: Baker Book House, 1981), 155–157; Fairbairn, *Typology of Scripture*, 1:65–66; Goppelt, *Typos*, 180, 183, 218n37; James L. Kugel and Rowan A. Greer,

snake in the wilderness, which is an obvious allusion to Num 21:6–9. The typological relationship in this instance rests upon a NT text's use of an OT text, which juxtaposes two historical situations in order to highlight their connections. In this instance, the OT event is a type of Christ and his cross and its saving efficacy. Jesus establishes two notable points of connection between the OT event (i.e., the type) and himself (i.e., the antitype): (1) the lifting up of the serpent on the pole corresponds with the lifting up of Jesus on the cross and (2) the promise of life to the Israelites who looked up to the serpent corresponds with the promise of life to whoever believes in Jesus.[61] These two correspondences are not superficial or incidental but primary and significant to both Scriptural contexts.

In relating the OT event to himself and his redemptive work, the transition from the type to the antitype shows a clear increase or climax. There is movement from the lesser event to the greater and more important event in redemptive history. The Son of God being "lifted up" on the cross transcends the bronze serpent being "lifted up" on a pole, and the spiritual/eternal life granted to whoever looks to Jesus in faith surpasses the physical/temporal life given to the Israelite who looked up to the serpent.[62] That Jesus understands this event to be more than a mere analogy appears plain from his use of the

---

Early Biblical Interpretation (Philadelphia: Westminster, 1986), 133–34; M.-J. Lagrange, *Évangile selon Saint Jean*, 5th ed. (Paris: J. Gabalda, 1936), 81–87; R. C. H. Lenski, *The Interpretation of St. John's Gospel* (Columbus, OH: Lutheran Book Concern, 1942), 254–258; Martin Luther, *Sermons on the Gospel of St. John: Chapters 1–4*, vol. 22 of *Luther's Works*, trans. Martin H. Bertram (Saint Louis: Concordia Publishing House, 1957), 339–345; Mickelsen, *Interpreting the Bible*, 237; Terry, *Biblical Hermeneutics*, 250–251; Virkler and Ayayo, *Hermeneutics*, 182; Bernhard Weiss, *Das Johannes-Evangelium*, 9th ed., KEK 2 (Göttingen: Vandenhoeck und Ruprecht, 1902), 118–120.

61 Bernhard Weiss observes these two points of comparison, writing, "Das Num 218 erzählte Ereignis bietet nach der Auffassung des Evangelisten offenbar einen doppelten Vergleichungspunkt, sowohl das Emporgerichtetwerden (der bekannten ehernen Schlange an der Stange und Jesu am Kreuze), als das Gerettetwerden (zur Genesung durch den Hinblick auf die Schlange und zur ewigen ζωή durch den Glauben an den Gekreuzigten) ("In the evangelist's view, the event told in Num 21:8 apparently offers a double point of comparison, both being raised [the well-known iron serpent on the pole and Jesus on the cross] and being saved [for recovery with regard to the serpent and for eternal ζωή through faith in the crucified one]" [my translation]). Weiss, *Johannes-Evangelium*, 118. See also D. A. Carson, *The Gospel According to John*, PNTC (Grand Rapids: Eerdmans, 1991), 201–202; Mickelsen, *Interpreting the Bible*, 237.

62 The escalation or heightening from the type to the antitype naturally brings to the forefront how the former contrasts with the latter and greater event. Both events resemble each other in the notions of "lifting up" and "life." But, the meaning of these ideas rises to a new level of truth with regards to the Christ-event. First, the verb "lifted up" (ὑψόω) carries a double meaning here in the FG in connection to Jesus, referring both to his crucifixion and his resurrection-exaltation. Carson, *John*, 201–202. Second, the gift of "life" promised is spiritual and eternal in nature, rather than solely physical as in the OT context. Third, the scope of salvation extends to all people who believe in Jesus (i.e., "whoever") and not only to believing Israelites who were in focus in the original event. Andreas J. Köstenberger, *John*, BECNT (Grand Rapids: Baker Academic, 2004), 128.

verb δεῖ ("it is necessary/must"), which typically indicates divine necessity and some element of prophecy.[63] Thus, the divine plan of God for Jesus' death on the cross and salvation through him was anticipated in advance by means of the OT prefiguration, whose typological import becomes clear in light of NT revelation. Ultimately, Jesus teaches in this passage that the OT event was a prefiguration "planned by the foreseeing eye of God with special respect to the coming realities of the Gospel."[64] Jesus and his cross and the salvation it provides, then, are the perfect fulfillment of what the imperfect OT type was anticipating and, thus, predicting.[65]

Traditional Typology: Comparison with the Modern View

The previous pages provide a definition and explanation of traditional typology, the classical view which values a prophetic element. In NT scholarship, various modern definitions of typology exist, each of which differs from the traditional explanation of typology.[66] Of these various modern views, analogical typology is the most common way of understanding the biblical concept. In fact, contemporary NT scholarship identifies analogical typology along with traditional typology as the two primary views in biblical scholarship.[67] Since analogical typology is one of the primary conceptions of the subject, it is necessary to summarize this view briefly to show how it compares and contrasts with traditional typology.

The analogical view of typology agrees with the traditional view on certain points.[68] Hoskins identifies three basic points of common ground

---

63 Weiss, *Johannes-Evangelium*, 118. Other evidence in the FG supports understanding this OT text as providing a prophetic pattern in connection to Jesus and his death. This evidence includes the statements (1) that Moses wrote about Jesus specifically in the Law (John 1:45), (2) that the *Scriptures* testify about him (John 5:39), and (3) that Moses wrote about him in his *writings* (John 5:46).

64 Fairbairn, *Typology of Scripture*, 65. According to Calvin, "[W]hen Christ compares Himself to this serpent which Moses lifted up in the wilderness, (John iii. 14) it was not a mere common similitude which He employs, but He teaches us, that what had been shewn forth in this dark shadow, was completed in Himself." Calvin, *The Four Last Books of Moses*, 156. On the predictive sense of this typological relationship, see also Martin Luther, *Sermons*, 339–345; Terry, *Biblical Hermeneutics*, 250–251.

65 Jesus' clear allusion to Num 21:6–9 in John 3:14–15 is revelatory in function, revealing the OT basis for the divine necessity of Jesus' suffering to fulfill God's redemptive plan. Goppelt, *Typos*, 180. Consequently, for this passage to function in a revelatory manner means that a text describing an OT historical event provides a predictive pattern for a future, similar but greater NT event, the death of Jesus.

66 For a list of these modern definitions of typology, see the section "Definition and Description of Traditional Typology" above in this chapter.

67 Baker, *Two Testaments*, 180–181; Beale, *Handbook on the New Testament*, 13–14; Davidson, *Typology in Scripture*, 94; Hoskins, *Jesus as the Fulfillment*, 18–19.

68 The label "analogical" fits with C. A. Evans's classification of typology as a form of "ana-

between the two views.[69] Both views tend to stress the element of correspondence between OT and NT events. Both views emphasize escalation in the transition from the type to the antitype, which identifies the latter as the greater redemptive reality. Both views also understand a framework of salvation history to be central to the biblical concept.[70]

Even with these points of similarity, analogical typology differs from traditional typology in several significant ways.[71] The first difference is that the analogical view of typology is not necessarily tied to the biblical text in the same way traditional typology is. Admittedly, most proponents of the analogical view take seriously the biblical text and the events recorded therein, agreeing that typology involves connections between actual historical referents in the Old and New Testaments.[72] Yet, not all proponents of the analogical view insist upon the historicity of the events in typology.[73] If the events in typology possess no real historical basis and prove artificial, then this essentially relegates typology to a purely literary or theological phenomenon in Scripture.[74] The traditional view of typology sets itself apart from the analogical view in that it always interprets the biblical texts to be relaying actual historical events that correspond in salvation history.

logical interpretation," which denotes the NT's use of the OT for purposes of establishing simple comparisons. Typology, as analogical interpretation, stands separate from prophetic interpretation. C. A. Evans, "Old Testament in the Gospels," *DJG*, 579, 582–583.

69 Hoskins, *Jesus as the Fulfillment*, 18–21.

70 This framework of salvation history includes a few basic points of agreement as well as specific differences in the total understanding of what salvation history truly entails.

71 Hoskins, in his discussion of the analogical conception, links these issues of concern directly to the influence of the historical-critical hermeneutic. Hoskins, *Jesus as the Fulfillment*, 27–31. Cf. Davidson, *Typology in Scripture*, 74, 88–93, 111–12; Von Rad, "Typological Interpretation of the Old Testament," 22–25.

72 E.g., see comments by Baker, *Two Testaments*, 195; Dunn, *Unity and Diversity*, 93; R. T. France, *Jesus and the Old Testament: His Application of the Old Testament Passages to Himself and His Mission* (Vancouver, British Columbia: Regent College Publishing, 1998), 39–41; Donald Guthrie, *New Testament Theology* (Downers Grove: Inter-Varsity, 1981), 956–957; Christopher J. H. Wright, *Knowing Jesus Through the Old Testament* (Downers Grove: InterVarsity Press, 1992), 114–116.

73 Davidson, *Typology in Scripture*, 96. Gerhard von Rad exemplified well this tendency. Von Rad described OT typology primarily as a theological construct, consisting of confessional tradition rather than actual history. Von Rad, "Typological Interpretation of the Old Testament," 20. The problem with von Rad's understanding of history in typology is that the correspondences/analogies between the two testaments are not based upon *actual* history but upon *theologized* history. Consequently, typology in both the OT and NT is not grounded in an authentic history. Instead, typology rests upon an artificial history, because the OT and NT writers impose a theological interpretation upon actual events to the end that what is recorded and remains is exaggeration and inflation. Ibid., 20, 32–39. On the relationship between tradition history and salvation history in von Rad's theology, see Cullmann, *Salvation in History*, 54, 88. For a summary and critical analysis of von Rad's construal of typology, see Stek, "Biblical Typology," 142–159.

74 Cf. Hoskins, *Jesus as the Fulfillment*, 29–31.

A second concern with the analogical view of typology is that some of its proponents limit textual meaning solely to the human author's intention.[75] This principle of biblical study means that NT typology does not involve interpretation of the OT but only its application.[76] Since the text can only mean what the OT author had in mind when recording historical narratives, those texts cannot possess a future reference. The traditional proponent of typology finds this problematic, for it does not give proper place to the doctrine of inspiration and a canonical approach to biblical interpretation.[77] Consequently, God's intent as the ultimate author and unifier of the Scriptures is not considered in the interpretive process, and final NT revelation is not allowed to interpret and clarify God's previous revelation in the OT. In the analogical view of typology, therefore, there appears to be no allowance for OT types to point beyond themselves to future NT events, since human authorial intent (rather than divine intent within the unity of the total canon) determines the ultimate meaning of the biblical text.

The exclusion of the predictive significance of types is the third concern with the analogical conception of typology. In fact, analogical typology's omission of a prophetic element is frequently singled out as what sets it apart from the traditional view. Beale brings this issue to light: "One major question at issue here is whether typology essentially indicates an analogy between the OT and NT or whether it also includes some kind of forward-looking element or foreshadowing."[78] For the proponent of the analogical view, typology does not possess any kind of prophetic thrust. For example, Donald Guthrie says, "The use of type must be distinguished from the use of prediction, in that type carries with it no necessary reference to the future."[79] In the same way, R. T. France argues, "A type is not a prediction; in itself it is simply a person, event, *etc.* recorded as historical fact, with no intrinsic reference to the future. Nor is an antitype the fulfillment of a prediction."[80] So, as the label "analogical" signifies, typology stands separate from prediction. Type and

---

75 As pointed out by France, *Jesus and the Old Testament*, 41–42. According to Hoskins (*Jesus as the Fulfillment*, 23), this principle reflects "one of the norms of historical critical hermeneutics."

76 So France, *Jesus and the Old Testament*, 41–42. Cf. Baker, *Two Testaments*, 190.

77 Osborne explains, "A canonical approach . . . states that any biblical text can be explicated in terms of its total canonical context." Osborne, "Type; Typology," 4:931. For a good explanation of inspiration and the canonical approach to interpretation in connection to typology, see Hoskins, *Jesus as the Fulfillment*, 23–27.

78 Beale, *Handbook on the New Testament*, 13–14. Cf. Sidney Greidanus: "The basic issue in this discussion, therefore, is the question: Is an Old Testament type predictive as prophecy is or is it discovered retrospectively?" Greidanus, *Preaching Christ*, 251.

79 Guthrie, *New Testament Theology*, 956.

80 France, *Jesus and the Old Testament*, 39–40. See also R. T. France, "Relationship between the Testaments," *DTIB*, 669. Baker argues against a prophetic view of typology, stating

antitype relate not as prophecy and fulfillment, but simply as mere analogies or comparisons between the OT and NT.

God's consistent activity in salvation history supplies the basis for the analogical view of the type and antitype relationship being only comparative in nature. That is, OT and NT events correspond with each other because "there is a consistency in God's dealings with men. Thus his acts in the Old Testament will present a pattern which can be seen to be repeated in the New Testaments events."[81] David L. Baker maintains this very point:

> The fundamental conviction which underlies typology is that God is consistently active in the history of the world—especially in the history of his chosen people—and that as a consequence the events in this history tend to follow a consistent pattern. One event may therefore be chosen as typical of another, or of many others.[82]

Christopher J. H. Wright provides the same line of argument, concluding:

> Typology, then, to sum up, properly handled is a way of understanding Christ and the various events and experiences surrounding him in the New Testament by analogy and correspondence with the historical realities of the Old Testament seen as patterns and models. It is based on the consistency of God in salvation-history.[83]

Proponents of the analogical view, then, stress that typology concerns mere analogy, a comparison between an earlier historical event and a later one. Davidson rightly observes, "This is far different from the traditional understanding of typology in which God not only acts consistently but also has ordained and superintended specific persons/events/institutions to mutely predict the coming of Christ."[84]

Davidson goes on to explain why the analogical view lacks a predictive understanding of types in comparison with traditional typology:

> Throughout the latter nineteenth and early twentieth centuries typology was considered by most critical scholars as a relic of the past, no longer ac-

---

that "typology is retrospective whereas prophecy is prospective." Baker, *Two Testaments*, 190. Cf. Dunn, *Unity and Diversity*, 93.

   81 France, *Jesus and the Old Testament*, 39.
   82 Baker, *Two Testaments*, 195; see also 188.
   83 Wright, *Knowing Jesus Through the Old Testament*, 116.
   84 Davidson, *Typology in Scripture*, 95.

ceptable or relevant within the modern world view. But in recent decades an amazing instauration of interest in typology has occurred among noted advocates of the historical-critical method within the Biblical Theology Movement. The 'post-critical neo-typology' is not, however, a return to the traditional views. It is based upon a different understanding of history and revelation which has little room for the predictive element. Typology is viewed as a common way of thinking in terms of concrete analogies which in Scripture (and in modern typological interpretation) involves the retrospective recognition of God's consistent 'revelation in history.'[85]

What Davidson underscores is that analogical typology developed initially from a rationalistic explanation of biblical history and divine revelation to accommodate modern critical scholarship.[86] Rationalistic philosophy "completely changed" the view of biblical history, which undergirded typology in pre-critical interpretation.[87] So, when typology reemerged as a viable method of interpretation in the mid-twentieth century, a transcendent view of God in biblical history and revelation was no longer tenable to those who rejected pre-critical presuppositions but embraced a more scientific interpretive method.[88] Instead, analogical thinking was offered as the explanation for the correspondences between OT and NT history. In the final outcome, human reflection on the consistent activity of God (rather than the actual intervention of God) in history became the explanation for why later events are comparable to prior ones in salvation history.

---

85 Ibid., 111–112. Davidson defines "revelation in history" as the concept that "God's revelation is not in ideas, conceptions, statements or propositions, but in historical acts. The Bible is a history book in that it witnesses to these divine acts. But the history presented in Scripture is theologically informed and not intended to be historically accurate or objective." Ibid., 73n2.

86 Von Rad admits that the more traditional understanding of typology "came to a sudden end in rationalism" and that "our present theological point of view concerning the Old Testament still exhibits throughout the character imparted to it by the revolution brought about by rationalism." Von Rad, "Typological Interpretation of the Old Testament," 22.

87 Fritsch, "Biblical Typology," 419. The pre-critical view of biblical history acknowledged the transcendence of God in revelation and history. Ibid., 293–305.

88 Lampe captures this modern-critical attitude when he states, "The unity of the Bible ought never to mean the same thing for us as for the precritical generations. It must be sought in a collection of literature recognized to belong to very diverse times and circumstances, not in a single harmonious body of revealed truth expressing its complex pattern of interlocking themes, typological, allegorical, parabolic and prophetic, the one vast theme of the divine plan of creation and redemption." Lampe, "The Reasonableness of Typology," 17–18. Pre-critical interpretation acknowledged a biblical unity based upon the Holy Spirit's inspiration of the Scriptures and God's divine plan of redemption in Christ. Ibid., 14–15. These foundational presuppositions were rejected by modern-critical scholarship. Consequently, the traditional understandings of prophecy and typology were no longer suitable either. Ibid., 14–18.

Proponents of traditional typology, consequently, have reservations with the analogical view of typology because this understanding originated from the post-Enlightenment need to reinterpret the Bible in conjunction with the skeptical presuppositions of historical-criticism. Admittedly, the skepticism that started this new understanding of typology does not appear to be what is driving it in contemporary conservative scholarship. It appears that many supporters of the analogical view "[seem] to have generally accepted the understanding of typology elucidated by advocates of historical criticism in the 1950s" without challenging its "presuppositional shifts from the traditional understanding of typology."[89]

These presuppositional shifts resulted in a view of typology that designates typological relationships as simple analogies between biblical events.[90] Proponents of the analogical view, therefore, see no prospective nature in types. Furthermore, "fulfillment" language, since it makes typology sound more like prophecy, is usually excluded in the presentation of typology from the analogical perspective.[91] Since types are only retrospectively discerned and not prospective in nature, they do not really exist as types in their OT contexts and, consequently, have no fulfillment.

France, however, is one analogical proponent who attempts to deal with the concept of fulfillment, which he identifies as "inherent in New Testament typology."[92] His treatment recognizes the importance of the concept to NT typology, but it is not without its struggles. France states clearly that antitypes are not fulfillments in the predictive sense.[93] He, then, qualifies what fulfillment means in typology. Fulfillment in typology denotes imperfect OT patterns viewed from the life of Jesus as "more perfectly re-embodied, and thus brought to completion."[94]

---

89 Davidson, *Typology in Scripture*, 92.

90 One finds such language as correspondences, patterns, consistencies, models, illustrations, paradigms, and rhythms in the discussion of analogical typology. Baker, *Two Testaments*, 179–199; France, *Jesus and the Old Testament*, 38–43, 76; Wright, *Knowing Jesus Through the Old Testament*, 110–116. Whatever language appears, the analogical view intends typological links to be understood as simple analogies between biblical events.

91 For example, neither Baker (*Two Testaments*, 190) nor Wright (*Knowing Jesus Through the Old Testament*, 110–116) discuss typology and its relationship to the concept of "fulfillment" in the NT.

92 France, *Jesus and the Old Testament*, 40.

93 Ibid. Types "have no intrinsic reference to the future," they do not "point forward to an antitype," and they do not have any initial "forward reference." France, *Jesus and the Old Testament*, 39–42. Cf., however, Beale, who supports a traditional view of typology and discusses the use of πληρόω formulas in the Gospels and how they indicate historical events in NT typology as being prophetically fulfilled. Beale, "Positive Answer to the Question," 396n27, 397.

94 France, *Jesus and the Old Testament*, 40; Richard N. Longenecker, "Negative Answer to the Question "Who is the Prophet Talking About?" Some Reflections on the New Testament's

Even with this qualification, exactly how simple analogies and the concept of fulfillment can be brought together remains unclear. For example, how can something that is simply an analogy be fulfilled? NT typology, therefore, must involve something more than purely analogous events, when considering the notion of NT fulfillment. The fact that France sees the idea of "completion" as a part of typology argues against types being mere analogies. Analogical typology, unlike traditional typology, fails to account sufficiently for the NT concept of fulfillment.[95]

In sum, proponents of traditional typology find analogical typology lacking in its explanation of the concept.[96] Specifically, the traditional view defines the concept in terms of prophecy, while the analogical view defines it strictly in terms of analogy. I. Howard Marshall's evaluation of traditional typology and analogical typology underscores this distinction. The center of the discussion concerns whether OT types were "deliberately planned" in relation to their antitypes, or whether they exist "merely because God works consistently in OT and NT times."[97] The former understands types to be predictive of their future fulfillments. The latter understands types only to form comparisons with later events. Thus, the proponent of the traditional view of typology maintains an understanding quite distinct from the proponent of analogical typology.

TRADITIONAL TYPOLOGY: PRINCIPLES FOR EXEGETICAL CONTROL

This section delineates the principles commonly used to discern cases of NT typological interpretation.[98] These principles do not represent a fixed

---

Use of the Old," in *The Right Doctrine from the Wrong Texts: Essays on the Use of the Old Testament in the New*, ed. G. K. Beale (Grand Rapids: Baker Books, 1994), 378–379.

95 I appreciate my doctoral advisor, Paul Hoskins, directing my attention to the inability of the analogical view to treat adequately the concept of fulfillment in the NT. See also Beale, who notes the concept of NT fulfillment leads many scholars to "conclude that typology is more than mere analogy but includes some kind of prophetic sense, as viewed from the NT perspective." Beale, *Handbook on the New Testament*, 17.

96 Bock writes, "Analogy compares; typology escalates. It is often the case in other studies in this area that this second classification is not sufficiently distinguished from the first classification of typology. It is, however, *misleading* [emphasis added] to call both types of texts typological . . . . Typology is prophetic while analogy is not." Bock, *Proclamation*, 50.

97 I. Howard Marshall, "An Assessment of Recent Developments," in *It is Written: Scripture Citing Scripture. Essays in Honour of Barnabas Lindars*, ed. D. A. Carson and H. G. M. Williamson (Cambridge: Cambridge University Press, 1988), 16.

98 Delineating these principles serves two purposes. First, these principles demonstrate that typology is not without exegetical controls—a negative assessment sometimes leveled against typology by its critics. G. P. Hugenberger, "Introductory Notes on Typology," in *The Right Doctrine from the Wrong Texts? Essays on the Use of the Old Testament in the New*, ed. G. K. Beale (Grand Rapids: Baker Books, 1994), 333–336. Second, these principles reflect those which

methodology for typology in the NT per se.⁹⁹ Rather, these principles denote guidelines for analyzing possible instances of NT typology.¹⁰⁰ There are four key principles to consider.¹⁰¹

This first principle of typological interpretation is to identify the NT's use of an OT text. NT typology concerns typological relationships that the NT authors had in mind.¹⁰² Thus, a real connection to the OT must be identified in the NT passage that is under evaluation.¹⁰³ The NT varies its mode of referencing the OT, appealing to it sometimes formally (i.e., quotations) and sometimes informally (i.e., allusions).¹⁰⁴ Importantly, then, the first step to

---

will be used in the exegesis of the Psalms quotations in John and Acts in chapters 4 and 5 of this work.

99 Typology has no formal methodology. A few reasons that help explain the absence of a formal typological methodology include: (1) the NT itself does not delineate a prescriptive formula in a type of systematic presentation and (2) there has not been enough thorough exegetical study of typology in both the OT and NT. Cf. Davidson, *Typology in Scripture*, 423–424; Fairbairn, *Typology of Scripture*, 1:140–141. Even though no formal typological methodology exists presently in biblical scholarship, guiding principles have been identified, which aid in evaluating the possibility or probability of cases of typology in the NT. On this point, Beale rightly concludes: "Whether an interpreter has made a legitimate typological connection is a matter of interpretive possibility or probability. . . . We must also remember that the conclusions of all biblical interpretation are a matter of degrees of possibility and probability; the conclusions of typology must be viewed in the same way." Beale, *Handbook on the New Testament*, 23–24.

100 One could make the case that these principles are a *working method* for detecting typology. Austin Farrer cautions against the establishment of a set of rules in typology that appears to guarantee correct interpretive analysis. Yet, he is comfortable speaking of "a method of looking for 'typical' meaning, to see whether it is there, or not" and "a method of judging whether a piece of typology we think we have detected was in the sacred author's mind when he wrote, or merely in ours when we read him." Austin Farrer, "Important Hypothesis Reconsidered," *ExpTim* 67 (May 1956): 228.

101 For a discussion on principles in typological interpretation, see John D. Currid, "Recognition and Use of Typology in Preaching," *RTR* 53 (1994): 121; Fairbairn, *Typology of Scripture*, 1:140–167; Osborne, "Type; Typology," 4:931; Ramm, *Protestant Biblical Interpretation*, 229–231; Terry, *Biblical Hermeneutics*, 250–256; Virkler and Ayayo, *Hermeneutics*, 185–187. See also Beale, who suggests a ninefold approach for interpreting the OT in the NT. Beale, *Handbook on the New Testament*, 42–43. He also lists several helpful guidelines for finding indicators of OT and NT typology. Ibid., 14–23, 57, 70–71. See also G. K. Beale, "Finding Christ in the Old Testament," *JETS* 63, no. 1 (2020): 29–43, where Beale further discusses criteria for discerning OT types.

102 Proponents of typology are ultimately interested in the NT author's intent in his use of the OT text. Thus, the proponent of typological interpretation readily agrees with Bock's statement: "The key in thinking through interpretations related to the use of the OT in the New is understanding *how* [emphasis original] the NT text is reading the OT text." Darrel L. Bock, "Use of the Old Testament in the New," in *Foundations for Biblical Interpretation: A Complete Library of Tools and Resources* ed. D. S. Dockery, K. A. Mathews, and R. B. Sloan (Nashville: Broadman & Holman, 1994), 109. As Osborne instructs, "Do not seek types where the context does not allow them." Osborne, "Type; Typology," 4:931.

103 Hoskins makes this point, when he states that "this [typological] import is open to verification, since the texts relevant to each type and antitype are found within the canon." Hoskins, *Jesus as the Fulfillment*, 26.

104 For an informative and practical article on the criteria to consider when attempting

substantiating a legitimate case of NT typology is the identification of a real appeal to the OT in the given NT passage.

This second principle of typological interpretation is to conduct thorough exegesis of the NT passage along with its OT reference. As with all biblical interpretation, the exegetical process of typological interpretation should examine both passages in their historical, literary, grammatical/syntactical, and theological contexts to discern the original, authorial intent of both texts.[105] Careful exegesis, therefore, should inform the overall interpretive conclusions about possible cases of NT typology.[106]

The third principle of typological interpretation is to identify the element(s) of typological correspondence, which were explained in detail above. Does the NT author appeal to an OT text that describes an historical person, event, or institution in order to juxtapose it with a person, event, or institution in the present context? What notable parallels are being made between the NT and OT persons, events, or institutions? Does the NT event in focus relate to the *telos* or goal of redemptive history: Christ and the realities of his gospel?[107] Finally, is there clear escalation or heightening from the OT event to the NT event, signaling that the NT event represents the fulfillment and, thus, the greater and more important reality belonging to salvation history?

The fourth principle of typological interpretation is to identify textual evidence that indicates a prophetic fulfillment attached to an OT historical narrative in the NT passage. Several OT and NT textual features serve as pointers to the prophetic significance of OT types. One, look for specific fulfillment formulas or similar kinds of formulas the NT authors may use to introduce an OT quotation or allusion that references a historical person,

---

to identify allusions to the OT in the NT, see Jon Paulien, "Elusive Allusions: The Problematic Use of the Old Testament in Revelation," *BR* 33 (1988): 37–48. For further discussion on suggested principles for evaluating OT quotations and allusions in the NT, see Beale, *Handbook on the New Testament*, 29–40; Roger Nicole, "The New Testament Use of the Old Testament," in *The Right Doctrine from the Wrong Texts? Essays on the Use of the Old Testament in the New*, ed. G. K. Beale (Grand Rapids: Baker Books, 1994), 18–25; Stanely E. Porter, "The Use of the Old Testament in the New Testament: A Brief Comment on Method and Terminology," in *Early Christian Interpretation of the Scriptures of Israel: Investigations and Proposals*, ed. Craig A. Evans and James A. Sanders, JSNTSup 148, SSEJC 5 (Sheffield: Sheffield Academic Press, 1997), 94–95.

105 Cf. Virkler and Ayayo, *Hermeneutics*, 185–187. Any text-critical questions should also be dealt with in the exegesis, as well as any questions pertaining to the textual source of the OT quotation or allusion (particularly the MT and LXX).

106 R. A. Markus explains: "It [typological exegesis] presupposes scrupulous care and attention to the literal meaning of the text and historical background: to whatever is relevant and capable of throwing light on what its writers had in mind in writing it." Markus, "Presuppositions," 445.

107 If not, the OT reference probably functions for simple analogy purposes and not as an indicator of typology.

event, or institution.[108] Introductory formulas, especially those with "fulfillment" language, are one way the NT authors reveal the fulfillment of both direct (i.e., verbal) and indirect (i.e., typological) prophecy.[109] Two, look for other language in the immediate context of the NT passage that conveys the ideas of prediction or fulfillment between the events in focus. Three, look for evidence in the broader context of the NT that may shed light on whether an OT event was viewed as a type that was forward pointing.[110] When Scripture is allowed to interpret Scripture in this way, the less distinct parts benefit from the clarification the wider NT canonical context provides.

Four, look for foreshadowing indications in the immediate OT context from which the NT author draws the quotation/allusion.[111] Also, investigate the broader OT corpus. In the broader context of the OT, the typological nature of an OT event is often already pre-expressed.[112] That is, one observes clear statements or strong clues in the OT that certain figures, events, and institutions anticipate a greater, future fulfillment.[113]

Summary

To recap, this chapter describes the traditional understanding of typology that is central to this study. To clarify traditional typology, this chapter, first, provides a clear definition, description, and illustration of the biblical concept. Then, it compares traditional typology with the other primary

---

108 Beale, *Handbook on the New Testament*, 17; Beale, "Finding Christ in the Old Testament," 30.

109 On "fulfillment" language in typology, see chapter 3 of this work.

110 Beale, *Handbook on the New Testament*, 19–20; Ramm, *Protestant Biblical Interpretation*, 229–230.

111 Beale, *Handbook on the New Testament*, 19–20, 23. In the immediate context, the OT author may indicate that he perceives the event to be a pattern anticipating a later fulfillment. The NT author, in turn, would have been aware of such contextual features in his use of the OT text.

112 Beale advises one to consider the following criteria when dealing with the broader OT context to discern if OT events may have been forward-looking in nature: (1) the clustered narratives that find only temporary fulfillments and continue to repeat [e.g., installation of prophets, priests, and kings], (2) OT figures that appear to be patterns of prior OT figures that are clearly types [e.g., Adam and Noah; Moses and Joshua], (3) the replication of major redemptive-historical events [e.g., new creation, new exodus, new temple], (4) the key theological message of a narrative, and (5) OT prophecies that model what is yet to come because they are only partially fulfilled [e.g., the Day of the Lord]. Beale, *Handbook on the New Testament*, 19–23.

113 For example, the OT looks forward to a second and greater David (cf. Isa 9:6–7; Jer 23:5–6; 30:9; 33:14–26; Ezek 34:23–24; 37:24–25), a new Moses (cf. Deut 18:15–19), an eschatological Exodus (cf. Isa 40–55), a new Temple (cf. Ezek 40–48), etc. On the OT basis for typology, see Foulkes, *The Acts of God*, 9–32; Greidanus, *Preaching Christ*, 215–216; Horace D. Hummel, "The Old Testament Basis of Typological Interpretation," *BR* 9 (1964): 38–50.

conception (i.e., analogical typology) to show how the two views differ. Finally, it delineates guidelines for discerning possible instances of NT typological interpretation.

As explained above, traditional typology involves the study of various OT persons, events, or institutions in salvation history that serve ultimately as predictive prefigurations of various NT goals fulfilled in Christ and the realities of his gospel. According to the traditional understanding, then, OT types and NT antitypes share an organic relationship in salvation history, relating to each other as a prophecy and fulfillment. Traditional typology, therefore, is a kind of biblical prophecy, where the prophecy takes the form of OT texts which describe events that the NT writers interpret as predictive patterns or models for corresponding NT counterparts. The value traditional typology places upon the prophetic relationship between types and antitypes distinguishes it from analogical typology, which defines the concept in terms of mere analogies or comparisons between the testaments.

3

Biblical and Historical Evidence in Support of Traditional Typology

Traditional typology, as defined in the previous chapter, recognizes that various OT persons/events/institutions act as prefigurations in the progress of God's redemptive plan, whereby God uses them to point forward to and, thus, predict corresponding NT goals fulfilled in Jesus Christ and the realities of his gospel. As also noted in chapter two, the emphasis upon a prophetic significance of types in salvation history sets traditional typology apart from modern analogical typology. Considering the distinctive notion of prediction that is essential to traditional typology, this chapter presents a brief overview of the biblical and historical evidence that support understanding biblical typology in a prophetic sense and not as simple analogy.

Biblical Evidence in Support of Traditional Typology

The proponent of the traditional view of typology appeals foremost to Scripture, especially the NT, to justify its prophetic sense. The NT clearly substantiates that Jesus and the apostles understood the OT to be prophetic.[1] To be noted is the fact that Jesus' and the NT writers' concept of OT prophecy appears to take the form of both verbal statements (i.e., direct prophecy) and also historical situations (i.e., typological prophecy). In fact, the NT presents both prophecy and typology without sharp distinction.[2] The biblical evidence that

---

1 For Jesus' prophetic understanding of the OT, see e.g., Matt 3:15; 5:17–18; 13:14; 11:13; 26:54, 56; Mark 1:15; 14:49; Luke 4:21; 22:44; 24:25–27, 44–47; John 5:39–47; 17:12. For the NT writers' prophetic understanding of the OT, see e.g., Matt 1:22; 4:14; 8:17; 12:17–21; 13:35; 21:4–5; Acts 3:17–24; 10:43; 13:27; 17:2–3; 28:23; Rom 1:2; 16:26; 2 Cor 1:20; 1 Pet 1:10–12; 2 Pet 1:19–21.

2 Gerhard Friedrich, "προφήτης κτλ," *TDNT* 6:834. In this entry, the term "typology" does not appear, but it is clear from the context that this is the concept Friedrich is comparing with prophecy. He writes, "The words of the prophets do not usually take the form of open predictions (→ 857, 25ff.) but often contain descriptions of existing situations or even deal with past

supports a prophetic understanding of NT typology includes: (1) Jesus' teachings and examples, (2) typology in the Epistle of Hebrews, (3) "fulfillment" language, (4), hermeneutical τύπος language, and (5) the OT basis of typology.

JESUS' TEACHINGS AND EXAMPLES

The influence of the OT in the NT by way of quotations, allusions, and themes along with the NT's consistent application of the OT to the gospel points to it as the "substructure of all Christian theology."[3] Thus, the NT makes plain the OT's status as the primary background for its study. As equally plain in the NT is Jesus' status as the normative authority on interpreting the OT. The NT identifies Jesus as the "source" and "paradigm" for the proper application and understanding of the OT.[4] Concerning how the early disciples learned to interpret the OT, C. H. Dodd contended:

> We are precluded from proposing any one of them for the honour of having originated the process.... But the New Testament itself avers that it was Jesus Christ himself who first directed the minds of His followers to certain parts of the scriptures as those in which they might find illumination upon the meaning of His mission and destiny.[5]

The importance of Jesus' role, then, as the source and paradigm for applying and understanding the OT cannot be overemphasized.

So, when attention is given to the distinctiveness of Jesus' teachings and examples on how to understand the OT, one observes a key interpretive axiom that sheds light on the proper way to understand NT typology. Specifically, Jesus taught the disciples in Luke 24:25–27, 44–47 to read the whole

---

events which the NT relates to the present, so that more is seen of *advance depiction* [emphasis added] than of true prophecy.... The NT sees no distinction between *depiction* [emphasis added] and prophecy." Ibid., 6:834. In the original, "advance depiction" is the translation of the German "Vorausdarstellungen." That "Vorausdarstellungen" refers to the concept of typology is certain because in the following sentence, Friedrich explains, "So werden zB die geschichtliche Aussage ... für Weissagungen angesehen" ("Thus, for example, the historical statement . . . are considered for prophecies" [my translation]). The NT examples he identifies (Matt 2:15, 17f.; 13:35; Mark 7:6; John 12:38) reference OT historical statements noted to be predictions by the NT authors. Gerhard Friedrich, "προφήτης κτλ," *TWNT* 6:835.

3 C. H. Dodd, *According to the Scriptures: The Sub-Structure of New Testament Theology* (1953; repr., Eugene, OR: Wipf & Stock), 127.

4 Richard N. Longenecker, *Biblical Exegesis in the Apostolic Period*, 2nd ed. (Grand Rapids: Eerdmans, 1999), 36, 61–62, 187–88.

5 Dodd, *According to the Scriptures*, 110.

OT as pointing forward to his person and mission.⁶ In this passage, Jesus referred the disciples to the whole of the OT (i.e., the Law, the Prophets, and the Psalms),⁷ which he claimed was predictive of himself and the realities of his gospel.⁸ One of the primary implications of Luke 24, as Vern S. Poythress notes, is that the whole OT points forward to Jesus, speaks of him, and prefigures him.⁹ What this implies for NT typology, then, is that the OT texts relaying historical incidents that apply to Jesus must in some sense bear a prophetic function in connection to him.¹⁰

In John 5:39–47, John records another instance of Jesus' teachings that complements what he taught in Luke 24. This passage offers insight that is also helpful for understanding typology. Jesus teaches in John 5:39 that the primary witness of the OT Scriptures concerns him. Jesus says, "and, it is these [the Scriptures] that testify about me."¹¹ He, then, indicts the unbelieving Jews with the charge that Moses accuses them before the Father (John 5:45). The reason Moses accuses them, Jesus explains, is "for he wrote about me" (John 5:46). So, Moses' writings bear witness to Jesus because Moses

---

6 On this "Christocentric" hermeneutic, see Vern S. Poythress, *The Shadow of Christ in the Law of Moses* (New Jersey: P&R Publishing, 1991), 284–286.

7 The plural οἱ προφῆται in Luke 24:25 is most likely a reference to all Scripture. See BDAG, s.v. "προφήτης." The references Μωϋσέως καὶ ἀπὸ πάντων τῶν προφητῶν διερμήνευσεν αὐτοῖς ἐν πάσαις ταῖς γραφαῖς in Luke 24:27 appear to be synonymous with οἱ προφῆται. Jesus expands "Moses and all the Prophets" even further in Luke 24:44 to "the Law of Moses and the Prophets and the Psalms." These various labels indicate that there is no single or uniform way the NT refers to the whole of the OT. The characteristic threefold division of the OT into the Law, the Prophets, and the Writings finds the closest parallel with Jesus' delineation of the OT into the Law of Moses, the Prophets, and the Psalms (Luke 24:44).

8 Several features in these two texts support the claim that Jesus understood the OT to be predictive of him. First, the rhetorical question in Luke 24:26 begins with the emphatic οὐχὶ. This expects an affirmative answer to the necessity that Jesus had to suffer and enter into his glory in accordance with what had been written about him in the OT. Second, the verb ἔδει (Luke 24:26) indicates the prophetic quality of the OT. Charles H. Cosgrove notes that Luke ties δεῖ to explicit prophecy in four instances (Luke 22:37; 24:26, 44; Acts 26:22–23). Charles H. Cosgrove, "The Divine ΔΕΙ in Luke-Acts: Investigations into the Lukan Understanding of God's Providence," *NovT* 26 (1984): 174. One of the important functions of δεῖ in Lukan theology is "to express the rootedness of the kerygmatic history . . . in God's plan. The hard core of that plan is the Old Testament's prophecies of the divinely-sanctioned events of this history." Ibid., 183; see also 189. The divine δεῖ, therefore, links Jesus' passion to the fulfillment of OT prophecy and grounds it in Scripture. Finally, διερμήνευσεν in Luke 24:27 means to "explain" or "interpret" the meaning of prophecies. BDAG, s.v. "διερμηνεύω." As for Luke 24:44–47, the prophetic quality of the whole OT to Jesus is demonstrated by (1) πάντα τὰ γεγραμμένα . . . περὶ ἐμοῦ in 24:44, (2) the repeat use of the verb δεῖ in 24:44, (3) and the "fulfillment" language (πληρωθῆναι) in 24:44, which notes the realization of divine prophecies (BDAG, s.v. "πληρόω.").

9 Poythress, *The Shadow of Christ*, 5.

10 That is, OT history that points to Jesus and prefigures him is rightly understood as functioning to predict him in some way.

11 Τὰς γραφάς ("the Scriptures," John 5:39) "designates collectively all the parts of Scripture." BDAG, s.v. "γραφή."

wrote specifically about Jesus. Importantly, it is clear that Jesus has in mind more than a single instance in which Moses wrote about him from the plural γράμμασιν ("writings," John 5:47). Moses' *writings* testify to Jesus. While Deut 18:15 (cf. John 1:21; 4:19; 6:14; 7:40) was likely a reference Jesus had in mind, a careful reading of John's Gospel weighs against a single passage and suggests a "certain *way* of reading the books of Moses."[12] The *way* Jesus understands the writings of Moses to testify to him is by means of various historical situations Moses recorded.

For example, Jesus alludes to the incident of Jacob and his vision at Bethel (John 1:51/Gen 28:12) and applies it to himself. It appears the OT event functions as a pattern that anticipates Jesus. Jesus replaces and fulfills the ladder in Jacob's vision, thus, identifying him as the true and eternal means of revelation between God and man.[13] In his encounter with Nicodemus, Jesus alludes clearly to the historical narrative recorded in Num 21:6–9 (John 3:14–15).[14] Just as the serpent was lifted up, according to Jesus, so must (δεῖ) the Son of man be lifted up. Jesus' language communicates that his imminent death and its saving efficacy recapitulates and fulfills what was prefigured in the OT event.[15] A few chapters later in John, Jesus describes himself as "the true bread out of heaven" (John 6:32). In contrast with the manna that God gave to Israel in the wilderness (Exod 16:4, 15), Jesus claims that he is the "true" (ἀληθινόν) bread from heaven. The term ἀληθινόν identifies Jesus as the perfect and greater reality, which was anticipated in advance by the imperfect

---

12 Concerning John 5:46, Carson comments, "If a particular one [i.e., specific passage] is in view, perhaps it is Dt. 18:15 . . . . But it is perhaps more likely that this verse is referring to a certain *way* [emphasis original] of reading the books of Moses (cf. notes on 1:51; 2:19) than to a specific passage." D. A. Carson, *The Gospel According to John*, PNTC (Grand Rapids: Eerdmans, 1991), 266.

13 Paul M. Hoskins, *Jesus as the Fulfillment of the Temple in the Gospel of John* (Eugene, OR: Wipf & Stock, 2006), 125–135. Cf. C. K. Barrett, *The Gospel According to St. John: An Introduction with Commentary and Notes on the Greek Text*, 2nd ed. (Philadelphia: The Westminster Press, 1978), 187.

14 On the typology of John 3:14–15, see the section "Illustration of Traditional Typology" in chapter 2 of this work.

15 The comparative conjunctions καθὼς and οὕτως in John 3:14 connect the episode of the lifting up of the serpent in the wilderness with Jesus' imminent lifting up on the cross. Jesus' use of δεῖ suggests that he intends more than a simple illustration or comparison. Throughout the NT, especially in Luke-Acts, δεῖ emphasizes the necessity of the events that must transpire in Jesus' life according to God's divine purpose. See Cosgrove, "The Divine ΔEI in Luke-Acts," 173–174; Walter Grundmann, "δεῖ," *TDNT* 2:21–25. The verb links the events of Jesus' life to the fulfillment of the Scriptures. It functions this way in John 3:14 (cf. John 20:9, where John uses δεῖ to stress the necessity of Jesus' resurrection according to the Scriptures). Grundmann, "δεῖ," *TDNT* 2:24.

shadow, the manna.[16] In light of the fact that Jesus taught that Moses' writings testify specifically about him, it seems correct to view these OT historical narratives as bearing a predictive thrust towards Jesus. Thus, these OT texts to which Jesus alludes provide prophetic patterns, which he interpreted as pointing forward to their fulfillments in him. These various OT types, therefore, possess a prophetic force, prefiguring and predicting similar but greater realities that climax in Christ.

TYPOLOGY IN THE EPISTLE OF HEBREWS

Of the various ways the writer of Hebrews interprets the OT, "perhaps no other element of biblical interpretation has been as often identified with the Book of Hebrews as typology."[17] Vos points out that typology in Hebrews concentrates on the relationship between the Old and New Covenants. Specifically, Hebrews shows that the "old prefigures the new" in the sense of "shadow" to "image."[18] The author's use of the shadow/image language portrays the OT Law as pointing forward to Christ (Heb 10:1). The Law itself and its sacrifices were merely a "shadow/foreshadowing" (σκιά) but not the very "form/image/appearance" (εἰκών) of what was to come.[19] This foreshadowing aspect means that the Law along with its sacrifices prefigured, and, thus, predicted future realities fulfilled in Christ.[20]

---

16 See BDAG, s.v. "ἀληθινός," where the term has the possible meaning of stressing the reality of something in contrast to its copy (cf. John 15:1; Heb 8:2; 9:24). Paul M. Hoskins informs, "The second term commonly used to differentiate types from antitypes is 'true.' 'True' (*alēthinos*) is sometimes used in the Gospel of John and in Hebrews to differentiate the true or complete realities from their imperfect, anticipatory shadows in the Old Testament.... This is probably applicable in the case of the true light (John 1:9), the true worshipers (4:23), the true bread from heaven (6:32), and the true vine (15:1)." Paul M. Hoskins, *That Scripture Might Be Fulfilled: Typology and the Death of Christ* (Longwood, FL: Xulon, 2009), 29–30.

17 Andrew W. Trotter, Jr., *Interpreting the Epistle to the Hebrews*, GNTE (Grand Rapids: Baker Books, 1997), 196.

18 Geerhardus Vos, *The Teaching of the Epistle to the Hebrews* (Grand Rapids: Eerdmans, 1956), 55.

19 BDAG, s.v. "σκιά" and "εἰκών." See also Richard M. Davidson, *Typology in Scripture: A Study of Hermeneutical Τύπος Structures*, AUSDDS 2 (Berrien Springs, MI: Andrews University Press, 1981), 352.

20 The prophetic anticipation can be seen in (1) the natural relationship the OT "foreshadowing" shares with the NT "form" and (2) in the participle τῶν μελλόντων in Heb 10:1, whose root characteristically means "future/to come" or denotes some necessary future action that must take place. BDAG, s.v. "μέλλω." Paul uses the participle in a synonymous manner in Col 2:16–17. There, he instructs that the OT regulations, festivals, and holy days were in essence σκιὰ τῶν μελλόντων. Christ, however, is the substance or reality (τὸ σῶμα), which these OT institutions prefigured.

The author of Hebrews also draws attention to the regulations of priestly worship associated with the OT tabernacle (9:1–10). The tabernacle served a typological function in that it was a "type/figure (παραβολή) for the present time" (9:9). As a "type" or "figure" of the present time,[21] the tabernacle and its regulations were only meant to be temporary until Christ, the great high priest, ushered in the corresponding New Covenant realities (9:10–11). Especially significant is the author's claim that the Holy Spirit was "indicating" (δηλοῦντος) future fulfillments associated with the tabernacle (9:8).[22]

There are several other instances where Hebrews uses and interprets the OT as containing prophetic prefigurations, even though the passages are not explicit predictions. Melchizedek pointed forward to Christ's high priesthood (5:6, 10; 6:20; 7:1–28), the rest of Israel prefigured a NT rest (3:7–4:13), and Isaiah and his children were predictive of Christ and his children (2:13).[23] In light of these examples and the clear statement on the foreshadowing function of the Law and its sacrifices, it is clear that the author of Hebrews understood the OT and NT to relate typologically. He regards the typologies as inherent relationships, where the OT types were prefiguring NT realities that were to come.

Fulfillment Language

One item of textual evidence which proves significant for a prophetic understanding of NT typology is Jesus' and the NT writers' use of πληρόω ("fulfillment") language. BDAG lists six primary senses for πληρόω in the NT.[24] Helpful to understanding typology is the meaning πληρόω conveys in the "fulfillment" of the OT Scriptures. In the Gospels and in Acts, πληρόω appears

---

21 BDAG, s.v. "παραβολή." Cf. Heb 11:19, where Isaac is designated as a παραβολή of Christ's death and resurrection. Ibid. Hoskins discusses παραβολή as a NT term associated with typology. Hoskins, *That Scripture Might Be Fulfilled*, 30.

22 Vos, *Epistle to the Hebrews*, 59. The verb δηλόω means to reveal, make clear, show, indicate, or report something. BDAG, s.v. "δηλόω."

23 Vos, *Epistle to the Hebrews*, 59–61.

24 BDAG defines these six senses as follows: (1) to make full, *fill (full)*, (2) to complete a period of time, *fill (up)*, *complete*, (3) to bring to completion that which was already begun, *complete, finish*, (4) to bring to a designed end, *fulfill* a prophecy, an obligation, a promise, a law, a purpose, a desire, a hope, a duty, a fate, a destiny, etc., (5) to bring to completion an activity in which one has been involved from its beginning, *complete, finish*, and (6) *complete* a number, pass. *have the number made complete*. BDAG, s.v. "πληρόω." Poythress points out that BDAG really only provides three distinct senses, since four of the six listed in BDAG are "virtually indistinguishable from one another." Poythress, *The Shadow of Christ*, 368. According to Poythress, entries two, three, five, and six represent one meaning, while entries one and four represent the other distinct meanings.

in numerous citation formulas.²⁵ One of the basic and established senses of πληρόω, when used to cite passages from the OT, is its emphasis upon prophetic fulfillment.²⁶ Πληρόω naturally signals the realization of a predictive notion in the OT references it introduces. This natural underscoring of the fulfillment of a prophetic notion by πληρόω, according to G. K. Beale, offers clarity in the conversation about typology and its predictive quality. Beale explains:

> The *ultimate* [emphasis original] equation of direct verbal prophecy and indirect typological prophecy is illustrated by the observation that introductory fulfillment formulas are attached to both. . . . Some scholars try to argue that "fulfill" has a different meaning when used of OT direct verbal predictions than when "fulfill" is used of OT persons, events, and institutions. But "fulfill" in both sets of uses appears naturally to refer to fulfillment of OT prophecy, whether that is a direct prophecy through a prophet's direct words or an indirect prophecy through a person, event, or institution that points forward to a greater person, event, or institution.²⁷

According to Beale's explanation, πληρόω identifies typology as a category of biblical prophecy, seeing that it is used to denote the fulfillment of both direct prophecy (i.e., OT texts that relay words) and typological prophecy (i.e., OT texts that relay events).

---

25 Cf. Matt 1:22; 2:15, 17, 23; 4:14; 5:17; 8:17; 12:17; 13:35; 21:4; 26:54, 56; 27:9; Mark 14:49; Luke 4:21; 24:44; John 12:38; 13:18; 15:25; 17:12; 18:32; 19:24, 36; Acts 1:16; 3:18; 13:27, 33 (here ἐκπληρόω).

26 See entry four in BDAG, s.v. "πληρόω." See Thayer's, s.v. "πληρόω." John also uses πληρόω in two instances to note the fulfillment of Jesus' own words (John 18:9, 32).

27 G. K. Beale, *Handbook on the New Testament Use of the Old Testament: Exegesis and Interpretation* (Grand Rapids: Baker Academic, 2012), 58. For a list of Scripture references Beale uses to support this claim, see Ibid. Cf. Beale's statement that "the πληρόω formulas prefixed to citations from formally non-prophetic OT passages in the gospels *decisively* [emphasis added] argue against" those who claim that typology has no predictive quality. G. K. Beale, "Positive Answer to the Question: Did Jesus and His Followers Preach the Right Doctrine from the Wrong Texts? An Examination of the Presuppositions of Jesus' and the Apostles' Exegetical Method," in *The Right Doctrine from the Wrong Texts? Essays on the Use of the Old Testament in the New*, ed. G. K. Beale (Grand Rapids: Baker Books, 1994), 396n27. See also, Todd A. Scacewater, "The Predictive Nature of Typology in John 12:37–43," *WTJ* 75, no. 1 (2013): 143, who argues that John's use of "fulfillment" language in his Gospel with both typological fulfillment and direct prophetic fulfillment seems to indicate that John did not sharply distinguish between the two concepts and "suggests that the traditional view of typology may be the correct position with regard to the predictive element." See also, Craig L. Blomberg, *A New Testament Theology* (Waco, TX: Baylor University Press, 2018), 353–356; 694, who seems to understand Matthew's and Luke's use of "fulfillment" language with Scripture citation to indicate that those Scriptures are predictive, whether directly or typologically. Note especially that Blomberg discusses Matthew's use of the direct fulfillment and typological fulfillment of Scripture under the heading "Fulfilling Specific Prophecies." Ibid., 354–356.

Some scholars diverge with Beale, as he points out, where they find it necessary to define πληρόω differently, depending upon the kind of OT text it introduces in NT formula citations.²⁸ Particularly, some scholars resort to a non-prophetic meaning for πληρόω, when it is used in the citation of OT texts that relay historical events. Why do scholars opt for a non-prophetic sense of πληρόω in these cases? One of the more obvious answers is that they find a problem reconciling how πληρόω can denote prophetic fulfillment of seemingly non-predictive OT passages (i.e., texts describing events).²⁹

So, the primary question that must be answered is: "Can πληρόω legitimately indicate the fulfillment of prophecy in OT texts that are event-based?" There is evidence to suggest it can. According to D. A. Carson, "The verb 'to fulfill' has a broader significance than mere one-to-one prediction . . . . Not only in Matthew but elsewhere in the NT, the history and laws of the OT are perceived to have a prophetic significance" in connection to Christ.³⁰ Fulfillment, then, must be understood in light of OT history that *points* to Christ.³¹ Douglas J. Moo also says that πληρόω in introductory formulas does not always indicate the fulfillment of direct prophecy. Moo explains:

> But, in fact, *plēroō* cannot be confined to so narrow a compass. The word is used in the New Testament to indicate the broad redemptive-historical relationship of the new, climactic revelation of God in Christ to the preparatory, incomplete revelation to and through Israel. . . . What needs to be emphasized, then, is that the use of *plēroō* in an introductory formula need not mean that the author regards the Old Testament text he quotes as a direct prophecy.³²

Just because direct prophecy is not in view with the use of πληρόω, this does not mean a prophetic force is altogether absent in connection to the relevant

---

28 For example, R. T. France clearly distinguishes between the idea of fulfillment when used with NT typology and prophecy. With typology, fulfillment language identifies a previous pattern of God's working reaching "completion" or "culmination," but fulfillment language with prophecy signals the realization of a "predictive" or "forward-looking" element. R. T. France, *Jesus and the Old Testament: His Application of the Old Testament Passages to Himself and His Mission* (Vancouver, British Columbia: Regent College Publishing, 1998), 38–43, 83.

29 See e.g., J. R. Daniel Kirk, "Conceptualising Fulfilment in Matthew," *TynBul* 59 (2008): 80.

30 D. A. Carson, "Matthew," in EBC 8, ed. Frank E. Gaebelein (Grand Rapids: Zondervan, 1984), 92; see also, 142–145. See also, Douglas J. Moo, *The Old Testament in the Gospel Passion Narratives* (Sheffield, Eng.: The Almond Press, 1983), 383–387; C. F. D. Moule, "Fulfillment-Words in the New Testament: Use and Abuse," *NTS* 14 (1967–68): 293–320.

31 Carson, "Matthew," 92.

32 Douglas J. Moo, "The Problem of *Sensus Plenior*," in *Hermeneutics, Authority, and Canon*, ed. D. A. Carson and John D. Woodbridge (Grand Rapids: Zondervan, 1986), 191.

OT text. The explanation Moo gives of πληρόω actually elucidates that the broader sense of the verb witnesses to a prophetic character in the relationship OT revelation shares with NT revelation. Put simply, πληρόω highlights the climax of revelation in Christ, which indicates that OT revelation was preparing the way for him, anticipating, and, thus, predicting him.

The study by C. F. D. Moule adds further insight on how πληρόω can be used to signify that OT texts describing events bear prophetic import to corresponding NT events. First, Moule notes that the NT writers clearly use πληρόω to mark the realization of straightforward predictions.[33] In addition to this sense, there is a deeper meaning to πληρόω. The deeper meaning of πληρόω, according to Moule, portrays "the 'Christ-event' in its relation to the entire design of God."[34] Basically, what Moule is saying is that the broader sense of πληρόω is teleological,[35] so that "Jesus is seen as the goal, the convergence-point, of God's plan for Israel, his covenant promise."[36] Associated with πληρόω, then, is the idea that salvation history contains a pattern that moves in the direction of a climax, namely, Jesus' life, death, and resurrection.[37] Moule explains this principle as follows:

> Those who are sensitive can recognize God's pattern of relationship as it shapes itself out of the different materials of successive generations, particularly in God's covenant-relation with Israel, and they can see that the pattern has a purpose and is developing 'teleologically' towards a goal.[38]

The implication of this understanding of πληρόω sheds light on NT typology. Essentially, πληρόω implies some kind of prediction-fulfillment notion for typology (i.e., OT texts that relay events), for the wider scope of the term recognizes a teleological force to OT history.[39] So, in addition to verifying explicit OT prophecies, πληρόω language also recognizes instances where OT events (i.e., OT types) serve as prophetic paradigms that anticipate respective NT

---

33 Moule, "Fulfillment-Words," 297–298, 301–302, 317–318.
34 Ibid., 295.
35 Ibid., 298–299.
36 Ibid., 301.
37 Moule, "Fulfillment-Words," 298–301.
38 Ibid., 298.
39 Carson claims, "Most NT uses of *plēroō* in connection with Scripture, however, require some teleological force . . . and even the ambiguous uses presuppose a typology that in its broadest dimensions is teleological, even if not in every detail . . ." Carson, "Matthew," 143. This teleological force accords with the definition BDAG provides for πληρόω relation to the fulfillment of divine prophecies: "to bring to a designed end." BDAG, s.v. "πληρόω."

goals or fulfillments (i.e., NT antitypes).⁴⁰ These OT paradigms are considered predictive in force, because they are pointing to climactic NT goals. Carson summarizes this point well:

> But when it [πληρόω] refers to the fulfilling of Scripture, it does not lose all teleological force except in rare and well-defined situations. But opinion varies as to exactly how these OT scriptures point forward. Sometimes the OT passages cited are plainly or at least plausibly messianic. Often the relation between prophecy and fulfillment is typological: . . . . Yet the perception remains constant that the OT was preparing the way for Christ, anticipating him, pointing to him, leading up to him.⁴¹

Πληρόω, therefore, brings to light that typology amounts to more than mere analogy.⁴² Such "fulfillment" language shows that OT texts relaying events are interpreted as pointing forward to Christ and his gospel, which means they ultimately predict him and have a prophetic quality.

Looking at some NT examples of πληρόω will help illustrate how it shows OT events as pointing forward to or predicting NT events. In his Gospel, Matthew combines πληρόω language with OT Scripture to signal the fulfillment of direct verbal prophecies (cf. 1:22; 4:14; 8:17; 12:17; 21:4–5). In addition, he also employs the verb to highlight typological prophecy, when he cites OT passages that describe events and have no apparent predictive quality on the surface level.⁴³ On Matthew's fulfillment formulas, Thomas R. Schreiner observes:

> In some instances prophecy and fulfillment appear to be rather direct. . . . Other texts in Matthew conceive of the fulfillment of prophecy differently. The OT event functions as a model or type of that which is fulfilled in Jesus. Hence, the OT text is fulfilled in a typological fashion.⁴⁴

For example, in Matt 2:15 Matthew states, "in order that it might be fulfilled which was spoken by the Lord through the prophet, saying, 'Out of Egypt I called my son.'" Quoting from Hos 11:1, the passage in its original context recalls God's love for Israel and the deliverance he brought about in the exodus

---
40 Cf. Moule's brief discussion of typology as an important concept in the NT that witnesses to Jesus as the climactic goal of salvation history. Moule, "Fulfillment-Words," 298–299.
41 Carson, "Matthew," 28.
42 Beale, *Handbook on the New Testament*, 17.
43 Cf. Matt 2:15, 17; 13:34–35; 27:9–10. Matthew 1:22 may also be typology (see Thomas R. Schreiner, *New Testament Theology: Magnifying God in Christ* [Grand Rapids: Baker Academic, 2008], 73–75.), but Carson thinks it is more likely direct prophecy. Carson, "Matthew," 76–81.
44 Schreiner, *New Testament Theology*, 70–71.

from Egypt (cf. Exod 4:22–23; 12:40–41). Matthew, however, sees some kind of meaningful connection between this event and Jesus' departure from Egypt after the death of Herod (Matt 2:13–23). In fact, he states that Jesus' calling out of Egypt "fulfills" this OT text. How does Jesus fulfill a seemingly non-prophetic text, a historical statement about Israel, though? It appears that Matthew sees typological correspondences between Israel and Jesus and their similar situations. Thus, he interprets Israel's exodus from Egypt as pointing forward to Jesus' exodus from Egypt.[45] This typology is not simply analogy in Matthew's assessment. His use of πληρόω reveals that the former event possessed significance beyond itself. The initial exodus of Israel was anticipating or predicting the climactic new exodus of Jesus, the true Israel and Son of God who fulfills God's promise of salvation.[46] So, since Jesus recapitulates and fulfills the OT event, he is signaled as the goal to which the OT event was pointing. Matthew's use of πληρόω in this citation, therefore, demonstrates in this example (and others, cf. Matt 2:17; 27:9) that he sees OT historical situations as patterns recapitulated and prophetically fulfilled in the life of Christ. In that he uses πληρόω with OT Scriptures to denote the fulfillment of direct prophecy and typology, Matthew appears to view typology as a form of OT prophecy.

John also uses πληρόω in the passion narrative of his Gospel in a way that suggests typology possesses a prophetic element. What makes John 19:36–37 such a compelling argument for prophetic typology is the double duty πληρόω serves in these two verses. Contextually, the preceding verses recount the facts that (1) Jesus' legs were not broken and (2) his side was pierced with a spear (19:31–35). After recounting these details, John writes, "For these things happened that the Scripture might be fulfilled (19:36). Two

---

45 Cf. Leon Morris, who contends that Matthew can apply Israel's experiences to Jesus on certain occasions because "the divine purpose runs through the whole of Scripture, and it all *points* [emphasis added] in some way to the climax, the coming of Christ." Leon Morris, *The Gospel according to Matthew*, PNTC (Grand Rapids: Eerdmans, 1992), 44.

46 On the prophetic nature of this typology, Schreiner writes, "We still wonder, though, how Matthew seizes upon Hosea 11:1 as prophetic, since the text refers to a historical event. . . . The exodus from Egypt functions as a type for what God will now do in Hosea's day. Just as he freed Israel from Egyptian bondage, so he will liberate them in a new exodus from Assyria. Hosea 11:1, therefore, is not merely a historical remembrance of God's work in the past; it points forward to God's promise for Hosea's day, to a new liberating work of God. Hosea himself, then, views Israel's history typologically. If what I have suggested is correct, then Matthew used typology just as Hosea did. Matthew believed that the return from exile promised in Hosea ultimately became a reality with the true son of Israel, Jesus Christ. In calling Jesus out of Egypt—in replicating the history of Israel—we see that Jesus is the true Israel, the true son of the promise, the fulfillment of God's saving purposes." Schreiner, *New Testament Theology*, 74–75; see also 73. See also Beale, *Handbook on the New Testament*, 60–64; Carson, "Matthew," 90–93; C. F. Keil, *Minor Prophets*, trans. James Martin, *Commentary on the Old Testament* 10 (repr., Grand Rapids: Eerdmans, 1977), 1:137.

OT quotations follow this πληρόω formula, one in the latter part of 19:36 and the other in 19:37.[47]

John 19:37 contains a quotation from Zech 12:10 (cf. also Rev 1:7). In Zech 12:10, God announces beforehand that his Shepherd-Messiah (cf. Zech 13:7) will be pierced. Zech 12:10 appears as a prophetic statement in its original OT context, and the πληρόω language calls attention to the completion of this direct prophecy in the piercing of Jesus' side. The quotation in John 19:36, however, does not reflect a scriptural passage with an obvious predictive force. Most likely, the quotation is taken from either Exod 12:46 or Num 9:12.[48] Both passages are found in the Law and pertain to the prescription that no bone of the Passover lamb was to be broken in observance of the Passover. Apparently, John sees a typological connection. He looks back to the Passover lamb and understands it to function as an advance presentation of Jesus, the perfect and final Passover sacrifice (cf. 1 Cor 5:7). In effect, then, the OT Passover is seen to be pointing forward to and predicting its goal, Jesus.

In sum, the single πληρόω formula of John 19:36 governs both OT quotations. Consequently, it appears exegetically sound to conclude, then, that John sees prophecies being fulfilled with both kinds of texts. The Zechariah quotation is a case of direct prophetic fulfillment. The Exodus/Numbers quotation, since it relays a historical narrative, is a case of typological prophetic fulfillment. The use of πληρόω with both quotations presents the OT Passover event as possessing a predicative quality in John's thinking.[49]

Hermeneutical Τύπος Language

Some scholars argue that the NT designates explicit cases of typology by use of the term τύπος ("type," Rom 5:14; 1 Cor 10:6) and its cognates τυπικῶς ("typically," 1 Cor 10:11) and ἀντίτυπος ("antitype," 1 Pet 3:21).[50] While the NT writers

---

47 Though the πληρόω formula appears in John 19:36 and not in 19:37, it is clear that the formula governs both Scripture citations. Craig A. Evans explains that the adverb πάλιν in 19:37 links back to the citation formula. Craig A. Evans, "Obduracy and the Lord's Servant: Some Observations on the Use of the Old Testament in the Fourth Gospel," in *Early Jewish and Christian Exegesis: Studies in Memory of William Hugh Brownlee*, ed. Craig A. Evans and William F. Stinespring, SPHS 10 (Atlanta: Scholars Press, 1987), 225n20.

48 Leon Morris, *The Gospel according to John*, NICNT, rev. ed. (Grand Rapids: Eerdmans, 1995), 727n108.

49 Beale argues, "Since these OT references [i.e., Exod 12:46/Num 9:12] are not prophecies but historical narratives and John sees them as *prophecy* [emphasis added] being fulfilled, it would appear best to say that this is an *indirect fulfillment* [emphasis original] of what John considered to be foreshadowed by the historical event involving the Passover lamb." Beale, *Handbook on the New Testament*, 17.

50 Τύπος appears a total of fifteen times in the NT (John 20:25 [twice]; Acts 7:43, 44; 23:25;

do not consistently designate typology by a special terminology,[51] Paul and Peter seem to employ τύπος language in this specific way. Τύπος in general refers to a mark, form, or pattern, resulting from a strike or blow of some sort.[52] What distinguishes the three passages noted above is the conjoining of τύπος terminology and the author's reference to and seeming interpretation of an OT historical reality in view a present NT reality (i.e., Adam/Christ in Rom 5:12–21; Israel/the Church in 1 Cor 10:1–13; the Flood/Christian baptism in 1 Pet 3:18–22).

Leonhard Goppelt noted, in his detailed treatment of the term, a technical, hermeneutical function of τύπος in Rom 5:14 and 1 Cor 10:6 and the same parallel meaning in its cognates in 1 Cor 10:11 and 1 Pet 3:21.[53] By technical, hermeneutical, Goppelt meant that Paul and Peter used τύπος terminology in a special way to signal the interpretation of OT events in light of corresponding NT realities. Essentially, then, Paul and Peter interpret the OT events they reference as "'advance presentation[s]' intimating eschatological events."[54] Müller also observes τύπος serving as a "hermeneutical concept in the interpretation of OT tradition" in the instances noted above.[55] Additionally, Richard Davidson's in-depth examination of NT τύπος terminology substantiates Goppelt's and Müller's initial contentions, concluding that τύπος and its cognates do function as "specific hermeneutical terms" in various hermeneutical contexts (i.e., 1 Cor 10:6, 11; Rom 5:14; 1 Pet 3:21; Heb 8:5; 9:24).[56]

Rom 5:14; 6:17; 1 Cor 10:6; Phil 3:17; 1 Thess 1:7; 2 Thess 3:9; 1 Tim 4:12; Titus 2:7; Heb 8:5; 1 Pet 5:3). The adverb τυπικῶς is a hapax, appearing in the NT only in 1 Cor 10:11 (see Davidson, *Typology in Scripture*, 185, 274, for the renderings "corresponding to a type" and "typically"). Ἀντίτυπος occurs only twice in the NT (1 Pet 3:21; Heb 9:24).

51 Patrick Fairbairn, *Typology of Scripture: Two Volumes in One* (New York: Funk & Wagnalls, 1900; repr., Grand Rapids: Kregel, 1989), 1:30.

52 Cf. BDAG, s.v. "τύπος;" Leonhard Goppelt, "τύπος κτλ," *TDNT* 8:246–259; Davidson, *Typology in Scripture*, 115–190. Its use throughout the NT varies but is generally clear in the given contexts. In the NT τύπος designates the following: (1) the *mark* or *imprint* left on Jesus' hands by the nails that pierced them—John 20:25, (2) *figures* which are *images* or *idols* of false worship—Acts 7:43, (3) a *pattern* or *model* to be followed in construction—Acts 7:44; Heb 8:5 (4) the *style*, *contents*, or *form* of a letter—Acts 23:25 and possibly Rom 6:17, (5) a *mold* which shapes something, specifically in the case of Christian doctrine which shapes or molds the believer—Rom 6:17, (6) a *model* to be imitated in the sense of an ethical *example*—Phil 3:17; 1 Thess 1:7; 2 Thess 3:9; 1 Tim 4:12; 1 Pet 5:3. For further discussion of the uses of τύπος in these contexts, see Goppelt, "τύπος κτλ" *TDNT* 8:246–259; E. Kenneth Lee, "Words Denoting 'Pattern' in the New Testament," *NTS* 8, no. 2 (1962): 169–171; Davidson, *Typology in Scripture*, 141–190.

53 Goppelt, "τύπος κτλ," *TDNT* 8:248–249, 251–256.

54 Ibid., 8:251–252.

55 H. Müller, "Type, Pattern," NIDNTT 3:905; see 905–906.

56 Davidson, *Typology in Scripture*, 419; see also 115n2, 414. A technical, hermeneutical sense can also be found in some of the primary Greek lexicons, for these various passages above. See BDAG, s.v. "τύπος" and s.v. "ἀντίτυπος;" Thayer's, s.v. "τύπος" and s.v. "ἀντίτυπος;" Louw-Nida, s.v. "τύπος" and s.v. "ἀντίτυπος."

Even with arguments in defense of a technical/hermeneutical sense of τύπος, this specific sense is still highly debated within NT scholarship.[57] Heinrich Ostmeyer represents one of the more recent challenges to Goppelt's hermeneutical understanding of τύπος. After examining Rom 5:14, 1 Cor 10:6, 11, and 1 Pet 3:21, Ostmeyer concludes:

> Ein besonderes „hermeneutisches Verständnis" des Terminus begegnet weder im Neuen Testament noch in der frühchristlichen Literatur. Eine Typologiedefinition wie die von L. Goppelt, die ein solches Verständnis des Begriffes τύπος voraussetzt, und eine sich darauf gründende Hermeneutik finden keinen Anhalt an den Quellen.[58]

Ostmeyer denies any hermeneutical sense of τύπος in these passages and in the NT for that matter.[59] Even so, his final analysis still recognizes the presence of typology. Most notably, he points to Paul's and Peter's typology as signifying God's "new creation."[60] Ostmeyer, then, actually falls in line with Goppelt's understanding of τύπος more so than he thinks. He sees typology connected with NT fulfillment. This element accords with Goppelt's hermeneutical explanation of τύπος and is also central to the prophetic thrust typology has in the traditional view.

The key question to ask concerning these three debated passages is whether a convincing case can be made exegetically for a hermeneutical understanding of τύπος. Do the texts themselves lend support for understanding these typologies with some kind of prophetic thrust? Davidson's semasiological study of τύπος (along with its cognates) and his exegesis of these three passages attempts to substantiate such textual support. If not definitively, at

---

57 Not a few scholars deny any special, interpretive significance of the term and its cognates in the NT. Cf. e.g., David L. Baker, *Two Testaments, One Bible: A Study of the Theological Relationships Between the Old & New Testaments*, rev. ed. (Downers Grove: InterVarsity Press, 1991), 185–187; Christopher J. H. Wright, *Knowing Jesus Through the Old Testament* (Downers Grove: InterVarsity Press, 1992), 111. Yet, others contend it functions this way in some but not in all the instances noted above. See e.g., G. Schunack, "τύπος," *EDNT* 3:372–376.

58 "A special, 'hermeneutical understanding' of the term is not encountered in either the New Testament or in early Christian literature. A definition of typology such as that of L. Goppelt, which presupposes such an understanding of the τύπος concept and a hermeneutic based on it, finds no evidence in the sources" (my translation). Karl-Heinrich Ostmeyer, *Taufe und Typos: Elemente und Theologie der Tauftypologien in 1. Korinther 10 und 1. Petrus 3*, WUNT 2, Reihe 118 (Tübingen: Mohr Siebeck, 2000), 199–200; cf. 52.

59 Contra Ostmeyer, Davidson's extensive exegesis of these passages in his monograph supports a hermeneutical understanding of τύπος in the NT. Davidson, *Typology in Scripture*, 193–336. Ostmeyer, however, makes no reference to the exegesis or conclusions reached by Davidson.

60 Ostmeyer, *Taufe und Typos*, 200.

the very least Davidson makes a compelling argument that Paul and Peter use τύπος language to indicate typology, where they interpret OT events as predictive prefigurations fulfilled in Christ.[61]

One must be cautious not to overweight the contributions hermeneutical τύπος terminology makes for a prophetic understanding of NT typology, especially in light of the debate surrounding the term. At the same time, however, it should not be altogether ignored. Davidson presents textual evidence that agrees with both Goppelt's and Müller's earlier treatments on NT τύπος terminology. He finds that τύπος terminology is hermeneutical in function. Thus, it designates the interpretation of OT types that were pointing beyond themselves to NT truths fulfilled in Christ and his church. If Davidson's conclusions are correct in these cases, then the technical, hermeneutical sense of τύπος can be seen as additional NT support for the traditional, prophetic view of typology.

The OT Basis of Typology

The OT basis for typology suggests a prophetic understanding of the concept. One notices when reading the OT that an eschatological expectation adheres to certain parts of its history.[62] There are indications in the OT, at times, that Israel and the prophets theologically interpreted their history as moving towards a teleological end.[63] Furthermore, there are indications that this theological interpretation looked upon various acts of God as demonstrations of climactic forthcoming acts.[64] Recognizing God's sovereign control over history, God's former acts were viewed as prophecy of future events that would be similar to but greater than the past.[65] In its essence, the OT "moves forward to the New" and its original context possesses a "witnessing intent" that is "a forward direction."[66]

---

61 Davidson, *Typology in Scripture*, 193–336. In his exegesis, Davidson notes the following: (1) τύπος in Rom 5:14 presents Adam as a prefiguration of Christ. Ibid., 307–310. (2) τύποι and τυπικῶς in 1 Cor 10:6, 11 identify Israel's Exodus salvation and judgments as pre-presentations of the church's salvation and potential judgments in the eschatological age. Ibid. 246–248, 250–255, 267–268, 280–297. (3) ἀντίτυπον in 1 Pet 3:21 identifies Christian baptism as the fulfillment of the OT flood event, which prospectively looked forward to the ultimate salvation in Christ and final judgment that baptism pictures. Ibid., 326–336.

62 David E. Aune, "Early Christian Biblical Interpretation," *EvQ* 41 (1969):90–92; Horace D. Hummel, "The Old Testament Basis of Typological Interpretation," *BR* 9 (1964): 42–50.

63 Aune, "Early Christian Biblical Interpretation," 90–92; Francis Foulkes, *The Acts of God: A Study of the Basis of Typology in the Old Testament* (London: The Tyndale Press, 1958), 32–35.

64 Foulkes, *The Acts of God*, 7–40.

65 Ibid. Cf. especially pp. 20, 23, 32–40.

66 Hans Walter Wolff, "The Hermeneutics of the Old Testament," *Int* 15 (1961): 456–457, 459–460.

For example, the OT anticipates a new but greater David (cf. Isa 9:6–7; Jer 23:5–6; 30:9; 33:14–26; Ezek 34:23–24; 37:24–25), a new but greater Moses (cf. Deut 18:15–19), an eschatological Exodus (cf. Isa 40–55), a new Temple (cf. Ezek 40–48), etc.[67] How the OT signals the forward-projecting nature of OT events varies.[68] Whatever the manner of expression, specific historical figures and events are depicted by the OT itself to be forward pointing. Not to be missed is the fact that there is some level of OT consciousness of the foreshadowing function of historical events. The OT's future anticipation of corresponding but more consummative acts in the future corroborates traditional typology's claim that the NT interprets instances OT history to be prophetic in force towards NT counterparts.

Historical Evidence in Support of Traditional Typology

Evidence from the history of pre-critical interpretation supplements the foregoing biblical evidence that typology was understood to be forward pointing and, thus, prophetic in nature. Specifically, analysis of the Church Fathers and the reformers Martin Luther and John Calvin brings to light how typology was conceived of in these periods preceding modern critical scholarship. Clear indicators are present that typology was recognized during these eras to be a form of biblical prophecy.

Patristic Era

Usually, the Patristic Era designates the time frame from the close of the first century and extends up to the fifth or even eighth century.[69] One of the values in patristic studies derives from what Christopher Hall designates as

---

67 For a more detailed discussion of these and other OT expectations, see Foulkes, *The Acts of God*, 9–33.

68 Beale discusses six key ways the OT makes known an historical event's prophetic function. See Beale, *Handbook on the New Testament*, 19–23. Sometimes, the OT signals such future expectations clearly in the immediate context of the passage. Sometimes, the OT signals such future expectations by repeating key episodes belonging to redemptive history (e.g., new exodus, new creation). Sometimes, the OT signals such future expectations in the sequences of institutions or offices that find only temporary fulfillments (e.g., sacrifices, priests, kings). Sometimes, the OT signals such future expectations in key figures patterned after prior key figures (e.g., Adam, Noah, David).

69 Gerald Bray, *Biblical Interpretation: Past & Present* (Downers Grove: InterVarsity Press, 1996), 77–79; Christopher Hall, *Reading Scripture with the Church Fathers* (Downers Grove, IL: InterVarsity, 1998), 51; A. Berkeley Mickelsen, *Interpreting the Bible* (Grand Rapids: Eerdmans, 1963), 30; Frances M. Young, "Patristic Biblical Interpretation," in *DTIB*, ed. Kevin J. Vanhoozer (Grand Rapids: Baker Academic, 2005), 566.

"hermeneutical proximity."[70] Hermeneutical proximity describes the nearness of the Fathers to the early Church from a temporal standpoint. Due to their closeness with the early church, the Fathers offer a vantage point to see some of the initial hermeneutical praxes at the close of the NT period.[71] The Church Fathers hermeneutical proximity, therefore, offers insights on an understanding of typology from a very early time in interpretive history.[72]

Typology was so much a part of the Fathers' interpretation of Scripture that John J. O'Keefe and R. R. Reno posit that "without typology it is difficult to imagine patristic theology and the concept of Christian orthodoxy it defined and supported as existing at all."[73] For the Fathers, typological interpretation was a focal hermeneutic because they found its origins in the Scriptures. Patristic typology followed suit with the NT's explicit identification of "types," which they considered "*a priori* evidence included in the primal Gospel event."[74] Typological interpretation contributed to their goal of a comprehensive reading of the Scriptures in light of Christ. Their comprehensive reading perceived a coherent unity in the Bible: a divine economy that only found clarity and fulfillment in Christ.[75] Typological interpretation recognized corresponding patterns within the divine plan of Scripture. These patterns were understood to be prefigurations, anticipating and finding ultimate meaning in Christ.[76]

One visible mark of patristic typology is that it regarded types to be predictive prophecy. In an article on typology, Stanley M. Gundry clarifies the consistent understanding of typology for post-apostolic Christians up through the Reformation period:

---

70 Hall, *Reading Scripture*, 38–41, 54. Hall cites Michael Casey as listing this factor among one of the important reasons for studying the Fathers. Casey explains, "In general, the earlier authors are valued because they are more proximate beneficiaries of the apostolic tradition." Michael Casey, *Sacred Reading: The Ancient Art of Lectio Divina* (Liguori, MO: Triumph Books, 1995), 105.

71 Cf. Hall, *Reading Scripture*, 35.

72 The parameters of this study obviously restrict a comprehensive treatment on typology during the patristic period. Consequently, this section attempts only to demonstrate that certain of the Church Fathers described typology as inherently predictive.

73 John J. O'Keefe and R. R. Reno, *Sanctified Vision: An Introduction to Early Christian Interpretation of the Bible* (Baltimore: The John Hopkins University Press, 2005), 69.

74 Charles Kannengiesser, *Handbook of Patristic Exegesis: The Bible in Ancient Christianity*, ed. D. Jeffrey Bingham (Leiden: Brill, 2004), 1:239.

75 O'Keefe and Reno, *Sanctified Vision*, 24–44.

76 Ibid., 69, 73, 84–88. Typology among the Church Fathers is not necessarily limited to the facet of finding "prefigurations" of Jesus and the church in the OT. O'Keefe and Reno state that it is more "wide ranging" than that. It is this practice of typology, however, that they identify as the "most central" to the Church Fathers. The other important facet of typology centered on using typology to explain personal Christian experiences. Ibid., 73–84.

That one point of agreement is that the essence of a type is that it is in some sense predictive, every bit as predictive as a verbal utterance of predictive prophecy. Typology was regarded as a species of predictive prophecy. The correspondence between type and antitype, whatever the nature of that correspondence, was not a mere analogy nor an artificially imposed scheme on the part of the writers of scripture; the Old Testament types were foreshadowings in a predictive sense of Christ and his saving person and work.[77]

Several examples can be cited that evidence a prophetic understanding to patristic typology. Jean Daniélou shows that Irenaeus conveyed such an understanding of biblical typology. Irenaeus' belief that the testaments depict a unified divine plan meant that "there is an imperfect order which prepares for and prefigures an order of perfection."[78] Irenaeus develops the Adam/Christ typology of the NT within this particular frame of thought. Adam resembles Christ because the doctrinal basis of typology (i.e., the unity of God's plan) ordains the correspondences between the preparatory figure (i.e., the first Adam) and the accomplishment (i.e., the New Adam).[79] Consequently, Irenaeus speaks of Adam as having been "as though the Word, who framed all things, had formed beforehand, with a view to himself, that Economy of Mankind which was to centre in the Son of God."[80] The Adam/Christ typology was not mere analogy for Irenaeus. It was theological and prospective in nature, pointing to and anticipating Christ from the beginning.

Hubertus R. Drobner summarizes Diodore of Tarsus's hermeneutic and why he allowed for typology in interpretation. Diodore of Tarsus found typology acceptable because he believed that in the literal meaning "historical realties may contain references to future salvific events."[81] Typology did not ignore the literal meaning of the text, but being based upon the literal meaning, typology explained an innate "prophetic expression based on its

---

77 Stanley M. Gundry, "Typology as a Means of Interpretation: Past and Present," *JETS* 12 (1969): 237. Cf. Hall's analysis that the typology practiced by the Fathers was the kind where they read the OT as containing predictive foreshadowings of Gospel realities. Hall makes a distinction between patristic typology and allegory, but he does so with reservation. He cautions that "for some fathers, the distinction between typology and allegory was blurred at best." Hall, *Reading Scripture*, 133. Even with this caution, he still admits to some differentiation between the two methods.

78 Jean Daniélou, *From Shadows to Reality: Studies in Biblical Typology of the Fathers* (London: Burns & Oates, 1960), 30–31.

79 Ibid., 30–47.

80 Irenaeus as quoted in Ibid, 39.

81 Hubertus R. Drobner, *The Fathers of the Church: A Comprehensive Introduction*, trans. Siegfried S. Schatzmann (Peabody: Hendrickson Publishers, 2007), 320.

[i.e., the literal meaning's] correspondence with salvation history."[82] Justin Martyr provides another example of a prophetic understanding of OT types. In his *Dialogue with Trypho*, Justin places prophecy and typology on the same level. He argues that "the Holy Spirit sometimes caused something that was to be a type of the future to be done openly, and on other occasions He spoke of things of the future as though they were actually taking place, or had already taken place."[83] The Holy Spirit, therefore, prophesies the future both by words (i.e., verbally) and by causing events (i.e., historically). Another Church Father, Junilius, advocated a familial relationship between prophecy proper and typology. According to Junilius, prophecy proper is verbal and "in types events are declared by events" so that "the type is a prophecy in events, insofar as the events are known as events."[84]

Chrysostom is another who articulates clearly a view of typology in prophetic terms. Jean-Noël Guinot suggests that Chrysostom demonstrates that the Antiochenes understood typology as a kind of prophecy.[85] The evidence for this, according to Guinot, is found in Chrysostom's distinction between "'prophétie figurative' (διὰ τύπου) et 'prophétie déclarative' (διὰ λόγου)."[86] The distinction is that Chrysostom "définit la prophétie 'figurative' comme une prophétie exprimée par les faits eux-mêmes (διὰ πραγμάτων), par opposition à la prophétie 'verbale' (διὰ ῥηάμτων), tout entière contenue dans les mots utilisés par le prophète."[87] So, for Chrysostom, prophecy includes typological prophecy by events as well as verbal prophecy by words.

In overview, there is evidence that typology was explained and described in prophetic terms during the Patristic Era. Various OT events/figures were understood by various Fathers to be prophetic expressions of future NT events.[88] This observation show, at the very least, that typology at the close

---

82 Ibid., 320–321.

83 Justin Martyr, *Dialogue with Trypho*, vol. 6 of *The Fathers of the Church*, trans. Thomas B. Falls (New York: Christian Heritage, 1948), 323–324. Cf. Ronald E. Heine, *Reading the Old Testament with the Ancient Church: Exploring the Formation of Early Christian Thought* (Grand Rapids: Baker Academic, 2007), 52.

84 Junilius as quoted in Robert M. Grant and David Tracy, *A Short History of the Interpretation of the Bible*, rev. 2nd ed. (Philadelphia: Fortress Press, 1984), 71.

85 Jean-Noël Guinot, "La typologie comme technique herméneutique," in *Figures de l'Ancien Testament chez les Pères*, Cahiers de Biblia Patristica (Strasbourg: Centre d'Analyse et de Documentation Patristiques, 1989), 10. Cf. Jacques Guillet, "Les Exégèsis d'Alexandrie et d'Antioch. Conflit ou malentendu?," *RevScRel* 34 (1947): 275–286, 297.

86 "'Figurative prophecy' (διὰ τύπου) and 'declarative prophecy' (διὰ λόγου)" (my translation). Guinot, "La typologie," 10.

87 The distinction is that Chrysostom "defines 'figurative' prophecy as a prophecy expressed by the facts themselves (διὰ πραγμάτων), as opposed to 'verbal' prophecy (διὰ ῥηάμτων) entirely contained in the words used by the prophet" (my translation). Ibid., 11.

88 Cf. Kannengiesser, *Handbook of Patristic Exegesis*, 1:228–232.

of the NT period and in the subsequent centuries of the Fathers was defined by some as prophetic interpretation. The Fathers' closeness to the NT writers *may* indicate and reflect that the principle way to understand biblical typology is in a predictive sense.

Reformation Era

One primary concern of the Reformation period centered on the return to literal, historical exegesis that the church had drifted away from during the Middle Ages.[89] Martin Luther and John Calvin championed this cause. As interpreters of the Bible, they were reacting against the allegorical or "fourfold" sense of interpretation of Scripture taught by Augustine and later embraced by theologians in the medieval church.[90] This "fourfold" sense recognized three spiritual senses in addition to the literal sense: (1) the allegorical, (2) the tropological, and (3) the anagogical.[91] In their efforts to reestablish the primacy of literal interpretation, typology continued to be recognized by them as a legitimate way of interpreting Scripture (albeit Calvin, more so than Luther, was inclined to interpret Scripture typologically). As the analysis demonstrates below, their conceptions of typology present it as having a prophetic thrust, so that OT figures are understood to point forward to their fulfillments in Christ.

In his quest to reassert the literal sense of Scripture, Luther denounced the allegorical method of interpretation as a general practice.[92] His stress upon the literal sense of the text, however, did not always prevent him from engaging in a "regulated" or "moderate" use of allegory on occasion.[93] Nor did it altogether preclude the recognition of typological interpretation.[94] Luther acknowledges the legitimacy of allegory and typology from time to time, first of all, because he was thoroughly committed to a Christological approach to interpretation.[95] To Luther, the literal and Christological meanings of the

---

89 Grant and Tracy, *A Short History*, 85; Gundry, "Typology," 235–236; Bernard Ramm, *Protestant Biblical Interpretation: A Textbook of Hermeneutics*, 3rd rev. ed. (Grand Rapids: Baker Book House, 1970), 38.

90 Ibid., 51–59; David C. Steinmetz, "John Calvin as an Interpreter of the Bible," in *Calvin and the Bible*, ed. Donald K. McKim (Cambridge: Cambridge University Press, 2006), 284–285.

91 Steinmetz, "John Calvin as an Interpreter of the Bible," 284.

92 Edwin Cyril Blackman, *Biblical Interpretation* (Philadelphia: The Westminster Press, 1957), 118–121; David S. Dockery, "Martin Luther's Christological Hermeneutics," *GTJ* 4 (1983): 190.

93 Heinrich Bornkamm, *Luther and the Old Testament*, trans. Eric W. Gritsch and Ruth C. Gritsch (Philadelphia: Fortress Press, 1969), 96.

94 See e.g., Ibid., 150, 208n472.

95 Grant and Tracy explain that "such a view requires the typological understanding of the Old Testament, and often permits allegorical interpretation . . ." Grant and Tracy, *A Short*

Scriptures were essentially one and the same.[96] Since all of the OT finds fulfillment in Christ and points toward him,[97] allegory and typology sometimes, though infrequently, were appropriate means of "spiritual" interpretation in concert with the "literal" interpretation of Scripture.[98] Secondly, Luther could not totally jettison allegory or typology, since he found Scriptural support for both approaches.[99]

Despite the limited role typology played in his overall hermeneutic, Luther still recognized its validity. This position is clear from Luther's typological understanding of Jesus' reference to the lifting up of the serpent in the wilderness in John 3:14–15. His sermon notes explain the passage as follows:

> I would never have ventured to interpret this story as Christ Himself did when He plainly related it to Himself, saying: "This is the bronze serpent; I, however, am the Son of man. Those people were asked to look at the serpent physically, but you must look at Me spiritually and in faith. Those people were cured of bodily poisoning; but you, through Me, will be delivered from eternal poison. They recovered from a physical ailment, but I bestow eternal life on those who believe in Me."[100]

Luther finds the application of this story to Christ to consist of "strange statements and sayings." Nevertheless, he clearly sees Jesus establishing correspondences between himself and the OT incident. The subsequent comments Luther makes about this passage are significant for seeing how he understands the overall nature of this typology. Luther writes:

> In this way the Lord shows us the proper method of interpreting Moses and all the prophets. He teaches us that Moses points and refers to Christ in all his stories and illustrations. His purpose is to show that Christ is the point and center of a circle, with all eyes inside the circle focused on Him. Whoever turns his eyes on Him finds his proper place in the circle

---

History, 93.

  96 Blackman, *Biblical Interpretation*, 122; Dockery, "Martin Luther's," 192.

  97 Blackman, *Biblical Interpretation*, 122–123; Dockery, "Martin Luther's," 192.

  98 Bornkamm, *Luther and the Old Testament*, 95. To be sure, neither allegory nor typology was predominant in Luther's Christological interpretation of the OT. He was, in fact, critical of both methods in general. Most characteristically, Luther argued for a direct prophetic application of the OT to Christ. Ibid., 96–120, 250–251.

  99 On allegory, see Ibid., 95–96. On typology, see Martin Luther, *Sermons on the Gospel of St. John: Chapters 1–4*, vol. 22 of *Luther's Works*, trans. Martin H. Bertam (Saint Louis: Concordia Publishing House, 1957), 339; Martin Luther, *Lectures on Titus, Philemon, and Hebrews*, vol. 29 of *Luther's Works*, trans. Walter A. Hansen (Saint Louis: Concordia Publishing House, 1968), 168.

  100 Luther, *Sermons*, 339.

of which Christ is the center. All the stories of Holy Writ, if viewed aright, point to Christ.... Thus, He also relates the figure of the serpent to Himself here. Thereby He opens the treasure chest of Moses and shows them the nugget concealed there. He shows that all the stories and illustrations of Moses point to Christ.[101]

Luther clearly views Jesus' application of this OT narrative as more than mere analogy. He states that the figure of the serpent "points" and "refers" to Christ and that Jesus reveals something that was previously "concealed." This typology contains comparisons that Jesus makes between himself and the serpent.[102] But, Luther sees more involved than just simple comparisons. He states, "In this serpent God thus prefigured His own Son for the people of Israel."[103] Furthermore, Luther argues that "the intention of both Moses and of John was to point to the deity of the Lord Christ."[104] There is clear evidence, therefore, that Luther understood OT types to point forward to Christ. In Luther's estimation, Christ taught that Moses and the prophets wrote with a directedness toward himself. Luther plainly asserts by this example, then, that his understanding of typology values an intentional forward-looking aspect, which means it is prophetic.[105]

What is particularly interesting about Calvin during the Reformation period is that typology factored into his hermeneutic in a significant way.[106] When it came to allegory, Calvin claimed it was "superficial" and even "diabolical."[107] Why, then, did Calvin affirm a typological interpretation of the Scriptures? Calvin affirmed typology because he considered it to be literal interpretation. David C. Steinmetz points out that typological interpretation was not problematic for Calvin because it was a "plain" or "natural" sense in his

---

101 Ibid., 339–340.
102 Ibid., 344.
103 Ibid., 343.
104 Ibid., 345.
105 Luther also clearly states the prophetic notion of typology in his comments on the use of Ps 95:7–11 in Heb 3:7–11. He explains, "In the first place, it is clear from this text that the prophets knew that the future was prefigured in the history of the Children of Israel." Luther, *Lectures on Titus, Philemon, and Hebrews*, 147.
106 For an excellent analysis of Calvin's typological hermeneutic, see David L. Puckett, *John Calvin's Exegesis*, Columbia Series in Reformed Theology (Louisville: Westminster John Knox Press, 1995), 113–124.
107 Calvin's disparaging criticism towards allegory, according to Puckett, stemmed from its disconnection to the text. Puckett writes that Calvin "calls interpretations 'allegorical' if they disregard the historical context or if they interpret the details of a biblical text apart from a consideration of the immediate literary context. Allegorical exegesis is the antithesis of historical exegesis." Ibid., 106–107.

assessment.[108] A typological reading stayed true to the literal sense of Scripture for Calvin, taking seriously the past and future reference of texts. A typological reading allowed him to explain the relatedness of OT events to their fulfillment in Christ in a natural way.

Typological interpretation preserved the significance of both the OT and NT contexts in a literal or natural way because Calvin saw it as prophecy and fulfillment. David L. Puckett writes, "Typology for Calvin is true prophecy, albeit shadowy and somewhat obscure."[109] He further elaborates that Calvin,

> counsels his fellow Christians that prophecy need not deny a historical referent in Old Testament times. That is just the point with typology. It has an Old Testament reference, yet its perfect fulfillment comes later in the person of Christ. This approach allows Calvin to guard the unity of scripture without requiring him to discard historical exegesis.[110]

Calvin illustrates his understanding of typology as prophecy most notably in his commentary on the Psalms. Psalm 2 relates a prophetic notion of David typology fulfilled in Christ, according to Calvin. Seeing David as a type of Christ, Calvin posits that "those things which David declares concerning himself are not violently, or even allegorically, applied to Christ, but were truly predicted concerning him."[111] Aspects of David's life and kingdom were a shadow describing Christ and his kingdom by the "spirit of prophecy." Calvin interprets Psalm 22 in the same typological manner, insisting that David knew himself to be "a type of Christ, whom he knew by the Spirit of prophecy."[112] Again, David's life events, in this case his sufferings, point in a prophetic way to the sufferings of Christ and find fulfillment in him. On Ps 22:18 and its description of the division of clothing and casting of lots, Calvin comments, "To teach us the more certainly that in this Psalm Christ is described to us by the Spirit of prophecy, the heavenly Father intended that in the person of his Son those

---

108 Steinmetz, "John Calvin as an Interpreter of the Bible," 284–285. Calvin's positive stance toward typology reflects the position of medieval interpreters such as Nicholas of Lyra, who defined the "literal" meaning in a double sense: literal-historical and literal-prophetic.

109 Puckett, *John Calvin's Exegesis*, 114. Hans W. Frei likewise observes that in Calvin's typological interpretation, the typology is forward looking (i.e., prospective) rather than backward looking (i.e. retrospective). Of importance then, the type existed in its original context with a forward reference. Hans W. Frei, *The Eclipse of the Biblical Narrative: A Study in Eighteenth and Nineteenth Century Hermeneutics* (New Haven: Yale University Press, 1974), 36.

110 Puckett, *John Calvin's Exegesis*, 119–120.

111 John Calvin, *Commentary on the Book of Psalms*, trans. James Anderson, vols. 4–6 of *Calvin's Commentaries* (Grand Rapids: Baker Book House, 1981), 4:11.

112 Ibid., 1:356.

things should be visibly accomplished which were shadowed forth in David."[113] Thus, Psalm 22 relates to Christ because the psalm predicts Christ's sufferings in the experiences of David.[114]

Clearly, Calvin's view of typology falls in line with the traditional view of typology. He explains the NT's use of OT texts that highlight typological relationships as being prophetic in nature. Typology, then, was a form of prophecy in Calvin's hermeneutic. By classifying typology as literal and prophetic interpretation, Calvin shows himself a successor to the early understanding of typology in the Patristic era. Calvin, however, did not justify typology based on the practice of the Church Fathers. Calvin justified his conception of typology as exemplary of Jesus' and the NT writers' use of the OT.[115]

Summary

To recap, this chapter presents both biblical and historical evidence to support the prophetic sense of typology, according to the traditional view. The biblical evidence (i.e., Jesus' teachings and examples, typology in Hebrews, NT "fulfillment" language, hermeneutical τύπος terminology, and the OT basis for typology) seems to validate that biblical typology possesses a predictive force. Likewise, the historical evidence (i.e., pre-critical interpretation of typology by the Church Fathers and by the Reformers, Martin Luther and John Calvin) shows that typology was delineated in terms of prophecy. Importantly, then, both the internal and external evidence identifies typology as more than mere analogy between the testaments. Consistent with the traditional understanding, typology consists of OT types which prefigure and predict their corresponding NT fulfillments in Christ.

---

113 Ibid., 1:376.

114 Wulfert de Greef, "Calvin as Commentator on the Psalms," in *Calvin and the Bible*, ed. Donald K. McKim (Cambridge: Cambridge University Press, 2006), 101; see also 99–106.

115 Puckett, *John Calvin's Exegesis*, 118.

4

Prophetic David Typology in John

THIS CHAPTER DEMONSTRATES THAT traditional typology best explains the Psalms quotations in John 13:18; 15:25; 19:24, 28. Specifically, this chapter argues that David typology in a traditional, prophetic sense accounts best for Jesus' (John 13; 15) and John's (John 19) application of Davidic psalms to the events of Jesus' suffering and death in the FG. This chapter consists of four main sections and a summary. Each main section presents the analysis of a single psalm quotation, each of which is examined in three steps.[1] Step one establishes the identification of the OT psalm reference in the NT passage. Step two identifies the typological correspondences established between David and Jesus. Step three identifies the evidence for a prophetic notion in the quotation.

Ps 41:9 in John 13:18

John appeals to a quotation from the OT in John 13:18 to establish a typological relationship between David and Jesus. He designates the OT quotation with the reference ἡ γραφή ("the Scripture")[2] and the quotation formula ἀλλ' ἵνα ἡ γραφὴ πληρωθῇ ("but *it is* that the Scripture may be fulfilled"). The formula ἵνα...πληρωθῇ is used by John in five other instances.[3] Here and in John

---

[1] The principles of typology delineated in chapter 2 of this work will be integrated into these exegetical steps.

[2] Ἡ γραφή is a common designation for the OT as a whole or for an individual passage. See Gottlob Schrenk, "γράφω κτλ," *TDNT* 1:749–761. In John 13:18, ἡ γραφή probably retains a singular sense, since a direct OT quotation follows. Douglas Moo notes that a single OT passage is the normal sense of γραφή in John. Douglas Moo, *The Old Testament in the Gospel Passion Narratives* (Sheffield: The Almond Press, 1983), 277. See also Rudolf Schnackenburg, *The Gospel According to St. John*, trans. Kevin Smyth, Cecily Hastings, et al. (New York: Crossroad, 1982), 3:46on60.

[3] John 12:38; 15:25; 17:12; 19:24, 36. Matthew is the only other NT writer to use this construct

15:25, John presents the ἵνα...πληρωθῇ formula as coming directly from the mouth of Jesus.[4]

The OT source of the quotation in John 13:18 is "universally accepted" to be Ps 41:9[5] (MT 41:10, LXX 40:10).[6]

John 13:18	ὁ τρώγων μου τὸν ἄρτον ἐπῆρεν ἐπ' ἐμὲ τὴν πτέρναν αὐτοῦ
	"He who eats my bread has lifted up his heel against me."[7]
MT Ps 41:10	גַּם־אִישׁ שְׁלוֹמִי אֲשֶׁר־בָּטַחְתִּי בוֹ אוֹכֵל לַחְמִי הִגְדִּיל עָלַי עָקֵב
	"Even my close friend in whom I trusted, who ate my bread, has lifted up *his* heel against me."[8]
LXX Ps 40:10	καὶ γὰρ ὁ ἄνθρωπος τῆς εἰρήνης μου ἐφ' ὃν ἤλπισα ὁ ἐσθίων ἄρτους μου ἐμεγάλυνεν ἐπ' ἐμὲ πτερνισμόν
	"For even the man of my peace, in whom I hoped, the one who eats my loaves made great deception against me."[9]

The textual correspondence John 13:18 shares with Ps 41:9 properly classifies Jesus' reference as a direct quotation, closer to the MT than the LXX.[10]

CORRESPONDENCE IN THE DAVID-JESUS TYPOLOGY

John 13:18 establishes a typological relationship between David and Jesus in

---

in formulas (cf. Matt 1:22; 2:15; 4:14; 12:17; 21:4).

4 Edwin D. Freed, *Old Testament Quotations in the Gospel of John* (Leiden: E. J. Brill, 1965), 89.

5 The psalms throughout this work will be referenced according to their English numeration.

6 Margaret Daly-Denton, *David in the Fourth Gospel: The Johannine Reception of the Psalms*, AGJU 47 (Leiden: Brill, 2000), 191.

7 Throughout I have cited OT texts from the *BHS*.

8 Throughout I have cited NT texts from the NA27.

9 Throughout I have cited the Septuagint or LXX from Alfred Rahlfs' *Septuaginta*. I have provided my own translations of the focal texts from the LXX.

10 A "direct" quotation means the "quotation is a general reproduction of the original text, sufficiently close... to establish unquestionably the passage from which it is taken." Merrill C. Tenney, *Interpreting Revelation: A Reasonable Guide to Understanding the Last Book in the Bible* (Peabody, MA: Hendrickson, 1957), 102. In this work, the terms "quotation" and "citation" are used interchangeably. On quotation divergences, see Roger Nicole, "The New Testament Use of the Old Testament," in *The Right Doctrine from the Wrong Texts? Essays on the Use of the Old Testament in the New*, ed. G. K. Beale (Grand Rapids: Baker Books, 1994), 17–25. Since John diverges only slightly from the MT, he probably draws his quotation from the Hebrew orignal. According to Adolf Schlatter, "Der Rückgriff auf die hebräische Formel ist deutlich" ("The use of the Hebrew formula is clear" [my translation]).

its use of Ps 41:9.[11] Before examining the analogous points of this typology, Psalm 41 needs to be summarized in its original context to see how the psalm relates to David.

Psalm 41 is best classified as a psalm of lament,[12] with an introduction (41:1–3), a body (41:4–10), and a conclusion (41:11–12).[13] The psalm recounts suffering experienced by David, who recalls a prayer he voiced to God in a time of sickness.[14] David acknowledges his sin and petitions God for mercy and healing (41:4). David is desperate for God's grace because external factors were intensifying his already difficult situation (41:5–9). While on his sickbed, his illness was exacerbated by the evil speech and scheming of his enemies (41:5–8). To make matters worse, one of his close friends betrayed him during this vulnerable time (41:9).[15]

Thus, Ps 41:9 records David's complaint to God about a close friend who had betrayed him while he was suffering with illness. In John 13:18, Jesus applies what was originally specific to David to himself pointing back to Ps 41:9 to explain his imminent sufferings from the background of what had once

---

11 This work assumes that John affirmed Davidic authorship of the psalms being examined and that those psalms were about David, even though he does not explicitly mention David's name in connection with the psalms citations in his Gospel. Margaret Daly-Denton, in fact, maintains this position is essential to a correct understanding of the use of these psalms in the FG. Daly-Denton, *David in the Fourth Gospel*, 110–111. Her research leads her to conclude: "Therefore, the fact that John does not directly mention David as author of the psalms needs to be evaluated in the light of his over-all pattern of scriptural reference. . . . [T]here is sufficient evidence in the literature of early Judaism and in the NT to allow us to presume that the Fourth Evangelist would have shared the commonly held belief that David 'wrote' the psalms, just as he shared the belief that Moses 'wrote' the Pentateuch (John 1:45; 5:46)." Ibid., 104; see also 59–113. Additionally, all focal passages under evaluation in John (i.e., John 13:18/Ps 41; John 15:25/Ps 69; John 19:24/Ps 22; John 19:28/Ps 69) contain quotations from psalms with a לְדָוִד superscription, which connects these psalms to David in their interpretation. The לְדָוִד ("by/of David") superscription seems most naturally to function as a *lamed auctoris*, informing the reader that David composed the psalm. See *GKC* §129.I(a); Joüon §130b; *IBHS* 206–207, 207n70. This Davidic authorial sense is the traditional way to understand the superscriptions (so Matthias Millard, *Die Komposition des Psalters: Ein formgeschichtlicher Ansatz*, FAT 9 [Tubigen: Mohr-Siebeck, 1994], 29) and is consistent with how Jesus and the NT writers understood them in relation to David (cf. Matt 22:43–45; Mark 12:36–37; Luke 20:42–44; Acts 1:20; 2:25–28, 31, 34–35; Rom 4:6–8; 11:9–10).

12 So A. A. Anderson, *The Book of Psalms*, NCBC (Grand Rapids: Eerdmans, 1972), 1:321–322; Sigmund Mowinckel, *The Psalms in Israel's Worship*, trans. D. R. Ap-Thomas, rev. ed. (Grand Rapids: Eerdmans, 2004), 2:1–2, 6, 9; Shepherd, "The Book of Psalms as the Book of Christ," 550, 550n33. According to A. A. Anderson, "Lamentation was man's response to God, in a situation of need and affliction." Anderson, *Psalms*, 1:37. Psalms of lament typically contain a "description of distress and misfortune" and "a prayer and cry for help and deliverance."

13 See, e.g., Anderson, *Psalms*, 1:321–27; Peter C. Craigie, *Psalms 1–50*, WBC 19 (Waco, TX: Word Books, 1983), 318–322; Kidner, *Psalms 1–72*, 179–181; Ross, *Psalms*, 1:876–878.

14 Apparently, the sickness was the result of some sin against God. Note the causal clause כִּי־חָטָאתִי לָךְ, where כִּי ("because/for") expresses cause or reason (Ps 41:4b).

15 Ross, *Psalms*, 1:883–884.

happened to David. Essentially, Jesus sees David's experience as a pattern for his own with three points of correspondence between them: (1) the royal status of the sufferer, (2) the identity of the antagonist, and (3) the nature of the offense.

In both Psalm 41 and John 13, the situations present the mistreatment of a "royal figure."[16] Andreas Köstenberger identifies "the person and kingship of David" as a primary focal point for applying the psalms of David to Jesus in the FG.[17] Just as Köstenberger understands Psalms 69 and 22 (John 2:17; 15:25; 19:14, 28) to be Davidic passages, "aligning Jesus and his ministry with the experience of a king,"[18] Psalm 41 functions in the same way. Bruce Waltke corroborates this point, identifying kingship as an important element in the NT's application of the psalms of lament to Jesus.[19] A royal dimension, he explains, is not limited solely to those Psalms scholars label as "royal psalms."[20] To the contrary, he writes:

> We conclude, therefore, that transcending the various types of psalms so laboriously analyzed and classified by Gunkel stands the more significant fact that in the original composition the king is the human subject of the psalms, whether they be lament, acknowledgement, praise, or belonging to various other types of psalms.[21]

Being a psalm of lament, Psalm 41 retains a notion of kingship. The one lamenting to God in Psalm 41 is David, Israel's king, the one chosen and anointed by God as ruler over his people.[22] Significant to the reading of Psalm 41, then, is its "portrait of a king at risk."[23]

---

16 Cf. Schuchard, *Scripture Within Scripture*, 114.

17 Andreas J. Köstenberger, *A Theology of John's Gospel and Letters: The Word, the Christ, the Son of God*, BTNT (Grand Rapids: Zondervan, 2009), 306.

18 Ibid., 411.

19 Bruce K. Waltke, "A Canonical Process Approach to the Psalms," in *Tradition and Testament: Essays in Honor of Charles Lee Feinberg*, ed. John S. Feinberg and Paul D. Feinberg (Chicago: Moody Press, 1981), 15–16.

20 Those labeled as "royal" psalms include: Psalms 2; 18; 20; 21; 45; 72; 89; 101; 110; 132; 144. See Ibid., 11–12.

21 Ibid., 12. Bruce Waltke explains further that "the intertestamental literature and the New Testament make clear, however, that the royal dimension of the lament psalms become lost during this period of time, and thus Israel lost sight of a suffering Messiah. Perhaps these psalms now become democratized in the synagogues and interpreted as references to everyman, as Mowinckel theorized. But . . . Jesus had to correct Israel's understanding back to their original intention." Ibid., 15.

22 See e.g., 1 Sam 16:1–13; 25:30; 2 Sam 5:1–4, 12; 6:21; 7:8–16; 12:7; 1 Kgs 8:16; 1 Chr 17:7–15; 18:14; 28:4; 29:26–27; Ps 78:70–72.

23 Wilson, *Psalms Volume 1*, 650–651. Wilson states further that this psalm underscores the "vulnerability of the human king." Geoffrey G. Grogan also suggests that the kingly mo-

A similar suffering-king motif resonates with Jesus in John 13. Early in John, Jesus is proclaimed to be God's Anointed One (i.e., Messiah) and the King of Israel (John 1:41, 49; cf. 7:26, 41–42; 9:22; 10:24–25; 11:27). In the second half of his Gospel, John draws attention to Jesus as the suffering king. Jesus enters Jerusalem, the city where his sufferings are to take place, acclaimed by the crowd as the promised "King of Israel" in John 12:13–15. Overall contextual features indicate that this scene celebrates Jesus' kingship as one of triumph through his death and resurrection.[24] Furthermore, it is important to remember that John 13:1 merges the themes of the Passover and Jesus' "hour." These themes emphasize the idea of suffering in John 13 and connect it with the kingship motif emphasized in 12:13–15 and the psalm quotation in 13:18.[25] Finally, attention is drawn explicitly to this royal-suffering motif in 18:33–19:22.[26] John intends, therefore, to portray Jesus' passion as narrating the suffering and death of Israel's King. The quotation of Ps 41:9 in John 13:18 clearly brings forth the suffering kingship notion that connects David and Jesus.[27]

Jesus' kingly status, though similar to David's, is not equivalent to his. David suffers in Psalm 41 as Israel's human king. In the FG, Jesus is not only the "King of Israel" but also the unique "Son of God."[28] Jesus' divinity accentuates the overall impact of the David typology. His unique position as the true Son of God sets him apart and identifies him as the promised, divine King, who is greater than David.[29]

The second point of correspondence between the situations of David

---

tif is significant to Psalm 41. Geoffrey W. Grogan, *Psalms*, THOTC (Grand Rapids: Eerdmans, 2008), 95.

24 L. A. Losie, "Triumphal Entry," *DJG,* 857–858.

25 Cf. Nash, "Kingship and the Psalms," 151, 209.

26 Various references to Jesus' kingly status characterize the narration of his sentencing, his beatings, and his crucifixion. Jouette M. Bassler writes, "Finally, the royal title, King of the Jews, dominates the trial and crucifixion narratives of all the Gospels." Jouette M. Bassler, "A Man for All Seasons: David in Rabbinic and New Testament Literature," *Int* 40 (1986): 169. He identifies this royalty motif as an "exact" connection between David and Jesus in his passion. Ibid.

27 See Nash, who concludes in his dissertation that the psalms in the FG underscore the "suffering king" connection between David and Jesus. Nash, "Kingship and the Psalms," 206–215.

28 Cf. John 1:1, 14, 34, 49; 3:16–18; 5:16–30; 8:36–59; 10:32–38; 11:27; 14:7–11; 15:23; 17:1–26; 19:7; 20:31. It is true that Israel's human king was considered God's "son" (cf. 2 Sam 7:12–16; Ps 2:7). This special title, however, was understood in terms of adoption (cf. Ps 89:27) and never implied claims to deity. See Ross, *Psalms*, 1:138–140. See also J. C. K. Hoffman, who argues that David's appointment as king and relationship to God as a son "typified Christ the Son of God." Hoffmann, *Interpreting the Bible*, 143.

29 Cf. Gen 49:8–10; 2 Sam 7:8–16; Isa 9:6–7; Dan 7:13–14, 27; Mic 5:2. Even in the foot washing scene, Jesus acknowledges the veracity of the disciples' address of him as "Lord" (John 13:13–14)—a title which almost certainly carries implications of his deity. Cf. Barrett, *John*, 443; Morris, *John*, 553.

and Jesus is seen in the description of the antagonist who commits treachery in each context. David speaks of one of his enemies as the one "who ate my bread" (אוֹכֵל לַחְמִי Ps 41:9b). This phrase describes a man who ate from David's table, which pictures the intimacy, fellowship, and hospitality one shares with a friend.[30] To David's surprise, the malefactor seeking his harm turned out to be a "close friend" (אִישׁ שְׁלוֹמִי Ps 41:9a) in whom he "trusted" (אֲשֶׁר־בָּטַחְתִּי בוֹ Ps 41:9a).[31]

Jesus borrows David's words from Ps 41:9b and designates his offender as ὁ τρώγων μου τὸν ἄρτον ("he who eats my bread"). The singular form of the participle ὁ τρώγων ("he who eats") along with the narrative's repetitive focus upon Judas confirms him as its proper and sole referent.[32] As in the case of David, the adversary of Jesus is a personal companion. Jesus' use of the clause, at the very least, describes his betrayer in terms of a friend with whom he has known close fellowship.[33] The fact that Jesus quotes "he who eats my bread" during the Last Supper seems to intensify its application to Judas's betrayal.[34]

Noticeably, Jesus omits the first half of Ps 41:9 in his reference. This omission is theologically relevant to the typology in that it draws a real distinction between Jesus and David. In Ps 41:9a, David prays to God as a helpless victim taken unaware by the treachery of a friend, whom he had truly "trusted" (note

---

30 Goldingay, *Psalms 1–41*, 1:586; Leupold, *Psalms*, 333; Ross, *Psalms*, 1:883–884; Wilson, *Psalms Volume 1*, 654.

31 אִישׁ שְׁלוֹמִי translates literally as "man of my peace" (Ps 41:9a). The construct "indicates the man was, or was thought to be, someone who was committed to his peace and welfare, a close friend who truly cared." Ross, *Psalms*, 1:883. F. Delitzsch explains the phrase as describing a "harmonious relationship." F. Delitzsch, *Psalms*, trans. Francis Bolton (Grand Rapids: Eerdmans, 1976), 2:48. Both Leupold (*Psalms*, 332–333) and Anderson (*Psalms*, 1:325) render the descriptive as "my bosom friend." אֲשֶׁר־בָּטַחְתִּי בוֹ translates literally as "whom I trusted in him." The clause describes a friendship in which David felt "secure" and had placed his "confidence." *HALOT*, s.v. "בטח."

32 Contra J. Ramsey Michaels, *The Gospel of John*, NICNT (Grand Rapids: Eerdmans, 2010), 740–741.

33 Morris, *John*, 553; Herman N. Ridderbos, *The Gospel According to John: A Theological Commentary* (Grand Rapids: Eerdmans, 1992), 467. That Jesus views Judas' actions as a most serious breach in relationship is clear from the syntax of the quotation. The position of the possessive μου ("my") before the direct object τὸν ἄρτον ("bread") is emphatic, which points to "the severity of Judas's treachery." Andreas J. Köstenberger, "John," in *CNTUOT*, ed. G. K. Beale and D. A. Carson (Grand Rapids: Baker Academic, 2007), 486.

34 John sets the stage for the meal and the foot washing scene that accompanies it with the statement that Jesus loved his disciples, Judas included, "to the end" (John 13:1). When Jesus dips the bread and gives it to Judas (13:26), an action which recalls the quotation in 13:18 (so Schnakenburg, *John*, 3:30), this is "a final gesture of supreme love." Carson, *John*, 474. According to Augustus Tholuck, Judas "arose from the *supper of love* [emphasis added] to consummate an act of betrayal." Augustus Tholuck, *Commentary on the Gospel of John*, trans. Charles P. Krauth (New York: Sheldon and Company, 1867), 324. Thus, Judas takes the morsel but rejects Jesus' final offer of friendship and love, choosing instead to side with Satan (13:27–30). Cf. Raymond E. Brown, *The Gospel According to John (13–21)*, AB 29A (Garden City, NY: Doubleday, 1970), 578.

אֲשֶׁר־בָּטַחְתִּי בוֹ).[35] Edwyn C. Hoskyns explains that Ps 41:9a is really "inapplicable" to Jesus, "since Jesus did not trust Judas."[36] In John 6:64, 70–71, John alerts the reader to the fact that Jesus never had confidence in Judas (cf. John 2:24–25). Even in John 13, John repeatedly stresses Jesus' perfect knowledge of Judas's treachery (13:1, 3, 10–11). Thus, the omission of Ps 41:9a contrasts David and Jesus. Jesus, unlike his counterpart David, is not deceived or a helpless victim in his suffering. To the contrary, he knows all things in advance and is, thus, sovereign over Judas and his malicious deed.

The remaining correlation between David and Jesus is seen in the crime committed against each. In Ps 41:9b, David says that his close friend הִגְדִּיל עָלַי עָקֵב ("he made great the heel against me"). Commentators differ as to the precise meaning of the expression in the Hebrew.[37] Even so, the whole of Ps 41:9 makes clear that the expression denotes an act of "treachery" or "betrayal."[38] Whether David had the incident with Ahithophel in mind or some other incident, the general idea is clear concerning the close friend's action.[39] The trusted confidant turned against David.

John attributes to Jesus the words ἐπῆρεν ἐπ' ἐμὲ τὴν πτέρναν αὐτοῦ ("has lifted up his heel against me") as his rendering of the latter part of Ps 41:9. John's wording agrees with the Hebrew fairly closely.[40] John's verbal modification may imply a "malicious kick"[41] and be a metaphoric expression for an

---

35 The overall tone of the prayer as well as the adverb גַּם ("even") commencing Ps 41:9 underscore David's helplessness and his state of surprise about his friend turned foe. The adverb גַּם is commonly employed to note additions (i.e., "also") or to note emphasis (i.e., "even"). Bill T. Arnold and John H. Choi, *A Guide to Biblical Hebrew Syntax* (Cambridge: Cambridge University Press, 2003), 132–133. The sense of "even" seems to be the preferable way to translate גַּם "when the additional event or statement is unexpected or illogical." Ibid., 132.

36 Hoskyns, *The Fourth Gospel*, 441. So Köstenberger, "John," 486–487; Menken, *Old Testament Quotations*, 137; Crawford Howell Toy, *Quotations in the New Testament* (New York: Charles Scribner's Sons, 1884), 89.

37 E.g., F. Delitzsch interprets it to mean "to give a great kick, *i.e.* with a good swing of the foot." Delitzsch, *Psalms*, 2:48. Leupold says that "the phrase is the epitome of vile dealing." Leupold, *Psalms*, 333. Craigie argues that "he who hinders you" is the more obvious sense. Craigie, *Psalms 1–50*, 319n10.c. Anderson suggests the ideas of "trampling on someone, or an act of violence in general." Anderson, *Psalms*, 1:325. Allen P. Ross connects the expression to treachery by deceiving and taking advantage of someone. Ross, *Psalms*, 1:884n30.

38 See e.g., Craigie, *Psalms 1–50*, 321; Ross, *Psalms*, 1:884; Willem A. VanGemeren, "Psalms," in EBC 5, ed. Frank E. Gaebelein (Grand Rapids: Zondervan, 1991), 327; Wilson, *Psalms Volume 1*, 654–655.

39 Early Rabbinic exegesis interpreted David's remarks in Ps 41:9 (as well as those in the parallel text of Ps 55:12–15) as a reference to David's counselor Ahithophel, who joined Absalom in his conspiracy to usurp his father's throne (2 Sam 15:12, 31, 34; 16:15, 20–23; 17:14, 21, 23). Menken, *Old Testament Quotations*, 132–133.

40 The only changes John makes is that he substitutes the verb ἐπῆρεν ("to lift up") in the place of הִגְדִּיל ("to enlarge") and makes explicit the pronoun αὐτοῦ ("his").

41 BDAG, s.v. "πτέρνα."

action of hostility or contempt against someone.[42] Whatever the exact meaning is, Moo rightly asserts that "certainly rejection and betrayal are connoted by the figure of speech."[43] Jesus clearly understands the language in this way by his use of παραδώσει in John 13:21, which means to hand someone over in the sense of betrayal.[44]

Again, although David experiences betrayal comparable to Jesus', the betrayal Jesus undergoes appears greater in its NT context. First, the metaphor "to lift the heel" takes on deeper meaning against the backdrop of the foot washing scene. Helen C. Orchard explains:

> Whatever the precise original meaning, it is evident that the metaphor used is a malignant one and in this context it is particularly appropriate: the feet that Jesus has washed respond with violence and a metaphorical kick. This accentuates the contempt of the betrayer and his rejection of Jesus' deed.[45]

The action of Judas, therefore, signals the rejection of Jesus' love and cleansing from sin. Second, John informs the reader that Judas is "a devil" (John 6:70–71) in conspiracy with the devil against Jesus (13:2, 27). His treachery is all the more scandalous, then, because he ultimately carries out the grand scheme of Satan. Third, Judas initiates the chain of events that ends decisively in Jesus' death. While God delivered David from his false friend (Ps 41:11–12), Judas's action culminates in the crucifixion of Jesus.

PROPHECY IN THE DAVID-JESUS TYPOLOGY

The foregoing examination demonstrates how the quotation of Ps 41:9 in John 13:18 sets forth a typological relationship between David and Jesus. The textual evidence suggests this typology constitutes something more than a mere analogy that simply compares David and Jesus.[46] Instead, the typology

---

42 Menken, *Old Testament Quotations*, 131n39.

43 Moo, *The Old Testament*, 238–239.

44 Cf. John 6:64, 71; 12:4; 13:2, 11; 18:2, 5; 19:11; 21:20. The verb παραδίδωμι, which the NT frequently uses to describe Judas's actions against Jesus, means "to hand over/turn over/give up" an individual. BDAG, s.v. "παραδίδωμι." According to Spicq, "The verb rather often also connotes this nuance of criminality: desertion to another camp, breach of sworn faith, betrayal of someone's trust. . . . To say that Jesus was handed over, then, means that he was betrayed." Ceslas Spicq, "παραδίδωμι," *TLNT* 3:21–22. Note also that Judas is given the title of a "προδότης" (i.e., "traitor/betrayer") in Luke 6:16. BDAG, s.v. "προδότης."

45 Helen C. Orchard, *Courting Betrayal: Jesus as Victim in the Gospel of John*, JSNTSup 161 (Sheffield: Sheffield Academic Press, 1998), 172.

46 Contra Fredrick C. Holmgren, *The Old Testament and the Significance of Jesus: Embrac-*

appears to possess a predictive quality, which links the Davidic event to Jesus in an intrinsic way. That is, this instance in David's life serves as a predictive model for what Jesus is to experience and is best explained as a case of prophetic David typology.[47] Four textual elements support this claim: (1) the ἵνα purpose clause, (2) the fulfillment language, (3) the contextual background of Jesus' "hour," and (4) Jesus' explanation in John 13:19.

The first piece of evidence that indicates a prophetic understanding of the David typology in John 13:18 is the introductory formula ἀλλ' ἵνα ἡ γραφὴ πληρωθῇ ("but [it is] that the Scripture may be fulfilled"). The adversative ἀλλά ("but"), when it introduces a Scripture citation, can function "to correct, qualify, or underscore a preceding statement or citation."[48] In this case, ἀλλά connects back to the immediately preceding statement: "I know the ones I have chosen."[49] Essentially, ἀλλά introduces a clause that clarifies the "meaning of Scripture" in regards to "I know the ones I have chosen."[50] To make sense of its connection to this sentence, most commentators agree that ἀλλά functions elliptically in relation to the subsequent ἵνα ("in order that/that").[51] Between

---

ing Change—Maintaining Christian Identity (Grand Rapids: Eerdmans, 1999), 38, 45–46

47 See e.g., Beale, *Handbook on the New Testament*, 60; John Calvin, *Commentary on the Gospel According to John*, trans. William Pringle (Grand Rapids: Eerdmans, 1949), 2:65; Carson, *John*, 470; Currid, "Recognition and Use," 126–127; Delitzsch, *Psalms*, 1:69; 2:45–46; Hofmann, *Interpreting the Bible*, 175–176. For commentators who describe Ps 41:9 as the fulfillment of prophecy but do not discuss typological aspects, see e.g., Bruce, *John*, 287; Craigie, *Psalms 1–50*, 322; Hoskyns, *The Fourth Gospel*, 441; Ridderbos, *John*, 467; J. N. Sanders, *A Commentary on the Gospel According to St. John*, BNTC (London: Adam & Charles Black, 1968), 311.

48 E. Earle Ellis, *Paul's Use of the Old Testament* (Eugene: Wipf and Stock, 1981), 84–85. Cf. Jakob K. Heckert, who explains that ἀλλά "introduces a correction of the expectation created by the first conjunct; an incorrect expectation is canceled and a proper expectation is put in its place." Jakob K. Heckert, *Discourse Functions of Conjoiners in the Pastor Epistles* (Dallas, TX: SIL International, 1991), 22. It seems here the contrast would be the expectation that Jesus would not have chosen Judas since He knew him, *but* He did choose Judas so that Ps 41:9 might reach its fulfillment.

49 Contra R. C. H. Lenski and Theodor Zahn, who argue for linking ἀλλά to the negative "I do not speak of all of you" statement that begins John 13:18. Lenski, *St. John's Gospel*, 931–932; Theodor Zahn, *Das Evangelium des Johannes*, Kommentar zum Neuen Testament 4 (Leipzig: Deichert, 1908), 532. This syntactical link is not preferable, however, since it turns "I know the ones I have chosen" into a parenthetical statement. Cf. Rudolph Bultmann, *The Gospel of John: A Commentary*, ed. R. W. N. Hoare and J. K. Riches, trans. G. R. Beasely-Murray (Oxford: Basil Blackwell, 1971), 477n9.

50 Ellis explains that the use of ἀλλά before a citation "represents an exegetical technique, a dialectical procedure by which apparent contradictions are resolved and the meaning of Scripture is drawn out or more precisely specified." Ellis, *The Old Testament*, 85.

51 So e.g., Barrett, *John*, 444; Bultmann, *John*, 477n9; Godet, *John's Gospel*, 812; Menken, *Old Testament Quotations*, 123; Moo, *The Old Testament*, 236; Morris, *John*, 552n43; Schuchard, *Scripture Within Scripture*, 107n2. BDF §448.7. For similar elliptical constructions in the FG, cf. John 1:8; 9:3; 15:24–25.

ἀλλά and ἵνα, a supplement along the lines of "but [this happened] in order that" needs to be supplied in order to complete the thought.[52]

With this supplement, the following ἵνα...πληρωθῇ ("that . . . may be fulfilled") subjunctive construction sheds light on what Jesus intends to emphasize with ἀλλά. Basically, the ἵνα clause supports a prophetic notion in the David typology. In the NT, ἵνα plus the subjunctive usually implies either "purpose, aim, or goal" (i.e., "in order that") or "result" (i.e., "so that").[53] When John uses this construct in his citation of Scripture,[54] the purpose or telic force seems most probable.[55] Even if one interprets the ἵνα as a purpose-result clause, the telic force still remains.[56]

The implication of the telic force in John 13:18 indicates why Jesus chose Judas.[57] According to Klaus Wengst,"Das war kein Versehen, sondern Absicht.

---

52 This ellipsis reading is recommended in BDF §448.7. The NASB supplies the supplement "*it is*." See also Godet, *John's Gospel*, 812; Moo, *The Old Testament*, 236; Ridderbos, *John*, 467.

53 BDAG, s.v. "ἵνα," 1, 3. While the ἵνα πληρωθῇ subjunctive can designate an imperative, this goes against the usual telic sense in John. Brown, *John (13–21)*, 2:553–554. So also, Barrett, *John*, 444.

54 Cf. John 12:38–40; 15:25; 17:12; 19:24, 28, 36–37. Except for John 19:28, each of these employs the ἵνα πληρωθῇ aorist subjunctive construct. In John 19:28, a virtually synonymous verb is used for the construct (i.e., ἵνα τελειωθῇ).

55 So Brown, *John (1–12)*, 1:483; Brown, *John (13–21)*, 2:553–554; Carson, "John and the Johannine Epistles," 250; Bruce M. Metzger, "The Formulas Introducing Quotations of Scripture in the NT and the Mishnah," *JBL* 70 (1951): 306n17; Morris, *John*, 81n61, 536n106. E. Stauffer also argues for a telic force to the ἵνα clauses in the FG, especially those in John's Scripture introductory formulas. The telic force of the ἵνα, Stauffer explains, is clear from John's teleological understanding of Jesus' passion. Jesus taught that his passion must take place to fulfill the Scriptures (cf. John 19:28; Matt 26:56). Consequently, when John references OT citations, his theological perspective is that the OT Scriptures point towards this ultimate *telos*, the cross. The use of the ἵνα construction to introduce Scripture citations, therefore, indicates that the corresponding events are the outworking of God's purposes in relation to the cross. E. Stauffer, "ἵνα," *TDNT* 3:323–328, 327–328n44–46.

56 Wallace treats purpose-result ἵνα clauses as a distinct category. Daniel B. Wallace, *Greek Grammar Beyond the Basics: An Exegetical Syntax of the New Testament* (Grand Rapids: Zondervan, 1996), 473–474. BDAG explains that "in many cases purpose and result cannot be clearly differentiated, and hence ἵνα is used for the result that follows according to the purpose of the subj[ect] or of God. As in Semitic and Gr[eek]-Rom[an] thought, purpose and result are identical in declarations of the divine will." BDAG, s.v. "ἵνα," 3, p. 477. Both purpose and result, according to BDAG, are present in the use of the ἵνα πληρωθῇ formula, "since the fulfillment is acc[ording] to God's plan of salvation." Ibid. Wallace explains a purpose-result clause as follows: "It indicates *both the intention and its sure accomplishment* [emphasis original].... What God purposes is what happens and, consequently, ἵνα is used to express both the divine purpose and the result." Wallace, *Greek Grammar*, 473. In this classification, therefore, there is still a sure emphasis upon the action in connection to divine purpose. See also C. F. D. Moule, *An Idiom Book of New Testament Greek*, 2nd ed. (Cambridge: Cambridge University Press, 1959), 142–143.

57 Accordingly, the ellipsis "but, [this happened] in order that" refers back to the verb ἐξελεξάμην ("I chose") of the preceding ἐγὼ οἶδα τίνας ἐξελεξάμην statement. Syntactically, then, the ἵνα modifies the verb ἐξελεξάμην, explaining the ultimate purpose for why Jesus chose a disciple whom he knew would betray him. Cf. the discussion by E. W. Hengstenberg, *Commentary on the Gospel of St. John*, (Edinburgh: T&T Clark, 1865), 2:152–153.

Was aber war diese Absicht bei der Wahl des Judas? Sie erfolgte deshalb, fährt der Text fort, 'damit die Schrift erfüllt werde.'"⁵⁸ That is, Jesus chose Judas even though he knew his treachery beforehand, because he knew Ps 41:9 had to be fulfilled (cf. John 6:64, 70–71).⁵⁹ The ἵνα clause, therefore, indicates that the ultimate meaning of Ps 41:9 had Jesus' betrayal by Judas in mind.⁶⁰ For Jesus to choose Judas *in order that* the Scripture might be fulfilled, Ps 41:9 must have been pointing beyond David's betrayal to this NT event in Jesus' life. One cannot, therefore, relegate the typology of John 13:18 to pure analogy, which is concerned only with comparisons. The typology of John 13:18, however, connects David and Jesus on a deeper level. If Jesus' choice of Judas was intentional with regard to Ps 41:9, as the purpose ἵνα clause seems to indicate, then Jesus views a text relaying David's experience as a prophetic pattern for his own experience.

The second piece of evidence that supports the prophetic understanding of the David typology in John 13:18 is the verb πληρωθῇ. NT πληρόω ("to fulfill") in connection to the fulfillment of the OT Scriptures is important for understanding the concept of typology.⁶¹ The NT writers clearly use πληρόω in introductory formulas to signal the fulfillment of specific, verbal prophecies in connection with Jesus. At the same time, they also use πληρόω to denote the fulfillment of OT texts that recount historical situations, which are not straightforward prophecies. G. K. Beale rightly contends that this interchange of πληρόω with both kinds of OT texts is the "the *ultimate* equation of direct verbal prophecy and indirect typological prophecy."⁶²

Πληρόω can be used to indicate prophetic fulfillment of texts relaying events because the wider scope of the verb encompasses the idea of

---

58 Wengst, *Das Johannesevangelium*, 2:99. "This was not an oversight, but intentional. But what was the intention in the choice of Judas? It was therefore done, the text continues, 'that the Scripture might be fulfilled'" (my translation).

59 Moo explains "that the choice has, in fact, been made in order to fulfill the Scriptures (cf. Jn. 6:64, 71)." Moo, *The Old Testament*, 236. See also Barrett, *John*, 444; Brown, *John (13–21)*, 554; Carson, *John*, 470; Hengstenberg, *St. John*, 2:152–153; Menken, *Old Testament Quotations*, 123; Schuchard, *Scripture Within Scripture*, 107; George Allen Turner and Julius R. Mantey, *The Gospel According to John*, ECB 4 (Grand Rapids: Eerdmans, 1964), 269. Contra Ridderbos, *John*, 466–467. Naturally, the ἵνα purpose clause raises questions regarding Judas's free will in the betrayal of Jesus. For a balanced discussion of the telic ἵνα and its implications for the issue of divine sovereignty and human freedom, see Borchert, *John*, 63–65.

60 Cf. Hengstenberg, *St. John*, 2:152–153.

61 On πληρόω language in typology, see the section "Fulfillment Language" in chapter 3 of this work.

62 Beale, *Handbook on the New Testament*, 58 (emphasis original). Thomas Schreiner observes the same feature occurring in Matthew's use of πληρόω in introductory formulas. Πληρόω indicates the fulfillment of prophecy in Matthew, but the prophetic fulfillment is sometimes direct and sometimes typological. Thomas R. Schreiner, *New Testament Theology: Magnifying God in Christ* (Grand Rapids: Baker Academic, 2008), 70–79.

fulfillment in teleological terms. That is, NT πληρόω language communicates that OT history was progressing purposefully towards a climactic goal: Jesus and his gospel. Consequently, when the NT uses πληρόω to cite OT passages describing events, the fulfillment concept reveals that those OT events possessed a predictive thrust toward their corresponding NT events. In other words, πληρόω identifies the stated NT events as the goals to which those OT event-based texts were pointing.[63] If OT event-based texts were pointing forward to NT goals, then they were predicting their NT goals.

John clearly uses πληρόω as a signpost for the fulfillment of OT predictions that are essentially both verbal and typological. One finds an example of the former kind of fulfillment (i.e., verbal prophecy) in John 12:37–38[64] and of the latter (i.e., typological prophecy) in John 19:36–37.[65]

Thus, the most consistent way to understand Jesus' use of πληρόω in John 13:18 is according to a prophetic frame of reference. The logic, then, is simple: the fulfillment language indicates that Ps 41:9 is a goal-oriented text in connection to Jesus. For Ps 41:9 to have Jesus' betrayal as its goal, this means that the text was interpreted as pointing forward to this climactic NT incident. Thus, Jesus shows that a passage about David's betrayal provides a prophetic foreshadowing of his similar, climactic betrayal. The Davidic episode is an event in salvation history that typologically prefigures and predicts a future fulfillment in Christ, a case of typological prophecy.

The theological theme of Jesus' "hour" (ὥρα) (cf. John 12:23, 27; 13:1) is the third piece of evidence that favors a prophetic view of the typology in John 13:18.[66] The "hour" in the FG "refers to the appointed time for either Jesus'

---

[63] Such a teleological or goal orientation for πληρόω accords with the definition BDAG supplies for the fulfillment of divine prophecies and promises: "to bring to a designed end." BDAG, s.v. "πληρόω."

[64] The πληρόω formula of this text indicates the fulfillment of Isa 53:1—a direct statement which predicted the unbelief of the Jewish people toward Jesus, the Servant of the Lord. See Beale, *Handbook on the New Testament*, 58–59; Carson, "John and the Johannine Epistles," 250–51.

[65] In John 19:36–37 a single introductory πληρόω formula introduces two OT quotations cited one after the other. It seems most exegetically sound to understand πληρόω as expressing a uniform sense for both OT quotations. What is interesting about John 19:36–37 is that the first OT quotation (John 19:36/Exod 12:46 or Num 9:12) describes an event that is predictive (i.e., typological prophecy), while the second OT quotation (John 19:37/Zech 12:10) records a straightforward prediction in words (i.e., verbal prophecy). For both OT texts, then, πληρόω indicates that prophetic fulfillment is in view, albeit one text is word-based and the other is event-based. For a fuller discussion of John 19:36–37, see the section on "Fulfillment Language" in chapter 3.

[66] Carson notes that the "hour" in John "always bears theological content," referring to Jesus' death and glorification. Carson, *John*, 307. John develops this theme throughout his Gospel (John 2:4; 4:21, 23; 7:30; 8:20; 12:23, 27; 13:1; 16:32; 17:1), moving from a future tense ("not yet;" cf. John 2:4) perspective in John 2–10 to a present tense ("has come;" cf. John 12:23) perspective from John 12–17.

sufferings in the Passion week or His glorification in the resurrection."[67] Leon Morris explains, "The 'hour' in this Gospel has about it the air of inevitability. It represents the doing of the Father's will."[68] So, the theme of the "hour" identifies the specific events of Jesus' sufferings to be key parts of the predetermined plan of the Father, which climaxes in the cross.[69] Jesus makes this much clear, when he identifies his hour as the purpose for which the Father sent him into the world (John 12:27).

Moreover, Raymond E. Brown observes, "the Johannine fulfillment texts are all in the context of 'the hour,' i.e., of the passion."[70] This is significant for understanding the function of John's Scripture citations. As John Christopher Thomas points out, "Collectively, these texts serve to highlight the divinely ordained sequence of events which make up the passion."[71] When Jesus introduces Ps 41:9 with πληρόω, the context of the "hour" means that the psalm reveals his betrayal as the outworking of the divine plan of God.[72] Daniel B. Stevick similarly explains the function of Scripture in the FG and in John 13:18 as follows:

> The Scripture citations in the later part of the Fourth Gospel tend to show that a plan or a determining order is at work in the events of Jesus' life (12:13–15, 38–40; 15:25; 17:12; 19:24, 28, 36, 37). The source of this intentionality which pervades the gospel narrative is the redemptive purpose of God, being carried forward by the Father's will and Jesus' obedience. . . Here Jesus' citation from the Jewish Scriptures seems to imply that events as they play out are within a *divine intention that has been foreshadowed* [emphasis added] in a Hebrew Psalm. . . . A larger meaning is suggested by the Scripture citation. Jesus says that the disciples will later remember not only this event and that he had predicted it but also the Psalm passage to

---

67 J. G. Gibbs, "Hour," *ISBE* 2:769.
68 Morris, *John*, 529.
69 The repetition of the hour in the FG, as Morris notes, points to the cross as the "intended climax" of Jesus' coming. Leon Morris, *New Testament Theology* (Grand Rapids: Zondervan, 1986), 270.
70 Brown, *John (13–21)*, 2:554.
71 John Christopher Thomas, *Foot washing in John 13 and the Johannine Community*, JSNTSup 61 (Sheffield: JSOT Press, 1991), 113.
72 Oscar Cullmann understands ὥρα in the FG as a reference to the predetermined events God planned for Jesus to accomplish in salvation history. He writes, "[It] has the same intention of reminding us that salvation proceeds within the framework of time whose Lord is God, and that within this time God has singled out the hours that bring salvation. . . . In John's Gospel the reference to the 'hour' that has not yet come stresses much more Jesus' link with the divine saving plan. Starting with 2.4, 'The hour has not yet come', the Gospel leads up to 12.23, 'The hour *has* come'." Oscar Cullmann, *Salvation in History*, trans. Sidney G. Sowers (Tübingen: Mohr-Siebeck, 1965), 276; cf. 275.

which he calls attention now. It was the coming together of the incident and the interpreting Scriptures that would reveal the rootage of Jesus and his mission in the deep purposes of God.[73]

John's use of Scripture citations, as Stevick clarifies, shows the "rootage" of the events of Jesus' sufferings "in the deep purposes of God." D. A. Carson similarly declares that in John "the OT citations in one way or another point to Jesus . . . grounding the details of his life and death in the Scriptures."[74] Therefore, to label the use of Ps 41:9 in John 13:18 as establishing only an analogy weakens the contextual force of God's purposes or divine program being *grounded* in the OT Scriptures.

Furthermore, as Stevick observes, the quotation of Ps 41:9 appears to substantiate "divine intention that has been foreshadowed." This means that the fulfillment of Ps 41:9 points to an intrinsic relationship between David's betrayal and Jesus' betrayal: that is David's experience was providing advance notice of one of God's purposes for Jesus within the larger context of his predetermined plan (i.e., the "hour"). Thus, the quotation of Ps 41:9 reveals that Jesus' betrayal was essential to God's plan, having been predicted in a typological way through David's betrayal.

Lastly, John 13:19 supports a predictive understanding of the David typology in John 13:18. Jesus says to the disciples ἀπ' ἄρτι λέγω ὑμῖν πρὸ τοῦ γενέσθαι, ἵνα πιστεύσητε ὅταν γένηται ὅτι ἐγώ εἰμι ("From now on I am telling you before [it] comes to pass, so that when it does occur, you may believe that I am [He]."). This statement in 13:19 communicates the expectation that a prophecy will be fulfilled. In this sentence, the subject of the articular infinitive πρὸ τοῦ γενέσθαι ("before [it] comes to pass") and the verb γένηται ("it does occur") may be a general "it" or "this," which would be a reference to Jesus' betrayal,[75] or, based on its grammatical proximity, it is possible that the quotation in 13:18 stands as the subject of πρὸ τοῦ γενέσθαι and γένηται.[76] Whether the event of

---

73 Daniel B. Stevick, *Jesus and His Own: A Commentary on John 13–17* (Grand Rapids: Eerdmans, 2011), 37–38.

74 Carson, "John and the Johannine Epistles," 246.

75 According to the temporal markers πρό ("before") and ὅταν ("when"), this would imply that John 13:18 records the prediction of Jesus' betrayal. Since Ps 41:9 records an event in David's life, this would mean that Jesus interprets the OT text as providing a predictive model.

76 Barrett, *John*, 445; Lenski, *St. John's Gospel*, 935. If this is the case, the temporal markers πρό ("before") and ὅταν ("when") indicate that Ps 41:9 is a prophecy awaiting its fulfillment. The sense of John 13:19, then, would be as follows: "From now on I am telling you before Ps 41:9 comes to pass, so that when it (i.e., Ps 41:9) does occur, you may understand my identity as expressed by ἐγώ εἰμι ('I am')." Once Jesus is betrayed, Stevick argues that Jesus intends for the disciples to understand his ἐγώ εἰμι expression and what it means for his identity in light of his interpretation of Ps 41:9. Stevick, *Jesus and His Own*, 38.

the betrayal or the psalm quotation is in view, John 13:19 reinforces the interpretation that Ps 41:9 relays an event that is prophetic of Jesus' betrayal.

Ps 69:4 in John 15:25

In John 15:25, John quotes from another OT psalm to highlight a David-Jesus typology. As in the case of John 13:18, John 15:25 is a fulfillment-formula quotation that Jesus speaks. The formula quotation reads ἀλλ᾿ ἵνα πληρωθῇ ὁ λόγος ὁ ἐν τῷ νόμῳ αὐτῶν γεγραμμένος ὅτι ("But [they have done this] to fulfill the word that is written in their Law"). Notably, Jesus again employs the ἵνα πληρωθῇ construction to denote the fulfillment of Scripture. The nouns ὁ λόγος ("the word") and τῷ νόμῳ ("the law") along with the participle γεγραμμένος ("that is written") signal an ensuing appeal to a specific OT citation.[77]

The formula introduces the brief quotation ἐμίσησάν με δωρεάν ("They hated me without a cause"). Psalm 35:19 (34:19 LXX) and Ps 69:4 (68:5 LXX) are the most likely source texts for the words under consideration.[78] Since both verses contain the same wording in the MT and the LXX, either Ps 35:19 or Ps 69:4 could be the source, but Menken discusses two factors that favor Ps 69:4.[79] First, John quotes from Psalm 69 elsewhere (John 2:17) and also alludes to it (19:28).[80] There are no references to Psalm 35 in the gospel. Similarly, the NT writers frequently appeal to Psalm 69, but they demonstrate no such dependence for Psalm 35.[81] In light of these factors,[82] Ps 69:4 stands as the most

---

77 The NT writers sometimes use ὁ λόγος to designate the "writings that are part of Holy Scripture." BDAG, s.v. "λόγος." See e.g., Luke 3:4; John 12:38; Acts 15:15; 1 Cor 15:54; 2 Pet 1:19. As for τῷ νόμῳ, it often serves as a general reference to the whole of Scripture (see BDAG, s.v. "νόμος.") and indicates here that Psalms could be denoted as "the Law" (cf. John 10:34). See Ellis, *The Old Testament*, 39. Considered together, the sense of the introductory formula indicates the ensuing quotation is a specific text (i.e., ὁ λόγος) that belongs to the larger context of the OT (i.e., τῷ νόμῳ). Cf. Schuchard, *Scripture Within Scripture*, 120n8. On the frequent use of γράφω in its indicative and participial (i.e., γεγραμμένος) forms to introduce Scripture quotations, see BDAG, s.v. "γράφω."

78 Menken, *Old Testament Quotations*, 142.

79 Ibid., 144–145.

80 These two additional references by John also convince Moo that Psalm 69 is the preferred psalm. Moo, *The Old Testament*, 243.

81 See also Christian Dietzfelbinger, who argues Psalm 69 is in view "weil er einer der für die neutestamentliche Passionsgeschichte maßgebenden Psalmen ist, was für Ps. 35 nicht gilt" ("because it is one of the relevant psalms for the New Testament passion events, which does not apply to Psalm 35" [my translation]). Christian Dietzfelbinger, *Das Evangelium nach Johannes*, Zürcher Bibelkommentare (Zürich: Theologischer Verlag, 2001), 2:128. See also Carson, who notes not only the frequent use of Ps 69 in the NT but also its consideration as a noted messianic psalm. Carson, *John*, 527. See also Bernard, *St. John*, 495.

82 Menken also adds a third consideration. He posits that the references to "persecution" and "hate" in John 15:20, 25 may reflect the parallelism of those same ideas in Ps 69:5a–5b. Menken, *Old Testament Quotations*, 144–145. Cf. Freed, *Old Testament Quotations*, 95. In addition to

likely source from which John draws.[83]

The small portion of Ps 69:4 quoted in John 15:25 is close but not identical to the wording of either the MT or the LXX.

John 15:25	ἐμίσησάν με δωρεάν
	"They hated me without a cause."
MT Ps 69:5	רַבּוּ מִשַּׂעֲרוֹת רֹאשִׁי שֹׂנְאַי חִנָּם עָצְמוּ מַצְמִיתַי אֹיְבַי שֶׁקֶר אֲשֶׁר לֹא־גָזַלְתִּי אָז אָשִׁיב
	"Those who hate me without a cause are more than the hairs of my head; Those who would destroy me are powerful, being wrongfully my enemies, What I did not steal, I then have to restore."
LXX Ps 68:5	ἐπληθύνθησαν ὑπὲρ τὰς τρίχας τῆς κεφαλῆς μου οἱ μισοῦντές με δωρεάν ἐκραταιώθησαν οἱ ἐχθροί μου οἱ ἐκδιώκοντές με ἀδίκως ἃ οὐχ ἥρπασα τότε ἀπετίννυον
	"Those who hate me without cause are increased above the hairs of my head. My enemies who persecute me unjustly are strengthened. What I did not take away, then, I repaid."

The part John appropriates differs from the MT and the LXX only in regard to a verbal change.[84] Since the LXX renders the MT exactly[85] and the quotation in John 15:25 provides an apt adaptation of either version, one must leave open the possibility that John cites from either the MT or the LXX.[86]

Correspondence in the David-Jesus Typology

The content and mood of Psalm 69 leads most commentators to designate its

---

Menken's arguments, Brown contends, "Moreover the context of Ps lxix is better for the meaning that John gives the citation." Brown, *John (13–21)*, 698.

83 E.g., Beasely-Murray, *John*, 276; Brown, *John (13–21)*, 698; Carson, *John*, 527; Daly-Denton, *David in the Fourth Gospel*, 202–203; Dodd, *According to the Scriptures*, 58; Köstenberger, "John," 467; Barnabas Lindars, *The Gospel of John*, NCBC (London: Oliphants, 1972), 495; Moo, *The Old Testament*, 243; Witherington, *John's Wisdom*, 261. Contra Francis J. Moloney, who prefers Ps 35:19. Francis J. Moloney, *The Gospel of John* (Collegeville, MN: The Liturgical Press, 1998), 430, 434. Contra Schuchard, who thinks both psalms may be in play but remains undecided as to the "preferred solution." Schuchard, *Scripture Within Scripture*, 123.

84 Where they use the substantival participles שֹׂנְאַי and οἱ μισοῦντές ("Those who hate"), John uses the finite verb ἐμίσησάν ("They hated").

85 That is, (1) οἱ μισοῦντές and שֹׂנְאַי are both plural participles with the lexical meaning "to hate," (2) δωρεάν and חִנָּם are both adverbs that mean "without cause," and (3) the first-person pronoun με agrees with the Hebrew first person suffix י.

86 Edwin D. Freed says that "it is impossible to tell whether it is from the Heb[rew] or Gr[eek] text." Freed, *Old Testament Quotations*, 95.

genre as a lament.[87] Structurally, Psalm 69 moves from the individual lament in 69:1–28 to a conclusion of thanksgiving in 69:29–36.[88] David supplies only enough details in Psalm 69 to reconstruct a general picture of the experience he recounts. In 69:1–4, David voices an urgent prayer to God for deliverance. His situation is so dire that he likens himself to a man who is drowning and about to sink permanently beneath the waters (69:1b–2). He feels completely worn out from his grief (69:3). The exact nature of David's dilemma becomes apparent in 69:4. He has enemies too numerous to count, who hate him "without cause" (69:4a). They accuse him falsely and are set on seeking his destruction (69:4b).[89]

David speaks to God in Ps 69:4 about his personal struggle against numerous enemies motivated by unjustified or groundless hate. Jesus applies this text about David's experience to himself when he quotes Ps 69:4 in John 15:25. As in the case with John 13:18, Jesus seems again to apply this psalm text based on David typology. That is, Jesus turns the disciples' attention once more to a time of suffering in David's life because in David and in his experience he finds a prefiguration that relates to his situation. The specific parallels John 15:25 establishes between Jesus and David include (1) the royalty status of the sufferer, (2) the multitude of the enemies, and (3) the motivation of the enemies.

The first point of correspondence is the same one discussed initially with Ps 41:9 in John 13:18. David and Jesus correspond in their status as suffering kings. Psalm 69 reflects a lament written by King David, which merges the topics of kingship and suffering[90] (the first-person pronominal suffix יִ ["me"] in Ps 69:4 clarifies King David as the sufferer). John 15 also combines suffering and kingship in regard to Jesus.[91] John 15:25 specifically discusses the hostility Jesus, Israel's King, encounters from the world. In quoting Ps 69:4, Jesus

---

87 Cf. e.g., Tremper Longmann III, *How to Read the Psalms* (Grand Rapids: InterVarsity 1988), 133–134; VanGemeren, *Psalms*, 454. On psalms of lament, see the summary of Ps 41:9 in the analysis of John 13:18 above in this chapter.

88 VanGemeren, "Psalms," 454, 461. For a detailed structural analysis of Psalm 69 as a whole and in unit sets, see Pierre Auffret, "'Dieu sauvera Sion': Étude structurelle du Psaume LXIX," *VT* 46 (1996).

89 The term שֶׁקֶר ("false witness/lying testimony/a lie;" *HALOT*, s.v. "שֶׁקֶר.") suggests David's enemies were persecuting him with false accusations. Cf. Wilson, *Psalms Volume 1*, 951. David's words in the latter part of Ps 69:4 (i.e., "What I did not steal, I then have to restore.") may reveal his enemies were accusing him of theft. If not, this statement may simply represent a common proverbial expression denoting his innocence. Cf. Anderson, *Psalms*, 1:501.

90 On the notion of suffering royalty in lament psalms, see the section "Typological Correspondence between David and Jesus" above in this chapter in the analysis of John 13:18.

91 In the analysis of the typology of John 13:18 above in this chapter, it was established that John presents Jesus entering into the events of his suffering as the King of Israel. John continues to emphasize the kingship theme up through Jesus' crucifixion.

assumes the place of David, so that the first-person accusative με ("me") now emphasizes himself as the object of suffering. The quotation of Ps 69:4, thus, serves as Jesus' way of linking himself with David to underscore their analogous relationship as suffering kings.[92] Nevertheless, the kingship of Jesus contrasts with David's, since Jesus is the one sent from the Father (John 15:21). His royal office, being divine in nature, therefore, transcends David's and represents the culmination of David's office.

Jesus and David are also parallel with regard to the multitude of their enemies. David clarifies in his lament that the plural subject (i.e., *"those* who hate") refers to the great number of his enemies. He describes them to God as being "more than the hairs of my head" (Ps 69:4a) and as being "countless" (69:4b).[93] In John 15:25, the plural subject (i.e., *"They* hated") of the psalm verse carries the same quantitative focus but has two frames of reference. The "they" to whom Jesus refers includes the Jews,[94] but the Jews represent only a part of a larger entity of the enemies of Jesus, which properly encompasses ὁ κόσμος ("the world," 15:18–19). ὁ κόσμος is used predominantly in John with negative force, and it stands for "the created order (especially of human beings and human affairs) in rebellion against its Maker."[95] King David had enemies who seemed numberless to him, but Jesus stands as the king whom all mankind opposes from generation to generation. Jesus as the antitype surpasses the type David in greatness, as is seen in the universal resistance to him and his rule.

The other significant point of contact Jesus shares with David is the motivation common to their enemies. David designates his enemies as שֹׂנְאַי חִנָּם ("Those who hate me without cause") in Ps 69:4. The adverb חִנָּם means "in vain," "without cause," and "undeservedly."[96] Essentially, the foes of David loathe him for no justifiable reason. His enemies harbor a groundless enmity for him, which motivates them in their various attacks (Ps 69:26).[97] Jesus reveals the same inward motivation to be the driving force of his opposition from the world at large and the Jews specifically. About them, Jesus says

---

92 Cf. Köstenberger, *John's Gospel and Letters*, 411–412.

93 The verb עָצְמוּ in Ps 69:4b can mean "to be powerful" or "to be countless." *HALOT*, s.v. "עָצַם." The latter sense seems preferable in this context, since it parallels with the quantitative emphasis of the hyperbole (רַבּוּ מִשַּׂעֲרוֹת רֹאשִׁי) in 69:4a. Anderson, *Psalms*, 1:500.

94 Jesus' references to "their law" (John 15:25) and the "synagogue" (16:2) clearly indicate that he has in mind the Jewish nation. Witherington, *John's Wisdom*, 261.

95 Carson, *John*, 123. He lists John 1:10; 7:7; 14:17, 22, 27, 30; 15:18–19; 16:8, 20, 33; 17:6, 9, 14, where the "world" carries this sense.

96 *HALOT*, s.v. "חִנָּם."

97 David's enemies were guilty of accusing him falsely (Ps 69:4b), seeking his destruction (69:4b), reproaching him (69:7, 9, 11–12), denying him mercy (69:20–21), and persecuting him (69:26).

ἐμίσησάν με δωρεάν ("They hated me without a cause," John 15:25).[98] This hatred of which Jesus speaks is "real hatred, and not, as in the Semitic idiom (cf. 12.25), a matter of liking less."[99] The adverb δωρεάν translates the Hebrew accurately, depicting the Jews as hating Jesus "undeservedly" or "without reason/cause,"[100] for no fault on Jesus' part contributes to the malice he experiences.[101] Both Jesus and David are hated by their enemies for no justifiable reason, yet the senseless hate Jesus encounters brings with it greater implications than it did in the person of David.

First, the hatred of Jesus cannot have only him as its object but necessarily includes the Father by extension (John 15:23–24; cf. 1 John 2:23).[102] Second, the hostile attitude of men toward Jesus continues to the present with ongoing results.[103] Third, hatred of Jesus entails eternal consequences, since it equates to rejection of God's perfect revelation through his Son (John 15:22–24).[104] Such hatred marks the "final ('eschatological') seriousness as the attitude of not wanting to 'know' the Messiah."[105] Thus, to hate Jesus equates to rejecting him, which "is sin, distinguished from all other sin. It is inexcusable. . ."[106] Lastly, the baseless contempt of the world brings with it not only acts of persecution and rejection (John 15:20), but in the end, it nails Jesus to the cross. He will no longer be with the disciples (15:26–27; 16:4) because the irrational hate of the world will procure his atoning sacrifice. Unlike David, therefore, Jesus dies as a result of the animus of his enemies.

---

98 The change to the finite aorist verb ἐμίσησάν ("They hated") in place of the original Hebrew participle is simply an adaptation to the NT context.

99 Barrett, *John*, 480. See also BDAG, s.v. "μισέω."

100 BDAG, s.v. "δωρεάν."

101 The sense of the adverb in relation to the main verb is: "'They hated me, but they didn't have reason for hating me,' or 'They hated me, but I had not done anything to cause them to hate me.'" Newman and Nida, *John*, 496.

102 B. F. Westcott expounds, "Hatred of the Son as Son carries with it hatred of the Father, in which character He had revealed God." Westcott, *St. John*, 224.

103 Cf. Morris, *John*, 602n44. The continuative character of the world's hate against Jesus is established by (1) the perfect tense verbs in John 15:18, 24 ("it has hated/they have hated"), which emphasize ongoing results, (2) the proclamation of the gospel (15:26–27), which continues to confront people with Jesus, and (3) the persecution of Christ's disciples, which the world ultimately does on account of Jesus (15:21).

104 On this, Herman N. Ridderbos writes: "'Hate' shares in the absoluteness of Jesus' words about sin . . . . To hate is to turn away from the way that God has opened for salvation. This hatred is the human "no" to the divine "yes" expressed in the mission of his Son. And this all the more because the power and authority that God has given the Son to speak and act in his name was so unmistakable that it should have convinced the world." Ridderbos, *John*, 525.

105 Ibid., 526. Cf. Barnabas Lindar's comment, where he explains the hatred of the world as "the rejection of the total message and work of Jesus." Lindars, *The Gospel of John*, 495.

106 Hoskyns, *The Fourth Gospel*, 481.

Prophecy in the David-Jesus Typology

The use of Ps 69:4 in John 15:25 juxtaposes David and Jesus to show a typological relationship in their persons and specific situations. The textual evidence suggests that the typology is not mere analogy but is prophetic in force, so that the type and antitype relate as a kind of prophecy and fulfillment.[107] Three pieces of evidence support a prophetic view of the David typology: (1) the ἵνα purpose clause, (2) the "fulfillment" language, and (3) the theological theme of Jesus' "hour."[108]

Jesus introduces the quotation of Ps 69:4 in John 15:25 with the formula ἀλλ᾽ ἵνα πληρωθῇ ὁ λόγος ὁ ἐν τῷ νόμῳ αὐτῶν γεγραμμένος ὅτι ("But [they have done this] to fulfill the word that is written in their Law"). The strong adversative ἀλλά ("but") signals that the psalm quotation clarifies Jesus' preceding words. Agreeing with Bultmann, ἀλλά appears to answer the unexpressed thought between John 15:24–25, concerning how unthinkable it is that the Jews would reject Jesus.[109] Ἀλλά and the ἵνα that immediately follows are best understood as an elliptical construct,[110] best completed along the lines of "But, [this occurred] in order that . . ." or "But [they have done this] to . . ."[111] The effect of the conjunction ἀλλά is to direct the minds of the disciples to an OT Scripture, which introduces "a new point of view in regard to the hatred

---

107 See e.g., Carson, "John and the Johannine Epistles," 249; Kidner, *Psalms 1–72*, 162; Moo, *The Old Testament*, 243–244, 299–300. Cf. Delitzsch who says, "The whole of Psalm [69] is typically prophetic, in as far as it is a declaration of a history of life and suffering moulded by God into a factual prediction concerning Jesus Christ, whether it be the story of a king or a prophet." Delitzsch, *Psalms*, 2:278. Cf. also Calvin who explains Ps 69 in terms of prophetic David typology, arguing: "But to whatever part of David's eventful life the psalm primarily refers, it may be concluded, from the frequency with which it is quoted and applied to Christ in the New Testament, that it was prophetic of him, of whom David, rejected and persecuted, was an eminent type." John Calvin, *Commentary on the Book of Psalms*, trans. James Anderson (Grand Rapids: Baker Book House, 1981), 5:45n1. Contra Sanghee Michael Ahn, "Old Testament Characters as Christological Witnesses in the Fourth Gospel" (PhD diss., Southern Baptist Theological Seminary, 2006), 144, who denies a David-Jesus typology in this passage.

108 These key pieces of evidence need only brief treatment here, since they were treated in detail in the initial examination of the prophetic elements of John 13:18. For each of these prophetic elements, see the relevant sections above in this chapter.

109 Bultmann, *John*, 551n6. That is, it is hard to imagine the Jews would hate Jesus, but they act in this way to fulfill the Scripture. See also Moo, *The Old Testament*, 243n1, who agrees with Bultmann's analysis.

110 So e.g., Barrett, *John*, 482; Bernard, *St. John*, 495; Lenski, *St. John's Gospel*, 1064; Menken, *Old Testament Quotations*, 141; Moo, *The Old Testament*, 243n2; Ridderbos, *John*, 525; Schuchard, *Scripture Within Scripture*, 120. See also BDF §448.7. Understanding the ἵνα subjunctive imperatively (i.e., "But, let the word be fulfilled . . .") is possible, but the ellipsis is the more likely sense in the FG. Barrett, *John*, 481–482.

111 Cf. Morris, *John*, 605; Ridderbos, *John*, 525n141; NASB.

of the Jews."¹¹² As in the case of John 13:18 above, the ἵνα πληρωθῇ ("to fulfill") construction that follows ἀλλά is a purpose clause. Syntactically, the ἵνα clause modifies the elided material ("they have done this"), which logically refers back to μεμισήκασιν ("they have hated") at the end of John 15:24.¹¹³ The ἵνα clause explains why the Jews responded in hate toward Jesus: essentially for the purpose of fulfilling the quotation of Ps 69:4.¹¹⁴ Describing Jesus' use of Ps 69:4 as a case of simple analogy fails to capture the telic force of this syntax. If there is a fulfillment of Ps 69:4, then the psalm verse foretold their hatred,¹¹⁵ while also recounting an event about David. In sum, Jesus points back to a David typology because he understands the psalm verse to anticipate and prefigure the hatred he would encounter from the world.

Moreover, the use of πληρωθῇ ("to fulfill") argues against a purely analogical description of the David typology in John 15:25. As noted above in John 13:18, πληρόω indicates prophetic fulfillment of texts relaying events. This is so because πληρόω communicates the idea that salvation history is teleological, developing towards a climactic goal. Thus, πληρωθῇ is best understood to be indicating that the OT experience of David in relation to the NT experience of Jesus constitutes a prophecy and its fulfillment. Jesus' and David's situations, therefore, connect on a deeper level than simple analogy; the original Davidic event functions as a prophetic pattern for the future experience of Jesus.

Finally, it is important to remember that John delineates the sufferings of Jesus in terms of the arrival of his "hour" (cf. John 13:1) in John 13–21. This is important because the theological sense of Jesus' hour pictures the specific events of his sufferings to be the outworkings of a divine program. The Scriptures cited in connection to specific events of Jesus' suffering show these sufferings to be grounded in the OT Scriptures and, thus, to be God's predetermined purposes for Jesus. Thus, Ps 69:4 is not cited in John 15:25 to make a mere comparison. Instead, it is more consistent to see the fulfillment of Ps 69:4

---

112 Hengstenberg, *St. John*, 2:270.

113 Since the quotation of Ps 69:4 focuses on "hate without cause," it seems best to understand the verb μεμισήκασιν at the end of John 15:24 as the proper referent of the ellipsis supplement. Cf. Lenski, *St. John's Gospel*, 1065.

114 In the citation formula of John 15:25, ὁ λόγος ("the word") is the grammatical subject of πληρωθῇ. Syntactically, the quotation stands in apposition to ὁ λόγος. The inference, then, is that the hatred of the Jews happens in order that "the word" (= the quotation of Ps 69:4) might be fulfilled.

115 Though the telic force of the ἵνα clause presents the reaction of the Jews as occurring for the purpose of fulfilling Ps 69:4, this does not support the radical notion of what Beasely-Murray terms "naked predestinarianism" or "irresistible reprobation." Beasely-Murray, *John*, 216. Jesus is not explaining the inner workings of divine sovereignty and human responsibility. He is showing that the intent of Ps 69:4 was to predict the hatred of the Jews (and the world) toward him in advance.

underscoring a prophetic function, whereby God was revealing an appointed event that Jesus was to experience through David's similar experience.

The fact that Jesus introduces the quotation as coming from "their Law" (τῷ νόμῳ αὐτῶν) makes it even clearer that he sees it as part of the realization of the divine plan grounded in the OT. Here, referring to the psalm verse as "Law" is probably a case where νόμος is used as a general reference to Holy Scripture (cf. John 10:34).[116] The possessive modifier αὐτῶν ("their") is used, as Hoskyns explains:

> not so much that [Jesus] may dissociate himself from [the law], as so many modern commentators maintain . . . but rather in order to rivet upon the Jews those scriptures in which they boast themselves so proudly, and then to prove those same scriptures prophetic of their apostasy.[117]

The Jews stand guilty, therefore, because their hateful rejection of Jesus was predictively foreshadowed through those who hated David in his time. In sum, only a prophetic view of the David typology of Ps 69:4 is able to represent accurately the fulfillment of a divine plan, which Jesus' "hour" and the reference to "their Law" emphasize.

Ps 22:18 in John 19:24

Another psalm quotation appears in John 19:24, which again John seems to understand to apply to Jesus typologically. John 19:24 differs from John 13:18 and 15:25 in that its formula and quotation represent the words of the evangelist rather than the words of Jesus. The formula John uses in 19:24 is ἵνα ἡ γραφὴ πληρωθῇ [ἡ λέγουσα] ("[this was] to fulfill the Scripture, which says"). Once again John employs ἵνα . . . πληρωθῇ ("to fulfill"). ἡ γραφὴ ("the Scripture") and the participle ἡ λέγουσα ("which says") designates that the fulfillment concerns a specific OT passage,[118] clearly Ps 22:18 (= Ps 22:19/MT and Ps

---

116 BDAG, s.v. "νόμος."

117 Hoskyns, *The Fourth Gospel*, 481. J. N. Sanders expounds, "The point of the quotation is to show that the Jews' gratuitous hatred of Jesus is shown up by their own Scripture (5:45ff), and thereby proved to be within the providence of God." Sanders, *John*, 345.

118 Concerning the participle ἡ λέγουσα, UBS4th places the clause in brackets and gives it a "C" rating in the textual apparatus. This "C" rating with brackets means that "the enclosed word, words, or parts of words may be regarded as part of the text, but that in the present state of New Testament textual scholarship this cannot be taken as completely certain." Barbara Aland, Kurt Aland, Johannes Karavidopoulos, Carlo M. Martini, and Bruce M. Metzger, eds., *The Greek New Testament* [UBS4th], 4th ed. rev. (Stuttgart: United Bible Societies, 2001), 2. As the accepted reading, ἡ λέγουσα functions as an explanatory clause, identifying the following statement as a direct citation. Cf. Bruce M. Metzger, *A Textual Commentary on the Greek New Testa-*

21:19/LXX).[119] The textual correspondence of John's quotation with both the MT and LXX is seen below.

John 19:24	διεμερίσαντο τὰ ἱμάτιά μου ἑαυτοῖς καὶ ἐπὶ τὸν ἱματισμόν μου ἔβαλον κλῆρον
	"They divided my outer garments among them, and for my clothing they cast lots."
MT Ps 22:19	יְחַלְּקוּ בְגָדַי לָהֶם וְעַל־לְבוּשִׁי יַפִּילוּ גוֹרָל
	"They divide my garments among them, and for my clothing they cast lots."
LXX Ps 21:19	διεμερίσαντο τὰ ἱμάτιά μου ἑαυτοῖς καὶ ἐπὶ τὸν ἱματισμόν μου ἔβαλον κλῆρον
	"They divided my garments among them, and for my clothing they cast lots."

This time, John quotes the whole psalm verse. Wengst observes, "Das Zitat entspricht genau dem Septuagintatext von Ps 21,19. Der ist seinerseits wörtliche Übersetzung des hebräischen Textes von Ps 22,19."[120] Thus, most scholars agree that the LXX is his source text,[121] and consequently John's quotation also follows the MT closely.[122]

Correspondence in the David-Jesus Typology

Psalm 22 is a psalm of lament.[123] Structurally, David's composition divides into two parts: (1) lament (22:1–21) and (2) praise or thanksgiving (22:22–31).[124]

ment: *A Companion Volume to the United Bible Societies' Greek New Testament* (*Fourth Revised Edition*), 2nd ed. (Stuttgart: United Bible Societies, 1994), 217.

119 Cf. Freed, who identifies this psalm verse as the "obvious source of the quotation." Freed, *Old Testament Quotations*, 99.

120 Wengst, *Das Johannesevangelium*, 2:255n209. "The quotation corresponds exactly to the Septuagint text of Ps 21:19. This is in turn a literal translation of the Hebrew text of Ps 22:19" (my translation). See also, Zahn, *Das Evangelium des Johannes*, 643n86.

121 See Schuchard, *Scripture Within Scripture*, 127n8, for a representative list of these scholars.

122 The only place where the LXX differs from the MT is its translation of the Hebrew imperfect verbs with aorist tense verbs. Cf. Freed, *Old Testament Quotations*, 100; Moo, *The Old Testament*, 253; Schuchard, *Scripture Within Scripture*, 127.

123 So e.g., Bullock, *Psalms*, 137, 139, 141–142; Mark D. Futato, *Interpreting the Psalms: An Exegetical Handbook*, ed. David M. Howard Jr., Handbooks for Old Testament Exegesis (Grand Rapids: Kregel Publications, 2007), 150; Richard D. Patterson, "Psalm 22: From Trial to Triumph," *JETS* 47 (2004): 216–217; Ross, *Psalms*, 1:526, 528; VanGemeren, "Psalms," 198; Wilson, *Psalms Volume 1*, 412.

124 Anderson, *Psalms*, 1:184–185; Craigie, *Psalms 1–50*, 197; Kidner, *Psalms 1–72*, 123, 126;

The lament portion of Psalm 22 has two subunits: 22:1–10 and 22:11–21.[125] In the first part of the lament, David opens with the complaint that he feels like God has abandoned him in his trouble (22:1–5), yet he retains confidence in God (22:6–10). In the second part of his lament, David pleads for God's help and nearness in his trouble (22:11). The general situation of David's distress comes to light in 22:12–21. Essentially, David is "describing a time when his enemies attempted to put him to death, a time of intense sufferings that left him almost dead."[126] Using hyperbolic, figurative language,[127] David depicts an execution scene.[128] He sees himself as a dying man surrounded by a gang of evil

Leupold, *Psalms*, 196; VanGemeren, "Psalms," 198. The change from "plea to praise" in Ps 22 represents the typical "positive to negative" movement of laments. Futato, *Interpreting the Psalms*, 151. See also Ellen F. Davis, "Exploding the Limits: Form and Function in Psalm 22," *JSOT* 53 (1992): 97.

125 Cf. e.g., James L. Mays, "Prayer and Christology: Psalm 22 as Perspective on the Passion," *ThTo* 42 (1985): 324–327; Patterson, "Psalm 22," 217, 219–224. David introduces his complaint in Ps 22:1–10, and then details the specifics of his situation in 22:11–21.

126 Ross, *Psalms*, 1:527; see also 1:526, 548–549. Some suggest the background of Ps 22 reflects a time of suffering by illness. See e.g., Anderson, *Psalms*, 1:185; Craigie, *Psalms 1–50*, 198; Sheldon Tostengard, "Psalm 22," *Int* 46 (1992): 167. But, as Leupold argues, "[The idea of a sick man] scarcely does justice to the statements of the psalm." Leupold, *Psalms*, 208. The overall imagery of Ps 22, instead, seems to depict the psalmist's near-death experience at the hands of his enemies. See e.g., Delitzsch, *Psalms*, 1:303–307, 316–317; Kidner, *Psalms 1–72*, 122; Waltke, Houston, and Moore, *The Psalms*, 397–398, 403–408.

127 A number of commentators "recognize that the words of Psalm 22 go beyond any individual experience of suffering in the Old Testament." Richard P. Belcher, Jr., *The Messiah and the Psalms: Preaching Christ from All the Psalms* (Fearn, Scotland: Mentor, 2006), 167. What one observes in Psalm 22 is the employment of poetic language (e.g., apostrophe, hyperbole, merism, metaphors, and similes). Patterson, "Psalm 22," 219. David's use of hyperbole or figurative expressions is important for a proper understanding of Psalm 22 in its original setting and for how it applies to Christ's death in John 19:24. Noting the role of poetic language in Psalm 22, Ross writes, "Because of the nature of the suffering the ascription of the psalm to David has been challenged. We know of no time in the life of David that even comes close to the event that is described here; if it came from his experiences, the language of the psalm must be poetic and somewhat hyperbolic in places. It may be difficult to connect such a specific and significant event to David's life; but it is not impossible that it came from that time, for we do not know all that he experienced." Ross, *Psalms*, 1:527; also see 1:548–549. Importantly, then, Psalm 22 can be understood to portray an historical experience of David's, but one must consider that "the language of the psalmist is natural for someone enduring intense agony at the hands of enemies and the apparent abandonment of God, but it is excessive." Ibid, 1:549. Mark H. Heinemann, therefore, appears correct in his assessment, when he avers, "And though it cannot be proven that his [David's] descriptions go beyond his own experience, they are clearly hyperbolic in nature." Mark H. Heinemann, "An Exposition of Psalm 22," *BSac* 147 (1990): 303. For further discussion of the use of hyperbole/figurative expressions in Ps 22, see Calvin, *Psalms*, 4:372–376; Delitzsch, *Psalms*, 1:306–07; see also, 1:69–70; Grogan, *Psalms*, 72; Heinemann, "Psalm 22," 300–303; Alexander Maclaren, *The Psalms*, The Expositor's Bible (London: Hodder & Stoughton, 1898), 1:211–212; Waltke, Houston, and Moore, *The Psalms*, 414–415.

128 Carson, *John*, 612; Kidner, *Psalms 1–72*, 122, who cites A. Bentzen for support; Köstenberger, "John," 501; Moo, *The Old Testament*, 254; Ross, *Psalms*, 1:526, 549. Cf. Craig C. Broyles, *Psalms*, ed. Robert L. Hubbard Jr. and Robert K. Johnston, NIBC (Peabody: Hendrickson, 1999), 116. Not enough details are given for one to be dogmatic on the exact nature of David's suffer-

men with murderous intent who have wounded him (22:12–17, 19–21). The reference to his enemies dividing his clothes and gambling for them indicates that they consider David as good as dead (22:18).[129] In his near-death state, David pleads for God's presence and rescue from the "sword" of his enemies (22:19–21). God answers David's prayer (22:21b) and delivers him from death.[130]

Thus, Ps 22:18 in its original context describes David's situation of suffering at the hands of his enemies. John applies Ps 22:18 to Jesus' death, pointing to its fulfillment in the soldiers' actions at the foot of the cross. Just as Jesus quoted from psalms in John 13:18 and 15:25 to highlight a Davidic typology that pointed to his specific sufferings, John makes use of Ps 22:18 in a similar way, apparently following Jesus' examples. The typological relationship between David's and Jesus' suffering has the following points of correspondence: (1) the royal status of the sufferer, (2) the distribution of the garments by the enemies, and (3) the scene of death by execution.

---

ings in Ps 22. In light of David's use of poetic imagery, two interpretations seem plausible. On one hand, it is possible the poetic imagery underscores David's intense emotional agony in physical terms. Cf. Heinemann, "Psalm 22," 294–295. If so, David is really describing what he *anticipates* from his persecutors upon falling into their hands. That is, once his enemies seize him, David "imagines himself enduring a cruel and unjust death." Waltke, Houston, and Moore, *The Psalms*, 397. Cf. John I. Durham, "Psalms," in BBC 4, ed. Clifton J. Allen (Nashville: Broadman Press, 1971), 214. On the other hand, the poetic imagery may indicate physical suffering or a combination of both emotional and physical suffering. Cf. Heinemann, "Psalm 22," 294–295. In this case, David may be describing a time when he fell into enemy hands. His enemies may very well have been "methodically putting him to death," and he uses poetic devices to describe the pain of that experience. Ross, *Psalms*, 1:526–527; see also 1:548–549. This latter view will be assumed in this work because "in Psalm 22 . . . the context of violence leads one to conclude that David was describing both emotional and physical suffering." Heinemann, "Psalm 22," 295. Nevertheless, whether the suffering is predominantly emotional or both emotional/physical in nature matters little in the overall interpretation of the psalm. In both cases, David is still describing a personal experience of suffering, even if he describes his suffering with exaggerated language that transcends his actual experience in some ways.

129 It is possible to understand David's description as a literal experience (i.e., having fallen into enemy hands, they actually stripped him of his clothing and were dividing it among themselves). But, given the prominence of poetic imagery, David is most likely speaking in figurative terms. Cf. Delitzsch, *Psalms*, 1:320. Regardless of whether it is literal or metaphorical in nature, the meaning of the imagery is the same. Delitzsch explains that "the parting of, and casting lots for, the garments assumes the certain death of the sufferer in the mind of the enemies." Ibid., 1:321. Ross similarly avers, "The last possession a person would retain was the garment—that was until he died. Here they were dividing up his property because they considered that he was a good as dead." Ross, *Psalms*, 1:541. According to Grogan, "Verse 18 suggests his death and shows his enemies cynically despoiling him." Grogan, *Psalms*, 73. Furthermore, in that David says in 22:17 that he could count his bones may also imply that he sees himself "stripped by his enemies." Alexander, *The Psalms*, 1:186.

130 The abrupt tonal change from lament to praise/thanksgiving in 22:21b–31 confirms David's prayer has been answered. Cf. Grogan, *Psalms*, 73–74; Wolfgang Reinbold, "Die Klage des Gerechten (Ps 22)," in *Die Verheißung des Neuen Bundes: Wie alttestamentliche Texte im Neuen Testament forwirken*, ed. Bernd Kollmann, Biblisch-theologische Schwerpunkte 35 (Göttingen: Vandenhoeck & Ruprecht, 2010), 144–145.

First, the regal status of both David and Jesus is a clear point of contact Ps 22:18 underscores in John 19:24.¹³¹ Psalms of lament, as explained in the analysis of John 13:18 above, contain a royal dimension. The human subject expressing lament to God in Psalm 22 is King David. In the reading of Psalm 22, therefore, there is the obvious idea of a suffering king. The regal theme of Jesus, which John develops throughout his Gospel, reaches its climax in John's passion narrative.¹³² Twelve times the term "king" (βασιλεύς) appears with reference to Jesus in John 18–19.¹³³ In response to Pilate's question "Are you the King of the Jews?" (18:33), Jesus affirms his kingship (18:37) and defines the nature of his "kingdom" (18:36).¹³⁴ Pilate thrice calls Jesus the "King of the Jews" (18:39; 19:14–15), while the Jews deny his kingship several times (19:12, 15, 21). Even the soldiers, though they do it in mockery of his royalty, crown him, robe him, and acclaim him (19:1–3).¹³⁵ Moreover, Pilate most clearly confesses Jesus' kingship with the trilingual placard he affixes to the cross (19:19, 21). In this context, the quotation of Ps 22:18 in John 19:24 reinforces John's overall theological presentation of the theme of Jesus' kingship. Jesus fits the pattern of David in Psalm 22: he is Israel's king undergoing suffering.¹³⁶

It is equally clear, however, that the kingship of Jesus contrasts with David's. In Psalm 22, David suffers as a human king, being victimized by his enemies. John presents Jesus in a different light, however. Jesus enters into his sufferings with perfect foreknowledge of what lies before him (John 18:4). Jesus questions his own interrogators, Annas and Pilate, thus, showing himself to be the real judge over his captors (18:19–24; 19:33–38).¹³⁷ Jesus is the preexistent one who has "come into the world" with a mission (19:37). He is "the Son

---

131 Cf. Köstenberger, *John's Gospel and Letters*, 411–412.

132 Nash writes, "In [John 18–19], the motif of Jesus' identity as 'king' becomes explicit and dominates the story line." Nash, "Kingship and the Psalms," 171. See also David E. Garland, "John 18–19: Life through Jesus' Death," *RevExp* 85 (1988): 485. For an excellent discussion of Jesus' kingship in John's passion narrative, see Burge, *John*, 484–548. Burge notes that the literary structure of John 18:28–19:16a contains parallelism, which functions on a "deeper level" to show "Jesus is actually being acknowledged as king" in his suffering. Ibid., 489. This kingship theme continues to develop in John 19:16b–42 in the events of Jesus' crucifixion and burial. Ibid., 523–526, 534–536, 539, 541–543.

133 Cf. John 18:33, 37 (twice), 39; 19:3, 12, 14, 15 (twice), 19, 21 (twice).

134 Jesus uses the term βασιλεία three times in John 18:36. Jesus means for his kingship and kingdom, as Dodd rightly points out, to be understood "in a non-worldly sense." Dodd, *Fourth Gospel*, 229.

135 The soldiers' actions in John 19:1–3 function within the story to depict "Jesus' coronation," as king. Burge, *John*, 489.

136 Nash well states, "By allusion and citation John reinforces the connection between Jesus and the rejected/suffering king of the lament psalms. The unfolding events are shown to happen in fulfillment of scripture and as such demonstrate Jesus' true identity." Nash, "Kingship and the Psalms," 174; see also 187–188.

137 Cf. Burge, *John*, 495–496, 501, 517; Garland, "John 18–19," 485.

of God" (19:7), which by implication means "he bears the authority of God himself" and, therefore, is the one with supreme authority over what is happening to him (19:10–11).[138] His kingship, as the trilingual placard reveals, is universal in scope. Jesus, therefore, is greater than David and is the true Messianic King, sovereign over his enemies and his suffering.

Another central identification in David's and Jesus' situations includes the focal action described by Ps 22:18: the acquisition of the sufferer's garments by the enemy. In its original context, Ps 22:18 contains synonymous parallelism:[139] "they divide" corresponds with "they cast lots," and "my garments" corresponds with "my clothing."[140] Essentially, then, the verse depicts David's enemies dividing up his clothing among themselves by means of gambling. Given the poetic imagery in Psalm 22, it seems more probable that he was speaking in metaphorical terms and not describing an actual event. If this is a case of metaphor, David is stressing that his situation is so serious that his enemies "treated him as already dead."[141] On the other hand, what was potentially metaphorical for David happens literally to Jesus. Ps 22:18 is quoted in John 19:24, connecting it to the soldiers' actions at the cross. John reports that the soldiers divide Jesus' garments among themselves into four equal parts and cast lots for his tunic. Given the parallelism of Ps 22:18, it is possible John identifies two separate actions by the soldiers, connecting them to Ps 22:18a and 18b, respectively.[142] Carson, however, thinks it is preferable to understand the quotation as applying to the event holistically:

---

138 Cf. Morris, *John*, 682.

139 By definition, "synonymous parallelism simply means that the thought pattern in one line conforms to the pattern in the successive line. That does not mean, of course, that the thought in the successive line will be absolutely parallel. There are often nuances in the second line that enhance or alter the terms of the first line, but they will not contradict it." Bullock, *Psalms*, 36.

140 To be noted, the parallelism in Ps 22:18 does not imply exact repetition. Instead, there is room for expansion of thought. Here, the shift from the plural "my garments" to the singular "my clothing" could possibly indicate distinction in clothing items. So Godet, *John's Gospel*, 945; Hoskyns, *The Fourth Gospel*, 529. Cf. Carson, *John*, 613. Similarly, the second verb "they cast lots" sheds light further on the initial verb "they divided." Interpretively, this would mean the second action (i.e., casting lots) indicates that the first action (i.e., dividing) also involved casting lots. Cf. Carson, *John*, 613–614; Hengstenberg, *St. John*, 2:412; Lindars, *The Gospel of John*, 577.

141 Westcott, *St. John*, 275.

142 That is, the distribution of Jesus' outer clothes would accord with Ps 22:18a and the gambling for his tunic would accord with Ps 22:18b. So e.g., Godet, *John's Gospel*, 945. Harvey D. Lange takes this view, explaining, "John noted the plural form in 'clothes' ἱμάτια (LXX/Ps. 21:19a) and the singular 'tunic' ἱματισμόν (LXX/Ps. 21:19b), and he wanted to explain the significance of this detail. Therefore he interpreted the plural form as reference to the four parts in which Jesus' clothes were divided and distributed among the four soldiers. The singular referred to the seamless tunic." Harvey D. Lange, "The Relationship Between Psalm 22 and the Passion Narrative," *CTM* 43 (1972): 619.

The Evangelist sees in the *entire* distribution of Jesus' clothes a fulfillment of *both* lines of Psalm 22:18, but mentions the peculiarity of the decision about the tunic because he was an eyewitness, and possibly because he saw something symbolic in the seamless garment.[143]

Whichever view is taken, the quotation alerts the reader to the fact that the soldiers' actions parallel the actions of David's enemies. Like David, Jesus suffers the cruel indignity of being stripped and treated as already dead by his captors who claim his clothes, but when compared to its original meaning for David, Ps 22:18 occurs at the climax in Jesus' life. In that Ps 22:18 happens to Jesus literally (and not merely metaphorical as with David), the experience of Jesus appears in the text as the true reality or fulfillment of David's experience.

In addition, Ps 22:18 in both its OT and NT contexts constitutes the actions of executioners.[144] Ross well observes, "In both settings the suffering in the psalm describes a death by execution at the hands of taunting enemies—its seriousness cannot be minimized."[145] When David speaks about his garments being divided up in Ps 22:18, this verse appears in the latter part of his lament, which describes his death by execution.[146] When John quotes Ps 22:18, Jesus is indeed being put to death by soldiers, who gamble for his clothing. Importantly, it is executioners that gamble for the clothes in both OT and NT contexts. Consequently, John naturally juxtaposes the execution scenes of David and Jesus through his quotation,[147] and those who distribute Jesus' clothes are putting to death the King of Israel.

---

143 Carson, *John*, 614. According to this view, all of Jesus' clothing items are distributed by means of casting lots and not just the tunic. Cf. Hengstenberg, *St. John*, 2:412. While it is possible the tunic held a symbolic meaning in John's eyes (see Witherington, *John's Wisdom*, 308–309, for a list of some of the commonly suggested symbolisms), "we have no way of knowing whether such references were in the evangelist's mind." Brown, *John (13–21)*, 922. It seems best, then, to understand John referencing the tunic because he was giving details to an eyewitness account, which he understood as a literal fulfillment of Ps 22:18. Cf. Ridderbos, *John*, 610n136.

144 Executioners claiming a right to the clothes of an executed man was common custom in NT times (see Bruce, *John*, 369) as well as OT times (see Anderson, *Psalms*, 1:191). So, the distribution of clothing clearly suggests the work of executioners.

145 Ross, *Psalms*, 1:526.

146 Cf. Moo, *The Old Testament*, 254. Unlike the Synoptics, John does not bring attention to Jesus' cry of derelicition (cf. Ps 22:1/Matt 27:46; Mark 15:34). Nash appears right in his comments that "[John] is not interested in drawing attention to the human despair experienced by Jesus, but only to the concrete fulfillment that serves to identify Jesus with the psalmist and so shows Jesus' experience fulfilled the scriptures." Nash, "Kingship and the Psalms," 184–185. See also Bruce, *John*, 370.

147 According to Andrew T. Lincoln, the quotation of Ps 22:18 calls attention to "those who put Jesus to death," which, thus, emphasizes the crucifixion of Jesus as being in accordance with God's will. Andrew T. Lincoln, *The Gospel According to Saint John*, BNTC (New York: Hendrickson, 2005), 476.

Nonetheless, the execution of Jesus goes beyond David's actual experience. David clearly uses figurative language to dramatize the gravity of his emotional and physical distress. What was figurative for David was "in many ways vividly fulfilled in Christ, which means that Christ's experience of suffering is greater than David's."[148] David uses hyperbole to describe a violent near-death episode (possibly by means of the "sword," Ps 22:20), but Jesus himself undergoes literal crucifixion and dies (John 19:30).[149] So, in David's case there is "deliverance *from* death" (i.e., rescue), but in Jesus' case there is "deliverance *through* death" (i.e., resurrection).[150] David and Jesus also suffer for different purposes.[151] There is in "John's theology of the cross . . . the idea that Jesus is a sacrifice dying on the cross."[152] Put simply, his death holds re-

---

148 Belcher, *The Messiah and the Psalms*, 171. Similarly Moo comments: "It is not clear that David would always have been aware of the ultimate significance of his language; but God could have so ordered his experiences and his recordings of them in Scripture that they become anticipatory of the sufferings of 'David's greater son.'" Moo, "The Problem of *Sensus Plenior*," 197. Cf. Delitzsch who explains Ps 22 as follows: "The rhetorical figure hyperbole . . . is here made use of by the Spirit of God. By this Spirit the hyperbolic element is changed into the prophetic. . . . For as God the Father moulds the history of Jesus Christ in accordance with His own counsel, so His Spirit moulds even the utterances of David concerning himself the type of the Future one, with a view to that history." Delitzsch, *Psalms*, 1:306–307. See also, Ross, *Psalms*, 1:548.

149 It is possible that David is describing the threat of execution by the means of his enemies' "sword" (Ps 22:20). If "sword" is not to be taken literally and is only metaphorical for a "violent death," then it remains unstated as to the means by which David's enemies plan to kill him. It seems safe to conclude that David's enemies were not planning to crucify him because "such a practice did not exist in David's day." Gren, "Psalm 22:16," 298. But, herein lays the significance of the Holy Spirit leading David to write in terms of hyperbole. The use of hyperbolic language allowed David to describe the severity of his own near-death experience in a way that could also be applied to the future reality of Christ's literal experience of crucifixion. See Delitzsch, *Psalms*, 1:305–307. For example, David's wounded (i.e., "pierced," Ps 22:16) hands and feet correspond with Jesus' hands and feet that were nailed to the cross. David's reference to "bones out of joint" (22:14a) corresponds to the pain in Jesus' body and to being stretched out on a cross. David's references to his failing heart (22:14b), weaning strength (22:15a), and dry tongue (22:15b; cf. John 19:28) correspond to the physical tolls crucifixion exacts upon the body. As Heinemann explains, "David's descriptions of his own suffering in this psalm closely correspond to what Jesus must have experienced during his scourging and execution. What David wrote fits well with the exhaustion, stretching, suffocation, and circulatory stoppage that occur during crucifixion." Heinemann, "Psalm 22," 302–03. Similarly, Delitzsch says, "It is the agonising situation of the Crucified One which is presented before our eyes in vers[es] 15–18," which is prefigured typologically in David's sufferings. Delitzsch, *Psalms*, 1:305; 306–307. See also Waltke, Houston, and Moore, *The Psalms*, 405.

150 Craigie, *Psalms 1–50*, 203.

151 VanGemeren writes, "Whereas David's suffering was for himself, Jesus' suffering was on behalf of sinners." VanGemeren, "Psalms," 199.

152 Burge, *John*, 539. Burge recognizes a real Passover motif in the FG, especially in John 19, which contributes to John's sacrificial, redemptive understanding of Jesus' death. Ibid., 532, 539, 543–544. Nash notes that John 19:13–14 links together the notions of "kingship" and "Passover," which "finally plays itself out as the king of the Jews dies as the Passover lamb." Nash, "Kingship and the Psalms," 175. For a fuller discussion of the Passover theme in the FG and its

demptive significance; he dies for no wrong of his own (cf. John 18:38; 19:4, 6) but lays his life down for the sins of the world (cf. John 1:29; 10:17–18).[153] Finally, David and Jesus suffer with different perspectives. While David seems to view his suffering solely as trouble and affliction (cf. Ps 22:11, 24), John presents the humiliation of the cross as the ultimate manifestation of Jesus' and the Father' glory.[154] Overall, the literal crucifixion of Jesus with all its redemptive significance marks Jesus' suffering as the climax of the pattern set forth by David's suffering.

Prophecy in the David-Jesus Typology

In quoting Ps 22:18 in John 19:24, John draws attention to a predictive typological relationship between David and Jesus.[155] Several elements in the text suggest that the typology retains a prophetic character: (1) the purpose ἵνα clause, (2) the fulfillment language, (3) the inferential οὖν in John 19:24, and (4) the contextual background of Jesus' "hour."[156]

John signals his quotation of Ps 22:18 with the introductory formula ἵνα ἡ γραφὴ πληρωθῇ [ἡ λέγουσα] ("to fulfill the Scripture [which says]"). The ἵνα πληρωθῇ (to fulfill) purpose clause[157] points to a prophetic understanding of

---

particular traces in John 19 to its fulfillment in Jesus' death on the cross, see Porter, "Literary Analysis of the Fourth Gospel," 401–428. See also J. B. Green, "Death of Jesus," *DJG*, 162; Köstenberger, *John's Gospel and Letters*, 419–420.

153   See Morris, *New Testament Theology*, 270.

154   Cf. Köstenberger, *John's Gospel and Letters*, 408–409, 418.
John uses of the verb ὑψόω ("lift up/raise high;" cf. John 3:14; 8:28; 12:32–34) to show "some intimate connection between Jesus' crucifixion and his exaltation." Green, "Death of Jesus," 162. Cf. BDAG, s.v. "ὑψόω," which says, "for J[ohn] this 'lifting up' is not to be separated fr[om] the 'exaltation' into heaven, since the heavenly exaltation presupposes the earthly." Morris aptly summarizes, "Supremely is glory to be seen in the Cross, for there One who had no need to die suffered on behalf of others. So, when John says that Jesus was 'glorified,' he often means that he was crucified (7:39; 12:16, 23; 13:31; cf. 21:19). To understand glory as John did is to see the Cross casting its shadow over the whole life of Jesus." Morris, *New Testament Theology*, 271; see also 235, 270–272.

155   See e.g., Calvin, *John*, 2:229–230; Calvin, *Psalms*, 4:376; Carson, "John and the Johannine Epistles," 250; Carson, *John*, 612; Delitzsch, *Psalms*, 1:303–308, 320; Heinemann, "Psalm 22," 301–302; Hoffmann, *Interpreting the Bible*, 177; 169; Ross, *Psalms*, 1:527–528, 541, 548, 548n41, 549–550; Tholuck, *Commentary on the Gospel of John*, 395; Waltke, Houston, and Moore, *The Psalms*, 112; 414–415. Contra Anderson, who denies a Davidic connection or a prophetic element. Anderson, *Psalms*, 1:185. Contra Ahn, who thinks David typology is "feasible" but "heavily overshadowed by the theme of divine sovereignty" in the context of John 19. Ahn, "Old Testament Characters," 145. Contra Lenski, who argues Psalm 22 "is not a typical Psalm but one that is entirely prophetic." Lenski, *St. John's Gospel*, 1289.

156   See the analysis of John 13:18 above in this chapter, where the items of the (1) the purpose ἵνα clause, (2) the fulfillment language, and (3) the contextual background of Jesus' "hour" and their prophetic significance are discussed in more detail.

157   E.g., Brown, *John (13–21)*, 903; Carson, "John and the Johannine Epistles," 250; Morris,

Ps 22:18. The ἵνα explains *why* the soldiers acted as they did,[158] and like in John 13:18 and 15:25, no principal verb precedes ἵνα.[159] To better clarify the sense of the clause, then, supply words such as *"This came to pass"* or *"This happened"* before ἵνα.[160]

Syntactically, *"This happened* in order that . . ."* could refer back to the main verb εἶπαν ("They said") that commences John 19:24,[161] or it may be more general, summarizing the entire act of the soldiers' distribution of Jesus' clothes in 19:23–24. In either case, the ἵνα clause indicates that the abasement of Jesus by the soldiers happens for the purpose of fulfilling Ps 22:18.[162] John does not ultimately attribute the soldiers' deeds to greed, cruelty, or their perquisites, though these things surely play a part; ultimately, the soldiers act as they do because of divine purpose, which Ps 22:18 reveals. Morris explains:

> John sees in this a literal fulfillment of Scripture (Ps. 22:18). He stresses that this is the reason for the soldiers' action. Once again we see his master thought that God was over all that was done, so directing things that his will was accomplished, not that of puny men.[163]

Along the same lines, Carson writes, "However customary this merciless bit of byplay was at ancient executions, in the case of Jesus' death it was nothing less than the fulfillment of prophecy: it occurred that the scripture might be fulfilled."[164]

In sum, John's use of Ps 22:18 proves to be more than mere analogy; the psalm text was predicting Jesus' suffering at their hands. According to Carson, "There can be little doubt that John understands the event in the FG to fulfill

---

John, 716n59.

158 Freed rightly notes that the soldiers' speech ends with ἔσται ("it shall be") and that ἵνα represents the words of the evangelist. Freed, *Old Testament Quotations*, 99n1.

159 On this construction with ἵνα, Morris explains, "It may be that John uses the construction as a way of hinting at the divine purpose working out in each of the passages where it occurs. The telic force in ἵνα would be favorable to such a significance." Morris, *John*, 82n61.

160 See Hengstenberg, *St. John*, 2:412; Newman and Nida, *John*, 588. NIV supplies *"This happened* to fulfill . . ." ESV and NASB supply *"This was* to fulfill . . ."

161 If *"this happened"* refers back to the main verb εἶπαν ("they said"), then ἵνα actually modifies εἶπαν. The syntax in this case informs the reader as to *why* the soldiers decided to cast lots for Jesus' tunic. Put simply, the telic force of the ἵνα indicates that the soldiers' actions occur to fulfill the prophecy of Ps 22:18.

162 In the introductory formula, ἡ γραφὴ ("the Scripture") is the grammatical subject of πληρωθῇ. Syntactically, the psalm quotation stands in apposition to ἡ γραφὴ. The inference, then, is that the action of the soldiers happens in order that "the Scripture" (= the quotation of Ps 22:18) might be fulfilled.

163 Morris, *John*, 716.

164 Carson, *John*, 612. See also, Bruce, *John*, 369–370.

prophecy," based on the customary telic force of ἵνα πληρωθῇ.¹⁶⁵ John, thus, intends for his readers to view the original situation of David's suffering as prophetic of Jesus' suffering in the framework of a prophetic David typology.

In addition to the purpose clause, John's use of "fulfillment" language further suggests Ps 22:18 involves the fulfillment of prophecy. In John 19:24, John again introduces a quotation with the verb πληρωθῇ, which signals the fulfillment of a prophecy in Ps 22:18 (as in John 13:18; 15:25). John uses πληρόω ("to fulfill") to cite the fulfillment of prophecies in the form of words (i.e., direct prophecy) and in the form of events (i.e., typological prophecy).¹⁶⁶ Though the soldiers are unaware of it, John says that the soldiers' actions fulfill Ps 22:18. Since πληρωθῇ implies a teleological perspective, it identifies Jesus' suffering as the goal of the psalm verse. This ultimately means David's experience in Ps 22:18 was pointing forward to the suffering of Jesus, as a prophecy to its fulfillment. God intended for Ps 22:18 both to record an event in David's experience and to provide a prophetic outline of what the soldiers would do in killing the Messiah.

The use of the inferential οὖν ("therefore") in the short sentence Οἱ μὲν οὖν στρατιῶται ταῦτα ἐποίησαν ("Therefore, the soldiers did these things") that immediately follows the psalm citation is a third piece of evidence that reinforces a prophetic understanding of the typology.¹⁶⁷ In this instance, οὖν could be paired with the preceding μὲν ("to be sure/indeed") to communicate a resumptive or transitional notion (e.g., "So . . ."),¹⁶⁸ or μὲν οὖν may form a compound with δέ ("but") in John 19:25 to emphasize a contrast.¹⁶⁹ A few considerations, however, suggest there is more than a mere continuative or contrastive force in view. First, μὲν οὖν is not a typical marker in John for mere narrative continuation, seeing that it occurs only here and in John 20:30.¹⁷⁰

---

165 Carson continues, "Once again, however, the undergirding hermeneutical axiom is probably David typology." Carson, "John and the Johannine Epistles," 250.

166 See the section "Fulfillment Language" in chapter 3 of this work. See also the discussions of fulfillment language in the analyses of John 13:18 and John 15:25 above in this chapter.

167 The sentence "Therefore [οὖν] the soldiers did these things" is included as part of John 19:25 by some translations (e.g., NASB), while others include it with John 19:24 (e.g., ESV, NIV).

168 According to Moule, μὲν οὖν most commonly carries a resumptive or transitional significance in the NT, and this is how he classifies it in John 19:24. Moule, *Idiom Book*, 162. For μὲν οὖν to be resumptive or transitional means it serves as a connective "in the continuation or resumption of a narrative." BDF §451(1).

169 BDAG explains μὲν οὖν functions in John 19:24 to introduce a concessive clause that connects to the adversative particle δέ in 19:25 to emphasize a contrast. BDAG translates μὲν οὖν . . . δέ as "(*now*) *indeed . . . but*." BDAG, s.v. "μέν." For those who support this primarily contrastive sense, see e.g., Beasely-Murray, *John*, 348; Westcott, *St. John*, 275. Contra Ridderbos and Brown, who argue against an adversative sense. Brown, *John (13–21)*, 903–904; Ridderbos, *John*, 610, 610n140.

170 John frequently uses οὖν alone as a temporal connective or with particles other than

Second, it is probable that μέν actually pairs with δέ in the following verse to note a contrast between the soldiers and the women standing by the cross, and the οὖν probably connects back to the previous sentence in John 19:24, indicating an inference.[171] (This position is consistent with μὲν οὖν . . . δέ in John 20:30–31.[172]) Since the Scripture citations are a focal point for John in the Passion narrative, οὖν probably connects to what immediately precedes, providing additional explanation for the psalm citation.[173] Along these lines, M.-J. Lagrange comments:

> Si Jo. a repris au v. 24: "ainsi donc agirent les soldats", c'est pour montrer l'Écriture accomplie et ménager un contraste entre ces soldats indifférents au supplice qu'ils ont exécuté, ne songeant qu'à en tirer profit, et le groupe de ceux qui ont le plus aimé Jésus et l'ont suivi au pied de la croix.[174]

So, on the one hand μέν . . . δέ (John 19:25) sets up a contrast between the soldiers and the bystanders at the cross, as John shifts to this new scene. On the other hand, οὖν indicates a logical inference between its clause and with what immediately precedes, namely, the fulfillment of the psalm citation. Craig S. Keener observes:

μέν to form compounds that signal narrative continuation. See BDAG, s.v. "οὖν." For a discussion of non-compound uses of οὖν and its frequency of use in John's narrative discourse, see Vern S. Poythress, "The Use of the Intersentence Conjunctions *De, Oun, Kai,* and Asyndeton in the Gospel of John " *NovT* 26 (1984): 327–330.

171 For the correlative use of μέν and δέ to indicate contrasts, see BDAG, s.v. "μέν;" BDF §447. According to Moule, even though μὲν οὖν usually carries a purely resumptive or transitional force, the particles can stand distinct from one another, so that οὖν designates an inference. Moule, *Idiom Book*, 162.

172 In John 20:30–31, this same combination appears (i.e., μὲν οὖν in John 20:30 is followed by the correlative δέ beginning 20:31). In this case, Carson explains μὲν οὖν as distinct particles, where οὖν has an inferential "therefore" sense, connecting back to the previous verse. And, μέν connects with δέ to form a contrast. Carson, *John*, 660–661. See also Saeed Hamid-Khani, *Revelation and Concealment of Christ: A Theological Inquiry into the Elusive Language of the Fourth Gospel*, WUNT 2 (Tübingen: Mohr Siebeck, 2000), 162–163; Köstenberger, *John*, 581.

173 Additionally, the attention John gives to the actions of the soldiers in combination with the telic force of the ἵνα, the fulfillment language, and the psalm citation suggests μὲν οὖν probably serves to further emphasize the fulfillment of Scripture in the actions of the soldiers. Cf. Ridderbos who writes, "But these words are rather meant to underscore the importance of the preceding passage, ... What these four unknown Roman soldiers did was nothing other and nothing less than fulfill what was written about Jesus, . . ." Ridderbos, *John*, 610.

174 Lagrange, Évangile selon Saint Jean, 492. See also Carson, *John*, 614–615, 615n1; Lindars, *The Gospel of John*, 578. "When John resumed in verse 24: 'and therefore the soldiers acted,' this is to show the scripture fulfilled and to make a contrast between these soldiers' indifference to the torture they performed, thinking only of their own benefit, and the group of those who loved Jesus the most and followed him at the foot of the cross" (my translation).

John's most central implication at this point, however, is the fulfillment of Scripture. His οὖν at the end of v. 24 ("this is why the soldiers did these things") reinforces the point: the soldiers may have acted according to custom and may have acted according to evil desires, but they ultimately were unwittingly fulfilling God's unbreakable word.[175]

Similarly, David E. Garland writes:

> Even this commonplace element of an execution turns out to be part of the divine plan of God. After citing the Psalm, the evangelist records: "then the soldiers did these things," which underscores the fact that soldiers are doing exactly as prophesied. The abasement of Jesus fulfills God's will.[176]

If οὖν points back to the psalm citation, then its inferential force "emphasizes that the soldiers unwittingly did exactly as prophesied."[177] Since Ps 22:18 records a description of David's suffering in its original context, this provides additional support that John is viewing this OT event-oriented text as predictive. The David typology here is a prophetic typology.

The final indicator of a prophetic notion of the David typology in John 19:24 is the contextual background of Jesus' "hour." The quotation of Ps 22:18 in John 19:24 is the first of four Scripture references John cites (cf. John 19:28, 36–37), as the theme of Jesus' "hour" reaches its climax in his suffering on the cross.[178] Central to a proper understanding of Jesus' "hour" is its depiction of the events of Jesus' suffering as the outworking of God's pre-determined will for the Son. Given this understanding, the context of the "hour" means the Scriptures John cites in connection to the events of Jesus' death show that the sufferings of Jesus represent God's plan.

The citation of Ps 22:18, therefore, involves more than pure analogical typology, since mere analogical typology establishes only comparisons and is not forward pointing in any way. In the context of Jesus' "hour," Ps 22:18, however, shows that soldiers' actions toward Jesus are a part of God's redemptive plan. Thus, David's situation of suffering is predicting Jesus' suffering.

---

175 Craig S. Keener, *The Gospel of John: A Commentary* (Peabody: Hendrickson, 2003), 2:1140. For others who maintain a similar inferential force in the μὲν οὖν sentence, see Carson, *John*, 612; Hoskyns, *The Fourth Gospel*, 412; Lenski, *St. John's Gospel*, 1290; Lindars, *The Gospel of John*, 578; MacGregor, *John*, 346; Morris, *John*, 716; Ridderbos, *John*, 610.

176 David E. Garland, "The Fulfillment Quotations in John's Account of the Crucifixion," in *Perspectives on John: Method and Interpretation in the Fourth Gospel*, ed. R. B. Sloan and Mikeal C. Parson (Lewiston, NY: Edwin Mellen Press, 1993), 236.

177 Brown, *John (13–21)*, 904.

178 Note that in John 12:27, 32 Jesus identifies his death on the cross (i.e., what he describes as being "lifted up") as the purpose for coming to this "hour."

Ps 69:21 in John 19:28

In 19:28, John introduces another quotation with a formula ἵνα τελειωθῇ ἡ γραφή ("to fulfill the Scripture"). Instead of the usual ἵνα πληρωθῇ, John utilizes ἵνα τελειωθῇ. Like with πληρόω ("to fulfill"), the basic sense of τελειόω ("to bring to an end/goal, to accomplish") in a citation formula "preserve[s] the emphasis on fulfilment, the bringing to pass of God's design announced earlier..."[179] That John has in mind the fulfillment of a specific OT passage stems from ἡ γραφή ("the Scripture"), which usually points to a specific passage in the FG.[180] Here the OT passage is alluded to, not quoted[181] and constitutes the background to Jesus' exclamation, "I am thirsty" (διψῶ).[182]

Jesus' statement διψῶ probably alludes either to Ps 22:15 or Ps 69:21. The former passage has a thirst motif, and John quotes from Psalm 22 earlier during the crucifixion scene (John 19:24). Nevertheless, "the verbal dissimilarity is against the allusion."[183] It seems more probable that John has Ps 69:21 (= Ps 69:22/MT and Ps 68:22/LXX) in view. In favor of Ps 69:21 is the association of this psalm verse with the synoptic accounts of Jesus' death.[184] In addition, John's prior references to Psalm 69 (John 2:17; 15:25) demonstrate his affinity for this psalm. Furthermore, there are verbal parallels in John 19:28–30,[185] which can be seen when compared with the MT and LXX.

John 19:28	διψῶ
	"I am thirsty."

---

179 Carson, "John and the Johannine Epistles," 252. See BDAG, s.v. "τελειόω," where "final fulfillment" and "to fulfill" are supplied for the meaning it has in connection to Scripture in John 19:28. So also Thayers, s.v. "τελειόω." Notably, John 19:28 is the only NT occurrence of the verb τελειόω in a citation formula to denote the fulfillment of Scripture. Freed, *Old Testament Quotations*, 104.

180 Moo, *The Old Testament*, 277; Schnackenburg, *John*, 3:286, 460n60. See also Beasely-Murray, *John*, 351. Contra J. Ramsey Michaels, who says the object of the fulfillment is "not a particular passage of Scripture about 'thirst,' but Scripture as a whole." Michaels, *John*, 961. Robert L. Brawley points out, however, that ἡ γραφή is unlikely a general reference to Scripture, since a specific OT text is in view in the other three fulfillment quotations in John 19:24, 36–37. Robert L. Brawley, "An Absent Complement and Intertextuality in John 19:28–29," *JBL* 112 (1993): 434.

181 "Allusions," according to Jon Paulien, "are limited to a word, an idea, or a brief phrase that can be traced to a known body of text." Paulien, "Elusive Allusions," 39.

182 Cf. Barrett, *John*, 553; Moo, *The Old Testament*, 277. The majority of commentators link Jesus' statement, "I am thirsty," to the OT passage being fulfilled. Köstenberger, *John*, 550n53.

183 Moo, *The Old Testament*, 277.

184 Daly-Denton, *David in the Fourth Gospel*, 219. Cf. Matt 27:48; Mark 15:36; Luke 23:36.

185 In terms of internal evidence, verbal parallels, along with thematic and structural parallels, are one of the three basic criteria for identifying allusions. Paulien, "Elusive Allusions," 41–44.

MT Ps 69:22	וַיִּתְּנוּ בְּבָרוּתִי רֹאשׁ וְלִצְמָאִי יַשְׁקוּנִי חֹמֶץ
	"They also gave me gall for my food, and for my thirst they gave me vinegar to drink."
LXX Ps 68:22	καὶ ἔδωκαν εἰς τὸ βρῶμά μου χολὴν καὶ εἰς τὴν δίψαν μου ἐπότισάν με ὄξος
	"And they gave me gall for my food, and for my thirst they gave me vinegar to drink."

First, thirst is explicitly mentioned in both contexts. John's verb διψῶ parallels the LXX's noun δίψαν ("my thirst") (LXX εἰς τὴν δίψαν μου = MT's וְלִצְמָאִי, "for my thirst").[186] Second, the references to ὄξους/ὄξος ("sour wine") in John 19:29–30 parallel the LXX's ὄξος (= MT's חֹמֶץ),[187] and in both passages a vinegar drink is given to quench thirst. According to Schlatter, "Die Tränkung mit Essig zeigt, daß Joh. an Ps. 69, 22 dachte."[188] In light of these verbal parallels, John 19:28 is probably an allusion to Ps 69:21.[189]

Correspondence in the David-Jesus Typology

When Ps 69:21 is analyzed in both its original context and in John 19:28, substantive parallels can be seen between Jesus and David and their similar situations. These parallels indicate again that David typology stands behind the application of the psalm verse to Jesus.

Psalm 69 was summarized in the analysis of Ps 69:4 in John 15:25 above. It is necessary, therefore, only to provide additional explanation for Ps 69:21 in its original application to David in his suffering. Basically, Ps 69:21 continues

---

186 Daly-Denton explains that John's choice of a verb over the prepositional phrase in the LXX is due to the present tense context of his narrative. She writes, "Since the fulfilment is in the unfolding of the event, it is logical that the psalm's εἰς τὴν δίψαν μου should be reformulated by the author as direct speech of Jesus, thus Διψῶ." Daly-Denton, *David in the Fourth Gospel*, 221.

187 The Hebrew חֹמֶץ refers to "vinegar." *HALOT*, s.v. "חֹמֶץ." "Ὄξος was a "sour wine/wine vinegar," that "relieved thirst more effectively than water and, being cheaper than regular wine, it was a favorite beverage of the lower ranks of society and of those in moderate circumstances." BDAG, s.v. "ὄξος."

188 Schlatter, *Der Evangelist Johannes*, 351. "The water with vinegar shows that John thought of Ps 69:22" (my translation).

189 E.g., Barrett, *John*, 553; Bultmann, *John*, 674n11; Calvin, *John*, 2:231; Carson, *John*, 619–620; Hengstenberg, *St. John*, 2:420; Köstenberger, *John*, 550; Lagrange, Évangile selon Saint Jean, 496; Lincoln, *The Gospel According to Saint John*, 477; Lindars, *The Gospel of John*, 581; Moo, *The Old Testament*, 277; Nash, "Kingship and the Psalms", 188–193; Newman and Nida, *John*, 591; Schnackenburg, *John*, 3:283; Tenney, *John*, 183; Wengst, *Das Johannesevangelium*, 2:259; Witherington, *John's Wisdom*, 310. Contra Freed, *Old Testament Quotations*, 106; Tholuck, *Commentary on the Gospel of John*, 396. Cf. Daly-Denton, who sees Ps 69:21 as the "primary reference" and also sees echoes to other psalms texts at play. Daly-Denton, *David in the Fourth Gospel*, 228–229.

Prophetic David Typology in John 99

to develop the severe distress of David's situation brought on by persecution from his countless enemies, who hate him without cause (69:4). The reproach of David's enemies has devastated him, leaving him in a heartbroken and weak state (69:20a). In this great distress, David looked for sympathy and comfort, but no such relief was to be found (69:20b). What he experienced was quite the opposite of the respite he needed. Instead of easing up, his suffering intensified. David says in 69:21 that his enemies gave him "gall" (רֹאשׁ) for his food and "vinegar" (חֹמֶץ) for his drink.[190] Common to the gall and vinegar here, as the parallelism of the verse indicates, is their unpalatably bitter, sour qualities.[191]

These words of David may be interpreted literally,[192] but more likely the language here is to be taken metaphorically.[193] David, then, is understood to be saying that his enemies "made things worse for him.... They did their best to aggravate his troubles."[194] As Leupold explains it, "This indicates that they continued their cruel attitude.... [and that] they intensified cruel treatment."[195] Essentially, then, David likens his suffering to the state of a hungry and thirsty man, who is given condiments "to aggravate his hunger and thirst instead of satisfying them."[196] In this context, therefore, the reference to

---

190 The term translated as "gall" refers to "a bitter and poisonous herb." BDB, s.v. "II. רֹאשׁ." The precise identification of the herb is not known, but the colocynth or hemlock plant is commonly suggested. Roland K. Harrison, "Gall," *ISBE* 2:392–393. Depending on the context, רֹאשׁ sometimes refers to "poison" and sometimes to "bitterness." John H. Walton, Victor H. Matthews, and Mark W. Chavalas, *The IVP Bible Background Commentary: Old Testament* (Downers Grove: InterVarsity, 2000), 539. The term, חֹמֶץ, refers to "vinegar" (*HALOT*, s.v. "חֹמֶץ."), which the context of Ps 69:21 insinuates was "a sour, undrinkable wine." J. W. Rogerson and J. W. McKay, *Psalms*, CBC (London: Cambridge University Press, 1977), 2:98. See also, Anderson, *Psalms*, 1:506. There were apparently differing kinds of vinegar beverages, some of which were less bitter and sour in their content and, thus, more drinkable (cf. Num 6:3). Cf. H. W. Heidland, "ὄξος," *TDNT* 5:288–289. In Ps 69:21, however, the vinegar appears undrinkable and is a "bitter, worthless vintage offered to the sufferer" (Walton, Matthews, and Chavalas, *Bible Background Commentary*, 539) in the place of drinkable wine. Mitchell Dahood, *Psalms II*, AB 17 (Garden City, NY: Doubleday, 1968), 162.

191 Cf. Walton, Matthews, and Chavalas, *Bible Background Commentary*, 539. See also Delitzsch, who explains that "bitter and poisonous are interchangeable notions in the Semitic languages." Delitzsch, *Psalms*, 2:283. Since Hebrew parallelism does not imply exact repetition, gall probably refers to both the bitter and poisonous qualities of the herb from which it was made. Furthermore, since the vinegar is linked with gall (i.e., bitter poison) in Ps 69:21, "the parallelism indicates clearly the unpalatable nature of vinegar." Gary A. Lee, "Vinegar," *ISBE* 4:987.

192 Cf. Grogan, *Psalms*, 129.

193 So Anderson, *Psalms*, 1:506; Calvin, *Psalms*, 5:65 in vol. 3; Kidner, *Psalms 1–72*, 266; Leupold, *Psalms*, 505; Longmann, *How to Read the Psalms*, 137; Rogerson and McKay, *Psalms*, 2:98; Tate, *Psalms 51–100*, 199; VanGemeren, "Psalms," 459.

194 VanGemeren, "Psalms," 459.

195 Leupold, *Psalms*, 505–506. Calvin similarly states, "Here he repeats that his enemies carry their cruelty towards him to the utmost extent of their power." Calvin, *Psalms*, 5:65 in vol. 3.

196 Charles A. Briggs and Emilie G. Briggs, *A Critical and Exegetical Commentary on the*

vinegar "not merely attests to its nauseous flavor but implies that it was used in punishment."[197] Put simply, when David longed for consolation in his distress, his enemies took advantage to increase his suffering all the more.

John alludes to this specific psalm verse in John 19:28 and signals that it finds its fulfillment in Jesus' thirst on the cross. The way he uses this psalm text seems to be consistent with the way references from Psalms have been shown to apply to Jesus in John 13:18; 15:25; 19:24: that is, David typology. The experience of suffering that David describes in Ps 69:21 provides a model for the suffering Jesus must experience in his death with the following notable correspondences: (1) the royal status of the sufferer, (2), the explicit reference to thirst in the context of suffering, (3) the giving of a vinegar drink by the adversaries for the sufferer's thirst, and (4) the notion of cruelty in the giving of the vinegar.

The first point of typological correspondence concerns the royal status of the sufferer. Psalm 69 reflects a personal lament of David, Israel's king. The allusions to Psalm 69 in John 19:28 and 15:25 assert the idea of a suffering king. The notion of Jesus' kingship pervades and reaches its climax in the passion narrative of John 18–19, and so, John's appeal to Ps 69:21 in Jesus' thirst on the cross again connects David and Jesus in their status as kings and in their situations of suffering.[198]

Their similarity in this royal connection, however, is not a one-to-one equality. John shows the reader in John 19:28 that Jesus, unlike David, is the sovereign King. Wengst observes, "Auch jetzt, wo er zum letzten Mal agiert, erscheint Jesus, obwohl ohnmächtig am Kreuz hängend, als Souverän."[199] So, even though he is dying on the cross, the irony is that Jesus remains in total command and is not a helpless victim. He possesses perfect awareness (εἰδώς, "knowing") of his suffering according to the Father's will, and he intentionally says διψῶ to set in motion the fulfillment of the events related to Ps 69:21.[200]

David and Jesus are also parallel in the specific reference to thirst in their sufferings. When David describes his malicious treatment at the hands of his enemies in Ps 69:21, he uses the imagery of a thirsty man metaphorically to

---

Book of Psalms, ICC (Edinburgh: T. & T. Clark, 1907), 2:119. Cf. Calvin, *Psalms*, 5:66.

    197 Roland K. Harrison, "Vinegar," *New Bible Dictionary*, 1225.

    198 Cf. Köstenberger, *John's Gospel and Letters*, 411–412.

    199 Wengst, *Das Johannesevangelium*, 2:259. "Even now, where he acts for the final time, Jesus appears, although hanging weak on the cross, as the Sovereign" (my translation).

    200 On the latter point, Wengst explains, "Er gibt gleichsam das Stichwort, damit die anderen am Geschehen Beteiligten ihren Part übernehmen: 'Ich habe Durst.'" Wengst, *Das Johannesevangelium*, 2:259. "He gives the key word, as it were, so that the other participants in the event assume their part: 'I'm thirsty'" (my translation).

portray the severity of his suffering. In John 19:28, the verbal cry "I am thirsty" (διψῶ), which Jesus speaks, corresponds with the LXX's phrase "for my thirst" (εἰς τὴν δίψαν μου) (Ps 68:22). Most likely, the use of the verb διψῶ in place of the noun δίψαν in the LXX is John's way of adapting the psalm verse to his present tense narrative. Notably, the thirst of Jesus on the cross is a physiological thirst, which, as Lagrange notes, was entirely natural given the circumstances.[201] Common to both David and Jesus in Ps 69:21, then, is the reference to physical thirst, yet Jesus experiences a real, literal thirst in contrast to what was figurative expression for David. Jesus' suffering, therefore, goes beyond that of David, for Jesus literally endured in his body the torment David merely invoked.

A third point of correspondence between David and Jesus in their sufferings centers on the drink they are given and the agents who administer it. David says in Ps 69:21, "they" gave me "vinegar" to drink. The "they" refers to the adversaries David has been complaining about throughout Psalm 69 (cf. 69:4, 14, 18–19, 22–28), and the "vinegar" (MT חֹמֶץ/LXX ὄξος) refers to a sour, undrinkable wine. Turning to the context of John 19:28–30, it is Jesus' tormenters, the soldiers, who lift up to him a sponge full of "sour wine" to wet his mouth. This "sour wine" (ὄξος) given to Jesus, though a popular thirst-quenching drink of the common people, was a cheaper and inferior beverage to "wine" (οἶνος), being that it was "sour and bitter."[202] When their situations are considered together, John demonstrates that Jesus experiences

---

[201] Lagrange, Évangile selon Saint Jean, 495. The fact that Jesus says the words, "I am thirsty," to fulfill the Scripture does not take away from the fact that he was literally thirsting as a result of the suffering he was enduring. Cf. Wengst, who says, "Die Darstellung bei Johannes, dass Jesus um der Schrifterfüllung willen redet, nimmt der Tatsächlichkeit seines Leidens nichts weg, sondern bringt zum Ausdruck, dass gerade in diesem Geschehen doch Gott sein Werk treibt und zu Ende führt." Wengst, *Das Johannesevangelium*, 2:260. "The presentation of John, that Jesus speaks for the sake of the fulfillment of Scripture, takes away nothing from the reality of his suffering, but brings to expression that exactly in these events, nevertheless, God does his work and superintends to the end" (my translation). Extreme thirst was one of the physiological effects of one experiencing hypovolemic shock due to the blood loss from flogging and crucifixion. Erkki Koskenniemi, Kirsi Nisula, and Jorma Toppari, "Wine Mixed with Myrrh (Mark 15.23) and Crurifragium (John 19.31–32): Two Details of the Passion Narratives," *JSNT* 27 (2005): 385–386. Considering the original meaning of Ps 69:21 and the context of suffering in John 19:28, therefore, it seems best to understand Jesus' thirst literally, not figuratively. Contra Witkamp, who allows for the literal but sees more of a spiritual interpretation of Jesus' thirst. Witkamp, "Jesus' Thirst in John 19:28–30," 489–510.

[202] H. W. Heidland, "ὄξος," *TDNT* 5:288–289. The LXX translates the Hebrew חֹמֶץ ("vinegar") with ὄξος. Both refer to a vinegar kind of drink, but there appears to be some distinction between the two. The "vinegar" David speaks of in Ps 69:21 appears to be an undrinkable beverage that does not satisfy thirst, but in John 19:29–30 the "sour wine" is a thirst-quenching drink of the day, although it still retains certain sour and bitter qualities. So, in both the OT and NT contexts, the vinegar drink in view is an inferior beverage in comparison to wine. Cf. Wengst, *Das Johannesevangelium*, 2:259n222.

what David described about himself in Ps 69:21: those persecuting him provide him with a sour, vinegar drink for his thirst.

The final point of typological contact is the cruelty associated with the giving of vinegar. There is no doubt in the original context of Ps 69:21 that David intends the imagery of the vinegar beverage to be understood as a malicious act on the part of his enemies. When he needed comfort and sympathy, his enemies scorned his needs. They, so to speak, gave him bitter vinegar to drink in his thirst, which, metaphorically, pictures them injuring him even further. In the case of Jesus, the provision of the sour wine-vinegar seems also to represent an act of cruelty on the part of Jesus' torturers, the soldiers.[203] Even though John does not state explicitly a hostile motive in the soldiers' actions, the context of Ps 69:21 naturally points to Jesus undergoing added mistreatment in this deed. H. W. Heidland explains that John "stresses the fact that the drink was bitter. In particular, ὄξος is set in light of the verse in Ps. 69:21 which speaks of the innocent suffer being given vinegar to drink."[204] Based on the context of Ps 69:21, then, John is underscoring by his allusion to the psalm verse that the vinegar given to Jesus was a harsh mistreatment, for it is a sour and bitter liquid given to one with burning thirst. Hoisting up a sponge full of cheap, sour wine to Jesus, who is agonizing in thirst, hardly comes across as a merciful deed.[205] More fitting with the context of suffering in Ps 69:21 and in John 19 is to understand the offering of vinegar as an intensifier of Jesus' suffering. Wilson explains:

---

203 Surprisingly, while most agree that the giving of the vinegar in the original context of Ps 69:21 represents an act of mistreatment, they view the soldiers' actions in John 19:29–30 as an act of compassion. See e.g., Michaels, *John*, 963–964; Moo, *The Old Testament*, 279; Newman and Nida, *John*, 591; Ridderbos, *John*, 617; Tholuck, *Commentary on the Gospel of John*, 396n2; D. Bernhard Weiss, *Das Johannesevangelium: als einheitliches Werk* (Berlin: Trowitzsch & Sohn, 1912), 338; Westcott, *St. John*, 277; Witherington, *John's Wisdom*, 311. Gerald H. Wilson, however, explains that the context of Psalm 69 argues against a "compassionate" application of Ps 69:21 to Jesus' suffering in the NT. Wilson, *Psalms Volume 1*, 955n24. In addition, it is hard to imagine that John intends this scene to be viewed as a benevolent act by the soldiers, who have just nailed Jesus to the cross and gambled for his clothing and who are about to pierce his side with a spear and are planning to break his legs (John 19:18, 24, 32–34). Furthermore, the sour wine was not given to relieve but to extend the pain of crucifixion. Bruce writes, "The present incident in John's narrative has its parallel in Mark 15:36, where the vinegar, far from dulling the senses, may be intended to preserve or revive full consciousness." Bruce, *John*, 373. On this point, Köstenberger explains that the "'wine vinegar' prolonged life and therefore pain." Köstenberger, *John*, 550. See also Nash, who assesses the giving of the drink as act of cruelty. Nash, "Kingship and the Psalms," 195.

204 H. W. Heidland, "ὄξος," *TDNT* 5:289.

205 Ridderbos states, "Admittedly, the manner in which the drink is offered does depict the extremity of Jesus' situation. A sponge soaked in sour wine is attached to the top of a stalk of hyssop and so held to Jesus' mouth as the only way to give him a drink." Ridderbos, *John*, 617.

Instead of comfort, his enemies [i.e., the psalmist's] provide only "gall" and "vinegar" to assuage his raging thirst (69:21). This painful lack of concern—even sadistic toying with the urgent needs of the suffering—is used in the New Testament to describe the scornful treatment of the suffering of Christ on the cross.[206]

So, the offering of sour wine to Jesus develops further John's depiction of the extreme agony of his death in accordance with the Scripture. As David's enemies did to him, so do Jesus' enemies: they exercise further cruelty on top of his existing suffering by wetting his mouth with a bitter drink. Considering that Jesus actually drinks the sour vinegar in his suffering while David simply used it as a metaphor, the literal occurrence of the event in the death of Jesus underscores that his suffering was on a different level than David's, for he truly experienced the torment David described.[207]

PROPHECY IN THE DAVID-JESUS TYPOLOGY

As with the other passages investigated in this chapter, the allusion to Ps 69:21 in John 19:28 evidences a typological relationship between David and Jesus that fits best with the traditional, prophetic concept of typology.[208] That is, the David typology possesses a prophetic force, for John interprets an OT text relaying an event in David's life to be predicting a NT event in the life of Jesus. Support for this prophetic understanding of the typology includes (1) the ἵνα purpose clause, (2) the "fulfillment" language, and (3) the contextual background of Jesus' "hour."

The introductory formula ἵνα τελειωθῇ ἡ γραφή ("to fulfill the Scripture"), which appears in John 19:28, like the similar constructions in John 13:18; 15:25; 19:24 highlights the prophetic force of the David typology by using a purpose

---

206 Wilson, *Psalms Volume 1*, 955.

207 Calvin summarizes the implications of this point well, stating: "It is, undoubtedly, a metaphorical expression, and David means by it, not only that they refused to him the assistance which he needed, but that they cruelly aggravated his distresses. But there is not inconsistency in saying that what had been dimly shadowed out in David was more clearly exhibited in Christ: for thus we are enabled more fully to perceive the difference between truth and figures, when those things which David suffered, only in a figurative manner, are distinctly and perfectly manifested in Christ." Calvin, *John*, 2:234–235.

208 Carson explains, "the hermeneutical assumption" behind the use of Ps 69:21 in John 19:28 "is that David and his experience constitute a prophetic model, a 'type', of 'great David's greater son.'" Carson, *John*, 620. Contra Brawley who writes, "There is no intrinsic relationship between the incident on the cross and the Johannine allusion to Psalm 69." Brawley, "John 19:28–29," 442. However, the prophetic nature of the typology presented below suggests the opposite. Because Ps 69:21 predicts the NT event, there exists an intrinsic relationship between the OT type and the NT antitype.

clause.²⁰⁹ In this passage, there is discussion on whether the purpose clause modifies the verb which precedes it (τετέλεσται) or follows (λέγει). While it is possible that the purpose clause depends on τετέλεσται ("had been accomplished"),²¹⁰ the second option, which understands the ἵνα clause to be subordinate to the succeeding verb λέγει ("said"), finds the majority of support.²¹¹ First, the singular ἡ γραφή ("the Scripture") tends to denote a specific Scripture passage in the FG, especially in fulfillment formulas. Since John shows concern in the passion narrative to demonstrate the details of Christ's suffering as specific fulfillments from the OT, B. F. Westcott maintains that it is more likely that the ἵνα clause connects to λέγει than to τετέλεσται.²¹² In addition, though it is normal for final clauses to relate to a preceding main verb, sometimes their main verb follows.²¹³ Moo explains that "ἵνα clauses can depend on a following verb, and the construction accords with Johannine usage elsewhere."²¹⁴ The pre-positioning of the clause actually serves a purpose. By placing the ἵνα clause in front of the main verb λέγει, John underscores the notion of fulfillment in Jesus' initiative from the cross.²¹⁵ Following the majority consensus, then, the ἵνα clause modifies λέγει.

What is the implication of this purpose clause for the typology established

---

209 See, Metzger, "Formulas Introducing Quotations of Scripture," 306n17.

210 See e.g., G. Bampfylde, "John 19:28: A Case for a Different Translation," *NovT* 11 (1969): 253; Tholuck, *Commentary on the Gospel of John*, 396–397. See also, Brown and Morris, who suggest that the ἵνα clause may modify either verb. Brown, *John (13–21)*, 908; Morris, *John*, 719. When the ἵνα clause is subordinated to τετέλεσται, the sense of the clause would be: "Jesus, knowing that all things had already been accomplished in order to fulfill the Scripture, said, 'I thirst.'"

211 See e.g., Barrett, *John*, 553; Beasely-Murray, *John*, 351; Borchert, *John*, 270–271; Bultmann, *John*, 673–674; Carson, *John*, 619; Garland, "John 18–19," 495; Godet, *John's Gospel*, 948; Hengstenberg, *St. John*, 2:419–420; Köstenberger, *John*, 550; Moo, *The Old Testament*, 276–278; Schnackenburg, *John*, 3:283, 460n59; Weiss, *Das Johannesevangelium: Als Einheitliches Werk*, 338; Westcott, *St. John*, 277; Witkamp, "Jesus' Thirst in John 19:28–30," 494; Zahn, *Das Evangelium des Johannes*, 649. See also, BDF §478; G. Delling, "τέλος κτλ," *TDNT* 8:82n16. In connection to λέγει, the sense is, "Jesus, knowing that all things had already been accomplished, said, 'I thirst' in order that the Scripture might be fulfilled."

212 Westcott, *St. John*, 277. If the ἵνα clause depends on τετέλεσται, then ἡ γραφή takes on a collective sense. Yet, the fulfillment John has in view is not "the entire revelation of God in the Scriptures" but "a particular Scripture passage." Beasely-Murray, *John*, 351. See also Bultmann, *John*, 674n11. That a collective sense of Scripture is not in view seems further clear in that John goes on to speak of two other OT passages being fulfilled in John 19:36–37.

213 BDF §478 explains that "it is to be noted that there is the possibility of shifting a final clause forward." As examples of such cases, BDF lists John 19:28, 31 and Rom 9:11. For other examples in John, where the ἵνα clause precedes the main verb, Witkamp also references John 1:31 and 14:31 for support. Witkamp, "Jesus' Thirst in John 19:28–30," 494.

214 Moo, *The Old Testament*, 277.

215 Cf. G. Delling, who explains, "The thought of the ἵνα clause is underlined by putting it first." G. Delling, "τέλος κτλ," *TDNT* 8:82n16. Contra Haenchen, who thinks the clause adds emphasis but is a later editorial redaction. Haenchen, *John*, 2:193.

by the quotation of Ps 69:21? It reveals that Jesus understood the text of Ps 69:21 to relate specifically to an event in his death and deliberately says διψῶ to bring the passage to its proper fulfillment.[216] Lagrange writes, "Le sens est simplement que Jésus, dévoré par la soif, trop naturelle en pareil cas, a exprimé sa souffrance pour réaliser une prophétie . . ."[217] Importantly, though, the allusion to Ps 69:21 in John 19:28 is not a case of verbal prophecy but typological prophecy. Since Ps 69:21 records an event about David, John shows the reader that Jesus understood David's description of his suffering to be a predictive paradigm for his own suffering. Thus, the nature of the typology is more intrinsic than just analogy, for the Davidic event prefigures and points forward to the Christ event.

In the purpose clause, John uses the verb τελειωθῇ ("to fulfill"), which differs from John's usual verb of choice, πληρωθῇ ("to fulfill"; cf. John 12:38–40; 13:18; 15:25; 19:36–37), to note the fulfillment of Scripture. What explains John's change in the fulfillment language here? Most likely, John changes to τελειωθῇ to complement the cognate verb τετέλεσται ("had been accomplished"), which appears twice in the immediate verses (John 19:28, 30).[218] It is possible that the verbal change amounts to nothing more than a stylistic matter, and τελειωθῇ serves as a virtual synonym for πληρωθῇ.[219] Or perhaps John selects τελειωθῇ to accompany the repeated use of τετέλεσται to make a theological point. That is, John pairs the verbs together to draw attention to "climactic fulfillment" in Jesus' words, "I am thirsty."[220] Both of the foregoing suggestions are viable

---

216 Hengstenberg writes, "According to John, Jesus uttered the word 'I thirst' in order to introduce a fulfilment of Scripture, the word of Ps. lxix. 21." Hengstenberg, *St. John*, 2:420. This fulfillment includes both the thirst of Jesus and the response of the soldiers, as depicted in Ps 69:21. Beasely-Murray, *John*, 351. Cf. Wengst, *Das Johannesevangelium*, 2:259.

Further reinforcing the idea that Jesus intentionally cries out to fulfill Ps 69:21 is John's emphasis upon Jesus' omniscience (cf. εἰδώς, John 19:28), which underscores his sovereignty in his death. If Jesus "knowingly" acted to fulfill Ps 69:21, as the evidence seems to indicate, Carson suggests the following understanding of the fulfillment clause: "'Jesus, knowing that all things had been accomplished, in order to fulfill [the] Scripture [which says 'They . . . gave me vinegar for my thirst'] said 'I thirst.'" Carson, *John*, 619.

217 Lagrange, *Évangile selon Saint Jean*, 495–496. "The meaning is simply that Jesus, devoured by thirst, too natural in such a case, expressed his suffering to fulfill a prophecy" (my translation).

218 Cf. Barrett, *John*, 553.

219 Moule, "Fulfillment-Words," 314–135, 318–319. This change from πληρωθῇ to τελειωθῇ, according to Moule, "is in keeping with a well-known tendency in the Fourth Evangelist to use synonyms, apparently simply for the sake of variety. . ." Ibid., 314–315. For others who think the verbs are basically synonyms, see e.g., Bultmann, *John*, 674n1; Craig A. Evans, "The Old Testament in the New," in *The Face of New Testament Studies: A Survey of Recent Research*, ed. Scot McKnight and Grant R. Osborne (Grand Rapids: Baker Academic, 2004), 140n35; Witkamp, "Jesus' Thirst in John 19:28–30," 505–506.

220 Moo, *The Old Testament*, 277. See also, Carson, "John and the Johannine Epistles," 252; Köstenberger, "John," 502. In other words, John might be drawing special attention to this "ful-

interpretations,[221] but the latter understanding may be slightly preferable, since this represents "the last explicit example of Jesus' *active* fulfillment of the Scriptures in John's gospel" before his culminating death.[222]

Regardless of the view taken, the notion of prophetic realization characterizes both understandings. According to Craig A. Evans, the ἵνα τελειωθῇ formula "in any event, is virtually identical in meaning to the *hina plērōthē* formula."[223] "[B]oth verbs [πληρωθῇ and τελειωθῇ] preserve the emphasis upon fulfilment, the bringing to pass of God's design announced earlier."[224] Underlying the root verb τελειόω is the idea of completing something, bringing it to its end or goal,[225] so, with respect to the fulfillment of Ps 69:21, τελειωθῇ indicates that the psalm verse reaches its completion or goal in Jesus' experience of thirst and the soldiers' response. It is thus right to understand the psalm text as pointing forward to this NT event in Jesus' suffering, which indicates that the typology between David and Jesus is fundamentally prophetic. The event recorded in Ps 69:21 prophetically anticipates the similar but greater suffering of Jesus.

Finally, the theme of Jesus' "hour" supports a prophetic rather than purely analogical view of the David typology in John 19:28. As explained in the analysis of John 13:18 above, the "hour" of Jesus envisages a pre-determined plan of the Father, which entails specific events of suffering Jesus must experience according to the will of God. If Ps 69:21 applies to a specific event in Jesus' life and substantiates this event as the will of God, then this psalm verse ultimately had Jesus in mind, pointing to a future reality that must be fulfilled in Jesus. Hence, the David typology bears a predictive thrust, since John appeals to an event-based psalm text to support biblically the suffering of the Messiah on the cross.

Summary

This chapter examined four psalms that John references by means of fulfillment formulas (John 13:18/Ps 41:9; 15:25/Ps 69:4; 19:24/Ps 22:18; 19:28/Ps 69:21).

---

fillment" of Scripture, because it represents his last, final act of obedience to complete the work the Father gave him to do as outlined in Scripture. Cf. Carson, *John*, 620. See also the discussion by Martin Hengel, "The Old Testament in the Fourth Gospel," in *The Gospels and the Scriptures of Israel*, ed. Craig A. Evans and W. Richard Stegner, JSNTSup 104 (Sheffield, Eng: Sheffield Academic Press, 1994), 393.

221 Cf. Freed, *Old Testament Quotations*, 105–106.
222 Moo, *The Old Testament*, 278.
223 Evans, "Obduracy and the Lord's Servant," 225–226.
224 Carson, *John*, 252.
225 BDAG, s.v. "τελειόω." BDAG suggests the possible senses of "final fulfillment" or "to fulfill" (i.e., in the sense of a specific prophecy) for John 19:28.

In each instance, the verse quoted relays a historical event specific to David, which Jesus (John 13:18; 15:25) or John (John 19:24, 28) appropriates to explain the specific events of Jesus' sufferings. Two primary observations emerged in the analysis of each psalm quotation: there is clear correspondence between David and Jesus, and the typology is prophetic. First, the appropriation of these OT quotations in their NT contexts juxtaposes two texts relaying events, and comparing these texts allows the reader to observe substantive correspondences between David and Jesus in their persons and similar situations of suffering. These correspondences affirm that in each case a David typology stands behind the use of the psalm reference in its application to Jesus.

Second, in each NT case there are several items of textual evidence that support a prophetic understanding of the quotations in their application to Jesus. Prominent in each example was a purpose clause involving "fulfillment" language and allusions to Jesus "hour." These repeated patterns suggest that Jesus' sufferings are not only similar to David's but are the intended fulfillment of prophetic typology. Jesus and John interpret various events in David's life as prophetic models for what Jesus was to experience in his suffering and death. By placing the Scripture citations with fulfillment formulas on the lips of Jesus (i.e., John 13:18; 15:25), John shows his readers that Jesus is the one who taught them how Psalms predicts his sufferings (cf. Luke 24:44). Specifically, Psalms records events that predict his sufferings typologically. Ultimately, then, it is the traditional view of prophetic typology—typology that is specifically Davidic in focus—that best explains how the Psalms quotations apply to the events of Jesus' passion. Collectively, the core hermeneutic of prophetic David typology identifies Jesus as the New and Greater David.[226]

---

226 Cf. 2 Sam 7:12–16; Jer 30:9; Ezek 34:23–24; 37:24–25; Hos 3:5.

5

Prophetic David Typology in Acts

The quotations from Psalms in Acts 1:20; 2:25–28, 34–35; 4:25–26 are also best explained by the traditional view of typology. Specifically, David typology, conceived of prophetically, best accounts for Peter's application of Psalms to the events of Jesus' suffering, resurrection, and exaltation. The analysis of Acts follows the same steps used to examine the quotations in John in chapter four.[1]

Pss 69:25 and 109:8 in Acts 1:20

Luke appeals to two OT psalm citations in Acts 1:20 to establish a David-Jesus typology. He uses the formula construct γέγραπται γὰρ ἐν βίβλῳ ψαλμῶν ("For it is written in the book of Psalms") to introduce his psalm references.[2] Ἐν βίβλῳ ψαλμῶν ("in the book of Psalms) clearly indicates the book of Psalms as the source of Luke's quotations.[3]

---

1 Each quotation from Psalms is examined in three steps: (1) establish the identification of the OT psalm reference, (2) identify the typological correspondences between David and Jesus, and (3) discuss evidence that indicates a prophetic notion in the quotation.

2 For a discussion of the various citation formulas in Acts, see I. Howard Marshall, "Acts," in *CNTUOT*, ed. G. K. Beale and D. A. Carson (Grand Rapids: Baker Academic, 2007), 522. This work accepts the traditional position that Luke authored both the Gospel of Luke and the book of Acts (see Darrell L. Bock, *A Theology of Luke and Acts: God's Promised Program, Realized for All Nations*, BTNT [Grand Rapids: Zondervan, 2012], 32–37; 55–61; Richard N. Longenecker, "The Acts of the Apostles," in EBC 9, ed. Franck E. Gaebelein [Grand Rapids: Zondervan, 1981], 231–232; 238–240). In Luke-Acts, Luke uses the perfect tense verb γέγραπται ("it is written") a total of fourteen times to cite Scripture (see Luke 2:23; 3:4; 4:4, 8, 10; 7:27; 10:26; 19:46; 24:46; Acts 1:20; 7:42; 13:33; 15:15; 23:5). The perfect-tense verb γέγραπται frequently appears in the NT to introduce OT quotations. See BDAG, s.v. "γράφω;" Gottlob Schrenk, "γράφω κτλ," *TDNT* 1:746–748.

3 Interestingly, Luke is the only NT writer who explicitly mentions Psalms in his references to the OT. As Peter Doble avers, "His [Luke's] overt references to this Book (Lk. 20:42; Acts 1:20), to 'Psalms' (Lk. 24:44) and to 'psalm' (Acts 13:33, 35) signal his unique use of the psalms."

Following the introductory formula in Acts 1:20, there is a "composite quotation of two quite separate texts."[4] The conjunction καί ("and") links together Ps 69:25 (=Ps 69:26/MT and Ps 68:26/LXX) and Ps 109:8 (=Ps 109:8/MT and Ps 108:8/LXX) under a single introductory formula.[5] Both of these verses correspond closely enough with their source texts to be considered direct quotations.[6] Beginning with Ps 69:25, one sees two modifications in Luke's translation in comparison to both the MT and LXX.

Acts 1:20	γενηθήτω ἡ ἔπαυλις αὐτοῦ ἔρημος καὶ μὴ ἔστω ὁ κατοικῶν ἐν αὐτῇ
	"Let his homestead be desolate, and let no one dwell in it."
MT Ps 69:26	תְּהִי־טִירָתָם נְשַׁמָּה בְּאָהֳלֵיהֶם אַל־יְהִי יֹשֵׁב
	"May their camp be desolate; May none dwell in their tents."
LXX Ps 68:26	γενηθήτω ἡ ἔπαυλις αὐτῶν ἠρημωμένη καὶ ἐν τοῖς σκηνώμασιν αὐτῶν μὴ ἔστω ὁ κατοικῶν
	"Let their homestead be made desolate, and let no one dwell in their tents."

Peter Doble, "The Psalms in Luke-Acts," in *The Psalms in the New Testament*, ed. Steve Moyise and Maarten J. J. Menken (London: T & T Clark, 2004), 87.

4   Steve Moyise, *Old Testament in the New: An Introduction* (London: T&T Clark International, 2001), 52.

5   C. K. Barrett, "Luke/Acts," in *It is Written: Scripture Citing Scripture. Essays in Honour of Barnabas Lindars*, ed. D. A. Carson and H. G. M. Williamson (Cambridge: Cambridge University Press, 1988), 240. Contra G. D. Kilpatrick, who argues for only a single psalm quotation, seeing καί ("and") as part of the quotation's third line. G. D. Kilpatrick, "Some Quotations in Acts," in *Les Actes des Apôtres: Traditions, rédaction, théologie*, ed. Jacob Kremer, BETL 48 (Gembloux: J. Duculot; Louvain: Leuven University Press: 1979), 86–88. The majority of scholars, however, agree that two psalm quotations are in view in Acts 1:20, namely, Pss 69:25 and 109:8. See e.g., Samuel Amsler, *L'Ancien Testament Dans L'Église: Essai d'herméneutique chrétienne*, Bibliothèque Thélogique (Neuchatel: Delachaux et Niestlé, 1960), 68; Darrell L. Bock, *Acts*, BECNT (Grand Rapids: Baker Academic, 2007), 85–87; Detlev Dormeyer and Florinzio Galindo, *Die Apostelgeschichte: Ein Kommentar für die Praxis* (Stuttgart: Katholisches Bibelwerk, 2003), 36; Jacques Dupont, "L'interpretation des Psaumes dans les Actes des Apôtres," in *Études sur les Actes des Apôtres*, LD 45 (Paris: Éditions du Cerf, 1967), 299–300; Rudolf Pesch, *Die Apostelgeschichte*, EKKNT (Zurich: Benzinger/Neukirchen-Vluyn: Neukirchener Verlag, 1986), 1:88–89; David G. Peterson, *The Acts of the Apostles*, PNTC (Eerdmans: Grand Rapids, 2009), 125–126; Erwin Preuschen, *Die Apostelgeschichte*, HNT 4:1 (Tübingen: Mohr [Siebeck], 1912), 8; G. J. Steyn, "LXX-Sitate in die Petrus- en Paulusredes van Handelinge," *SK* 16 (1995): 132; Crawford Howell Toy, *Quotations in the New Testament* (New York: Charles Scribner's Sons, 1884), 95–96. Furthermore, not only does καί indicate two separate quotations are in view but the expanded introductory formula seems to do so as well. On this point, see Pesch, *Die Apostelgeschichte*, 1:88–89.

6   Jacque Dupont observes, "Une première observation ne soulève aucune difficulté : il y a dans les Actes *sept citations explicites du psautier* [emphasis original]." ("A first observation raises no difficulty: in Acts there are seven explicit quotations from the Psalter" [my translation]). Dupont identifies two in Acts 1:20, two in Acts 2:25–28, 34, one in Acts 4:25–26, and two in Acts 13:33, 35. Dupont, "L'interpretation des Psaumes," 284.

Luke changes the plural reference "their" (ם ָ/αὐτῶν) to the singular "his" (αὐτοῦ). Also, Luke shortens the latter part of the verse by omitting "in their tents" (בְּאָהֳלֵיהֶם/ἐν τοῖς σκηνώμασιν αὐτῶν). He replaces these words with the prepositional phrase "in it" (ἐν αὐτῇ), which refers back to ἔπαυλις ("homestead"). Given these divergences, it is not decisively clear whether Luke translated from the MT or paraphrased the LXX.

As for the second quotation, one can see below that Luke quotes only the second half of Ps 109:8. In addition, Luke uses the imperative λαβέτω instead of the LXX's optative λάβοι. Aside from this change of mood, Luke's quotation mirrors the LXX.

Acts 1:20	τὴν ἐπισκοπὴν αὐτοῦ λαβέτω ἕτερος
	"Let another man take his office."
MT Ps 109:8	יִהְיוּ־יָמָיו מְעַטִּים פְּקֻדָּתוֹ יִקַּח אַחֵר
	"Let his days be few; Let another take his office."
LXX Ps 108:8	γενηθήτωσαν αἱ ἡμέραι αὐτοῦ ὀλίγαι καὶ τὴν ἐπισκοπὴν αὐτοῦ λάβοι ἕτερος
	"Let his days be few, and may another take his office."

THE DAVID-JESUS TYPOLOGY: THE ELEMENT OF CORRESPONDENCE

In David's life, Pss 69:25 and 109:8 relay events of his own suffering. In Acts 1:20, Peter applies them to Jesus' suffering at the hands of Judas, giving these recent events an explicit biblical rationale. The basis for applying these verses to Jesus in this way rests upon a typological connection between David and Jesus. Before analyzing the key correspondences between David and Jesus relevant for Acts 1:20, a short overview of these verses in their original contexts demonstrates how they apply to David in their original settings.

A general summary of the content and structure of Psalm 69 was provided in chapter 4 in the analysis of Ps 69:4 as it appears in John 15:25 and 19:28; thus, only the meaning of Ps 69:25 in its original context needs further comment. Psalm 69 is a psalm of lament containing the superscription לְדָוִד ("by/of David"), which attributes authorship of the psalm to David and therefore instructs the reader to view its content as representing David's experiences.[7]

Psalm 69:25 belongs to the larger unit of 69:22–28, which is the concluding

---

7 On psalms of lament, see the summary of Ps 41:9 in the analysis of John 13:18 above in chapter 4 of this work. On the Davidic authorship understanding of לְדָוִד in the Psalms superscripts, see the section "The David-Jesus Typology: The Element of Correspondence" in the analysis of John 13:18 in chapter 4 of this work.

section of David's lament. These verses constitute the imprecations or curses David prays against his enemies.[8] The words of David in 69:25 represent a poetic case of synonymous parallelism.[9] In 69:25a, David states תְּהִי־טִירָתָם נְשַׁמָּה ("May their camp be desolate"), which calls for the enemies' dwelling-place to be uninhabited.[10] David continues in 69:25b with בְּאָהֳלֵיהֶם אַל־יְהִי יֹשֵׁב ("May none dwell in their tents"), with the implication "may they and their families perish."[11] Thus, David's curse upon his enemies in 69:25 entails a punishment from God that will bring about the desolation of their settlement and their death as well as the destruction of their families.[12]

Similarly, Psalm 109 is an individual lament,[13] again with לְדָוִד ("by/of David) in the psalm's heading. Psalm 109 has four basic sections: (1) 109:1–5: David's initial lament, (2) 109:6–20: David's imprecations against his enemies, (3) 109:21–29: David's continued lament, and (4) 109:30–31: David's conclusion of praise.[14]

David begins with an outcry comprised of both praise and requests for help directed to God (Ps 109:1). The next four verses supply a general idea

---

8 Concerning imprecatory prayers, C. Hassell Bullock explains, "As the name implies, some of the Psalms contain extremely harsh judgments upon the enemies of the psalmists. The term 'imprecations' means 'curses' and suggests that the psalmists prayed that evil would befall their persecutors." C. Hassell Bullock, *Encountering the Book of Psalms: A Literary and Theological Introduction* (Grand Rapids: Baker Academic, 2001), 228; see also 228–238, for a detailed discussion of imprecatory psalms.

9 By definition, "synonymous parallelism simply means that the thought pattern in one line conforms to the pattern in the successive line." Bullock, *Psalms*, 36. The nouns "their encampment" and "their tents" parallel with one another, as do the verbs "may be desolate" and "may none dwell."

10 The term טִירָה refers to "an encampment protected by a stone wall." *HALOT*, s.v. "טִירָה." Delitzsch describes the word as "a designation of an encamping or dwelling place . . . taken from the circular encampments . . . of the nomads (Gen. xxv. 16). F. Delitzsch, *Psalms*, trans. Francis Bolton, Commentary on the Old Testament 5 (repr., Grand Rapids: Eerdmans, 1976), 2:284. The root of the niphal participle נְשַׁמָּה means to "be uninhabited," "be deserted," "be desolated." BDB, s.v. "שָׁמֵם;" *HALOT*, s.v. "שׁמם."

11 Anderson, *Psalms*, 1:507.

12 J. W. Rogerson and J. W. McKay, *Psalms*, CBC (London: Cambridge University Press, 1977), 2:99. Summarizing Ps 69:25, VanGemeren writes, "He [the psalmist] prays that the wicked may be homeless, childless, and without a future (v. 25; cf. 109:9–10). In the end they should have no part in the community of God's people on earth nor in the hereafter." VanGemeren, "Psalms," 460.

13 So e.g., Anderson, *Psalms*, 2:758; Richard P. Belcher Jr., *The Messiah and the Psalms: Preaching Christ from All the Psalms* (Fearn, Scotland: Mentor, 2006), 77; VanGemeren, "Psalms," 689; David P. Wright, "Ritual Anaology in Psalm 109," *JBL* 113 (1994): 392. Cf. Leslie C. Allen, *Psalms*, WBC 21 (Waco, TX: Word Books, 1983), 75.

14 So e.g., Anderson, *Psalms*, 2:758; Belcher, *The Messiah and the Psalms*, 77; Derek Kidner, *Psalms 73–150: A Commentary on Books III–V of the Psalms*, TOTC (Leicester, England: Inter-Varsity, 1975), 388–391; H. C. Leupold, *Exposition on the Psalms* (Columbus, OH: The Wartburg Press, 1959; repr., Grand Rapids: Baker Book House, 1969), 765–770. Cf. Walter Brueggemann, "Psalm 109: Three Times 'Steadfast Love'," *WW* 5 (1985): 144–146.

about David's affliction: he suffers from slanderous enemies, who attack and accuse him with wicked, deceitful, and hateful words (109:2–4a). Their malicious speech is groundless; David is innocent. In return for his love, prayers, and kindness, David's accusers have treated him with evil and hatred (109:4–5).

David proceeds in 109:6–20 to invoke several harsh judgments against his attackers. When speaking of his enemies, this section shifts from the plural subject in 109:2–5 to the singular in 109:6–19 and then back to the plural in 109:20. The shift may represent a Hebrew idiom, so that "'him' and 'he' are a way of saying 'each one of them'."[15] Another possibility, as favored by H. C. Leupold, understands the singular as referring to "one outstanding leader of the opposition against the psalmist, in whom the whole movement centered. He is particularly thought of, the rest are indirectly included."[16] Either of these views is viable.[17] The shifts may also function poetically (along with other features) to divide the section into smaller poetic units. Nevertheless, regardless of which interpretation one accepts, there is an inherent collective sense to the use of the singular, such that David addresses all of his enemies in 109:6–19.[18]

David wishes the most severe punishments upon his enemy, including the individual (109:6–8, 19), his family (109:9–10, 12–13), and his property (109:11).[19] Within this imprecatory context, David delivers two curses against his enemy in 109:8. First, David prays, "Let his days be few" (109:8a); that is, "let him die prematurely."[20] Next, David follows up this request with "Let another take his office" (109:8b).[21] Apparently, David's enemy occupied a place

---

15 Kidner, *Psalms 73–150*, 389. The return to the plural in Ps 109:20, according to Derek Kidner, supports this idiomatic understanding of the pervasive singular reference in 109:6–19. In this case, 109:20 is to be understood as "summarizing the passage." Ibid. For others who mention the singular reference may have a "collective" sense, see e.g., Allen, *Psalms*, 2:72n6a; Anderson, *Psalms*, 2:758–759; Wright, "Ritual Anaology in Psalm 109," 397, 399–400.

16 Leupold, *Psalms*, 766–767. So also Anderson, *Psalms*, 2:758; Grogan, *Psalms*, 183.

17 Cf. John Calvin, *Commentary on the Book of Psalms*, trans. James Anderson, vols. 4–6 of *Calvin's Commentaries* (Grand Rapids: Baker Book House, 1981), 6:274–275 in vol. 4; John I. Durham, "Psalms," in BBC 4, ed. Clifton J. Allen (Nashville: Broadman, Press, 1971), 394.

18 Cf. Wright, "Ritual Anaology in Psalm 109," 397. Ps 109:20 provides reasonable grounds for understanding the sense as a "collective singular." Wright, "Ritual Anaology in Psalm 109," 401. So, in the remaining discussion of Ps 109, David's reference to his "enemy" in the singular will be understood as an address to the entire group.

19 Cf. VanGemeren, "Psalms," 691–694. These punishments clearly climax in physical condemnation on earth and may possibly entail eternal implications (109:14–15).

20 Anderson, *Psalms*, 2:761. Cf. Pss 37:35–38; 55:23; Prov 10:27

21 The Hebrew term פְּקֻדָּתוֹ can refer to "things laid up" (see BDB, s.v. "פְּקֻדָּה."), thus, denoting material possessions and allowing for a possible sense of Ps 109:8b as found in the RSV translation: "May another seize his *goods*." Durham, "Psalms," 394. But, most commentators agree that in 109:8b פְּקֻדָּתוֹ retains the more common meaning of "office" (*HALOT*, s.v.

of leadership ("office"),[22] and David seeks for his enemy to be removed from his leadership position and for another to replace him.[23] Calvin summarizes the central thought of 109:8:

> Now . . . the brevity of human life is here introduced as a mark of God's disapprobation; for when he cuts off the wicked after a violent manner, he thus testifies that they did not deserve to breathe the breath of life. And the same sentiment is inculcated when, denuding them of their honour and dignity, he hurls them from the place of power and authority.[24]

Both Pss 69:25 and 109:8 recount personal experiences of suffering in David's life with regard to his enemies. In Acts 1:20, Peter applies these two psalms to Jesus to explain his suffering at the hands of Judas. That a typological relationship between David and Jesus is in view becomes apparent from the substantive correspondences the text establishes between David and Jesus.[25] The formal parallels between David and Jesus in Acts 1:20 center on the following: (1) the royal status of the sufferer, (2) the persecution or betrayal by an enemy, and (3) the judgments upon the enemy's property, life, and office.

First, David and Jesus are aligned in their status as regal sufferers. Peter explicitly introduces David into the interpretive context of these quotations,

---

"פְּקֻדָּה."). See e.g., Allen, *Psalms*, 73n8a; Anderson, *Psalms*, 2:761; Calvin, *Psalms*, 6:278 in vol. 4; Mitchell Dahood, *Psalms III*, AB 17A (Garden City, NY: Doubleday, 1970), 102; Delitzsch, *Psalms*, 3:178–179; Kidner, *Psalms 73–150*, 390; Leupold, *Psalms*, 767, 770n8. The sense of "office" seems to be the preferred sense in light of the following considerations: (1) the LXX translates פְּקֻדָּתוֹ with τὴν ἐπισκοπὴν, (2) David curses his enemy's possessions in a later verse, Ps 109:11, and (3) Peter clearly understands the term to mean "office," as his application of Ps 109:8b to Judas in Acts 1:20–26 evidences.

22 VanGemeren, "Psalms," 691.

23 Considering the poetic parallelism of Ps 109:8, the request in 109:8b reinforces the initial request in 109:8a while adding some additional thought. Put simply, the office of his enemy will be open for replacement because of his untimely death. So, imbedded in David's plea for his enemy to be replaced in his place of leadership is David's desire for him to experience premature death.

24 Calvin, *Psalms*, 6:277–278 in vol. 4.

25 On this point Yuzuru Miura summarizes: "Here Jesus is presented in parallel with David as righteous suffering king. The persecution of David by his enemies (in a general sense) is typologically paralleled with the persecution of Jesus by Judas." Miura, *David in Luke-Acts*, 159. Contra Craig S. Keener who suggests Pss 69:25; 109:8 apply to Judas's betrayal of Jesus based on a "righteous sufferer" motif found in various psalms which means Jesus is the righteous sufferer "par excellence." Craig S. Keener, *Acts*, New Cambridge Bible Commentary (New York: Cambridge University Press, 2020), 118. Contra also L Scott Kellum, who thinks that Ps 69:25 is applied to Jesus' suffering typologically, while Ps 109:8 seems best understood as Peter's use of analogy. L. Scott Kellum, *Acts*, EGGNT (Nashville: B&H Academic, 2020), 25). The fact that Peter explicitly mentions David in Acts 1:16 in connection with the psalm citations, however, suggests both texts apply to Jesus' suffering by means of a specific David typology rather than a general righteous sufferer motif or just a general analogy.

Prophetic David Typology in Acts 115

when he states in Acts 1:16 that the Holy Spirit spoke them διὰ στόματος Δαυὶδ ("by the mouth of David"). As King David laments to God about his enemies, the notions of his kingship and suffering combine to depict a portrait of a suffering king.[26] A similar kingly suffering motif characterizes Jesus in Peter's speech as well. The references to Judas' betrayal and the resulting arrest of Jesus (Acts 1:16) clearly recalls the specific events that ultimately end in Jesus' death.[27] So, these verses clearly place Jesus in David's place, based on how they compare Judas with David's enemies. Moreover, Acts 1:16–20 contains certain textual features that support Jesus as a *kingly* sufferer.[28] Peter's language in Acts 1:16 "the Scripture had to be fulfilled" (ἔδει πληρωθῆναι τὴν γραφὴν) connects back to Jesus' words in Luke 24:44 "all things which are written must be fulfilled" (δεῖ πληρωθῆναι πάντα τὰ γεγραμμένα).[29] Thus, Peter follows Jesus' pattern of interpreting Psalms as bearing witness to the sufferings of Jesus, the Messiah (cf. Luke 24:44–47). Also, Peter's explicit reference to David in Acts 1:16 suggests that Peter is comparing David and Jesus, which naturally evokes the royal status common to both.[30] Lastly, "substructurally, Acts 1:15–20 extends Luke's Passion Narrative."[31] This narrative relationship means that the stress Luke lays upon Jesus as Israel's suffering King in the passion narrative of his Gospel also extends to Peter's speech in Acts 1.[32]

---

26 On the king as the subject of psalms of lament, see the section "The David-Jesus Typology: The Element of Correspondence" in the analysis of John 13:18 in chapter 4 of this work.

27 Even so, one might question how these quotations speak of Jesus' specific sufferings? The answer seems to be that, since Judas suffers the curses of David's enemies (see discussion below), these Scriptural judgments indicate that Judas's betrayal of Jesus and his consequent suffering were foreseen in these verses. For God to punish Judas with the curses of David's enemies proves that Judas was an enemy of Jesus and guilty of persecuting him.

28 Cf. Jipp, "Messiah," 266–269.

29 Tannehill, *Luke-Acts*, 2:20. See also, Jipp, "Messiah," 266–267.

30 On the mention of David in connection to these quotations in Acts 1, Jipp writes, "One is thereby given a hint as to how the early Christians read the psalms, namely, as royal texts that foreshadow the life and experiences of David's royal son." Jipp, "Messiah," 267.

31 Doble, "Psalms," 116; see also 89n10. Doble sees Acts 1:15–20 as extending Luke's Passion Narrative "because not only is Judas the guide for Jesus' captors, but Psalm 68 is a traditional element in the Passion story." Ibid., 116. For other various narrative connections between Luke 24 and Acts 1, see Robert C. Tannehill, *The Narrative Unity of Luke-Acts: A Literary Interpretation*, Volume One: *The Gospel according to Luke* (Minneapolis: Fortress Press, 1986), 1:277–301.

32 Luke draws explicit attention to the theme of the kingship of Jesus throughout his Gospel: Jesus' birth (Luke 1:31–33; 2:4–7), his entry into Jerusalem (Luke 19:28–40), his trial before Pilate (Luke 23:1–7), and his crucifixion (Luke 23:33–43). For a discussion on the various ways Luke presents the regal status of Jesus his Gospel, see Darrell L. Bock, "Luke, Gospel of," *DJG*, 503–504; Bock, *Luke and Acts*, 141–143, 149–159, 166–169, 177–198, 415. Green points out that it is especially in Luke's passion narrative, where Luke clearly underscores Jesus' status as Israel's King. Joel B. Green, *The Gospel of Luke*, NICNT (Grand Rapids: Eerdmans, 1997), 818–819, who cites Brawley for support. See also, 682–688; 817–823. See also Jipp, "Messiah," 259–260. According to Jipp, Luke's use of the psalms of David to explain Jesus' suffering in his Gospel present Jesus as a royal sufferer. Jipp, "Messiah," 259–260. It is in the psalms of David where "the

The quotations of Pss 69:25 and 109:8 in Acts 1:20, therefore, connect David and Jesus in terms of kingship and suffering, but their experiences are not identical. For instance, Jesus is superior to David in his kingship; this is suggested by Peter's address of Jesus as "the Lord Jesus" in Acts 1:21.[33] This Christological title (κύριος "Lord") in Luke-Acts signifies both Jesus' divinity and authority,[34] which identifies him as the greater suffering King.

There is a second correspondence between David and Jesus in Acts 1:20. In both their OT and NT contexts, the situations of suffering involve some form of enemy persecution: multiple enemies in David's case and a single enemy in Jesus' case.[35] In Ps 69:25, David directs his curse against his adversaries (69:19), those who hate him without just cause (69:4a) and persecute him in various ways (69:4b, 16–21, 26, 29). In Ps 109:8, David again prays judgment upon his enemies, who wrongly attack and accuse him (109:1–5, 16–20, 28–29). Moreover, in Ps 109:4–5 this persecution may be all the worse because it really amounts to betrayal, being carried out by men David considered his friends.[36] In the context of Acts 1:16, Jesus is similar to David in that he also

---

paradoxical combination of kingship and righteous suffering" present David not simply as the "righteous sufferer" but as the "righteous suffering *king* [emphasis original]." Ibid., 259. Consequently, when Luke applies the psalms of David to Jesus in his Gospel to explain Jesus' passion, he depicts both notions of suffering and kingship in relation to Jesus. Ibid., 259.

33 On Jesus as "Lord," cf. Luke 1:43; 20:41–44; 24:34; Acts 1:6, 21; 2:36; 4:33; 7:59; 8:16; 9:17, 35, 42; 11:17, 20; 15:11, 26; 16:31; 19:5, 13, 17; 20:21, 24, 35; 21:13; 28:31.

34 On the full thrust of the Christological title "Lord" in Luke-Acts, see Bock, *Luke and Acts*, 155–156, 166–176, 185, 197–198.

35 One notices in the original context of Ps 69:25 that David's prayer in both the MT and LXX contains the possessive pronoun "their" (ם‎ָ/αὐτῶν), denoting a plurality of enemies. But, when Peter quotes the psalm verse he employs the singular "his" (αὐτοῦ), so that the verse speaks of a single enemy. What justifies Peter's change of Ps 69:25 from the plural in its OT context to the singular in its NT use? Clearly, Peter uses the singular pronoun in order to appropriate the psalm verse specifically to the individual enemy of Jesus, namely, Judas (Acts 1:16). There appears to be a theological rationale behind the change. Put simply, the typological relationship Peter understands David and Jesus to share means that the *enemies* of David in Ps 69:25 can legitimately foreshadow the *enemy* of Jesus. Cf. Marshall, *Acts*, 67–68; Peterson, *Acts*, 125. It is important to remember that Peter claims that Ps 69:25 finds its "fulfillment" in Judas. By the notion of fulfillment, Peter shows, first, that the Holy Spirit (Acts 1:16) intended for David's original description of his enemies in this verse ultimately to apply to Judas. Thus, Peter personalizes the text to Judas with the singular "his." Furthermore, Peter emphasizes by the use of the singular "his" that the "fulfillment" actually signals a climax or escalation in the typology in connection to Jesus (on "escalation" in typology, see the section "Typology As Correspondence" in chapter 2 of this work). That is, Peter reveals that there is a real progress from David's original situation of suffering to Jesus' experience of suffering. In the end, the singular draws attention to the unique status of Judas among the wicked. The thought seems to be that Judas stands in as the supreme representative of all of David's wicked enemies. Cf. Calvin, *Acts 1–13*, 42. The same understanding also applies to Ps 109:8, where David's singular reference to his enemy most likely bears a collective sense for all his enemies. See the summary of Ps 109:8 above.

36 According to C. Hassell Bullock, "His [David's] hurt had been compounded by the fact that the perpetrators of evil were his friends." Bullock, *Psalms*, 232. Bullock cites Pss 55:12–14;

experiences persecution from an enemy: Judas. Judas's treachery is only implicit in the quotation. That Judas reaps the consequences of the curses of Pss 69:25 and 109:8 proves his status as an enemy, one guilty of persecuting Jesus.[37] Peter delineates for his audience Judas's specific crime against Jesus in Acts 1:16, describing Judas's betrayal ("who became a guide") that sets in motion the events ("to those who arrested Jesus") ending in Jesus' death.[38] By means of the quotations, Peter shows that David's betrayal by his enemies parallels Judas' betrayal of Jesus.

Thus, David and Jesus are kingly figures, and both experience suffering brought on by their enemies, but the typological pattern reaches a climax in Jesus. This climactic progression is seen in that (1) Judas, as the fulfillment of David's enemies, stands as the chief representative of the wicked[39] but also (2) the treachery of Judas results in Jesus' death. Consequently, Jesus' suffering goes beyond that of David's.

In addition, there are curses common to both David's enemies and to Judas. The ways in which David desires God to punish his enemies for their evil serve as the model for how God punishes Judas for his treachery. There are three correspondences along these lines. First, David curses his enemies' camp, requesting that their property become desolate and uninhabited in Ps 69:25a.[40] Peter, applying this text to Judas in Acts 1:20, phrases it as γενηθήτω ἡ ἔπαυλις αὐτοῦ ἔρημος ("Let his homestead be made desolate").[41] Luke's parenthetical comments in Acts 1:18–19 alert the reader to the literal fulfillment of this judgment for Judas, when he relates that Judas's "field" became known as

---

109:4–5 to support this statement. The notion that David's persecutors were *false-friends* stems from the repeat expression תַּחַת־אַהֲבָתִי ("in return for my love") in 109:4a, 5b. Belcher writes that "Psalm 109 arises out of a situation of great betrayal where the psalmist is mistreated, deceived, and lied about." Belcher, *The Messiah and the Psalms*, 78; see also, 77n48, 80–81. Belcher argues that David's friendship and covenant language (cf. Ps 109:4a, 21, 26) suggests that "the one who has betrayed David is a member of the covenant community." Ibid., 80. Cf. Dupont, who avers that the context of a disloyal friend in Ps 109 made for easy application of the verse to Judas in Acts 1:20. Dupont, "L'interprétation des Psaumes," 300.

37 If, however, David's enemies in the context of Ps 109 were false-friends who betrayed him, then it would seem logical that Peter would be connecting the betrayal of David's enemies with the betrayal of Judas in his quotation of Ps 109:8 in Acts 1:20.

38 Luke also recalls for the reader Judas's betrayal, when he describes it as "wickedness" in his parenthetical note in Acts 1:18.

39 Cf. Calvin, *Acts 1–13*, 42. See also the discussion above.

40 For a discussion of this verse, see the summary of Ps 69:25 in its OT context above in this section.

41 On the change to the singular "his" to personalize Ps 69:25 to Judas, see the discussion above. The term ἡ ἔπαυλις refers to "property that serves as a dwelling place whether personally owned or by contract, to a farm, homestead, residence." BDAG, s.v. "ἔπαυλις." This is the same term the LXX uses to translate the Hebrew טִירָה. The adjective ἔρημος, when modifying a place, means "isolated/unfrequented/abandoned/empty/desolate." BDAG, s.v. "ἔρημος."

the "Field of Blood." [42] This fulfills the curse of Ps 69:25a because "der Blutacker bleibt unbewohnbar für die Lebenden." [43]

Consequently, the punishment David requested for his enemies falls upon Judas: the piece of land associated with him became an empty, desolate ground upon which no one lived. [44]

Second, David curses not only his enemies' habitation but also their very lives. He prays that they and their families might perish (Pss 69:25b; 109:8b). The quotation of these two verses in Acts 1:20 points to this grave fate as the punishment Judas was to suffer. [45] That Judas experienced this punishment is verified in Acts 1:18, where Luke depicts Judas's gruesome death. [46]

The final imprecation David directs against his enemy is for someone to replace him in his office (Ps 109:8). Peter renders this in Acts 1:20 as τὴν ἐπισκοπὴν αὐτοῦ λαβέτω ἕτερος ("Let another man take his office"). The term τὴν ἐπισκοπὴν refers to a "position of responsibility" and points to Judas's position as an apostle. [47] As David's persecutor was one in a leadership position,

---

42 The term χωρίον in Acts 1:18 refers to a "place/piece of land/field." BDAG, s.v. "χωρίον." The chief priests apparently bought a field in Judas's name with his betrayal money (cf. Matt 27:3–8), thus, associating legal ownership of the field to Judas. See Bruce, *The Acts of the Apostles*, 109; Longenecker, "The Acts of the Apostles," 263. Since the term ἡ ἔπαυλις in Acts 1:20 refers to a "dwelling place," the chief priests may have bought a piece of land that had a building on it. Cf. Johnson, *Acts*, 36. The reader learns that Judas's property was indeed cursed, since it was publicly known as "The Field of Blood" (Acts 1:19; for explanations of the name "Field of Blood," see e.g., French L. Arrington, *The Acts of the Apostles: An Introduction and Commentary* [Peabody: Hendrickson, 1988], 14; Marshall, *Acts*, 69; Peterson, *Acts*, 124). Cf. William J. Larkin, Jr., *Acts*, IVPNTCS (Downers Grove: InterVarsity, 1995), 45–46. Cf. Matthew 27:7, where Matthew explains that the field the chief priests purchased became a burial ground for strangers.

43 Dormeyer and Galindo, *Die Apostelgeschichte*, 38. ". . . the blood field remains uninhabitable for the living" (my translation).

44 Cf. Marshall, *Acts*, 70.

45 Peter's citation of Ps 69:25b reads καὶ μὴ ἔστω ὁ κατοικῶν ἐν αὐτῇ ("And let no one dwell in it"). The modification from the MT and LXX's reading of "in their tents" to Luke's reading of "in it" is just a "simplified rendering of the passage." Bock, *Acts*, 86. To ask that no one dwell in Judas's property is a way of requesting his death. Also, it is important to realize that the curse of Ps 109:8 ("Let another man take his office") implies the loss of physical life as well. Contra Alfons Weiser, who states that "das Zitat selbst hat nichts mit dem Tod des Judas zu tun" ("the quotation itself has nothing to do with the death of Judas" [my translation]). Alfons Weiser, *Die Apostelgeschichte: Kapitel 1–12*, Ökumenischer Taschenbuchkommentar zum Neuen Testament 5.1 (Gütersloh: Gütersloher Verlagshaus Mohn, 1981), 65. This interpretation, however, ignores the Hebrew parallelism of the Ps 109:8a–b. For Judas to be replaced in his office (Ps 109:8b) is first of all a request for his death, which Ps 109:8a makes clear ("Let his days be few"). See the summary of Ps 109:8 above in this section.

46 Also, it is to be noted from Acts 1:25 that Judas went to his own "place," which "in this case the term most likely refers to a place of punishment after death." B. J. Oropeza, "Judas' Death and Final Destiny in the Gospels and Earliest Christian Writings," *Neotestamenica* 44.2 (2010): 352–353. So, Judas's judgment is far greater than just physical death, seeing that it also includes eternal death.

47 BDAG, s.v. "ἐπισκοπή." Τὴν ἐπισκοπὴν accurately translates the meaning of the Hebrew word פְּקֻדָּתוֹ ("office") in Ps 109:8 and is also the same word the LXX uses in its translation.

so the persecutor of Jesus occupies a prominent office, namely, an apostleship. Furthermore, as David prayed for his persecutor to be replaced in his office, so God replaces Judas with Matthias (Acts 1:21–26).[48] In sum, Judas experiences the judgments David described for his own enemies in Psalms 69:25 and 109:8, which indicates that David's curses in these instances were viewed by Peter as a pattern for what Judas was to suffer.

The David-Jesus Typology: The Element of Prophecy

The correspondence between David and Jesus show that typology undergirds Peter's application of Psalms 69:25 and 109:8 to Jesus' betrayal by Judas. In addition, Peter ascribes a prophetic force to the David typology.[49] The textual evidence that supports this kind of prophetic understanding of the David typology includes the use of (1) δεῖ, (2) fulfillment language, and (3) προεῖπεν ... περὶ Ἰούδα.

In Acts 1:15–26, Peter twice uses δεῖ: the imperfect ἔδει in Acts 1:16 and the present δεῖ in 1:21. This is important because it casts the David typology established by Psalms 69:25 and 109:8 as necessarily bound to happen, for δεῖ carries the basic meaning of "to be under necessity of happening."[50] In many of its NT occurrences, particularly in Luke's writings, that which is "necessary" is theological in nature and actually reveals God's will or plans.[51] Charles H. Cosgrove's study of δεῖ in Luke-Acts points out that Luke often uses the term in conjunction with Scripture to emphasize its prophetic nature:[52] "Δεῖ

---

48 On the nature of the punishment David prays in Ps 109:8 as it relates to Judas in Acts 1:20, Calvin argues: "Indeed this [i.e., replacement by a successor] increases the gravity of the punishment, that the office which was taken from the man who was unworthy is given to another. . . . So after wishing that the wicked man may be deprived of his life, he adds that he should be robbed of his honour; not only so, but that another should succeed, thereby doubling the punishment . . ." Calvin, *Acts 1–13*, 43.

49 See Bock, *Acts*, 85–86; Miura, *David in Luke-Acts*, 160; Calvin, *Acts 1–13*, 40–43; Delitzsch, *Psalms*, 2:277; 3:177. Dormeyer and Galindo also appear to understand a prophetic function of the Scriptures in this passage because "die Schriftzitate fügen den unbegreiflichen Verrat mit seinen Folgen in den Heilsplan Gottes ein" ("the Scripture quotations add the incomprehensible betrayal with its consequences in the plan of God") [my translation]. Dormeyer and Galindo, *Die Apostelgeschichte*, 38. Cf. F. F. Bruce, who does not use prophetic typology terminology but seems to come close to the concept. F. F. Bruce, *The Book of Acts*, rev. ed., NICNT (Grand Rapids: Eerdmans, 1988), 44–45. Contra Johnson, who classifies Peter's use of these psalms as a case of pure prophecy and fulfillment. Johnson, *Acts*, 35. Contra also Kellum, who thinks with regards to Ps 109:8 "[i]t is best to understand that Peter made an analogy in the face of God's judgement rather than a promise-fullment pattern." Kellum, *Acts*, 25.

50 BDAG, s.v. "δεῖ."

51 Walter Grundmann, "δεῖ," *TDNT* 2:21–25.

52 Cosgrove, "The Divine ΔΕΙ in Luke-Acts," 173–174. He adds, "Furthermore, a number of other texts fall within the purview of these Scripturally-grounded 'musts' according to content. Specifically, there are eleven references to the necessity of Jesus' passion in Luke-Acts. Four of these are explicitly linked to Scripture prophecy, with the result that the set of passion musts

is therefore a typical Lukan vehicle for describing the necessity that God's plan, as expressed in Scripture, be fulfilled."[53] According to Bock, Luke "underscores divine design" with δεῖ, particularly in regard to the necessity of Jesus' sufferings in relation to OT Scripture.[54] Importantly, then, the stress that δεῖ places on "necessity" underlines an inherent predictive quality in the OT texts to which it is applied; they are ultimately being shown to express the fulfillment of God's predetermined plan.[55] When Peter uses δεῖ in Acts 1:16–22, he does so in the context of referencing Scripture.[56] Peter uses the imperfect tense in the initial clause of his speech: ἄνδρες ἀδελφοί, ἔδει πληρωθῆναι τὴν γραφήν ("Brethren, the Scripture had to be fulfilled . . ."). Syntactically, the infinitive phrase πληρωθῆναι τὴν γραφήν serves as the subject of the verb ἔδει (lit. "To fulfill the Scripture was necessary").[57] In that ἔδει communicates that the fulfillment of the Scripture had to occur (i.e., divine necessity), this verb inherently indicates a prophetic view of the Scripture about which Peter is speaking.[58] The subsequent relative clause ἣν προεῖπεν τὸ πνεῦμα τὸ

as a whole is Scripturally grounded." Ibid. 174. Cf. Lk 9:22; 13:33; 17:25; 22:37; 24:7; 24:26; 24:44, 46; Acts 1:16, 21; 17:3; 26:22–23.

53 Ibid., 174.
54 Bock, *Luke and Acts*, 140.
55 Cf. Haenchen, who explains: "In Luke δεῖ implies that God wills something and that it therefore must happen. Such instances of the divine will can be recognized from the fact that they are prophetically expressed by the Spirit in holy scripture." Haenchen, *Acts*, 159n8.
Cosgrove summarizes: "The term δεῖ is not a *terminus technicus* in Luke-Acts but carries a wide range of meaning. There is, however, within this circle of broad usage a motif of the divine 'must' that is crucially important to Luke. . . . First, this divine δεῖ points back to God's ancient plan (the βουλή τοῦ θεοῦ) and so grounds the kerygmatic history in divine sanction. That plan is expressed fundamentally in Old Testament prophecy, hence the δεῖ of Scripture proof." Cosgrove, "The Divine ΔΕΙ in Luke-Acts," 189. See also Johnson, *Acts*, 35; Peterson, *Acts*, 122–123, 122n84; Polhill, *Acts*, 91.
56 Peter's use of the divine δεῖ in Acts 1:16, 21 recalls Jesus' use of the same term in Luke 24:44, where he refers to the scriptural necessity of his sufferings. So Tannehill, *Luke-Acts*, 2:20.
57 Impersonal verbs such as δεῖ commonly have an infinitive or infinitive phrase as their subject. See C. F. D. Moule, *An Idiom Book of New Testament Greek*, 2nd ed. (Cambridge: Cambridge University Press, 1959), 27; Stanley E. Porter, *Idioms of the Greek New Testament*, 2nd ed., Biblical Languages: Greek 2 (London: Sheffield Academic Press, 1999), 77–78; 195. While the infinitive phrase acts as the true subject in the clause, the accusative τὴν γραφήν stands as the direct object of πληρωθῆναι.
58 Some debate exists as to what passage(s) τὴν γραφήν ("the Scripture") in Acts 1:16 refers exactly. Dupont observes this issue and identifies four possibilities. He writes, "La question se pose de savoir si «l'Écriture» du v. 16 vise la première de ces citations, ou la seconde, ou les deux prises ensemble, ou bien encore une autre Écriture. Ces quatre hypothèses ont chacune leurs partisans" ("The question arises as to whether the 'Scripture' of v. 16 refers to the first of these quotations [Ps 69:25], or the second [Ps 109:8], or the two taken together, or to another Scripture. These four hypotheses each have their supporters." [my translation]). Dupont, "La destinée de Judas," 309. Of these four possibilities Dupont discusses, contemporary NT scholarship consistently argues for either the first or third option identified by Dupont. See Yuzuru Miura, *David in Luke-Acts: His Portrayal in the Light of Early Judaism*, WUNT 2, Reihe 232 (Tübingen: Mohr Siebeck, 2007), 155n71. Accordingly, τὴν γραφήν in Acts 1:16 refers only to Ps

ἅγιον διὰ στόματος Δαυὶδ ("which the Holy Spirit foretold by the mouth of David") modifies τὴν γραφὴν ("the Scripture"), attributing it to David. This reference to David looks forward to the reference to ἐν βίβλῳ ψαλμῶν ("in the book of Psalms") in 1:20,[59] a verse which begins with the introductory phrase γέγραπται γάρ ("for it is written"). This explanatory γάρ ("for") connects back to 1:16. Thus Pss 69:25 and 109:8 are the specific Scriptures spoken through David that had to be fulfilled concerning Judas.[60] ἔδει, then, informs the reader that these Psalms texts in some way predicted future NT events related to Christ.[61] Thus OT texts relaying experiences of suffering in David's life at the

---

69:25 in Acts 1:20a (see e.g., Dupont, "La destinée de Judas," 315–319; Johnson, *Acts*, 35; Pesch, *Die Apostelgeschichte*, 1:87; Polhill, *Acts*, 91) or to both Pss 69:25; 109:8 in Acts 1:20a–b (see e.g. Alexander, *Acts*, 24; Marshall, "Acts," 529; Miura, *David in Luke-Acts*, 155; Williams, *Acts*, 32). The latter option seems preferable since both quotations, as shown in the typology section above, establish overlapping correspondences between David's and Jesus' situations to show the Scriptural basis of Judas's betrayal and Jesus' suffering and death. Those who disagree with this option usually raise two objections. First, it is argued that the singular τὴν γραφὴν indicates a single passage is in view, and, thus, refers only to the first quotation in Acts 1:20a. This objection, however, ignores that the singular γραφή can bear a collective sense (cf. BDAG, s.v. "γραφή.") and may refer to more than a single passage (cf. e.g., Mk 12:10; Lk 4:21). See Alexander, *Acts*, 24. Second, others (see e.g., Polhill, *Acts*, 91) contend that since Peter uses the imperfect ἔδει ("it was necessary") in Acts 1:16, the past tense must connect to Ps 69:25 because it is the only quotation that has already been fulfilled. Furthermore, since Ps 109:8 justifies the replacement of Judas and remains unfilled at this point in the narrative, this explains why Peter uses the present tense δεῖ ("it is necessary") in Acts 1:21 to stress the prophetic necessity for selecting Judas's successor. While this argument has its strengths, it ignores an important point. Specifically, it is possible for Peter to use ἔδει in Acts 1:16 to indicate that both texts have already been fulfilled in a sense, when one understands that Peter could have still considered Ps 109:8 to possess one element of typological correspondence that remained unfulfilled. Cf. Tzvi Novick, who argues that ἔδει in this instance could mean "that some element of the cited Scripture was fulfilled," while implying another element awaits fulfillment. Tzvi Novick, "Succeeding Judas: Exegesis in Acts 1:15–26," *JBL* 129 (2010): 799.

59 Alexander, *Acts*, 24, 29; Wilcox, "The Judas-Tradition," 444.

60 Soards rightly explains, "The introductory phrase γέγραπται γάρ ("for it is written") relates to v. 16, which provides an explanation, as the γάρ ("for") indicates." Soards, *The Speeches in Acts*, 28. See also, Barclay M. Newman and Eugene A. Nida, *A Handbook on the Acts of the Apostles*, Helps for Translators (New York: United Bible Societies, 1972), 28. The distance between Acts 1:16 and 1:20 raises questions on the connection between these two verses and their "natural flow of thought." Wilcox, "The Judas-Tradition," 444; see also, 442. The γάρ most logically connects these verses together, however. And, the distance is not as great as it seems. I. Howard Marshall reminds that "the long gap before the actual quotation is due to the way in which verses 18–19 have been inserted as a parenthesis which does not form part of Peter's speech." Marshall, *Acts*, 69.

61 The imperfect tense of ἔδει places the fulfillment of the Scripture in Acts 1:16 in past time. Cf. Newman and Nida, *Acts*, 25. An important question, then, is "what does Peter understand as having already been fulfilled 'concerning Judas' with regards to Pss 69:25; 109:8?" The answer to this question must consider carefully how the quotations contribute to the typological correspondences discussed in the typology section above. In that section, it was shown that both quotations converge to provide a Scriptural basis for (1) Jesus' sufferings, (2) Judas's role as Jesus' persecutor, which implies his betrayal, and (3) the curses upon Judas's property and life. Since Ps 109:8 speaks of both Judas's death and his replacement with a successor, the latter

hands of his enemies constitute a prophetic foreshadowing of what Jesus had to suffer from Judas and also foreshadow the judgment Judas would suffer.

As for the present tense δεῖ ("it is necessary") that Peter uses in Acts 1:21, the inferential οὖν ("therefore") shows that the contents of 1:21–26 connect back to Ps 109:8 in 1:20.[62] Peter understands Ps 109:8 to point "to another person assuming his [Judas's] place of leadership,"[63] and thus Ps 109:8 possesses a predictive element not yet fulfilled.[64] By acting to replace Judas with a successor on Scriptural grounds, the δεῖ in 1:21 provides an example where "prophecy functions as a divine mandate in Luke-Acts."[65] The prediction is typological, meaning that the curse against David's enemy provided a predictive outline for the judgment God intended Judas, Jesus' enemy, to experience as a consequence of his defection.

In addition to δεῖ, Peter's language of fulfillment in Acts 1:16 also indicates that the David typology is predictive in nature.[66] He employs the infinitive phrase πληρωθῆναι[67] ιτὴν γραφὴν ("to fulfill the Scripture"); the accusative τὴν

---

typological element remains to be fulfilled. So, some elements of Ps 109:8 have been fulfilled, while one element (i.e., appointing Judas's successor) still awaits fulfillment. This understanding of Ps 109:8 explains how Peter can speak of both its past fulfillment (i.e., ἔδει) in Acts 1:16 and also its need for present fulfillment (i.e., δεῖ) in 1:21. Contra David R. Bauer, who discusses Peter's citation of Ps 109:8 only in terms of the future fulfilment "which the community is to embrace through obedient action." David R. Bauer, *The Book of Acts as Story: A Narrative Critical Study* (Grand Rapids: Baker Academic, 2021), 78.

62 Cf. Haenchen, *Acts*, 161.

63 Polhill, *Acts*, 91. Essentially, Peter understands Ps 109:8 to be a typological prophecy that Judas must be replaced. So, he leads the group to fulfill this prophetic mandate to find the one God has chosen (Acts 1:24) to occupy Judas's place. One notices that Peter's quotation of Ps 109:8 contains the imperative λαβέτω ("let another take"), while the LXX uses the optative form of the verb ("may another take") and the MT uses the jussive יִקַּח אַחֵר ("let another take"). If Luke drew his translation from the LXX, G. J. Steyn explains the change and its implications as follows: "'n Uitstaande kenmerk hier is die verandering van die optatief na die imperatief. Dit verbind nie net die gesiteerde teks met die voorafgaande een nie, maar vervul ook die funksie van 'n goddelike bevel" ("A prominent feature here is the change from the optative to the imperative. It connects not only the quoted text with the previous one, but also fulfills the function of a divine command" [my translation]). Steyn, "LXX-Sitate," 132. On the other hand, the change to the imperative may simply represent Luke's way of laying stress upon Peter's clear understanding of the prophetic nature of the text, whether based off the MT or the LXX.

64 On this, see the discussion of ἔδει and δεῖ above in this chapter.

65 Cosgrove, "The Divine ΔΕΙ in Luke-Acts," 174. Cf. Jack T. Sanders, who contends that Luke interprets God's expression of "the divine will" from Scripture to be "prophetic." Jack T. Sanders, "The Prophetic Use of the Scriptures in Luke-Acts," in *Early Jewsih and Christian Exegesis: Studies in Memory of William Hugh Brownlee*, ed. Craig A. Evans and William F. Stinespring, SPHS (Atlanta: Scholars Press, 1987), 193.

66 See the section "Fulfillment Language" in chapter 3 of this work. Also see the discussion of fulfillment language in each analysis of the quotations from Psalms in John in chapter 4 of this work.

67 For Luke's use of πληρόω in connection to the fulfillment of OT Scripture, cf. Luke 4:21; 24:44; Acts 1:16; 3:18; 13:27, 33 (here ἐκπληρόω). Cf. also Luke 18:31; 22:37; Acts 13:29, where Luke

γραφὴν is the direct object of πληρωθῆναι. This identifies the Scripture as what must be fulfilled. "The Scripture" refers to Psalms 69:25 and 109:8 cited in Acts 1:20, and the fulfillment language shows that God was using these Psalms texts to give advance notice of the similar but greater events of suffering Jesus must experience.[68] A third and final indicator that Peter conceived of the typology as fundamentally prophetic stems from his use of the verb προεῖπεν ("foretold") in Acts 1:16. προλέγω means "to say someth[ing] in advance of an event, tell beforehand,"[69] generally denoting a prediction.[70] προεῖπεν in Acts 1:16, according to Samuel Amsler, points to the prophetic quality of Scripture in Acts. Amsler states, "Or ce qui caractérise le témoignage de l'Ecriture par rapport à celui des apôtres, c'est qu'il a été *prononcé à l'avance*."[71]

Προεῖπεν appears in the relative clause ἣν προεῖπεν τὸ πνεῦμα τὸ ἅγιον διὰ στόματος Δαυὶδ περὶ Ἰούδα τοῦ γενομένου ὁδηγοῦ τοῖς συλλαβοῦσιν Ἰησοῦν ("which the Holy Spirit foretold by the mouth of David concerning Judas, who became a guide to those who arrested Jesus"). This relative clause modifies τὴν γραφὴν ("the Scripture") and functions adjectively, describing the Psalms texts Peter has in mind. First, τὸ πνεῦμα τὸ ἅγιον ("the Holy Spirit") is the subject of προεῖπεν, and thus the Holy Spirit—the ultimate author of these Psalms texts according to Peter—is seen as the one foretelling or predicting something.[72] David, as the prepositional phrase διὰ στόματος Δαυὶδ ("by the mouth of David") indicates, was the means or instrument the Spirit used to make his prophecy.[73] περὶ Ἰούδα ("concerning Judas") gives the specific sub-

---

expresses fulfillment with the interchangeable term τελέω. Cf. Mogens Müller, "The Reception of the Old Testament in Matthew and Luke-Acts: From Interpretation to Proof from Scripture," *NovT* 43 (2001): 323.

68 Note that πληρωθῆναι ("to fulfill") is in the passive voice. Here, this use of the passive voice is known as a divine passive, which identifies God as the agent acting to bring about the Scripture's fulfillment. So, it is correct to say that God brought Pss 69:25;109:8 to their fulfillments or goals.

69 BDAG, s.v. "προλέγω." A second definition BDAG supplies is "to say/express someth[ing] at a point of time that is prior to another point of time, state beforehand/earlier." Ibid. On this latter sense, cf. 2 Cor 7:3; 13:2 [twice]; Gal 1:9; 5:21 [twice]; 1 Thess 3:4; 4:6; Heb 4:7. Of the fifteen occurrences of προλέγω in the NT, several instances of what is said in advance clearly refers to a prediction (cf. Matt 24:25; Mark 13:23; Acts 1:16; Rom 9:29; 2 Pet 3:2; Jude 1:17).

70 Cf. Thayer's, s.v. "προλέγω," where the definition "to predict" is supplied.

71 Amsler, *L'Ancien Testament Dans L'Église*, 66. "But what characterizes the testimony of Scripture in relation to that of the apostles is that it was *pronounced* in *advance*" (my translation). Along with Acts 1:16, Amsler also cites Acts 3:18 in its use of προκατήγγειλεν and Acts 7:52 in its use of προκαταγγείλαντας. Ibid. See also Müller, "Reception of the Old Testament," 324.

72 Bruce rightly sees this reference to the Holy Spirit as an express indication of the inspiration of OT Scripture. Bruce, *The Acts of the Apostles*, 108–109. See also, Peter Stuhlmacher, *Vom Verstehen des Neuen Testament: Eine Hermeneutik*, 2nd ed., GNT 6 (Göttingen: Vandenhoeck & Ruprecht, 1986), 53.

73 The prepositional phrase διὰ στόματος Δαυὶδ modifies προεῖπεν, indicating that David was the means or instrument used to accomplish the verbal action. Cf. Moule, *Idiom Book*,

ject matter concerning which the Holy Spirit prophesied:[74] the prophecy was about Judas's betrayal and Jesus' resulting suffering and death.[75]

Thus Peter, by claiming the Holy Spirit "predicted" (in Pss 69:25 and 109:8) what was to happen "concerning Judas," regards these as prophecies. What must be noted in classifying them as prophecies is the form the prophecies take: they appear in event-based Psalms texts, which properly classifies them as typological prophecies. Essentially, Acts 1:16 communicates that the Spirit guided David to speak about his own enemies as notice of Judas's role as Jesus' betrayer.

Ps 16:8–11 in Acts 2:25–28

In Acts 2:25–28, Peter cites a psalm passage which also highlights David-Jesus typology. Peter introduces the passage in Acts 2:25 with the formula Δαυὶδ γὰρ λέγει εἰς αὐτόν ("For, David says of Him"), identifying David as the author of the quotation he cites (cf. 2:30–31). The conjunction γάρ ("for") formally connects the quotation with the preceding verses that speak of Jesus death and resurrection (Acts 2:23–24). εἰς αὐτόν ("of Him") indicates that what David said in the quotation had reference to "Jesus the Nazarene" in some way (2:22).

Acts 2:25–28 is a direct quotation of Ps 16:8–11b (= Ps 16:8–11/MT and Ps 15:8–11/LXX). A comparative analysis of Peter's quotation with the both the MT and LXX reveals how closely it corresponds with both texts.

Acts 2:25–28	προορώμην τὸν κύριον ἐνώπιόν μου διὰ παντός, ὅτι ἐκ δεξιῶν μού ἐστιν ἵνα μὴ σαλευθῶ. διὰ τοῦτο ηὐφράνθη ἡ καρδία μου καὶ ἠγαλλιάσατο ἡ γλῶσσά μου, ἔτι δὲ καὶ ἡ σάρξ μου κατασκηνώσει ἐπ' ἐλπίδι, ὅτι οὐκ ἐγκαταλείψεις τὴν ψυχήν μου εἰς ᾅδην οὐδὲ δώσεις τὸν ὅσιόν σου ἰδεῖν διαφθοράν. ἐγνώρισάς μοι ὁδοὺς ζωῆς, πληρώσεις με εὐφροσύνης μετὰ τοῦ προσώπου σου.
	"I saw the Lord always in my presence, for he is at my right hand, so that I will not be shaken. Therefore my heart was glad, and my tongue exulted; moreover my flesh also will live in hope; because you will not abandon my soul to hades, nor allow your holy one to undergo decay. You have made known to me the ways of life; you will make me full of gladness with your presence."

56–57. Cf. Luke 1:70; Acts 3:18, 21; 4:25; 15:7, where Luke uses "mouth" with a similar instrumental sense.

74 Alexander, *Acts*, 24–25.

75 Peter clarifies that the Holy Spirit spoke in advance "concerning Judas" and further specifies with the adjectival participial clause "who became a guide to those who arrested Jesus" that it was Judas's betrayal and Jesus' suffering which he foretold in the quotations.

MT Ps 16:8–11	שִׁוִּיתִי יְהוָה לְנֶגְדִּי תָמִיד כִּי מִימִינִי בַּל־אֶמּוֹט: לָכֵן שָׂמַח לִבִּי וַיָּגֶל כְּבוֹדִי אַף־בְּשָׂרִי יִשְׁכֹּן לָבֶטַח: כִּי לֹא־תַעֲזֹב נַפְשִׁי לִשְׁאוֹל לֹא־תִתֵּן חֲסִידְךָ לִרְאוֹת שָׁחַת: תּוֹדִיעֵנִי אֹרַח חַיִּים שֹׂבַע שְׂמָחוֹת אֶת־פָּנֶיךָ נְעִמוֹת בִּימִינְךָ נֶצַח:
	"I have set the Lord continually before me; Because he is at my right hand, I will not be shaken. Therefore my heart is glad and my glory rejoices; My flesh also will dwell securely. For you will not abandon my soul to Sheol; Nor will you allow your holy one to undergo decay. You will make known to me the path of life; In your presence is fullness of joy; In your right hand there are pleasures forever."
LXX Ps 15:8–11	προωρώμην τὸν κύριον ἐνώπιόν μου διὰ παντός ὅτι ἐκ δεξιῶν μού ἐστιν ἵνα μὴ σαλευθῶ. διὰ τοῦτο ηὐφράνθη ἡ καρδία μου καὶ ἠγαλλιάσατο ἡ γλῶσσά μου ἔτι δὲ καὶ ἡ σάρξ μου κατασκηνώσει ἐπ' ἐλπίδι, ὅτι οὐκ ἐγκαταλείψεις τὴν ψυχήν μου εἰς ᾅδην οὐδὲ δώσεις τὸν ὅσιόν σου ἰδεῖν διαφθοράν. ἐγνώρισάς μοι ὁδοὺς ζωῆς πληρώσεις με εὐφροσύνης μετὰ τοῦ προσώπου σου τερπνότητες ἐν τῇ δεξιᾷ σου εἰς τέλος
	"I saw the Lord always before me, for he is at my right hand that I may not be shaken. Therefore my heart was glad, and my tongue rejoiced; moreover my flesh also will live in hope. For you will not abandon my soul to Hades, nor allow your holy one to see corruption. You have made known to me the ways of life; you will make me full of joy with your presence; at your right hand are pleasures forever."

Except for its omission of Ps 16:11c ("at your right hand are pleasures forever"), the quotation of Ps 16:8–11 in Acts 2:25–28 agrees verbatim with the LXX translation.[76] Furthermore, while A. Schmitt identifies several differences between the LXX and MT,[77] these differences are mostly stylistic and consistent with the original sense of the MT.[78]

---

76 Martin Rese points out, as do the many scholars, "Fast keine Probleme bietet der Text des Zitats; er stimmt bis auf Kleinigkeiten wörtlich mit der LXX überein." ("Almost no problems are offered by the text of the quote; except for small things, it literally agrees with the LXX" [my translation].) Martin Rese, "Die Funktion der alttestamentlichen Zitate und Anspielungen in den Reden der Apostelgeschichte," in *Les Actes des Apôtres: Traditions, rédaction, théologie*, ed. J. Kremer, BETL, no. 48 (Leuven: Leuven University Press, 1979), 73. So also e.g., Bock, *Proclamation*, 172; Doble, "Psalms," 91; Dormeyer and Galindo, *Die Apostelgeschichte*, 51; Marshall, "Acts," 537; Miura, *David in Luke-Acts*, 140; A. Schmitt, "Ps 16, 8–11 als Zeugnis der Auferstehung in der Apg.," *BZ* 17 (1973): 243.

77 Schmitt, "Ps 16, 8–11," 232–243.

78 Bock provides a substantive analysis of each of Schmitt's six noted differences in the LXX's translation of the MT. He demonstrates convincingly that in each instance the concep-

THE DAVID-JESUS TYPOLOGY: THE ELEMENT OF CORRESPONDENCE

Again, David typology is the best way to understand how the quotation of Ps 16:8–11 applies to Jesus in Acts 2:25–28.[79] Psalm 16 is a psalm written by David, as לְדָוִד indicates.[80] Scholars tend to categorize Psalm 16 as a psalm of confidence/trust.[81] The psalm's eleven verses can be organized into three sections: (1) 16:1–4, (2) 16:5–7, and (3) 16:8–11.[82] While the psalm does not supply enough detail to ascertain a precise historical background, the general message of Psalm 16 is clear: David "exemplifies a deep trust in the Lord in both life and death."[83] In Ps 16:1–4, David asks for protection and confesses his trust in God and then transitions to praise in 16:5–7. Having stated his trust in God in the present (16:1–7), David concludes by stating his trust in God for the future in 16:8–11.[84] Psalm 16 builds to these verses (8–11), in which

---

tual point of the MT remains intact. While the LXX may represent an idea more vividly or concretely with some of its changes, it still accurately reflects the understanding inherent to the Hebrew. The LXX changes are mostly stylistic in nature, and, importantly, it can be argued that in each instance there is equivalence of meaning with the MT. Bock, *Proclamation*, 172–177. Cf. Walter C. Kaiser, *The Uses of the Old Testament in the New* (Chicago: Moody Press, 1985), 40; see also 36–40. See also, Trull, "Peter's Interpretation," 435; Peterson, *Acts*, 148n64.

79 Contra Youngmo Cho and Hyung Dae Park, who write, "... Peter is certain that this particular psalm should be read messianically. Under the inspiration of the Spirit, Peter explains that David in this song was not speaking about himself but was prophesying about his later descendent, the Messiah." Youngmo Cho and Hyung Dae Park, *Acts—Part One: Introduction and Chapters 1–12*, NCCS (Eugene, OR: Cascade Books, 2019), 60. Keener discusses Ps 16:8–11 in Acts 2 applying to Jesus "par excellence" on the basis of the righteous sufferer theme common to various psalms. Keener, *Acts*, 157. Kellum recognizes that some scholars understand Ps 16:8–11 to function typologically in Acts 2. But, he agrees with Marshall that "it is unlikely that typology exists where the pattern (not seeing decay) is not true of the 'type' (David)." Kellum, *Acts*, 38. But, the discussion that follows shows that what David says in Ps 16:8–11 can be understood to be true not only of himself but also ultimately of Jesus, thus, establishing typology as the most likely way the passage applies to Jesus.

80 On the Davidic authorship understanding of לְדָוִד in superscripts in Psalms, see the section "The David-Jesus Typology: The Element of Correspondence" in the analysis of John 13:18 in chapter 4 of this work. David's authorship of Ps 16 is not in dispute, for Peter explicitly identifies David as the author in Acts 2:25–31.

81 So e.g., Anderson, *Psalms*, 1:140; Craig C. Broyles, *Psalms*, ed. Robert L. Hubbard Jr. and Robert K. Johnston, NIBC (Peabody: Hendrickson, 1999), 96; Bullock, *Psalms*, 170; Craigie, *Psalms 1–50*, 155–156; Mark D. Futato, *Interpreting the Psalms: An Exegetical Handbook*, ed. David M. Howard Jr., Handbooks for Old Testament Exegesis (Grand Rapids: Kregel Publications, 2007), 161–162; Grogan, *Psalms*, 62; Ross, *Psalms*, 1:399–400. Psalms of confidence "express a deep confidence in God and his goodness." Bullock, *Psalms*, 166. While other psalm types may express trust in God, "the sentiment of trust dominates a few psalms and singles them out as special expressions of confidence in God." Ibid.

82 Ross, *Psalms*, 1:401.

83 VanGemeren, "Psalms," 153.

84 Trull observes that Ps 16 moves towards a climax from beginning to end. Accordingly, Ps 16:1–6 focuses on David's *present* relationship with the Lord, while Ps 16:8–11 concerns his *future*. Psalm 16:7 serves as a transitional verse in this progression. Gregory V. Trull, "An Exegesis

David's trust in God extends beyond the grave, revealing his hope in a future resurrection and eternal life.[85] In 16:8, David declares his confidence in God's protection because of God's faithful presence with him.[86] His confidence in the protection of God leads him to a "climactic conclusion" in verses 9–11,[87] in which David concludes that "his whole being shall enjoy security" (16:9):[88] both the security of his immaterial, spiritual person (16:9a) and of his material, physical body (16:9b).[89] Psalm 16:10 begins with the causal particle כִּי ("because"),[90] supplying the basis of David's confident assertion about the security of his body in 16:9b, "for You will not abandon my soul to Sheol, nor will You allow Your Holy One to undergo decay" (16:10). In the first of these two synonymously parallel lines, God is the subject of the verb לֹא־תַעֲזֹב ("You will not abandon").[91] The object of the verb, נַפְשִׁי ("my soul"), denotes David's person (i.e., "me"),[92] while "to Sheol" (לִשְׁאוֹל)[93] references "the place of the dead, the grave."[94] In the second line (16:10b), David enhances the basic idea

of Psalm 16:10," *BSac* 161 (2004): 305–307. Cf. Léonard Ramaroson, who also observes Ps 16:9–11 marks a shift from the present to the future. Léonard Ramaroson, "Immortalité et Résurrection dans les Psaumes," *ScEs* 36 (1984): 288.

85 Trull, "An Exegesis of Psalm 16:10," 306–307. The repetition of "right hand" (Ps 16:8, 11) signals that Ps 16:8–11 forms a textual unit. Ibid., 306.

86 Calvin, *Psalms*, 4:228; Ross, *Psalms*, 1:408.

87 Waltke, Houston, and Moore, *The Psalms*, 327.

88 Leupold, *Psalms*, 151. Commentators rightly note that Ps 16:9 brings into view David's "whole being" or "whole person," as evidenced by the references to the heart, soul, and body. See e.g., Alexander, *The Psalms*, 1:117; Belcher, *The Messiah and the Psalms*, 163–164; Charles A. Briggs and Emilie G. Briggs, *A Critical and Exegetical Commentary on The Book of Psalms*, ICC (Edinburgh: T. & T. Clark, 1906; repr., Nabu Press), 1:121; Goldingay, *Psalms 1–41*, 1:232; VanGemerem, "Psalms," 159n9.

89 כְּבוֹדִי translates as "my glory" and is understood as a poetic expression for "the inner man, the noblest part of man." BDB, s.v. "כָּבוֹד." The term לִבִּי ("my heart") refers to "man's immaterial personality functions." Andrew Bowling, "לֵב," *TWOT* 1:466. בְּשָׂרִי bears the basic sense of "flesh," which can stand for part of the body or the whole body itself. BDB, s.v. "בָּשָׂר;" *HALOT*, s.v. "בָּשָׂר." Here, in Ps 16:9 the term primarily stands for the "external, material aspect of a human being. It denotes the body's fleshy consistency and the whole exterior form of a living being." Waltke, Houston, and Moore, *The Psalms*, 334.

90 Waltke and O'Connor, *Syntax*, 640.

91 BDB, s.v. "עָזַב."

92 See Bruce K. Waltke, "נֶפֶשׁ," *TWOT* 2:590, which states, "It comes as no surprise, then, that in some contexts *nephesh* is best rendered by 'person,' 'self,' or more simply by the personal pronoun." Both the NIV and RSV translate נַפְשִׁי in Ps 16:10 with the personal pronoun "me." See also Briggs and Briggs, *Psalms*, 1:121; Goldingay, *Psalms 1–41*, 1:233; VanGemeren, "Psalms," 159–160n10.

93 The לְ prefix can be translated as "in" to denote a location or as "to" to signify motion to a location. Waltke and O'Connor, *Syntax*, 205. But, either rendering (i.e., "in" or "to") can denote a location, since they are so close in meaning. Trull, "An Exegesis of Psalm 16:10," 311.

94 VanGemeren, "Psalms," 572. VanGemeren continues, "When the psalmist refers to Sheol, he thinks of the tomb, the place where speaking, laughing, and the praise of God are absent." Ibid. On this general sense of "Sheol" in Ps 16:10, see Belcher, *The Messiah and the Psalms*, 164; Calvin, *Psalms*, 4:230–32; Leupold, *Psalms*, 151; Ross, *Psalms*, 1:267n22; 409; Waltke, Hous-

of the first line.⁹⁵ Again God is the subject of the main verb לֹא־תִתֵּן ("Nor will You allow"). This time the idea is completed by an infinitive construct לִרְאוֹת ("to undergo"), a figurative expression that means "to get to know/to experience something."⁹⁶ The substantival adjective חֲסִידְךָ ("your holy one") is the object of the verb and stands as David's reference to himself as one who is "faithful," "godly," or "pious."⁹⁷ The term the NASB translates as "decay" is שָׁחַת, which refers to the "pit/grave."⁹⁸ Ross explains:

> The word refers to the grave; and calling it a pit may suggest something like a dungeon in *sheol*, i.e., an inescapable region of death. The pit, i.e., the grave, is where the body decays, and so by referring to the pit David probably understood it with all its implications, as the place of death and decay.⁹⁹

So, "the pit" parallels "Sheol" and also bears the connotation of corruption that the grave has on the physical body.¹⁰⁰

---

ton, and Moore, *The Psalms*, 335. For more detailed discussions, see D. K. Stuart, "Sheol," *ISBE* 4:472; R. Laird Harris, "she'ôl," *TWOT* 2:892–893.

95 In synonymous parallelism, the second line (Ps 16:10b) repeats the basic idea of the first line (16:10a) but adds some additional kind of meaning. See Bullock, *Psalms*, 36.

96 *HALOT*, s.v. "רָאה."

97 BDB, s.v. "חָסִיד;" *HALOT*, s.v. "חָסִיד." This substantive use of the adjective denotes the following: "one who is set apart unto the Lord" (Leupold, *Psalms*, 152), "God's servant" (Van-Gemeren, "Psalms," 159–160n10), and "one who is beloved of the LORD, a member of the covenant" (Ross, *Psalms*, 1:410). Some translations capitalize חֲסִידְךָ (i.e., "Holy One;" see e.g., NIV; NASB) in Ps 16:10, seeing it not as referring to David but "to a more specific Holy One—the coming Messiah." Wilson, *Psalms Volume 1*, 313. This does represent a possible interpretation of the term in Ps 16:10. But, it is does not seem to be the most fitting, because "according to the superscript, parallelism, and use of *ḥāsîd* in Psalm 4:3[4], the reference is to David." Waltke, Houston, and Moore, *The Psalms*, 336. Cf. Marshall, "Acts," 538; Ross, *Psalms*, 1:410; Wilson, *Psalms Volume 1*, 313. Both the ESV and RSV translate חֲסִידְךָ in Ps 16:10 in lowercase ("holy one" and "godly one," respectively), viewing David as the referent. In accordance with the Hebrew parallelism of the verse, David's use of חֲסִידְךָ adds additional thought to the previous line. According to Leupold, for death not to reign over a man, "The subjective condition to be met by man finds stronger expression; a man must be one who may be classed as a 'holy one' (AV) or 'godly one,' according to our translation. That means one who is set apart to the Lord." Leupold, *Psalms*, 152. Thus, it seems best to take "holy one" in Ps 16:10 as David's description of himself. With that said, the term חָסִיד may also bear messianic implications, recalling God's covenant promise to David and, thus, his future seed. See Kaiser, *Uses*, 32–41; Trull, "An Exegesis of Psalm 16:10," 313–315. If such a messianic sense is present in the term, this would mean that what David says in regard to himself in Ps 16:10 would allow for his statement easily to transfer also to his future descendent, the Messiah (even if he did not use the term with the Messiah in mind).

98 *HALOT*, s.v. "שָׁחַת."

99 Ross, *Psalms*, 1:410.

100 This additional thought of "corruption" is consistent with the Hebrew parallelism, which repeats but enhances the idea of the first line. Some argue that שַׁחַת can only refer to a physical place (i.e., "pit") and not to a physical experience (i.e., "corruption"). This is due to dis-

Some think Ps 16:10 presents simply "the hope of not dying."[101] While this is possible, the psalm's context, language, and tone suggest it is not merely a declaration of God's protection *from* death (i.e., premature death) but *in* death (i.e., beyond the grave).[102] Accordingly, Ps 16:10 discloses David's expectation of death and burial (as Charles A. Briggs and Emilie G. Briggs state, "He [the poet] expects to die and to go to Sheol"[103]) but also demonstrates that David believes in some kind of "rescue after death."[104]

What kind of rescue after death does David envision here? Probably the

---

agreements on the exact etymology of the term, whether it is derived from one or two verbal roots. Bock, *Proclamation*, 175. But, the term can mean either "pit" or "destruction/corruption," depending on its context. So VanGemeren, "Psalms," 572. In that both the LXX (Ps 15:10) and the NT (Acts 2:27; 13:35) render שַׁחַת in Ps 16:10 with the noun διαφθορά (i.e., "the condition or state of rotting or decaying, destruction, corruption;" BDAG, s.v. "διαφθορά."), this suggests the reference to the place (i.e., "the pit/grave") in Ps 16:10b was understood also to possess a connation to its effects (i.e., "corruption/decay"). Cf. Calvin, *Acts 1–13*, 68; Goldingay, *Psalms 1–41*, 1:233; Kaiser, *Uses*, 35, 40. Or, this suggests that the primary meaning of the term is "corruption." So Trull, "An Exegesis of Psalm 16:10," 315–320; Waltke, Houston, and Moore, *The Psalms*, 323n76, 339. In either case, the use of שַׁחַת in Ps16:10b seems to emphasize the concept of corruption. Cf. Ross, *Psalms*, 1:399n15.

101 Delitzsch, *Psalms*, 1:228. So also, e.g., Anderson, *Psalms*, 1:145–146; Craigie, *Psalms 1–50*, 158; Krodel, *Acts*, 85; Johannes Lindblom, "Erwägungen zu Psalm 16," *VT* 24 (1974): 194; Pesch, *Die Apostelgeschichte*, 1:122; Gustav Stählin, *Die Apostelgeschichte*, NTD 5 (Göttingen: Vandenhoeck & Ruprecht: 1980), 47; Toy, *Quotations in the New Testament*, 100–101; Wilson, *Psalms Volume 1*, 1:313. This view, accordingly, understands both lines of Ps 16:10 to reveal David's confidence that God is going to protect him from an untimely or premature death in his present situation.

102 In terms of context, Geoffrey W. Grogan argues, "Verse 10 may refer to preservation from (premature) death, but clear contextual support for this is lacking as the psalm does not suggest imminent peril of death, and the petition of verse 1 in no way dominates it. It can therefore be read, quite naturally but startlingly, as rescue after death." Grogan, *Psalms*, 63. In terms of tone, David's attitude throughout Psalm 16 is predominantly one of peace and joy, with no sense of fear of an enemy. This overall tone argues against a seeing Ps 16:10 as preservation from premature or sudden death. So Ramaroson, "Immortalité," 289–290. In terms of language, Calvin says, "Moreover, it is to be observed, that David's language is not to be limited to some particular kind of deliverance ... but he entertains the undoubted assurance of eternal salvation, which freed him from all anxiety and fear. It is as if he had said, There will always be ready for me a way of escape from the grave, that I may not remain in corruption." Calvin, *Psalms*, 4:230. Similarly, Belcher rightly points out that "the language of the psalm presses toward an unbroken relationship with the LORD beyond this life.... [T]he idea of not abandoning my soul to Sheol means that God will not leave the psalmist in Sheol, which generally refers to the place of the dead. Certainly this includes more than deliverance from death in this life. There is expressed here a confident hope beyond this life and beyond the grave." Belcher, *The Messiah and the Psalms*, 164. See also, Alexander, *The Psalms*, 1:117–119; Leupold, *Psalms*, 152; Waltke, Houston, and Moore, *The Psalms*, 338–339.

103 Briggs and Briggs, *Psalms*, 1:21.

104 Grogan, *Psalms*, 63. Ross explains: "He found comfort in the fact that in the final analysis God was not going to abandon him to the grave .... David knew, as all the saints have known, that God did not establish a covenant with him and provide for him and guide throughout his life, only to abandon him at the moment of his greatest need, death." Ross, *Psalms*, 1:409.

hope of a future resurrection.[105] The concept of a general bodily resurrection does find expression in the OT,[106] although the clearest texts were written after David lived.[107] Bruce K. Waltke, James M. Houston, and Erika Moore argue that the parallelism of Ps 16:10 suggests the idea of personal resurrection; specifically, the hyperbolic language of Ps 16:10b clarifies the intended sense of 16:10a. They write:

> Possibly David is using hyperbole with reference to his own body in order to imply several truths. First, that he will not see decay entails he envisions himself in the grave, not merely as being delivered from a premature death. (If the Old Testament has no hope beyond the grave, as is often alleged, the Old Testament is an anomaly in ancient Near Eastern religions.) Second, it implies that God raises his body from the grave. If his body goes to the grave and does not decay, then beyond any cavil God must have raised it. Third and correlatively, it implies God's presence with his saint even in the grave.[108]

---

105 See e.g., Kaiser, *Uses*, 35–41; Kidner, *Psalms 1–72*, 103; Trull, "An Exegesis of Psalm 16:10," 320; Waltke, Houston, and Moore, *The Psalms*, 336, 339. Cf. also Ross, who thinks David's words could be understood in terms of individual resurrection but is not certain if David understood that exact notion. Ross, *Psalms*, 1:410n36. See also Trull's substantial list of those who hold to a "personal resurrection" understanding of Ps 16:10. Trull, "An Exegesis of Psalm 16:10," 308n11.

106 See e.g., Isa 26:19; Dan 12:1–2, 13. Admittedly, the OT does not provide a detailed presentation of the doctrine of personal resurrection, but the doctrine does find expression in the OT. See e.g., P. S. Johnston, "Afterlife," *DOTP*, 1–5; M. J. Harris, "Resurrection, General," *NDT*, 581–582; R. Laird Harris, "she'ôl," *TWOT* 2:892–893. Furthermore, concerning Ps 16 speaking of a resurrection from death, Jürgen Roloff states, "In der Tat war das bereits die Meinung des pharisäischen Judentums." ("In fact, this was already the opinion of Pharisaic Judaism," [my translation]). Jürgen Roloff, *Die Apostelgeschichte*, NTD 5 (Göttingen and Zürich: Vandenhoeck & Ruprecht, 1988), 57. On Rabbinic literature which seems to interpret Ps 16:10 in terms of David's hope of resurrection, see Miura, *David in Luke-Acts*, 142–143.

107 Barnabas Lindars admits the more literal meaning of Ps 16:10 could apply "to the expectation of the resurrection of the dead which appears in Dan. 12:2 (cf. Matt. 27.52f.)." Barnabas Lindars, *New Testament Apologetic: The Doctrinal Significance of the Old Testament Quotations* (Philadelphia: The Westminster Press, 1961), 40. Patrick Fairbairn takes this position of Ps 16:10, explaining: "The Psalms, which are so full of the experiences and hopes of David, and other holy men of old, while they express only fear and discomfort in regard to the state after death, not unfrequently point to the resurrection from the dead as the great consummation of desire and expectation: 'My flesh also shall rest in hope: for Thou wilt not leave my soul in hell; neither wilt Thou suffer thine Holy One to see corruption.'" Patrick Fairbairn, *Typology of Scripture: Two Volumes in One*, (Funk and Wagnalls, 1900; repr., Grand Rapids: Kregel, 1989), 1:341.

108 Waltke, Houston, and Moore, *The Psalms*, 336; see also, 339. Ross notes also that David's language in Ps 16:10b seems hyperbolic (i.e., "extravagant" or "excessive"). Ross, *Psalms*, 1:410–411. Cf. Kidner, *Psalms 1–72*, 103. Accordingly, David's use of such hyperbolic language allows him to state emphatically the specific way he believes God will deliver him from the grave (i.e., by resurrection). As hyperbole, David's words allow for the idea of experiencing some kind of *temporary* corruption but just not *eternal* corruption. That is, David's use of hyperbole provides the sense that "he would not experience all that the pit signified." Ross, *Psalms*, 1:410.

In a similar assessment of David's language in Ps 16:10b, Ross avers, "In any case, his words are extravagant for his own experience."[109] These extravagant or hyperbolic words appear to be the way David more forcefully declares his hope of a resurrection, for not being abandoned to the grave (16:10a) is a reference to bodily rescue out of the grave.[110] Admittedly, David's language is not an explicit statement of personal resurrection, but "David expressed at least a veiled hope for resurrection: his flesh would not be abandoned in the grave."[111] Thus, Ps 16:10 may express hyperbolically a hope in a future, bodily resurrection.[112] The final verse, Ps 16:11, makes explicit David's hope of eternal life upon rescue of his body from the grave.[113] David has confidence that he[114] will overcome death to be in God's presence forever.

Before examining the specific points of correspondence between David and Jesus, there are two points of clarification. First, Peter's quotation of Ps 16:8–11 in Acts 2:25–28, which agrees with the LXX, is an accurate translation of the original Hebrew.[115] Second, in Acts 2:25–28 Peter cites four verses from

---

Calvin's explanation that David would "not *remain* [emphasis added] in corruption" seems to capture the thought. Calvin, *Psalms*, 4:230. Trull admits that hyperbole is an interpretive option for Ps 16:10 but argues instead for a literal sense of the words. Trull, "An Exegesis of Psalm 16:10," 320. The fact that David uses metaphorical language in Ps 16:5–6 and seeming hyperbole in 16:8 (see comments on these verses above), however, strengthens the case that he is using hyperbole in 16:10b. The hyperbole, then, has bearing for a typological application of Ps 16:10 to Jesus. Cf. J. A. Motyer, "The Psalms," in *New Bible Commentary: 21st Century Edition*, ed. D. A. Carson, R. T. France, J. A. Motyer, and G. J. Wenham (Downers Grove: InterVarsity, 1994), 495; Ross, *Psalms*, 1:411.

109   Ross, *Psalms*, 1:410.
110   Cf. Waltke, Houston, and Moore, *The Psalms*, 339.
111   Trull, "An Exegesis of Psalm 16:10," 320. Trull thinks David's speaks of himself in Ps 16:10a but speaks of the Messiah's resurrection in Ps 16:10b. Ibid. See also, Trull, "Peter's Interpretation," 448. The parallelism of Ps 16:10, however, makes this interpretation seem unlikely.
112   Such hope of a future resurrection does not necessarily imply that David fully understood how God would accomplish it (i.e., through the resurrection of Christ). Cf. Ross, *Psalms*, 1:410n10.
113   Ps 16:11 envisages God's presence with David beyond the grave. David says that God will make him to know "the path of life," which is a reference to eternal life. So Belcher, *The Messiah and the Psalms*, 164; Mitchell Dahood, *Psalms I*, AB 16 (Garden City, NY: Doubleday, 1965), 91; Kaiser, *Uses*, 35; Kidner, *Psalms 1–72*, 103; Waltke, Houston, and Moore, *The Psalms*, 324n77; 337–338. Contra Anderson, *Psalms*, 1:146. That David has in mind life everlasting with God seems clear from his description of perfect joy in God's presence and eternal pleasures at God's right hand. Ramaroson, "Immortalité," 289–290, 294.
114   See e.g., Moyise, *Old Testament in the New*, 53; Waltke, Houston, and Moore, *The Psalms*, 338.
115   This point deserves mention because some contend that Peter's application of Ps 16:8–11 in Acts 2:25–28 depends upon the LXX translation, since the LXX supposedly changes the original sense of the MT into a resurrection sense. So e.g., Schmitt, "Ps 16, 8–11," 244. While Peter's translation does agree with the LXX, to claim that the LXX translation changes the sense of the original Hebrew overlooks the evidence (as shown in the summary above) that Ps 16:10 can be understood in its original context as expressing David's hope of resurrection. Furthermore,

Psalm 16, but, as Trull rightly points out, "he focused on verse 10 for his argument. He repeated the two lines of verse 10 exactly except for two changes."[116] Gustav Stählin argues:

> Von den angeführten vier Versen wird nur einer, V. 27 (= Ps. 16,10), auf Christus gedeutet (V. 31); vgl. zu V. 21. Darüber, wie man die übrigen Verse mit Jesus in Verbindung brachete, können wir nur Vermutungen anstellen .... Aber das folgende zeigt, daß es dem Verfasser nur auf Verse 27 ankam.[117]

There is warrant, therefore, that Peter applies only Ps 16:10 and not all four verses of the passage to Jesus. This understanding takes seriously Acts 2:31, where Peter identifies Ps 16:10 it as the main verse of the passage in its application to Jesus and his resurrection.[118] In addition, this understanding avoids speculation about how the other psalm verses may or may not apply to Christ. This understanding also accords with Peter's prior quotation of Joel 2:28–32 in Acts 2:17–21, where he applies only select verses rather than the entire quotation.[119] Thus, it may be that Peter simply quotes all of Ps 16:8–11 to give context to the main verse (Ps 16:10) that he intends to apply to Jesus.[120] The two main points of typological contact between David and Jesus in Ps 16:10 center on: (1) their regal status and (2) the notion of bodily resurrection.

David and Jesus share regal status. David speaks concerning himself in

---

this claim overstates the case that the differences between the LXX and MT are substantive in nature, rather than simply stylistic (see discussion above).

116 Trull, "Peter's Interpretation," 446.

117 "Of the four verses mentioned, only one, v. 27 (= Ps. 16:10), is interpreted as referring to Christ (v. 31); cf. v. 21. We can only make assumptions about how the other verses were connected with Jesus.... But the following shows that the author only cared about verse 27" (my translation). Stählin, *Die Apostelgeschichte*, 48. Contra Dupont, who believes the whole passage applies to Christ. Dupont, "L'interprétation des Psaumes," 286. Even so, Dupont admits that Ps 16:10 is the verse Peter bases his argument upon. Ibid.

118 On Ps 16:10 standing as the key verse of the psalm quotation in Peter's speech, see e.g., Alexander, *Acts*, 73; Bock, *Acts*, 123; Dupont, "L'interprétation des Psaumes," 286; Peterson, *Acts*, 147n63; Polhill, *Acts*, 113; Preuschen, *Die Apostelgeschichte*, 15. It is clear Peter repeats Ps 16:10 in Acts 2:31 because he understands this verse to predict Christ's resurrection.

Jacques Dupont also recognizes this point, stating, "Pierre cite quatre versets du psaume (vv. 8–11); en fait cependant toute la démonstration repose sur les terms du v. 10." ("Peter quotes four verses from the psalm (vv. 8–11); in fact, however, the whole demonstration is based on the terms of v. 10," my translation.) Dupont, "L'utilisation apologétique," 266. Dupont also writes, "Le Ps 16,10 constitue la pièce capitale de l'argument scripturaire du discours de Pierre le jour de la Pentecôte (2,25–31)..." ("Ps 16:10 is the central piece of the scriptural argument of Peter's speech on the day of Pentecost [2:25–31]..." [my translation]). Ibid., 265.

119 Trull explains, "In quoting Joel 2:28–32 in Acts 2:17–21 Peter focused on only the beginning and the ending of that Old Testament passage. He did not address the great day of the Lord (v. 20)." Trull, "Peter's Interpretation," 447.

120 So Alexander, *Acts*, 73.

Psalm 16, and so the reader naturally interprets it as being about Israel's king. Peter underscores David's authorship (Acts 2:25, 30–31) and also refers to David's throne (τὸν θρόνον αὐτοῦ Acts 2:30). Likewise, Peter underscores the importance of Jesus' identity as Israel's king in connection to the psalm.[121] First, Peter alludes to Ps 132:11 to identify Jesus as the promised descendent who is to sit on David's throne (Acts 2:30–31). Next, he identifies Jesus as the Christ and Lord (Acts 2:31, 36), titles which emphasize Jesus' kingship and rule.[122] Finally, he declares him to be the exalted one who sits at God's right hand as co-regent in fulfillment of Ps 110:1 (Acts 2:33–35). Thus, the reader of Acts 2:25–36 becomes aware that Ps 16:10 relates not only to the biography of King David but also to his royal son, King Jesus. At the same time, David and Jesus are not equal in regal status, for—as Peter points out in Acts 2:33–34—the promised seed of David is superior to David.

The main point of typological correspondence between David and Jesus centers on bodily resurrection. Peter brings this to light most explicitly in Acts 2:29–32. Here, Peter recites Ps 16:10 (Acts 2:27) and explains that David spoke of the resurrection of the Messiah, Jesus. Now, the most natural way to understand Ps 16:10 in its original setting is as David's statement about himself. David uses hyperbolic language to emphasize his idea of a bodily resurrection in 16:10a. "Not experiencing corruption" is David's way of expressing confidence that God will rescue his body from the grave. Further indication that this verse speaks of resurrection comes from Peter's application of Ps 16:10 to Jesus' resurrection. This is clear from the explanatory γάρ ("for") that links Ps 16:8–11 in Acts 2:25–28 with Acts 2:24.[123] Furthermore, Peter singles out Ps 16:10; in this verse David ἐλάλησεν περὶ τῆς ἀναστάσεως τοῦ Χριστοῦ ("spoke of the resurrection of the Christ" Acts 2:31).[124]

---

[121] Donald Juel argues that "the centrality of Jesus' identity as Messiah-King is stressed in Peter's speech in Acts 2." Donald Juel, *Messianic Exegesis: Christological Interpretation of the Old Testament in Early Christianity* (Philadelphia: Fortress Press, 1988), 83. See also Victor McCracken, "The Interpretation of Scripture in Luke-Acts," *ResQ* 41 (1999): 202.

[122] Cf. Bock, *Luke and Acts*, 185–187, 197–198.

[123] Technically, the initial γάρ of Acts 2:25 is causal in connection to 2:24, signaling that in the psalm quotation in 2:25–28 David expresses why death could not keep Jesus in its power and why Jesus had to be raised from the dead. Cf. Larkin, *Acts*, 55; Peterson, *Acts*, 147; Trull, "Peter's Interpretation," 437. Put simply, Jesus had to be raised from the dead (Acts 2:24), because David spoke of Jesus' resurrection in Ps 16:8–11.

[124] The subsequent ὅτι clause (ὅτι οὔτε ἐγκατελείφθη εἰς ᾅδην οὔτε ἡ σὰρξ αὐτοῦ εἶδεν διαφθοράν) is appositional, clarifying that Ps 16:10 refers to resurrection of the Christ. Peter makes three changes to Ps 16:10 in Acts 2:31. First, Peter replaces "my soul" with "he" (16:10a), which clarifies the application of the verse to Jesus. Miura, *David in Luke-Acts*, 146. Second, Peter changes the future tense verbs to the aorist tense (16:10a–b). Lastly, he substitutes "your holy one" with "his flesh" (16:10b). These latter two changes emphasize the fulfillment of the Ps 16:10 in connection to Jesus' resurrection and clarify that the psalm text was pointing to a physical or *bodily* resurrection, respectively. See Bock, *Proclamation*, 178–179; Peterson, *Acts*, 149.

How exactly does Peter apply Ps 16:10 to Jesus' experience, if David was originally speaking about himself? Peter applies the text typologically: David's experience provides a prefigurement of Jesus' experience. In Acts 2:29–31, Peter first explains that David died, was buried, and is still entombed (2:29). Thus, David's words in Ps 16:10 "could only apply to David in a general sense of a future resurrection,"[125] but Peter claims that David spoke prophetically, which means that his words were inspired by the Holy Spirit.[126] Consequently, King David's words describing his own personal hope of resurrection could, at the same time, be intended by the Spirit to prefigure (and predict) the resurrection of the future Davidic king, Jesus.[127] David's hyperbolic language in its most literal sense provides the precise pattern for the resurrection of Jesus. Ross explains:

> The language of Psalm 16 was excessive for the author's understanding but became literally true for Jesus Christ. In fact, Peter declares that David said these things about Christ (Acts 2:25–28). In other words, the New Testament writers bring this passage forward, knowing what the Spirit of God had intended when David wrote them. The apostles make it clear that these words could only apply to David in a general sense of a future resurrection, for his body had been in the grave for a thousand years; but they apply it to the Lord in the precise and fullest sense, for by the resurrection he did not see the effects of being in the grave that were true of every human being.[128]

What, then, is "the precise and fullest sense" of Ps 16:10? For David, the verse simply speaks of his confidence in a general, future bodily resurrection. Peter interprets "the literalness of the imagery" of Ps 16:10[129] to be about Jesus' special, immediate bodily resurrection. As Bock notes:

> The concept of an immediate resurrection within history was a fresh idea in Judaism. The Jews believed in a general bodily resurrection at the end of time for all the righteous and wicked together before the judgment (Isa. 66; Dan. 12:1–2; 2 Macc. 7) but did not have an expectation of an earlier,

---

125 Ross, *Psalms*, 1:411.
126 See Miura, *David in Luke-Acts*, 145.
127 Since Peter identifies David as an inspired OT prophet in Acts 2:30–31, Peter establishes that what David wrote about himself could have typological import, even if David did not comprehend that typological import. Cf. Hoskins, *Jesus as the Fulfillment*, 24–26.
128 Ross, *Psalms*, 1:411.
129 Bock, *Proclamation*, 176.

immediate, special resurrection for anyone. This new idea of a resurrection before the end was revealed by Jesus's resurrection. In this speech Peter is arguing that Scripture predicted it, as all can now see.[130]

Peter points out to his audience that the precise, ultimate, and fullest sense of Ps 16:10 is an immediate, bodily resurrection, which Jesus' resurrection fulfills, demonstrating that "the text is not only about the patriarch David."[131]

This typology also contrasts Jesus and David. First, Jesus' resurrection is special and immediate, which contrasts with the general and future nature of David's.[132] The nature of Jesus' resurrection, since it fulfills the precise sense of Ps 16:10, identifies him as the Messiah to whom the Holy Spirit ultimately intended David's words to apply (Acts 2:30–32). Additionally, Jesus' resurrection makes possible David's future resurrection, guaranteeing "that David, and all of the saints, would be raised from the dead."[133] Lastly, since Jesus' immediate resurrection fulfills the precise sense of Ps 16:10, the title of "holy one" applies to Jesus in a unique way, identifying him as "the ultimate 'type' of faithful servant who was not abandoned by God to Sheol and decay."[134] Furthermore, if "holy one" bears messianic implications,[135] then it reinforces even more that Jesus is the Son of David that God promised to seat on David's throne (Acts 2:30). Thus, the resurrection of Jesus identifies him as the Davidic Messiah, who is "God's Holy One *par excellence*."[136]

THE DAVID-JESUS TYPOLOGY: THE ELEMENT OF PROPHECY

The previous section demonstrated that Peter applies Ps 16:10 to Jesus based on David typology. As Peter presents it, the typology is more than a mere analogical construct. Instead, it provides a predictive pattern in its connection to Jesus.[137] The evidence for this includes: (1) the relationship of Ps 16:10 to the

---

130 Bock, *Acts*, 125. For a more detailed discussion, see Bock, *Proclamation*, 176–181. To be noted, Bock takes a different position on the original sense of Ps 16:10 than is maintained in this work. Whereas this work argues that bodily resurrection was the original sense to David's words in Ps 16:10, Bock thinks that a bodily resurrection sense is more conceptual than explicit. Ibid., 174, 177.

131 Ibid., 126.

132 Though he does not argue for a typological framework in Peter's understanding of Ps 16:10, Trull still discusses how the verse compares Jesus with David. He points out that Jesus' resurrection before any bodily decay ultimately set Jesus apart from David and his still future resurrection. Trull, "Peter's Interpretation," 446–447.

133 Ross, *Psalms*, 1:411–412. See also Delitzsch, *Psalms*, 1:230.

134 Wilson, *Psalms Volume 1*, 313.

135 See the summary of Ps 16:8–11 in its OT context above in this section.

136 Peterson, *Acts*, 150n71.

137 For those who argue that a prophetic David typology stands behind Peter's use of Ps

plan of God, (2) the introductory phrase to the quotation, and (3) the reference to David's prophetic status.

First, the relationship of Ps 16:10 to the plan of God is important for discerning the prophetic character of the typology established by the psalm. Peter quotes Ps 16:8–11 within the context of the claim that Jesus' suffering and death were part of God's saving plan. In Acts 2:23, Peter refers to τῇ ὡρισμένῃ βουλῇ καὶ προγνώσει τοῦ θεοῦ ("the predetermined plan and foreknowledge of God"). On the significance of this phrase for Peter's sermon, Marion L. Soards comments:

> [I]n v. 23 one encounters the phrase τῇ ὡρισμένῃ βουλῇ καὶ προγνώσει τοῦ θεοῦ ("the definite plan and foreknowledge of God"), which is the first explicit reference in Acts to the important idea of ἡ βουλὴ τοῦ θεοῦ, "the plan of God" (2:23; 4:28; 13:36; 20:27). The qualifying of ἡ βουλὴ τοῦ θεοῦ ("the plan of God") with the participle form of ὁρίζειν ("to decide" or "to determine") emphasizes God's control in determining events, especially the future.... Thus, the cross is not cast as a scandal, for the crucifixion of Jesus at the hands of the lawless is viewed as the fulfillment of God's plan.[138]

By referring to the plan of God, Peter establishes that the events of Jesus' suffering, particularly his death and resurrection, reflect divine design.[139] Peter makes this point explicit by immediately quoting the passage containing a specific verse (i.e., Ps 16:10/Acts 2:31) important for his point.[140] Peter quotes Ps 16:8–11, as Doble rightly observes, not as one of his "isolated proof texts" but as a text which "carried God's plan revealed in scripture."[141]

16:8–11, see e.g., Bock, *Acts*, 123; Miura, *David in Luke-Acts*, 154. To be noted, Bock apparently changed his position, for his early work argued for a direct prophecy understanding of the psalm passage. See Bock, *Proclamation*, 180. Cho and Park maintain that "David in this song was not speaking about himself but was prophesying about his later descendent, the Messiah." Cho and Park, *Acts*, 60. Kellum appears also to classify Ps 16:8–11 as a case of direct prophecy. Kellum, *Acts*, 38.

138 Soards, *The Speeches in Acts*, 34. The reference to God's "foreknowledge" reinforces the notion of God's sovereignty in connection to his plan. Cf. Peterson, *Acts*, 146.

139 When Peter places Jesus' death under the umbrella of God's plan, as Trull points out, "This focus also applies to Jesus' resurrection." Trull, "Peter's Interpretation," 436.

140 In Luke-Acts, Bock informs, "The 'plan' is said to be present in Scripture, usually expressed in generic terms (Luke 24:43–47), but sometimes in the specific texts on a given theme (Acts 2 and the use of Joel 3:1–5; Pss 16:8–11; 132:11; 110:1)." Bock, *Luke and Acts*, 124.

141 Doble, "Psalms," 95. Krodel also picks up on the revelatory function of the psalm passage, stating, "Psalm 16:8–11 is cited to demonstrate that the resurrection is according to God's plan as set forth in the Scriptures." Krodel, *Acts*, 84–85. Cf. Larkin, *Acts*, 55; Roloff, *Die Apostelgeschichte*, 56; Weiser, *Die Apostelgeschichte*, 93.

If Ps 16:10 reveals that the resurrection of Jesus fulfills God's sovereign plan, this means it was predicting his resurrection. Thus, Peter is showing that a text which relays a personal experience in David's life serves as a prophecy for a corresponding fulfillment in Jesus' life. God intended David's written hope for a future resurrection to be a predictive paradigm for Jesus' immediate resurrection.

Second, the phrase Peter uses to introduce Ps 16:8–11 also indicates that the passage was predictive of him. Acts 2:25 commences with the introductory statement Δαυὶδ γὰρ λέγει εἰς αὐτόν ("For, David says of Him"). The conjunction γάρ ("for") links the quotation in Acts 2:25–28 with the previous verse (2:24).[142] The quotation, then, supplies the cause or reason as to why death could not keep its hold on Jesus (2:24),[143] because in Ps 16:8–11 David spoke εἰς αὐτόν ("of Him"). Here, after a verb of saying (λέγει), BDAG says that εἰς means "with reference to."[144] The antecedent of the pronoun αὐτόν is Ἰησοῦν τὸν Ναζωραῖον ("Jesus the Nazarene"), who is first mentioned in Acts 2:22 and who "bleibt thematisch im Mittelpunkt" in 2:22–24.[145] There are two possible ways to understand Jesus as the referent of what David says in Ps 16:10. Jesus could be the "exclusive" referent or the "ultimate" referent of the verse.[146] Since David is clearly speaking about himself in the original context, Jesus cannot be the "exclusive" referent.[147] Consequently, Peter's introductory statement points to Jesus as the "ultimate" referent of the passage, for Ps 16:10 possesses a typological import. In other words, the verse describes an event specific to David in its original context but points beyond itself to a more specific event in connection to Jesus.

Thus, by introducing Ps 16:8–11 with a phrase explaining that David spoke about Jesus in the psalm, Peter establishes that the passage contains a fundamentally typological prophecy concerning Jesus' resurrection. David's experience is shown to have been foreshadowing, anticipating, and predicting Jesus' experience.

Third, Peter refers to David's prophetic status and explains its implications concerning David's statement in Ps 16:10. The inferential οὖν ("therefore")

---

142 See BDAG, s.v. "γάρ."

143 On this causal sense of γάρ, see Larkin, *Acts*, 55; Peterson, *Acts*, 147; Trull, "Peter's Interpretation," 437.

144 BDAG, s.v. "εἰς." Cf. ESV's "concerning him;" NIV's "about him;" NASB's "of him."

145 "remains thematically at the center" (my translation). Schmitt, "Ps 16, 8–11," 244.

146 Trull, "Peter's Interpretation," 439.

147 For Jesus to be the "exclusive" referent would mean that Ps 16:10 had Jesus as its single and only referent in the original context of the psalm. If this is the case, David is understood as directly prophesying about Jesus. But, as demonstrated in the summary above, the most natural way to read Ps 16 in light of the evidence is with regards to David. David is the subject and is clearly speaking about himself in the original context of Ps 16:10.

identifies 2:30–31 to be a deduction from the preceding verse (2:29).[148] By means of three causal participles which modify the main verb ἐλάλησεν ("he spoke") in 2:31,[149] Peter makes the case that David spoke prophetically in Ps 16:10 about Jesus' resurrection. F. Delitzsch summarizes Peter's line of thinking well:

> The apostolic application of this Psalm (Acts ii. 29–32, xiii. 35–37) is based on the considerations that David's hope of not coming under the power of death was not realized in David himself, as is at once clear, to the *unlimited extent* [emphasis added] in which it is expressed in the Psalm; but that it is fulfilled in Jesus, who has not been left to Hades and whose flesh did not see corruption; and that consequently the words of the Psalm are a prophecy of David concerning Jesus, the Christ, ... David . . . becomes the prophet of Christ; but this is only indirectly, for he speaks of himself . . . . After his hope has found in Christ its full realization in accordance with the history of the plan of redemption, it receives through Christ its personal realization for himself also. For what he says, extends on the one hand far beyond himself, and therefore refers prophetically to Christ . . . . But on the other hand that which is predicted comes back upon himself, to raise him also from death and Hades to the beholding of God.[150]

Importantly, there is room in David's language for his words to apply to himself but also to extend beyond himself. Peter, therefore, is not saying that David's words in Ps 16:10 do not apply to him in some sense. Instead, as Peter sees it, the language David initially used regarding himself finds a more perfect or literal realization in the experience of Jesus. This Psalm text can point beyond itself in its language, according to Peter, because of David's prophetic status.[151]

Peter clarifies David's prophetic status in three ways. First, Peter explains

---

148 The deduction of Acts 2:29, as explained above in the discussion of the typology, is that Ps 16:10 can only apply to David in the sense of a future resurrection, since he is still entombed and his body has undergone decay.

149 See Trull, "Peter's Interpretation," 441. The three modifying participles include (1) "because he was"/ὑπάρχων in v. 30, (2) "knew"/εἰδὼς in v. 30, and (3) "he looked ahead"/προϊδὼν in v. 31.

150 Delitzsch, *Psalms*, 1:229–230. For clarity's sake, Delitzsch provides this explanation, assuming that the original sense of Ps 16:8–11 referred to preservation from death (i.e. David's hope of not dying) and, thus, experienced only a limited fulfillment in David's life. Ibid., 1:228. Even so, his explanation still works in the case of understanding David's original words as referring to a future resurrection, as this work maintains. In both cases, David's language is seen to be in reference to himself but also to go beyond his own experience to find perfect realization or fulfillment in Jesus' experience.

151 Note that Bock explains Peter's prophetic application of Ps 16:10 based on David's "language." Bock, "Proclamation," 177.

in Acts 2:30, David was a προφήτης ("prophet"),[152] "a person inspired to proclaim or reveal divine will or purpose,"[153] "who proclaimed in advance what was later fulfilled in Christ."[154] Second, Peter alludes to Ps 132:11, stating that David knew of God's promise to seat one of his descendents upon his throne (Acts 2:30). This claim need not necessarily imply that David knowingly or self-consciously prophesied about the Messiah based on his knowledge of God's promise.[155] Instead, it can be seen as a statement, which provides David's credentials as one who could speak as a prophet about the Messiah. Accordingly, Peter's reference to David's awareness of God's promise substantiates the basis of David's prophetic status.[156] Also, by stating that David knew of God's promise, "David is cast as an authority on the Messiah here."[157] Finally, Peter states in Acts 2:31 that David's prophetic status enabled him to "foresee" (προϊδών), which indicates that David's statement in Ps 16:10 was predicting something in advance.[158] When Peter re-quotes Ps 16:10 in Acts 2:31, the

---

[152] On David as a "prophet," see Joseph A. Fitzmeyer, "David, 'Being Therefore A Prophet . . .,'" *CBQ* 34 (1972).

[153] BDAG, s.v. "προφήτης."

[154] Gerhard Friedrich, "προφήτης κτλ," *TDNT* 6:832; see 6:832–833.

[155] Gregory V. Trull takes this statement to mean that David made a self-conscious prophecy of the Messiah's resurrection based on his knowledge of God's promise of an heir. Trull, "Peter's Interpretation," 443–446. See also Krodel, *Acts*, 86. Such an understanding, however, does not fit well with the original context of Ps 16:10, where it is most natural to see David speaking with reference to himself in the psalm verse. Furthermore, the fact that David had knowledge of God's promise to seat one of his descendents upon his throne does not necessarily mean that he understood this promise to imply a resurrection of the Messiah. See Trull, "Peter's Interpretation," 443–444, where even he acknowledges that David could have had knowledge of God's promise but not have understood its messianic implications.

[156] Miura takes this position, arguing, "David's awareness of God's promise in the Davidic covenant (v. 30) (based upon Ps 131:11 [cf. 2 Sam 7:12–16; Ps 88:4–5, 29–38]) might indicate a reason for Peter to simply believe David's prophetic status, such as the way that Josephus saw David's direct contact with God as a reason for David's prophet-like character." Miura, *David in Luke-Acts*, 145. Thus, David should be considered in the status of a prophet because God gave David special revelation, a fact made clear by God's personal promise to him concerning his heir.

[157] Soards, *The Speeches in Acts*, 35. According to Bruce, David "prefigured" the Messiah. Bruce, *Acts*, 65. David could, therefore, be understood as an authority on the Messiah from a typological standpoint. That is, since David had personal knowledge of God's promise concerning his future descendent, what David says concerning himself could anticipate truths fulfilled ultimately by his promised descendent whom he prefigures.

[158] See Gerhard Friedrich, "προφήτης κτλ," *TDNT* 6:833. Προϊδών means "to see in advance/foresee." BDAG, s.v. "προοράω." According to W. Michaelis, "This can hardly mean that he [David] prophetically (cf. 2:30) 'saw' the future resurrection of Jesus in advance; what is meant is that as a prophet he had advance knowledge of it." W. Michaelis, "ὁράω κτλ," *TDNT* 5:381. Importantly, when Peter says that David "foresaw," this does not necessarily mean that David knowingly prophesied about Messiah's resurrection in Ps 16:10. Marshall writes, "The fact that David had prophetic knowledge (Acts 2:30a) presumably applies not to his knowledge about his descendent (2:30b), but rather to his own statement about the Messiah (2:31)." Marshall, "Acts," 538. He adds further, "David is credited with 'seeing what was to come.' Thus the statement in

prepositional phrase περὶ τῆς ἀναστάσεως τοῦ Χριστοῦ ("of the resurrection of Christ") modifies the main verb ἐλάλησεν, clarifying that David predicted in advance the Messiah's resurrection.[159] Understanding that the ὅτι ("that") clause stands in apposition to τῆς ἀναστάσεως τοῦ Χριστοῦ in v. 31, this means Ps 16:10 refers to the resurrection of the Christ.

In sum, by referring to David's prophetic status, Peter is making a case that "David's words are inspired"[160] by the Holy Spirit (cf. 2 Sam 23:2; Matt 22:43–45; Mark 12:36–37; Luke 20:42–44; Acts 1:16; 4:25; 13:33–37).[161] Thus, David's words could bear a predictive significance, even if he was not cognizant of their prophetic force. This means the Holy Spirit guided David to use exaggerated or hyperbolic language in Ps 16:10, so that David's self-described experience might point forward to a more precise, future NT fulfillment in Jesus. Waltke, Houston, and Moore explain:

> Though David, the human author may be using hyperbole, God, the divine Author, speaks prophetically of David's greater Son, his heir, to validate his claim to be the promised Christ. Moreover, by his death and resurrection he proved the truths that the putative hyperbole infers.[162]

So, when David clarified his hope of a future, bodily resurrection using hyperbolic language in Ps 16:10, the Spirit of God intended ultimately to use this language for the purpose of predicting the immediate, bodily resurrection of the Messiah, who would rule on David's throne in fulfillment of God's covenant promise (Acts 2:30). Since Jesus was raised up in the way David described the Messiah's resurrection, the resurrection identifies Jesus as the Messiah (Acts 2:32).

Ps 110:1 in Acts 2:34–35

In Acts 2:34–35, Luke shows Peter quoting another psalm. Acts 2:34b contains the short introductory formula λέγει δὲ αὐτός ("but he himself says").[163]

---

the psalm is understood to be prophetic. But exactly what David foresaw is not stated." Ibid., 540. Since he was a prophet, Peter seems to be saying that David "foresaw" the resurrection of the Messiah in his statement in Ps 16:10.

159 After a verb of speaking (here ἐλάλησεν), the preposition περί ("about/concerning") denotes the object of the verbal activity. See BDAG, s.v. "περί."

160 Miura, *David in Luke-Acts*, 145.

161 For Rabbinic literature which speaks of David's psalm composition taking place under the inspiration of the Holy Spirit, see Jouette M. Bassler, "A Man for All Seasons: David in Rabbinic and New Testament Literature," *Int* 40 (1986): 159–160.

162 Waltke, Houston, and Moore, *The Psalms*, 336.

163 Barrett, "Luke/Acts," 238.

The antecedent of the pronominal subject imbedded in the verb λέγει ("he says") is Δαυίδ ("David"), whom Peter mentions in the initial part of the verse (2:34a).[164]

The words Peter attributes to David in Acts 2:34–35 are a quotation of Ps 110:1, which the NT refers to more often than any other OT text.[165] As can be seen below, Acts 2:34–35 reproduces the first verse of Psalm 110 (= Ps 110:1/MT and Ps 109:1/LXX).

Acts 2:34–35	εἶπεν [ὁ] κύριος τῷ κυρίῳ μου· κάθου ἐκ δεξιῶν μου, ἕως ἂν θῶ τοὺς ἐχθρούς σου ὑποπόδιον τῶν ποδῶν σου
	"The Lord said to my Lord, sit at my right hand, until I make your enemies a footstool for your feet."
MT Ps 110:1	נְאֻם יְהוָה לַאדֹנִי שֵׁב לִימִינִי עַד־אָשִׁית אֹיְבֶיךָ הֲדֹם לְרַגְלֶיךָ
	"The LORD says to my Lord: Sit at my right hand, until I make Your enemies a footstool for Your feet."
LXX Ps 109:1	εἶπεν ὁ κύριος τῷ κυρίῳ μου κάθου ἐκ δεξιῶν μου ἕως ἂν θῶ τοὺς ἐχθρούς σου ὑποπόδιον τῶν ποδῶν σου
	"The Lord said to my lord, sit at my right hand, until I make your enemies a footstool for your feet."

Two observations are apparent. First, the LXX provides an accurate translation of the MT.[166] Second, since Luke's quotation closely mirrors the LXX,[167] it seems reasonable to conclude that he used the LXX for his purposes because it correctly renders the MT.

THE DAVID-JESUS TYPOLOGY: THE ELEMENT OF CORRESPONDENCE

Peter uses Ps 110:1 in Acts 2:34–35 to explain the exaltation of Jesus, and the way in which Peter appropriates this text again rests upon David typology. The superscript לְדָוִד מִזְמוֹר ("A psalm of David") introducing Psalm 110

---

164 To emphasize the identity of David as the author/speaker, Peter includes the intensive αὐτός ("himself"). On the intensive use of αὐτός, see BDAG, s.v. "αὐτός."

165 Jacques Dupont, "'Assis à la droite de Dieu': l'interprétation du Ps 110, 1 dans le Nouveau Testament," in *Nouvelles Études sur Les Actes Des Apôtres*, LD 118 (Paris: Éditions du Cerf, 1984), 210.

166 There is only one difference between the LXX and the MT. The LXX reproduces the name of Yahweh with the term κύριος. Pesch, *Die Apostelgeschichte*, 1:118.

167 Ibid. The only variation between the LXX and Acts 2:34–35 is the article ὁ before κύριος. Dupont, "L'interprétation des Psaumes," 291n22.

identifies David as the psalm's author.[168] Based on its king motif, OT scholars tend to classify this as a royal psalm.[169] The oracular statements of Ps 110:1 ("The LORD says...") and 110:4 ("The LORD has sworn...") suggest a two-part division for the psalm's seven verses: (1) 110:1–3 and (2) 110:4–7.[170]

Psalm 110:1 breaks down into three basic parts: introduction (110:1a), exaltation/enthronement (110:1b), and subjection of enemies (110:1c).[171] The introductory words נְאֻם יְהוָה לַאדֹנִי ("The LORD says to my Lord") contain a prophetic formula.[172] Here, David occupies the role of a prophet, declaring the inspired word of God.[173] The sense of the prophetic formula is that David declares the message of Yahweh (יְהוָה) to his "lord" or "master" (לַאדֹנִי).[174] Who is David calling "my lord"? As Paul M. Hoskins points out, there are two commonly suggested referents:[175] some claim David prophesies directly of

---

168 On the Davidic authorship understanding of לְדָוִד in the superscripts in Psalms, see the section "The David-Jesus Typology: The Element of Correspondence" in the analysis of John 13:18 in chapter 4 of this work. The NT writers also affirm David's authorship of Ps 110. See Matt 22:43–45; Mark 12:36–37; Luke 20:42–44; Acts 2:34, where both Jesus and Peter attribute Ps 110 to David.

169 Herbert W. Bateman, IV, "Psalm 110:1 and the New Testament," *BSac* 149 (1992): 438. Those psalms typically categorized as royal psalms include eleven in total (Pss 2; 18; 20; 21; 45; 72; 89; 101; 110; 132; 144). See e.g., Bullock, *Psalms*, 178–80; Herman Gunkel, *The Psalms: A Form-Critical Introduction*, trans. Thomas M. Horner, Facet Books, BS 19 (Philadelphia: Fortress 1967), 23–24; Westermann, *The Psalms*, 105–107. As a category, royal psalms "share the common motif of the king" and focus upon "some momentous occasion in the life of the king, occasions such as his coronation, his wedding, the charter by which he would rule, or his greatest military campaigns in which the LORD gave the victory to his servant the king." Ross, *Psalms*, 1:137. See also Futato, *Interpreting the Psalms*, 181–182. The idea of kingship in royal psalms may be expressed by (1) referring to the "king," (2) referring to the "anointed," (3) referring to David, or (4) referring to activities of the king. Bullock, *Psalms*, 178–179. In the content of Ps 110, neither the term "king" nor the term "anointed" appears. Yet, as Bullock explains, "Psalm 110 uses language that obviously refers to the king, speaking of him as 'my lord' (v. 1) and referring to his 'scepter' (v. 2)." Ibid., 179.

170 So e.g., Allen, *Psalms*, 85; Belcher, *The Messiah and the Psalms*, 143; Dahood, *Psalms III*, 113; Durham, "Psalms," 396–397; VanGemeren, "Psalms," 697; Waltke, Houston, and Moore, *The Psalms*, 500.

171 Martin C. Albl, *"And Scripture Cannot Be Broken": The Form and Function of the Early Christian Testimonia Collections*, NovTSup 96 (Leiden: Brill, 1999), 217.

172 The phrase נְאֻם יְהוָה is "an almost completely fixed technical expression introducing prophetic oracles." *HALOT*, s.v. "נְאֻם."

173 Cf. Waltke, Houston, and Moore, *The Psalms*, 499. On David as a "prophet," see Acts 2:29–30.

174 VanGemeren explains, "The MT uses the phrase אֲדֹנִי (*'adōnî*, "my master") to denote the lord-vassal relationship between the king and his people (cf. 1 Sam 22:12; 26:18; 1 Kgs 1:13; 18:7)." VanGemeren, "Psalms," 697n1. (For a list of the numerous instances where אֲדֹנִי refers to an earthly king, see Bateman, "Psalm 110:1," 448nn44–46, n48.) Cf. also Mitchell Dahood, who says "my lord" was a Hebrew phrase "used by a subject when addressing a superior." Dahood, *Psalms III*, 113.

175 Paul M. Hoskins, *That Scripture Might Be Fulfilled: Typology and the Death of Christ* (Longwood, FL: Xulon 2009), 149–150.

the future Messiah,[176] while others see David speaking about his sons, the future kings that would come from his line.[177] Although a purely Messianic view is possible, the latter view seems preferable considering the royal nature of the psalm and its overall content.[178] Accordingly, in Ps 110:1 "David presents an inspired picture that God has revealed to him about God's anointed king."[179] Since God's anointed king comes from the line of David (cf. 2 Sam 7:13–16), this means that David addresses one of his sons as "lord."[180] Why would David refer to one of his sons in this exalted manner? Hoskins explains:

> The resolution to the tension probably lies in 2 Samuel 7:14 and Psalm 2:7. According to these verses, when a son of David becomes king, he becomes the son of God as well. In Psalm 2:7, God tells the king on the day of his anointing, "You are my son, today I have begotten you" (NASB). The king is no longer merely David's son. When he becomes king, David's son becomes God's son in a special way as well. As a result, when David writes Psalm 110 about the king at God's right hand, he rightly recognizes that this ruler will be God's king and not merely David's son. He rightly deserves to be addressed as "lord," even by David.[181]

Thus, David is "writing about the great kings who will rule after him."[182] Moreover, "The king of Psalm 110 is not the beginning of the line of similar kings.

---

176 See e.g., Belcher, *The Messiah and the Psalms*, 146–149; Barry C. Davis, "Is Psalm 110 A Messianic Psalm?," *BSac* 157 (2000): 160–173; Delitzsch, *Psalms*, 3:183–188; Grogan, *Psalms*, 184; Elliott E. Johnson, "Hermeneutical Principles and the Interpretation of Psalm 110," *BSac* 149 (1992): 432–433; Kidner, *Psalms 73–150*, 391–392. The sense of Ps 110:1, then, is "The LORD says to my Lord (i.e., Messiah) . . ."

177 In Ps 110, VanGemeren explains, "The Psalmist speaks of the promise of God pertaining to David and his dynasty. The promise pertains to the covenant between the Lord (*ʾadōnî*) and the one in authority over the people of God, the Davidic king." VanGermen, "Psalms," 697. Cf. Allen, *Psalms*, 83–85; Broyles, *Psalms*, 414; Durham, "Psalms," 396; Rogerson and McKay, *Psalms*, 3:66.

178 Leslie Allen writes, "One respects the worthy motives of those who seek to restrict the psalm to a messianic intent from the beginning. But it hardly accords with the pattern of historical and theological development discernible in the royal psalms in general and with ancient culture and historical royal references in Ps 110." Allen, *Psalms*, 84. Cf. Bullock, who notes also that the original, historical focus of the royal psalms concerned Israel's human king. Bullock, *Psalms*, 180–186.

179 Hoskins, *That Scripture Might Be Fulfilled*, 150.

180 That David has in mind an *earthly* king seems supported by the fact that the suffixed form לַאדֹנִי ("to my lord") in Ps 110:1 occurs 21 other times in the OT, none of which designate a divine reference. Bateman, "Psalm 110:1," 448n44.

181 Hoskins, *That Scripture Might Be Fulfilled*, 151.

182 Ibid., 151.

Psalm 110 describes this king as being like David himself. . . . David passes on to his sons an inspired picture of what it means to be a king like David."[183]

The first part of God's message is for the king to שֵׁב לִימִינִי ("Sit at my right hand"). This divine directive pictures David's son being enthroned as king by God.[184] The verb שֵׁב ("sit")[185] calls for the king to be enthroned at God's right, which may be taken metaphorically or symbolically.[186] In either case, to be seated at God's right hand means the king has been exalted to a position of authority and honor to serve as God's vice-regent.[187] This means that the Davidic king possesses an "incontrovertible authority" (cf. Ps 2:1–9),[188] which the latter half of the oracle in Ps 110:1 declares. The "footstool" imagery ("until I make your enemies a footstool [הֲדֹם] for your feet") conveys the king's "complete power and authority" over his enemies.[189] To the son of David, then, God promises to subdue his enemies.[190]

---

183 Ibid. Hoskins refers the reader to Pss 18:43–50; 89:19–29, where similar language is used to describe David and his kingship.

184 The importance of this divine directive to the newly installed king would be to recognize the commencement and legitimacy of his rule from God. Cf. Bernd Kollmann, "Der Priesterkönig zur Rechten Gottes (Ps 110)," in *Die Verheißung des Neuen Bundes: Wie alttestamentliche Texte im Neuen Testament fortwirken*, ed. Bernd Kollmann, Biblisch-theologische Schwerpunkte 35 (Göttingen: Vandenhoeck & Ruprecht, 2010), 157–158.

185 The basic meaning of the imperative שֵׁב is "sit/remain/dwell." BDB, s.v. "יָשַׁב." The verb is often used to denote kings sitting on thrones (cf. e.g., 1 Kgs 1:13, 17, 20, 35, 46, 48; 2:12; 1 Chr 29:23), or with reference to God in the sense of him being "enthroned" (cf. 1 Sam 4:4; 2 Sam 6:2; Ps 2:4; 9:7, etc.). See BDB, s.v. "יָשַׁב;" *HALOT*, s.v. "יָשַׁב;" Walter C. Kaiser, "יָשַׁב (yāshab) sit, remain, dwell," *TWOT* 1:411–413. Dahood translates שֵׁב in Ps 110:1 as "Sit enthroned." Dahood, *Psalms III*, 113.

186 Rogerson and McKay, *Psalms*, 3:67. Allen takes sitting on the right hand of God as a simple metaphor. Allen, *Psalms*, 80n11.c, 86. If the imagery is more symbolical, sitting at the right hand of God might refer to a ritual performed in the temple (cf. 2 Kgs 11:14; 23:3; 2 Chr 23:13; 34:31). Anderson, *Psalms*, 2:768. Or, "more probably God's right hand refers to the throne hall, the Hall of Judgment, where the kings sits to judge (1 Kings 7:7). The temple housing *I AM's* earthly throne, the ark (1 Sam. 4:4; Isa. 66:1; cf. Matt. 5:34), faces eastward in the great courtyard. The Hall of Judgment housing the king's throne seems to be on the south side, to the right of God's throne, facing northward in the great courtyard." Waltke, Houston, and Moore, *The Psalms*, 503.

187 So Bateman, "Psalm 110:1," 451; Broyles, *Psalms*, 414; Kollmann, "Der Priesterkönig zur Rechten Gottes (Ps 110)," 158; Waltke, Houston, and Moore, *The Psalms*, 503.

188 Durham, "Psalms," 396.

189 Waltke, Houston, and Moore, *The Psalms*, 504. Allen writes, "The human king is picturesquely promised dominion over his national foes. Yahweh would fight on his behalf." Allen, *Psalms*, 86. The preposition עַד ("until") indicates that "the subjection of enemies is incomplete and continuing." Rogerson and McKay, *Psalms*, 3:67.

190 This language concerning the subjection of enemies depicts David's son being a king in the pattern of David. Hoskins writes, "David elsewhere talks about God dealing with his enemies in ways that are similar to Psalm 110 (Psalm 18:43–50). Another psalmist makes similar claims about what God promised to David regarding his enemies (Psalm 89:19–29). On one level, then, in Psalm 110, David passes on to his sons an inspired picture of what it means to be a king like David." Hoskins, *That Scripture Might Be Fulfilled*, 151.

Thus, Ps 110:1 in its original context recalls a moment in the life of David when he delivered a prophetic message to his lord, a future Davidic king, who would assume the throne after him. In Acts 2:34–35, Peter claims that David spoke these words with reference to Jesus. Peter shows that the text relaying David's description of the enthronement of one of his sons as king serves as the ultimate pattern and description [191] for Jesus' enthronement as king.[192] The typological connections Acts 2:34–35 establishes in its quotation of Ps 110:1 center on the following main points: (1) the exaltation or enthronement of a son of David to God's right hand and (2) the subjection of enemies to the king.

First, a son of David is exalted to the right hand of God. In the original context of Ps 110:1a–b, David speaks about the exaltation of one of his own sons to God's right hand. When David says, "The LORD says to my lord, 'Sit at my right hand . . . ,'" David assumes the role of a prophet and declares God's word to his son, Solomon.[193] The divine directive ("Sit at my right hand") pictures David's son's coronation or enthronement as Israel's new king and God's earthly vice-regent. David then calls him "my lord," a title which shows that David understands "this ruler will be God's king and not merely David's son."[194]

According to Peter's argument in Acts 2:33–36, David spoke Ps 110:1a–b with reference to Jesus' exaltation to the right hand of God (2:33). So, when David says, "The LORD [195] said to my Lord, 'Sit at my right hand . . . ,'" the ultimate referent of τῷ κυρίῳ μου ("my Lord") in Ps 110:1a–b in Acts 2:34 is Jesus.[196] Thus, God the Father is inviting David's promised Messianic descendent (cf.

---

191 It is correct to see David typology in view, even though David actually describes the enthronement of one of his sons. This is the case, because, as noted above, David actually describes his son's enthronement in Ps 110:1 with a view to himself and what it meant to be a king like him.

192 George Eldon Ladd explains, "The exaltation of Jesus to the right hand of God means nothing less than his enthronement as messianic King." George Eldon Ladd, *A Theology of the New Testament*, ed. Donald A. Hagner, rev. ed. (Grand Rapids: Eerdmans, 1974; repr., 1993), 372. So, the terms exaltation and enthronement will be used interchangeably in this section.

193 Although Solomon may be the primary focus here, the typological pattern of being a king like David only begins with him but does not end with him. Solomon is the initial exemplar who would be succeeded by David's future sons.

194 Hoskins, *That Scripture Might Be Fulfilled*, 151.

195 Peter's quotation follows the LXX, using [ὁ] κύριος ("The LORD") in the place of יְהוָה ("Yahweh").

196 Herbert W. Bateman makes an important point on Jesus as the "ultimate" referent to Ps 110:1, as seen in the NT. He writes, "[S]hould the New Testament be the determining factor . . . in seeking to identify the recipient of Psalm 110? No, the New Testament certainly defines the psalm's unique significance as it pertains to the ultimate Referent, Jesus Christ, but it does not 'unpack' all the psalm's meaning. Clear historical connections with David's world are evident in the psalm, connections that are *applicable* also to Jesus Christ." Bateman, "Psalm 110:1," 452. Accordingly, Peter is simply showing that God intended for the verse to apply ultimately to David's future son, Jesus Christ.

Acts 2:30) and superior son, Jesus Christ, to sit at his right side. Thus, Peter understands Ps 110:1a–b to reach its fulfillment in describing the enthronement of King Jesus, David's heavenly Lord and God's heavenly coregent. How does Ps 110:1a–b show Jesus' enthronement to be superior to and to fulfill the pattern set forth in David and his sons? First, Jesus' exaltation is superior in the manner of his installation. The way in which the Davidic king was installed as king of Israel was by God's appointment (cf. 2 Sam 7:12–16; 1 Kgs 1:48; 5:5; 8:20; 1 Chr 28:5–6; 29:1; 2 Chr 6:10),[197] and typically one of the sons of the former king was crowned to rule in his place. While Jesus descends from the line of David (Acts 2:30), he does not ascend to the throne of David over Israel merely by Davidic succession; instead God enthrones Jesus as king through his resurrection and ascension (Acts 2:31–33). In fact, as Dupont writes, "La résurrection de Jésus est son intronisation."[198] The resurrection has two parts: a raising up from the grave (Acts 2:24, 31–32) and a raising up to heaven (2:33–34). Thus, Jesus' resurrection-ascension is a "transcendental event," which distinguishes Jesus' enthronement from being "simply a renewal of David's earthly dominion."[199] Since Jesus takes the throne in a new way (i.e., by his resurrection-ascension), this introduces a heavenly and eternal rule that fulfills God's covenant promise to David.[200]

Second, Jesus is superior because he rules in heaven, not Jerusalem. The throne that God invited David's son to sit upon was located in Jerusalem (Ps 110:2). The Davidic king sat on "the throne of the LORD" (1 Chr 29:23) and at "[the LORD's] right hand" (Ps 110:1), but such language was understood either metaphorically or symbolically. The enthronement of Jesus, however, shifts from an earthly to a heavenly venue.[201] Peter stresses in Acts 2:33–34a that Jesus' resurrection was ultimately an ascension to heaven to be exalted to God's right side.[202]

Peter interprets the language of Ps 110:1a–b literally: Jesus' ascension to heaven means that he literally shares the throne of God and literally remains

---

197 Ross explains, "In order for the king to rule legitimately he had to be elected or chosen by the LORD. . . . Once the covenant was made with David (2 Sam 7:5–16), every Davidic king was considered to be elected by God." Ross, *Psalms*, 1:138. Cf. Ps 132:10–12.

198 "The resurrection of Jesus is his enthronement" (my translation). Dupont, "L'utilisation apologétique," 267.

199 Peterson, *Acts*, 152.

200 Cf. Ibid.

201 Hoskins observes this fulfillment in the David typology in connection to Christ. He writes, "David probably was not envisioning one of his sons literally sitting in heaven at the right hand of God (Psalm 110:1, Hebrews 10:12)." Hoskins, *That Scripture Might Be Fulfilled*, 152.

202 Cf. Ladd, *Theology*, 372–373. See Bock, who also notes that "locale is a major topic" in Peter's application of Ps 110:1 to Jesus. Bock, *Acts*, 134.

in God's presence at his right side.[203] This accentuates the fact that Jesus is the son of David who is greater than both David and Solomon (cf. Matt 12:42; Luke 11:31), neither of whom ascended to heaven to satisfy Ps 110:1a–b in its fullest sense.[204]

Third, Jesus' exaltation is superior in terms of lordship. David originally addressed one of his sons as "my lord" in Ps 110:1a–b to recognize his son as God's anointed. Israel's king was considered the son of God, yet the Davidic king was not considered divine in any sense.[205] The lordship of Jesus, however, clearly transcends that of a mere son of David because his is divine in nature. Rudolf Pesch explains, "In der Schriftauslegung, die Petrus vorträgt, ist der 'Sohn Davids' also als 'Sohn Gottes' und 'Menschensohn' begriffen."[206] Clearly, Acts 2:24–36 emphasizes Jesus' "divine sonship."[207] Jesus is not merely a descendent of David but the unique, divine Son of God, which the resurrection-ascension declares with power (cf. Rom 1:1–4). Consequently, Peter understands "my Lord" in Ps 110:1a–b to declare Jesus' superior status in a divine sense.[208] Bruce states that "the title κύριος as henceforth applied to Jesus has a higher value than the strict exegesis of Ps. 110:1 would imply; it is not inferior in dignity to the ineffable name of God."[209] In light of Jesus'

---

203 Cf. Bruce, *Acts*, 67; Haenchen, *Acts*, 183; Johnson, *Acts*, 55. For Jesus to be at the right side of God is literal in the sense of Jesus being in the very presence of the Father in heaven. At the same time, as Bock points out, the language is still somewhat figurative, "since God does not have a limited location or a right hand." Bock, *Acts*, 134.

204 Peter stresses Jesus' superiority to David by explicitly stating that it was not David who ascended to heaven but Jesus (Acts 2:34a).

205 See 2 Sam 7:12–16 (cf. 1 Chr 28:5–6; Ps 2:7), where God tells David that the one who would sit on his throne after him would be his "son." The Israelite king, though he was called God's "son," was not considered divine. See Ross, *Psalms*, 1:139–140.

206 "Thus, in Peter's interpretation of Scripture, the 'Son of David' is understood as the 'Son of God' and the 'Son of man'" (my translation). Pesch, *Die Apostelgeschichte*, 1:123.

207 Eduard Schweizer, "The Concept of the Davidic 'Son of God' in Acts and Its Old Testament Background," in *Studies in Luke-Acts: Essays presented in honor of Paul Schubert Buckingham Professor of New Testament Criticism and Interpretation at Yale University*, ed. Leander E. Keck and J. Louis Martyn (London: S.P.C.K., 1966), 187.

208 Jesus makes this very point in his interpretation of Ps 110:1 in Matthew 22:41–46 (cf. Mark 12:35–37; Luke 20:41–44). What Jesus argued before the Pharisees was that, while the Messiah was the son of David, he was more than merely his human descendent. In that David called the Messiah "my Lord," this meant that he was more than David's son. Ultimately, the Messiah was both the human son of David and the divine Son of God. See D. A. Carson, "Matthew," in EBC 8, ed. Frank E. Gaebelein (Grand Rapids: Zondervan, 1984), 466–469. Importantly, Jesus' interpretation of Ps 110:1 does not necessarily imply that in the original setting David was not addressing his earthly "lord," the king(s) to follow him. Jesus stresses that David spoke these words by the Holy Spirit (Matt 22:43). That being the case, Jesus can be understood to be pointing out the ultimate sense of what the Spirit intended by David's words. Put simply, while David addressed one of his sons "my lord" to recognize him as God's chosen king, the Holy Spirit intended ultimately for David's address to underscore the divine status of the promised Messiah and King.

209 Bruce, *The Acts of the Apostles*, 55. The "Lord" motif in Ps 110:1 as it applies to Jesus

resurrection-ascension to God's right hand, "Jesus's position suggests an intimate connection between Jesus and the Father and an equality between them."[210] Significantly, then, Jesus is not only the promised Messiah (Acts 2:31), but "he can be called *Lord* in the full sense that God is."[211] Lastly, Jesus' exaltation is functionally superior. "To sit at God's right" meant that Israel's king functioned as God's earthly vice-regent, but the Davidic king's authority as God's representative on earth was limited, for Yahweh reigned from heaven, and the earthly vice-regent was "dependent on Yahweh (Pss 80:17; 89:20–24)."[212] The Davidic king represented God's rule, but "this power is far inferior to being exalted to the right side of God."[213] For Jesus literally to sit at God's right hand describes him as enthroned to function as God's heavenly coregent, who "shares God's presence and glorious position."[214] This means that Jesus possesses a universal and eternal authority equal to the Father's over all things in heaven and earth. Especially important, as Peter points out, is Jesus' lordship over salvation. Jesus is both Lord and Messiah, who pours out the gift of the promised Holy Spirit and grants salvation to those who call upon his name (Acts 2:21, 33–38). Herbert W. Bateman summarizes:

> There is no other Davidic king like Jesus Christ. He is the anointed Messiah, the son of David. . . . He is literally in Yahweh's presence and at His right hand. . . . His authority extends over the earth and in heaven over angels, authorities, and powers (Eph 1:20–21; Col 1:15–20; 2:9–10; 2 Peter 3:22). He is "Lord" in the sense that He shares the name of Yahweh and distributes His salvific benefits to those who believe (Acts 2:14–36; Col. 1:15–2:6; Heb 1:5–13).

Thus, the first point of typological correspondence between these passages is the enthronement of Jesus as the ultimate son of David to God's right hand.

A second point of typological correspondence emerges in Acts 2:35, where Peter quotes Ps 110:1c: ἕως ἂν θῶ τοὺς ἐχθρούς σου ὑποπόδιον τῶν ποδῶν σου ("until I make Your enemies a footstool for Your feet"). When David

---

links back to the use of "Lord" in the Joel quotation in Acts 2:21, equating Jesus with the Yahweh of the OT on whom to call for salvation. On this, see the section "Literary Context of Acts 2:25–28" above in this chapter.

210 Bock, *Acts*, 134.

211 Peterson, *Acts*, 152. While Ps 110:1 establishes the equality between God the Father and Jesus, Peterson rightly notes that the text also distinguishes them as two distinct persons. Ibid.

212 Bateman, "Psalm 110:1," 451.

213 Calvin, *Acts 1–13*, 75. Calvin says this originally with respect to David, but it would apply to all successive human Davidic kings.

214 Bock, *Acts*, 133.

originally spoke this for the enthronement of one of his sons, he envisioned his absolute power and authority as Israel's king over his physical enemies, the neighboring nations and their kings (110:1–3, 5–6). Peter quotes Ps 110:1c to show that Jesus' enthronement also includes the promise from God to place all his enemies under his feet (Acts 2:35), though Peter provides no explicit interpretation about the identity of Jesus' enemies.[215] Even so, the context allows one to infer who the enemies are. On the one hand, they include all people who do not repent and call upon the Lord Jesus for forgiveness and salvation (Acts 2:21, 38–39).[216]

On the other hand, Barnabas Lindars rightly observes that Jesus' heavenly enthronement (Ps 110:1a–b in Acts 2:34) implies that the subjection of enemies also includes all spiritual enemies (cf. Eph 1:22; 1 Cor 15:25; Heb 2:5–8; 10:13; 1 Pet 3:22).[217] Jesus' rule, therefore, surpasses the human Davidic king's rule: it includes victory not just over national enemies but even the subjugation of all spiritual enemies. Furthermore, although the subjection of Jesus' enemies is still an ongoing process,[218] Jesus' heavenly and eternal rule guarantees the consummation of what was prefigured initially in the reign of the Davidic king.

The David-Jesus Typology: The Element of Prophecy

It is clear from the immediate context that the David typology that undergirds Peter's application of Ps 110:1 in Acts 2:34–35 possesses a prophetic force. Perhaps instead of a royal psalm, Psalm 110:1 is best classified as a typological-prophetic psalm.[219] The evidence for prophecy includes (1) the relationship between Ps 110:1 and the plan of God, (2) the introductory phrase, and (3) the reference to David's prophetic status.

Just as Ps 16:10 (above) provides a prophetic paradigm pointing forward to a similar but climactic event in Jesus' life, the same kind of inference equally applies to the quotation of Ps 110:1 in Acts 2:34–35. In Acts 2:33 Peter interprets the resurrection not only to denote Jesus' rising from the grave but

---

215 So Bruce, *The Acts of the Apostles*, 127–128.
216 Cf. Roloff, *Die Apostelgeschichte*, 60.
217 Lindars, *Apologetic*, 50. Lindars states, "His presence at the right hand of God necessarily entails the conquest of the spiritual powers." Ibid.
218 The preposition ἕως ("until") in Acts 2:35, as the immediate contexts makes clear, indicates that Jesus is ruling and God is making his enemies subject to him. Newman and Nida, *Acts*, 57–58.
219 Bateman, "Psalm 110:1," 453; Hoskins, *That Scripture Might Be Fulfilled*, 149–153. Contra Keener, who says in Ps 110 that David does not speak of himself but that "he explicitly speaks instead of his Lord (Acts 2:34)." Keener, *Acts*, 160.

also his rising (or ascending) to God's right side in heaven. This means, therefore, that when Peter initially spoke of the resurrection as part of God's plan for Jesus (Acts 2:23–31), the wider scope of the resurrection-ascension was also in mind, and it is fitting to see Ps 110:1 functioning in the same way as Ps 16:10. Put simply, Ps 110:1 reveals Jesus' exaltation to be an integral element of God's saving plan, and the verse was predicting an event with respect to Jesus. Hence, the typology connecting Jesus with the other Davidic kings is a prophetic typology, whereby David's description about one of his sons serves as a pattern pointing forward to its NT goal: God's enthronement of David's future son, Jesus.

Peter's introductory phrase λέγει δὲ αὐτός ("but he himself says" Acts 2:34b) also supports understanding the David typology in a prophetic way. In context David is the subject of the verb λέγει ("he says"). The purpose of the introductory phrase is to show that David predicted the exaltation of Jesus, the Messiah and Lord (2:32–33, 36). Peter begins with the premise that David did not ascend into heaven "as Jesus did" (Acts 2:34a).[220] Nevertheless, David did speak about one who was exalted by God to his right hand. Thus, Peter intends for his audience to understand that David's words refer specifically to the exaltation of Jesus, who did ascend to heaven to share God's throne. This is significant, for it means that the psalm had Jesus in mind, anticipating and pointing forward to him. David's original description of the enthronement of Solomon and his descendents, therefore, foreshadows predictively the enthronement of Jesus.

The most obvious evidence for a prophetic view of the typology is Peter's identification of David as a prophet in Acts 2:30–31, which was discussed above.[221] Peter reinforces the fact that the words David spoke in Pss 16:10 and 110:1 were under the inspiration of the Holy Spirit. Jesus himself, when he referenced Ps 110:1 in his discussion with the Pharisees, clearly states that David spoke these words ἐν πνεύματι ("in/by the Spirit" Matt 22:43; cf. ἐν τῷ πνεύματι τῷ ἁγίῳ Mark 12:36).

Given that David is called a prophet whose words were inspired by the Holy Spirit, the typology established by Ps 110:1 can be understood as possessing an inherent prophetic force. Admittedly, when David originally spoke the words of Ps 110:1 he may have understood them only with reference to the enthronement of one of his earthly sons after him, but, since the Holy Spirit was guiding David to declare God's revelation to the future Davidic king, David's

---

220 Acts 2:34a implies the contrast between David and Jesus, which the supplement "as Jesus did" makes clear. Newman and Nida, *Acts*, 57.

221 For a discussion of David's status as a prophet, see the section "The David-Jesus Typology: The Element of Prophecy" in the analysis of Acts 2:25–28 above in this chapter.

words could have meaning beyond his context. The Holy Spirit ultimately intended for these words to describe more fully the future, heavenly enthronement of Jesus.

Ps 2:1–2 in Acts 4:25–26

In Acts 4:25–26 the community of believers together cite a Psalms quotation in prayer, and again the quotation applies to Jesus typologically. Luke introduces the OT quotation in Acts 4:25b with the formula ὁ τοῦ πατρὸς ἡμῶν διὰ πνεύματος ἁγίου στόματος Δαυὶδ παιδός σου εἰπών ("who by the Holy Spirit, through the mouth of our father David Your servant, said"). The agent of the participle εἰπών ("said") is the pronoun σύ ("You") in 4:24, God.[222] How did God speak through the Scripture? The prepositional phrase διὰ πνεύματος ἁγίου ("by the Holy Spirit") identifies the Holy Spirit as the primary agent, while the genitival phrase στόματος Δαυὶδ ("through the mouth of David") identifies David as the secondary agent. So, as seen in prior texts (cf. Acts 1:16, 20; 2:25–28, 31, 34–35), "David is identified as the human author of the psalm, but what he uttered is regarded as the word of God because God's Spirit was speaking through him."[223]

The words of Acts 4:25b–26 represent a direct quotation from Ps 2:1–2, and the comparative analysis below demonstrates its close correspondence with both the MT and LXX.

Acts 4:25b–26	ἱνατί ἐφρύαξαν ἔθνη καὶ λαοὶ ἐμελέτησαν κενά; παρέστησαν οἱ βασιλεῖς τῆς γῆς καὶ οἱ ἄρχοντες συνήχθησαν ἐπὶ τὸ αὐτὸ κατὰ τοῦ κυρίου καὶ κατὰ τοῦ χριστοῦ αὐτοῦ
	"Why did the Gentiles rage, and the peoples devise futile things? The kings of the earth took their stand, and the rulers were gathered together against the LORD and against his Christ."
MT Ps 2:1–2	לָמָּה רָגְשׁוּ גוֹיִם וּלְאֻמִּים יֶהְגּוּ־רִיק יִתְיַצְּבוּ מַלְכֵי־אֶרֶץ וְרוֹזְנִים נוֹסְדוּ־יָחַד עַל־יְהוָה וְעַל־מְשִׁיחוֹ
	"Why are the nations in an uproar and the peoples devising a vain thing? The kings of the earth take their stand, and the rulers take counsel together against the LORD and against His Anointed."

---

222 Cf. Pesch, *Die Apostelgeschichte*, 1:176.
223 Peterson, *Acts*, 199.

LXX Ps 2:1–2	ἵνα τί ἐφρύαξαν ἔθνη καὶ λαοὶ ἐμελέτησαν κενά παρέστησαν οἱ βασιλεῖς τῆς γῆς καὶ οἱ ἄρχοντες συνήχθησαν ἐπὶ τὸ αὐτὸ κατὰ τοῦ κυρίου καὶ κατὰ τοῦ χριστοῦ αὐτοῦ
	"Why did the Gentiles rage, and the peoples conspire in vain? The kings of the earth stood, and the rulers were gathered together against the Lord and against his Christ."

In comparing Acts 4:25b–26 with Ps 2:1–2 in the MT and LXX, Pesch's assessment is sound: "Ps 2,1f ist in Übereinstimmung mit der LXX-Fassung zitiert, die freilich vom hebräischen Text nicht abweicht."[224] Thus, Acts 4:25b–26 is a clear quotation of Ps 2:1–2, with no authorial emendations.

The David-Jesus Typology: The Element of Correspondence

Peter quotes Ps 2:1–2 in his prayer with the gathered body of believers.[225] After quoting the passage, Peter immediately interprets it in connection to the passion of Jesus (Acts 4:27–28). An examination of the psalm and how Peter applies it to Jesus and his suffering evidence a hermeneutic of David typology.

Like Psalm 110, OT scholars commonly classify Psalm 2 as a royal Psalm.[226]

---

224 "Ps 2:1f is quoted in accordance with the LXX version, which, of course, does not deviate from the Hebrew text" (my translation). Pesch, *Die Apostelgeschichte*, 1:176.

225 In the examination of Acts 4:25–26, I attribute the quotation to Peter, seeing him as the most likely one who is voicing the prayer. Peter is clearly the one who cites Psalms in Acts 1:20; 2:25–28, 34–35. But, in Acts 4:25–26, the psalm quotation appears in a prayer that Luke reports was voiced collectively by the community of believers, which Peter and John joined after their release from jail (Acts 4:23–24). So, the text does not explicitly identify Peter as the speaker in this passage. Even so, three considerations provide warrant for seeing Peter as directly responsible for the quotation. First, up to this point in the narrative Luke has consistently placed the Psalms quotations on the lips of Peter. Thus, it seems logical to conclude that Peter is once again the source of the quotation in Acts 4:25–26. Second, according to Doble, the introductory words of Acts 4:23 show that "this prayer is organically linked with Peter's speech and with Luke's longer narrative unit (3:1–5:42)." Doble, "Psalms," 102. So, there is textual evidence that Luke intends for the community's prayer to be an extension of Peter's defense speech (cf. Acts 4:8–12, 19–20), thus, connecting the quotation to Peter. Third, as Darrell Bock points out, "One person probably prays here with the whole community sharing in the spirit and nature of the request." Bock, *Acts*, 203–204; so also, Peterson, *Acts*, 198. Since Peter takes on the role of spokesman in these early chapters of Acts (see Gaventa, *The Acts of the Apostles*, 69), it seems probable that he led the group in their prayer. See Joshua W. Jipp, "Luke's Scriptural Suffering Messiah: A Search for Precedent, a Search for Identity," *CBQ* 72 (2010): 272–273. Admittedly, one cannot be dogmatic that Peter was the direct source who quoted Ps 2:1–2. But, in the very least, Luke intends for the reader to connect Peter with the citation, even if indirectly, since he was a part of the communal prayer. Thus, whether directly or indirectly, Luke connects Peter to the reference in Acts 4:25–26.

226 See e.g., Craigie, *Psalms 1–50*, 64; VanGemeren, "Psalms," 64; Wilson, *Psalms Volume 1*, 107.

Prophetic David Typology in Acts 153

There is no superscript prefixed to the Psalm, so the original text lacks any authorial notations. The NT, however, attributes Psalm 2 to King David (Acts 4:25). The Psalm's precise historical setting is uncertain, but the general message of Psalm 2 is clear: David "writes about the authority of the Lord's king over the nations."[227]

Scholars observe that God's covenant promise to David (2 Sam 7:5–16) stands in the background of Psalm 2.[228] As VanGemeren explains, "God's relationship with David and his sons, who were also 'anointed,' involves the promise that through the Davidic dynasty God will establish his universal rule over the earth."[229] The context of the Davidic covenant, then, is significant to interpreting Psalm 2, for David knows that God's covenant promise is to him and his heirs (2 Sam 7:5–16), the Davidic kings who will succeed him.[230] Put simply, God stands behind the authority of David and his sons to rule, which means that the nations of the earth cannot successfully oppose him or his sons.[231]

The first section of the psalm (2:1–3) describes a scenario of futile rebellion by the nations and their kings against God's king. The first verse begins with לָמָּה ("why"), asking a rhetorical question,[232] the two parallel lines of which complement each other in their similar subjects (i.e. "nations"/"peoples")[233]

---

227 Hoskins, *Jesus as the Fulfillment*, 24.

228 VanGemeren writes, "It is preferable to read the psalm in the light of Nathan's prophecy of God's covenant with David (2 Sam 7:5–16)." VanGemeren, "Psalms," 64; see 64–65. Similarly, Belcher says, "It is preferable to read it [Psalm 2] in light of the covenant with David in 2 Samuel 7, where the greatness of David's name and kingdom are affirmed, the concept 'son' is given to those who follow in the Davidic line of kingship, and God's choice of David and his line matches up to 'his anointed' as God's chosen representative (Ps. 2:2)." Belcher, *The Messiah and the Psalms*, 123. See also Rogerson and McKay, *Psalms*, 1:19. Cf. Ross, *Psalms*, 1:199.

229 VanGemeren, "Psalms," 65. Similarly, Belcher states, "The structure of Psalm 2 supports the basic message of the psalm that God will establish his reign through his anointed king." Belcher, *The Messiah and the Psalms*, 123.

230 Belcher, *The Messiah and the Psalms*, 123; Hoskins, *That the Scripture Might Be Fulfilled*, 151–52; Rogerson and McKay, *Psalms*, 1:19.

231 Hoskins, *That Scripture Might Be Fulfilled*, 151–152. Hoskins adds, "David's inspired picture of himself as God's king over the nations may appear grandiose to us, because we know the full history that shows the limited extent to which David and his sons lived up to the inspired picture. Yet David did not know this history. He faithfully created an inspired picture of his great kingship and the greater kingship of his sons after him." Ibid., 152. Cf. Belcher, who notes that the "affirmations" of Ps 2 assume the Davidic king's "obedience" to God. Belcher, *The Messiah and the Psalms*, 123; see also 125.

232 The rhetorical question says something about the nations efforts to resist God's king: it "makes clear that the nations' attempt is vain." VanGemeren, "Psalms," 66.

233 גּוֹיִם in Ps 2:1a commonly translates as "nations" (*HALOT*, s.v. "גּוֹי."), referring always to "foreign nations" in its occurrences in the Psalms. Waltke, Houston, and Moore, *The Psalms*, 164. לְאֻמִּים in 2:1b can also be rendered as "nations" (see *HALOT*, s.v. "לְאֹם") but more commonly translates as "peoples" (see BDB, s.v. "לְאֹם"), with the sense here again of "foreign peoples." Waltke, Houston, Moore, *The Psalms*, 164. Together, these parallel terms denote pagan,

and verbs ("uproar"/"devising").[234] The picture that David paints is clearly one of enemy rebellion. Foreign nations and their various peoples assemble together in an uproar to attempt an "empty thing" (רִיק): to overthrow the rule of God's king.[235] In verse two,[236] those taking the initiative to plot a devious rebellion against God's king include the nations' leaders, designated by the synonymous terms of "kings" (2:2a) and "rulers" (2:2b).[237] In a unified effort, these leaders "take their stand" (יִתְיַצְּבוּ)[238] and "get together" (נוֹסְדוּ־יָחַד).[239] The twice-repeated preposition "against" (עַל) in 2:2c clarifies that these actions are fundamentally "antagonistic" in nature,[240] entailing opposition against "the LORD" and against "his anointed" (2:2c).[241] Importantly, then, David un-

---

non-Israelites with a slight distinction. The former term (i.e., "nations") envisages "political entities with recognizable boundaries," while the latter term (i.e., "peoples") designates "ethnically related people groups within these national boundaries." Wilson, *Psalms Volume 1*, 109n9; see also 725n2. Bock notes, "In an original reading of the psalm, most Jews would argue that these opponents are completely Gentile." Bock, *Acts*, 206. Contra Miura (*David in Luke Acts*, 162–166) who follows Calvin (*Psalms*, 4:10) in suggesting that these adversaries comprised both Gentiles and Jews.

234 The basic sense of the verb רָגְשׁוּ is "to be restless" or "to be in tumult or commotion." BDB, s.v. "רגשׁ;" *HALOT*, s.v. "רגשׁ." In that the nominal form of this verb designates a "throng," Goldingay explains that the verbal idea suggests a "disorderly ruckus." Goldingay, *Psalms 1–41*, 1:97. Ross says that "here it [the verb] refers to the tumultuous meeting of rebels to plan an attack." Ross, *Psalms*, 1:202. The parallel verb יֶהְגּוּ means "to plot" or "imagine/devise." BDB, s.v. "הגה;" HALOT, s.v. "הגה." This second verb, according to the parallelism, sheds light on the initial verb, picturing the meetings of the nations being commotions because they are discussing various schemes to rebel against God's king.

235 רִיק means "a vain thing/an empty thing." Ross, *Psalms*, 1:203.

236 It is possible that Ps 2:2 parallels the rhetorical form of 2:1. David may have intended for the interrogative "why" in 2:1 to be read with the second verse also. See Anderson, *Psalms*, 1:65.

237 The designations "the kings . . . the rulers are synonyms, and denote the leaders of the enemies of God (cf. [Ps.] 76:12 (M.T. 13), 102:15, 148:11; see also Jg. 5:3; Isa. 40:23; Hab. 1:10)." Ibid. See also Waltke, Houston, and Moore, *The Psalms*, 158n47. The term "kings" translates from the noun מַלְכֵי, which means "king/ruler." *HALOT*, s.v. "מֶלֶךְ." The second term translates the participle וְרוֹזְנִים, a substantive which means "dignitary" or "rulers/potentates." BDB, s.v. "רָזַן;" *HALOT*, s.v. "רוּזן."

238 Associated with this verb is the idea of "'taking a stand *against* [emphasis original]' someone in resistance." Wilson, *Psalms Volume 1*, 110n13. See also *HALOT*, s.v. "יצב," where the sense of the verb in Ps 2:2 is defined in terms of "to resist." According to Anderson, the verb communicates that the nations are readying themselves for a battle. Anderson, *Psalms*, 1:66.

239 *HALOT*, s.v. "II יסד." In addition to the meaning "to get together," *HALOT* also provides the sense of "to conspire" for the verb נוֹסְדוּ in Ps 2:2. Thus, the verb seems to picture a gathering together to scheme or to plan. Many translations bring this idea to the forefront by rendering the verb as "take counsel together" in Ps 2:2 (see e.g., ESV, NASB, RSV).

240 Ross, *Psalms*, 1:203.

241 Here, the substantival adjective מְשִׁיחוֹ ("anointed one") "refers to any anointed king who was seated on the throne of David." VanGemeren, "Psalms," 66–67. For David to be God's "anointed one" emphasizes that he stands in "special relationship" to God as his chosen king, acting "as God's agent or vice-regent." Victor P. Hamilton, "māshîaḥ," *TWOT* 1:531. Importantly, as Schreiner explains, the term "messiah" or "anointed one" applies to David and his heirs in

derstands something which escapes the enemies' awareness and, thus, nullifies their insubordination: to oppose Israel's chosen king is to oppose God himself.[242] What would motivate nations to rise against the Davidic king's authority and fight against God's plan? According to 2:3, "they saw their domination by the king in Jerusalem as bondage ... thus they came rushing together to plot their strategy of breaking free."[243]

This explanation of Psalm 2 helps clarify the David-Jesus typology in Acts 4:25–26. Peter applies Ps 2:1–2 directly to Jesus to explain his suffering in Acts 4:27–28.[244] Essentially, Peter understands the scene David describes in Ps 2:1–2, which originally applied both to him and his sons after him, to be a prefigurement of what the promised Son of David, Jesus, would experience.[245] The correspondences of the David-Jesus typology center on the following: (1) the royal status of the sufferer, (2) the rebellion of the nations against God's anointed, and (3) the futility of the nations' rebellion.

The royal status of the sufferer marks the first point of typological correspondence between David and Jesus in Acts 4:25–28. Psalm 2 is classified as a royal psalm, and the opening verses (Ps 2:1–3) depict God's king facing a rebellion from earthly kings and their nations. These two elements of the psalm naturally allow the reader to see God's chosen king of Psalm 2—David—as a suffering king (cf. Acts 4:25a). Jesus, like David, appears as a kingly sufferer in this present context (Acts 4:27). The logical connective γάρ ("for") beginning 4:27 indicates that the verse provides an interpretation of the previous

---

the context of the Davidic covenant and God's saving purposes. Thus, the term gave rise to the OT expectation of a future Messiah or Anointed King from David's line who would fulfill God's promise to David. Schreiner, *New Testament Theology*, 197–213.

242 So Calvin, *Psalms*, 4:10; Leupold, *Psalms*, 47; Waltke, Houston, and Moore, *The Psalms*, 164–165. As Ross puts it, "For the surrounding nations to attempt to throw off the authority of the anointed king would be to try to overthrow the plan of God." Ross, *Psalms*, 1:204.

243 Ross, *Psalms*, 1:204. The bondage language used here is not literal but figural in meaning. Ibid.

244 Acts 4:27 begins with the explanatory conjunction γάρ ("for"), indicating that what follows explains the fulfillment of the previous quotation. Cf. Kellum, *Acts*, 64.

245 The reference to "David" (i.e., Δαυὶδ παιδός σου, "David Your servant") in Acts 4:25a in connection to the quotation makes explicit the typological relationship Luke intends the reader to see between him and Jesus, whom he similarly designates as τὸν ἅγιον παῖδά σου Ἰησοῦν ("Your holy servant Jesus") in 4:27. For those who see a typological relationship between David and Jesus in the application of Psalm 2 in Acts 4, see e.g., Belcher, *The Messiah and the Psalms*, 125, 128; Calvin, *Psalms*, 4:9–13; Calvin, *Acts 1–13*, 124–126; Leupold, *Psalms*, 41–47; Miura, *David in Luke-Acts*, 173–174; Ross, *Psalms*, 1:202–203, 213–214.

Doble, though he does not use the language of typology, understands that the story of David tells the story of Jesus in the use of Ps 2:1–2 in Acts 2:25b–28. He argues that "this praying community has appropriated to Jesus the same Davidic position as that described in the psalm, a *christos* confronting a conspiracy against him. Here, in this prayer, Jesus' history is retold as *fulfilled* scripture." Doble, "Psalms," 103.

quotation, connecting it to Jesus and the recent events of his suffering and death. Peter's reference to Jesus as the one whom God "anointed" (ὃν ἔχρισας) recalls the language of the Ps 2:2 in Acts 4:26 (τοῦ χριστοῦ αὐτοῦ), which identifies Jesus as the anointed king (i.e., Messiah/Christ) of whom the psalm speaks.[246] Further emphasizing the regal status of Jesus is the royal title "your holy servant Jesus" (τὸν ἅγιον παῖδά σου Ἰησοῦν), a designation that parallels with "David your servant" (Δαυὶδ παιδός σου) in Acts 4:25a; here παῖς is used as a substitute for a term like "vice-regent."[247] Together, these titles point to Jesus as the chosen Davidic king, God's Messiah,[248] who suffers like David. Specifically, Peter explains in Acts 4:27 that the "Gentiles/nations" and "peoples" with their leaders united against Jesus in a violent effort that culminated in his passion. Thus, Peter has "appropriated to Jesus the same Davidic position as that described in the psalm, a *christos* confronting a conspiracy against him."[249] "Just as David had enemies, as Ps. 2 notes," according to Bock, "so did Jesus. Both figures, however, were God's chosen and anointed."[250] There is, then, the parallel picture of David and Jesus as kingly sufferers, as Ps 2:1–2 relates to each of them, respectively.

The regal status of Jesus, however, does not exactly parallel David's. Jesus is not just another "anointed one" from David's line. Peter's application of Ps

---

246 Acts 4:27 uses the verb χρίω ("to anoint") from which the noun Χριστός ("Anointed One/Christ/Messiah") derives. In Acts 4:26, τοῦ χριστοῦ αὐτου (i.e., his anointed one/his Christ) translates the corresponding Hebrew term מְשִׁיחוֹ (i.e., his anointed one/his messiah) of Ps 2:2. The title of "anointed one" in the original context of Ps 2 was simply a reference to the chosen human king, "derived from the fact that the king on his coronation is anointed (1 Kgs 1:45), an act symbolizing that he was set aside from other persons to perform a particular service." Craigie, *Psalms 1–50*, 66. See the summary of Ps 2:1–2 in its OT context above in this section, for the discussion of the "anointed one" (i.e., Messiah) as it relates to the promise-fulfillment scheme of the Davidic covenant and the OT expectation of a future Messiah King from David's line.

247 It is common for Acts commentators to explain Jesus' title of "servant" in Acts 4:27 (cf. also Acts 3:13, 26; 4:30) against the background of the suffering Isaianic Servant of God (see e.g., Arrington, *Acts*, 40–41, 49). But, the term παῖς ("servant," see BDAG, s.v. "παῖς.") as it used in reference to both Jesus and David (cf. also Luke 1:69; Acts 2:30) in Acts 4:25, 27 in association with Ps 2 appears to be "royal language, appropriate to David the king and to the Messiah-King." Juel, *Messianic Exegesis*, 131; see also 79, 85. See also, Dale A. Brueggemann, "The Evangelists and the Psalms," in *Interpreting the Psalms: Issues and Approaches*, ed. David Firth and Philip S. Johnston (Downers Grove: IVP Academic, 2005), 274n41; Jipp, "Messiah," 264–266, 273n66. "Servant of Yahweh," as Wilson explains, was a way to designate Israel's kings, specifically King David in Psalms. Wilson, *Psalms Volume 1*, 116 and 116n29, 335–336, 335n3. In sum, it seems best in the context of Acts 4:25, 27 to understand παῖς in royal terms as a designation for the Davidic king. It is possible, however, that Luke may intend the title to evoke designation not only of Jesus' royalty but also his suffering in connection to David's sufferings. Cf. Doble, "Psalms," 104.

248 Doble rightly observes that Luke formally links David and Jesus together in the interpretation of Ps 2:1–2 by means of the terms "anointed one" and "servant." Doble, "Psalms," 103.

249 Ibid.

250 Bock, *Acts*, 207.

2:1–2 suggests "a profound difference between David and Jesus," signaling "the identification of Jesus as the promised '*Anointed One*' (v. 26, *tou Christou*)."²⁵¹ Additionally, the adjective ἅγιον ("holy;" Acts 4:27) distinguishes Jesus' kingship from the kings of the Davidic dynasty, describing Jesus' unique relationship to God and identifying Jesus as God's appointed Messiah King.²⁵²

The second key typological correspondence concerns the identity and activity of the enemies. In the original context of Ps 2:1–2, David speaks about a coalition of foreign nations (i.e., nations and peoples) and their leaders (i.e., kings and rulers) coming together to conspire against him in a hostile effort to overthrow him. Peter applies these enemies specifically to people responsible for Jesus' death.²⁵³ Acts 4:27 indicts the following adversaries directly: Herod (who fills the role of the "kings"), Pontius Pilate (who fills the role of the "rulers"), the gentiles (who fill the role of the "nations"), and the peoples of Israel (who fill the role of "peoples").²⁵⁴ Similar to what David described, the opponents of Jesus comprised an evil alliance or coalition of peoples and their leaders who "gathered together" (συνήχθησαν Acts 4:27). The preposition "against" (ἐπί) indicates the gathering was "hostile opposition" directed toward Jesus.²⁵⁵ The repetition in Acts 4:27 of a verb and preposition quoted from Ps 2:2 in Acts 4:26 explicitly links Jesus' suffering with David's situation.²⁵⁶

---

251   Peterson, *Acts*, 199.

252   Cf. Marshall, *Acts*, 112; Peterson, *Acts*, 200–201. Cf. Alexander writes, "*Holy*, as here applied to Christ, denotes not only character but office, not only his exemption from all moral taint, but his peculiar consecration to the work which his Father gave him to do." Alexander, *Acts*, 168.

253   Weiser, *Die Apostelgeschichte*, 133. See also Gaventa, *Acts*, 96.

254   Pesch, *Die Apostelgeschichte*, 1:177. (1) Herod: Luke is the only evangelist to record Herod's role in passion events (cf. Luke 23:7–15; see Mark 6:14, where Herod is identified as "King Herod). (2) Pilate: Luke narrates Pilate's involvement in Jesus' death and his specific collaboration with Herod in Luke 23:1–25. (3) the Gentiles: The Greek term translated as "Gentiles" is ἔθνεσιν, which can mean "nations" or "gentiles." See BDAG, s.v. "ἔθνος." Johnson explains well: "The same Greek word (*ethnē*) is used here as was translated 'nations' in the psalm citation. The reason for the shift [to Gentiles] is that Luke in his application is clearly thinking of 'representatives' of the nations as figures playing a role in Jesus' death (see Luke 23:47; Acts 2:23), rather than 'the nations' as entities." Johnson, *Acts*, 84–85. Here, the Gentiles denote the Roman authorities who conducted Jesus' execution. See Bruce, *The Acts of the Apostles*, 158. (4) the peoples of Israel: Luke's use of the plural "peoples" (λαοῖς) conforms to the plural form of the same noun in the psalm citation in Acts 2:25. The sense of the plural "peoples of Israel" may be understood as a reference to the various tribes of Israel (so e.g., Calvin, *Acts 1–13*, 126; Weiser, *Die Apostelgeschichte*, 133), to individual Jews and their rulers (so e.g., Johnson, *Acts*, 85; Marshall, "Acts," 553), or to the tribes, individuals, and rulers of the Jews who participated in Jesus' death. On Luke's "repeat" emphasis of the Jews' responsibility for Jesus' death, see Jacob Jervell, *The Theology of the Acts of the Apostles*, New Testament Theology (Cambridge: Cambridge University Press, 1996), 101n196.

255   BDAG, s.v. "ἐπί."

256   Cf. Newman and Nida, who explain the verb "gathered together . . . against" in Acts 4:27 denotes "multiple concepts" in explaining the meaning of the psalm citation. Newman

This direct echo invites the reader to consider how Jesus' enemies "raged" (ἐφρύαξαν) and "conspired" (ἐμελέτησαν) against him, even though these verbs are not repeated.[257] What David describes concerning himself, then, is seen to be happening in the history of Jesus.

Nevertheless, the application of Ps 2:1–2 to Jesus shows that his passion goes beyond the event David originally described. First, Jesus' enemies are drawn from a greater variety of factions. David's enemies are the leaders and armies of foreign or pagan nations. Peter, however, interprets these verses "with a broader application" that includes the Jews and their rulers as well.[258] Jacob Jervell writes, "Enmity with Jesus unites Gentiles with Jews: the Jews co-operate with the enemies of Israel and God against the God of Israel and his Messiah."[259] Jesus' rejection stands climactic against David's, since both Gentiles and Jews collaborated as his adversaries. Second, Jesus' suffering surpasses David's in that the conspiracy against Jesus results in his death, while God intervenes on David's behalf before the rebels can do him lasting harm. Nevertheless, the very fact that Jesus overcomes the rebellion of the nations not by violence but by his death (and resurrection) indicates that his kingship is greater than David's.[260]

The last point of typological correspondence centers on the futility of the nations' rebellion against God's anointed one. David's opponents in Ps 2:1–2 act "in vain" (2:1), for resisting God's chosen king equated to resisting God himself (2:2c). In the application of Ps 2:1–2 to Jesus, Peter establishes the same truth. Marshall explains, "In the present context it is the opening words of the psalm which speaks of the fruitless plotting of the peoples and their rulers against the Messiah which were relevant to the immediate situation."[261] In Acts 4:25, the adjective κενά ("in vain) clarifies that the conspiracy of the Gentiles and Jews against Jesus was ultimately an effort of futility. Additionally, the rhetorical "why" (ἱνατί) at the beginning of the quotation in Acts 4:25b

---

and Nida, *Acts*, 106–107. Cf. Pesch, *Die Apostelgeschichte*, 1:177; Stählin, *Die Apostelgeschichte*, 77. Συνήχθησαν parallels the other verb παρέστησαν in Ps 2:2 in Acts 4:26, which speaks of standing against someone with "hostile intent." BDAG, s.v. "παρίστημι."

257 The former verb means "to be tumultuous/to rage" (Thayers, s.v. "φρυάσσω.") or "to be arrogant/haughty/insolent" (BDAG, s.v. "φρυάσσω."). The latter verb means "to mediate/to devise/to contrive" (Thayers, s.v. "μελετάω.") or "to think vain thoughts/to conspire in vain" (BDAG, s.v. "μελετάω.").

258 Ross, *Psalms*, 1:203. Peterson describes this aspect of Psalm 2, the inclusion of the Jews among those who took a stand against the Lord's Anointed One, a "surprising fulfillment." Peterson, *Acts*, 200. By explicitly naming the Jews in this way, Peter makes clear that all those who reject Jesus become God's enemies, whether they are Gentiles or Jews. See Bock, *Acts*, 206.

259 Jervell, *Theology of the Acts*, 101.
260 Craigie, *Psalms 1–50*, 69.
261 Marshall, *Acts*, 112.

implies that the conspiracy Jesus' adversaries plan to execute against him will end in failure.[262]

There are two explicit reasons for the failure of the conspiracy. One, as Acts 4:26c reveals, Jesus' enemies were rebelling "against the Lord and against his Christ." On this, Calvin writes, "The Spirit here teaches us that all who refuse to submit to Christ are making war against God."[263] Commenting on Acts 4:27, Gustav Stählin similiarly states, "Der Zweck jenes Zusammenschlusses der Gegner war der Kampf gegen Gott und gegen Jesus."[264] Consequently, all the plotting against Jesus was truly in vain, because the enemy of Jesus is the enemy of God.

Two, as Acts 4:28 reveals, all that Jesus' opponents plotted against him was in accordance with the predetermined plan of God. Here, the reference to God's plan establishes that the Roman and Jewish persecution of Jesus was no surprise to God. Instead, their actions fulfill what Ps 2:1–2 foreshadowed. All who conspired against Jesus, "ohne es zu wissen, zu Werkzeugen Gottes bei der Durchsetzung seines Heilsratschlusses."[265] Furthermore, when he raised Jesus from the dead and seated him in glory, "Gott spottete seiner Feinde."[266] In the end, God triumphed over his enemies eternally through King Jesus, who overcame death through his resurrection-ascension and fulfilled God's sovereign plan of redemption.

The David-Jesus Typology: The Element of Prophecy

The use of Ps 2:1–2 in Acts 4:25–26 rests upon David typology. There are several reasons to believe that typology is prophetic, including: (1) the Holy Spirit's inspiration of and intentions for Ps 2:1–2 and (2) the relationship of Ps 2:1–2 to the plan of God.

The first argument for interpreting the typology of Acts 4:25–26 prophetically stems from the reference to the Holy Spirit's inspiration of Ps 2:1–2. The introductory formula in Acts 4:25a corresponds closely to the one in Acts 1:16,[267] which introduces Peter's quotations of Pss 69:25 and 109:8 (Acts 1:20). In both passages Peter establishes the dual authorship of the Psalm quotation in the introductory formula. David is the human author who spoke the

---

262 Marshall, "Acts," 553.
263 Calvin, *Acts 1–13*, 125.
264 "The purpose of this association of opponents was the fight against God and against Jesus" (my translation). Stählin, *Die Apostelgeschichte*, 77.
265 "without knowing it, they become instruments of God in the enforcement of his saving counsel" (my translation). Roloff, *Die Apostelgeschichte*, 87.
266 "God mocked his enemies" (my translation). Pesch, *Die Apostelgeschichte*, 1:177.
267 Weiser, *Die Apostelgeschichte*, 132.

words of Psalm 2 διὰ πνεύματος ἁγίου ("by the Holy Spirit"). By means of this introductory formula, Peter presents Ps 2:1–2 "als Gottesrede" in that "Gott sprach 'durch den Heiligen Geist'" and "sein Heiliger Geist sprach durch 'Davids Mund.'"[268] The reference to the Holy Spirit emphasizes the divine inspiration of Psalm 2,[269] acknowledging the Spirit to be the ultimate author of the words that David wrote.

This is important for understanding how Peter can transfer this originally Davidic psalm text in Acts 2:27–28 so directly to Jesus's passion. The comments in Acts 2:27–28 make clear, Peter views it as "a prophecy fulfilled in the events leading to the Passion: Jesus is the Messiah of whom the Psalm speaks."[270] Similarly, Amsler notes that Acts 2:27 substantiates that the events of Jesus' passion represent "une vérification (*en vérité*) de ce qui a été dit dans l'Ecriture."[271] Thus, Ps 2:1–2 is understood to be an OT prophecy given by the inspiration of God, foretelling the opposition Jesus would suffer.[272]

It is significant to define, however, precisely what form the prophecy takes in Ps 2:1–2. This passage is an event-based text, relaying originally David's depiction of hostile rebellion of the nations against God's king. Thus, the prophecy is clearly not verbal prediction but typological prediction.[273] John D. Currid observes:

> Note that Luke understands the gathering together of the persecutors of Jesus as having been typologically predicted in Psalm 2. In other words, the plotting and revolt of the heathen nations against the Davidic king in Psalm 2 serve as a prefiguration of the scheming of Herod and others to kill the Son of David, the true king of Israel.[274]

---

268 Peter presents Ps 2:1–2 "as divine speech" in that "God spoke 'through the Holy Spirit'" and "his Holy Spirit spoke through 'David's mouth'" (my translation). Pesch, *Die Apostelgeschichte*, 1:176.

269 Cf. Peterson, *Acts*, 199; Polhill, *Acts*, 149.

270 Haenchen, *Acts*, 226–227. According to Walter Brueggemann, Peter "considers David's words prophetic, since his words came 'by the Holy Spirit.'" Brueggemann, "The Evangelists and the Psalms," 274n41.

271 "A verification (in truth) of what has been said in Scripture" (my translation). Amsler, *L'Ancien Testament Dans L'Église*, 68.

272 Cf. e.g., Larkin, *Acts*, 79; Polhill, *Acts*, 149.

273 In his analysis of Psalm 2, Ross explains how it applies to Christ in the NT. He writes, "The psalm is essentially prophetic. It applies first to any Davidic king who came to the throne, but ultimately to the King of Kings. It is therefore not directly prophetic, but typologically so." Ross, *Psalms*, 1:213.

274 John D. Currid, "Recognition and Use of Typology in Preaching," *RTR* 53 (1994): 124.

Calvin also maintains that Ps 2:1–2 prophesies about Christ by way of typology, so that what David declares about himself actually predicts truth concerning Christ.[275] David may have had understanding of the typological import of what he was writing,[276] but such an understanding on the part of David is not necessary, when one takes seriously the Holy Spirit's inspiration of Ps 2:1–2 and his ultimate intention to use what David describes as a prophetic pattern for Christ's experience.[277] Peter interprets the passage he quotes as a prophecy. Furthermore, by quoting a text that records David's depiction of an event, this evidences that Peter understood the prophecy in this instance to be essentially typological.

In addition, what Peter says in Acts 4:28 also supports a prophetic interpretation of Ps 2:1–2 in connection to the events of Jesus' death and suffering. Peter states ποιῆσαι ὅσα ἡ χείρ σου καὶ ἡ βουλή [σου] προώρισεν γενέσθαι ("to do whatever Your hand and Your purpose predestined to occur"). Ποιῆσαι ("to do") is a purpose infinitive that modifies the main verb συνήχθησαν ("they were gathered together") in the previous verse.[278] This infinitive indicates why Herod, Pilate, the Gentiles, and the Jews came together against Jesus: in order to do ὅσα ("whatever/everything"),[279] an accusative pointing back to the hostile actions of Jesus' adversaries against him as outlined in 2:27. Importantly, ὅσα serves also as the object of the clause ἡ χείρ σου καὶ ἡ βουλή [σου] προώρισεν γενέσθαι ("Your hand and Your purpose predestined to occur"). This subsequent clause "shows with all possible clarity the conviction that the passion transpired by divine necessity and that God works in relation to human events with final authority."[280]

The reference to God's "hand" (ἡ χείρ) is frequently a symbol of God's mighty deeds in the OT.[281] This expression denotes God's power and is "added to stress God's sovereignty in all these events."[282] The reference to God's "plan" (ἡ βουλή),[283] which Peter used earlier in Acts 2:23 in his citation of Ps

---

275 Calvin, *Psalms*, 4:9–12.
276 So Ibid., 11.
277 Cf. Hoskins, *Jesus as the Fulfillment*, 24–25.
278 Cf. Newman and Nida, *Acts*, 107.
279 BDAG, s.v. "ὅσος."
280 Soards, *The Speeches in Acts*, 49. Because God was sovereignly acting in the events that transpired, "die Herrschenden und Machthaber, die aus eigener Willkür zu handeln glaubten, wurden so, ohne es zu wissen, zu Werkzeugen Gottes bei der Durchsetzung seines Heilsratschlusses" ("The rulers and potentates, who believed themselves to act arbitrarily, thus became, without knowing it, instruments of God in enforcing his salvation decree" [my translation]). Roloff, *Die Apostelgeschichte*, 87.
281 Roloff, *Die Apostelgeschichte*, 87.
282 Peterson, *Acts*, 201.
283 The basic sense of βουλή is "plan/purpose/intention" referring in Acts 4:28 (see also,

16:8–11,²⁸⁴ indicates that Jesus' passion was according to God's purpose or will.²⁸⁵ Peter qualifies the plan of God further with the verb προώρισεν ("decide upon beforehand/predetermine"),²⁸⁶ which draws attention to the fact that God's plan of salvation consists of future events previously established by God that were fulfilled in Jesus.²⁸⁷

Overall, then, Peter's quotation of Ps 2:1–2 in Acts 4:25–28 clarifies that God's plan of salvation entailed a united conspiracy against Jesus.²⁸⁸ Rightly, then, the David typology established by Ps 2:1–2 bears a prophetic thrust, pointing forward to its fulfillment in Jesus' passion.

Summary

This chapter examined five Psalms quotations that Peter quotes in speeches recorded by Luke in Acts 1:20 (Pss 69:25; 109:8), 2:25–28 (Ps 16:8–11), 2:34–35 (Ps 110:1), and 4:25–26 (Ps 2:1–2). In each passage, the quotation comes from a psalm of David, where David is describing an experience specific to him (i.e., Pss 16; 69; 109) or to him and his descendents (i.e., Pss 2; 110). Peter references these specific psalms to provide the biblical basis for events specific to Jesus: his suffering and death (Acts 1:20; 4:25–26), his resurrection (2:25–28), and his exaltation (2:34–35).

From the analysis of these Psalms quotations, as in chapter 4 of this work, two primary observations came to light, namely, that David typology and prophecy coalesce. Peter juxtaposes psalm texts relaying events with recent events in Jesus life, thus substantiating textually that real correspondences are being made between David and Jesus and their experiences. This affirms that Peter applies these quotations to Jesus based on David typology. Second, ample evidence was noted in each passage that Peter understood the Psalms quotations to apply to Jesus in a prophetic way. The quotations do

---

Acts 2:23; 13:36; 20:27) to 'the divine will.' BDAG, s.v. "βουλή."

284 See the section "The David-Jesus Typology: The Element of prophecy" in the analysis of Acts 2:25–28 above in this chapter.

285 Dormeyer and Galindo, *Die Apostelgeschichte*, 79.

286 BDAG, s.v. "προορίζω." According to Erwin Preuschen, "προώρισεν (s. zu Rom 829) ist streng genommen nur mit βουλή zu verbinden; aber für den Frommen ist der Ratschluß und die ihn ausführende Kraft eine Einheit. Der Gedanke wie 223" ("προώρισεν [see Rom 8:29] is strictly speaking only to be associated with βουλή; but for the pious the counsel and the power exercising it is a unity. The thought is like 2:23" [my translation]). Preuschen, *Die Apostelgeschichte*, 26.

287 Cf. Pesch, *Die Apostelgeschichte*, 1:177.

288 Concerning the conspiracy against Jesus in Acts 2:27, Doble says, "But this is within God's plan revealed in scripture (Acts 4:28)—here revealed through Psalm 2." Doble, "Psalms," 101.

not function as simple analogies which merely compare David and Jesus but constitute prophecies that reach their goals or fulfillments in Jesus, indicating that the OT passages are properly understood as predictive prefigurations of Christ and his experiences. In these instances, Luke shows his readers that Peter follows Jesus' example and teaching about how to understand the Psalms as predictive of his passion events (cf. Luke 24:44). Since the history of Jesus is shown to fulfill what the history of David was anticipating, traditional, prophetic David typology seems to explain best how the Psalms quotations apply to the events of Jesus' life in Acts 1, 2, and 4. Jesus is presented as the New David who is greater than David.[289]

---

289 This contention supports Dupont's claim that David represents a typological figure of Christ in Acts, even though he evaluates Luke's typologies as "une typologie d'ailleurs peu élaborée" ("a typology that is not well developed" [my translation]). Jacques Dupont, "L'utilisation apologétique de l'Ancien Testament dans les discours des Actes," in Études sur les Actes des Apôtres, LD 45 (Paris: Éditions du Cerf, 1967), 276. The David typology in Acts, however, appears to be more developed than Dupont thinks, considering the substantial typological correspondences the verses from Psalms highlight between David's and Jesus' stories in the texts examined in this chapter. On Peter's quotation of Ps 16:8–11 in Acts 2, Dormeyer and Galindo state, "Der christologische Mittelpunkt der Rede erklärt Jesus zum neuen David und stellt ihn zugleich über David" ("The Christological center of the speech declares Jesus to be the new David and at the same time places him above David" [my translation]). Dormeyer and Galindo, *Die Apostelgeschichte*, 54. The same can be said for each of the Psalms quotations examined in this chapter—they present Jesus as the New and Greater David.

6

Conclusion

This work argues that prophetic David typology best explains the appropriation of psalms of David to Jesus in the select passages examined in John and in Acts. In these focal passages, Jesus (John 13:18; 15:25), John (John 19:24, 28), and Peter (Acts 1:20; 2:25–28, 34–35; 4:25–26) each quote from various psalms written by David, interpreting texts originally about David also to concern Jesus. Together, Jesus, John, and Peter reinforce a common way of understanding how David's psalms can ultimately be transferred to Jesus. Put simply, these texts about David's experiences ultimately provide predictive foreshadowing of corresponding (and climactic) NT events fulfilled in Jesus' experiences: his passion, his resurrection, and his exaltation.

By using event-based psalm texts in NT contexts, the NT authors show that David and Jesus share a typological relationship. That is, David and his experiences stand as OT types, providing prophetic patterns that point to future goals to be fulfilled in Jesus, the NT antitype. Thus, these event-based texts relate in their OT and NT contexts as prophecies and fulfillments. The David typology, therefore, is not simple analogical typology that merely compares David with Jesus. Instead, the typology possesses a prophetic dimension. Furthermore, since the typology consistently presents Jesus as not merely repeating but fulfilling the pattern of David in the scope of salvation history, the prophetic David typology identifies Jesus as great David's greater Son. Thus, Jesus is the New David and promised Messiah of OT expectation.

The objective of this chapter is fourfold. First, it reviews the main points of chapters 1–5, giving primary attention to the exegetical analysis that identifies prophetic David typology as the way in which the Psalms quotations in John and Acts apply to Jesus. Second, it compares John's and Luke's uses of the psalms of David in their application to Jesus. Third, it identifies the important implications this study has for understanding how the concept of typology relates to biblical prophecy, how the psalms of David predict various events in Jesus' life, and how the psalms of David collectively provide a specific portrait of who Jesus is. Lastly, it provides suggestions for further research.

Review of Chapters 1 to 5

Chapter 1 states that the purpose of this work is to show that David typology in the traditional, prophetic sense best explains the way Jesus (John 13:18; 15:25), John (John 19:24, 28), and Peter (Acts 1:20; 2:25–28, 34–35; 4:25–26) apply the quotations from the psalms of David to the specific events of Jesus' passion, resurrection, and exaltation. The introduction highlights several reasons why this is significant for NT scholarship.

Chapter 2 sets forth an important foundation for this work, clarifying the traditional view of typology over against the modern analogical view. Proponents of the analogical view of typology define the concept primarily in terms of analogy between OT and NT events as they relate in salvation history. Proponents of traditional typology, however, define the concept as the study of the relationship between specific OT realities or "types" (i.e., events, persons, or institutions) and corresponding NT realities or "antitypes," whereby an OT type prefigures and predicts its NT antitype or fulfillment. Thus, type and antitype relate to each other as a kind of prophecy and fulfillment. So, unlike analogical typology, traditional typology values a predictive element in the biblical concept, and it recognizes that God shapes and uses OT historical events in the teleological orientation of salvation history to predict future, climactic NT goals to be fulfilled in Christ and the realities of his gospel.

Chapter 3 discusses some of the biblical and historical evidence that supports understanding typology according to a prophetic sense. In terms of biblical evidence, NT πληρόω (i.e., "fulfillment") language indicates that typology bears a predictive force. The NT writers commonly employ πληρόω in introductory formulas to note the prophetic fulfillment of OT texts that relay words (i.e., verbal predictions). Significantly, the NT writers also use πληρόω in introductory formulas with OT texts that relay events (i.e., typological predictions). When used in conjunction with event-based OT texts, πληρόω signals that these texts have reached their NT goals in Christ, which means that the text was anticipating and pointing forward to or predicting that goal. Accordingly, then, πληρόω implies prophecy in typology, so that OT event-based texts provide predictive models for respective NT goals or fulfillments.

Chapter 4 examines four passages where John uses clear references to psalms of David to provide the biblical rationale for the specific events of Jesus' suffering and death: (1) 13:18/Psalm 41:9, (2) 15:25/Psalm 69:4, (3) 19:24/Psalm 22:18, and (4) 19:28/Psalm 69:21. John records Jesus citing the first two Psalms texts (John 13:18; 15:25), while as narrator he cites the latter two (John 19:24, 28). Each of these quotations is in its original context a lament of King David, where he describes a situation of suffering induced by enemies. Both Jesus and John view these psalms as fitting descriptions of King Jesus' similar but greater experiences of suffering: the betrayal by Judas (John 13:18), the world's baseless hate toward him (John 15:25), the soldiers' execution of him and distribution of his clothing (John 19:24), and the soldiers' offering of a sour-wine drink on the cross (John 19:28). The references to these psalms juxtapose the original David event with the recent Jesus event. This juxtaposition of texts, in turn, establishes real textual correspondences between David and Jesus and their experiences of suffering, and it ultimately signals the presence of a David-Jesus typology. Thus, what David describes in these Psalms texts concerning his suffering serves to foreshadow corresponding but climactic events of suffering in the life of Jesus.

Clearly, however, these Psalms texts in the FG apply to Jesus in a way that sets forth more than mere comparisons or analogies with David and his experiences. Several items of textual evidence in each NT context indicate that the quotations are understood to possess a predictive thrust in connection to the NT events. One of these key textual items is the ἵνα purpose clauses, the telic force of which supports a prophetic notion in relation to Psalms and corresponding NT events. Another key textual item is the introductory "fulfillment" (i.e., πληρόω/τελειόω) formulas used in conjunction with these Psalms, which denote a prophetic fulfillment of these OT texts. Since the NT presents these event-based Psalms texts as predictions fulfilled in Jesus' passion, this means David's history provides a predictive model for Jesus' history in these instances. The David typology, therefore, connects formally to Jesus in the sense of prophecy and fulfillment.

Chapter 5 examines four passages in Acts where Luke also uses clear quotations from psalms of David to provide the OT basis for specific events in Jesus' life: (1) 1:20/Psalms 69:25 and 109:8, (2) 2:25–28/Psalm 16:8–11, (3) 2:34–35/Psalm 110:1, and (4) 4:25–26/Psalm 2:1–2. In each of these chapters, Luke records Peter appealing to these various Psalms verses in his speeches. Each of the quotations that Peter cites is a passage that recounts an event specific to David in its original setting, or to David and his sons. Though David describes his own personal experiences in these verses, Peter understands them to describe ultimately Jesus' similar but greater experiences: the treachery of Judas and his divine judgments (Acts 1:20), his bodily resurrection (Acts 2:25–28), the exaltation and enthronement to God's right side in heaven as Lord (Acts 2:34–35), and the futile rebellion of the nations and their leaders against God's Anointed One (Acts 4:25–26). In quoting these psalms, Peter brings together OT and NT texts that describe events original to David but re-appropriated to Jesus. Peter explicitly connects these Psalms quotations to David with repeated references (cf. Acts 1:16; 2:25, 29, 34; 4:25), reinforcing the David typology that undergirds the application of these OT texts to Jesus. Peter, therefore, understands the Psalms texts that describe events about David to foreshadow specific events concerning Jesus. Peter's use of this typology is not merely analogical, however; there is textual evidence demonstrating that Peter understands the Psalm verses to be predictions of the NT events in view, including the use of NT "fulfillment" language (Acts 1:16), reference to the Spirit's inspiration of the Psalms texts (Acts 1:16; 4:25), and reference to David's status as a prophet (Acts 2:30–31). The David typology, then, assumes a prophetic force, since these event-based Psalms texts are interpreted as prophecies fulfilled in Jesus' similar but climactic experiences. Ultimately, therefore, it is right to understand the David typology as possessing a prophetic force.

Comparing John and Acts

In comparing John and Acts, one first observes that John does not explicitly mention David's name in connection to the psalms he cites, but Luke explicitly references David (see Acts 1:16; 2:25, 29, 34; 4:25). Thus, whereas John establishes David typologies simply by quoting Davidic psalms, Luke establishes them by citing Davidic psalms and explicitly referencing David. This pattern may simply be a difference in how John and Luke prefer to cite Scripture, or Luke's repeat references to David may be his way to accentuate the typological relationships between David and Jesus.

Second, in both John and Acts, the royal status of David and Jesus is a correspondence that appears in each context to establish a typological relationship between them. Notably, while John and Luke both cite psalms to underscore Jesus' status as a king who suffers like David (i.e., Ps 41:9/John 13:18; Ps 69:4/John 15:25; Ps 22:18/John 19:24; Ps 69:21/John 19:28; Pss 69:25; 109:8/Acts 1:20; Ps 2:1–2/Acts 4:25–26), Luke uniquely cites them to highlight Jesus' divine deliverance through resurrection (Ps 16:10/Acts 2:25–28) and his exaltation to heaven (Ps 110:1/Acts 2:34–35). Thus, Luke uses David's psalms to show that Jesus is ultimately the Lord and Messiah, who defeats death (Acts 2:25–32), judges his enemies (Acts 1:20; 2:34–35; 4:25–26), and pours out the gift of the Holy Spirit, granting salvation to those who call upon his name (Acts 2:21, 33–38). Put simply, Luke's Psalms citations focus on Jesus' status as both the suffering *and* exalted king, while John's Psalms citations focus primarily on the events of Jesus' suffering and death: his betrayal (13:18), his rejection (15:25), his execution (19:24), and his thirst (19:28).

Third, John and Luke demonstrate a prophetic understanding of the Psalms in similar and different ways. John uses "fulfillment" language with ἵνα purpose clauses in each of his citation formulas to indicate the prophetic nature of the David-Jesus typologies (i.e., ἵνα πληρωθῇ in John 13:18; 15:25; 19:24/ ἵνα τελειωθῇ in John 19:28). Luke, however, appeals to "fulfillment" language only once and does so without a utilizing a purpose clause (i.e., πληρόω in Acts 1:20). But Luke, unlike John, communicates the necessity of prophetic fulfillment by means of δεῖ ("it is necessary"/Acts 1:16, 21). Additionally, John presents Jesus as a prophet (John 13:18–20) who declares the prophetic significance of Ps 41:9, while Luke presents David as a prophet inspired by the Holy Spirit to note the prophetic notion of David's psalms in Acts 1:16, 20; 2:30–31, 34–35; 4:25. Furthermore, both John and Luke point toward a specifically prophetic understanding of their typologies by relating the fulfillment of David's psalms in Jesus' life to the outworking of the divine plan and purposes of God. John does this by referencing his Psalms citations in connection with the theological theme of Jesus' "hour," which is a part of the overall context of all four John passages. Luke does this by explicitly referring to the "predetermined plan and foreknowledge of God" (Acts 2:23; 4:27–28), which relates to all five of his Psalms citations.

Fourth, when citing the Psalms, John refers to them as "Scripture" (John 13:18; 19:24, 28) and "word/Law" (John 15:25) in his introductory formulas. Similarly, Luke refers to the psalms he cites as "Scripture" in Acts 1:16, but he also overtly references "the book of Psalms" (Acts 1:20) to introduce his quotations—a feature that draws attention to his use of Psalms passages that predict events related to Jesus' life (cf. Luke 24:44 where Jesus teaches "that all things which are written about Me in . . . the Psalms must be fulfilled"). Lastly, one notices that John connects his Psalms quotations with nearby material using the adversative ἀλλά ("but"/John 13:18; 15:25) and the inferential οὖν ("therefore"/John 19:25), while Luke often uses the explanatory γάρ ("for"/ Acts 1:20; 2:25, 34; 4:27).

Implications of Study

The first implication of the use of these Psalms quotations in the select passages in John and Acts concerns the nature of biblical typology. Not only are there real points of correspondence or analogy between the OT type (i.e., David) and NT antitype (i.e., Jesus), but these correspondences introduce new, climactic truths in the progression from David to Jesus. This reveals Jesus to be the fulfillment or goal in God's redemptive plan. Most significantly, the points of typological correspondence are essentially textual, resting on clear references to the OT in each case.

The second implication of this study also pertains to the nature of biblical typology. The exegetical analysis of the Psalms quotations in John and in Acts demonstrates that the David typology possesses a predictive force in those contexts. This observation is significant because proponents of the modern view of typology sharply distinguish biblical typology from biblical prophecy, not allowing for any prospective or predictive quality in typological events. The findings in John and Acts, on the other hand, demonstrate that the concepts of typology and prophecy coalesce. At least in the passages examined here, typology and prophecy are not isolated constructs, which provides additional support for the traditional, prophetic understanding of typology.

The third implication sheds light on Jesus' hermeneutic regarding Psalms. Jesus taught the disciples in Luke 24:44–47 that Psalms predicted specific things about him and his passion that must be fulfilled. John 13:18 (Ps 41:9) and 15:25 (Ps 69:4) allow the reader to see one of the ways Jesus understood Psalms to predict his sufferings: events originally specific to David explain the biblical rationale for his own experiences. Thus, Jesus models a hermeneutic of prophetic David typology. Later John (John 19:24, 28) and Peter (Acts 1:20; 2:25–28, 34–35; 4:25–26) also apply event-based texts from David psalms to explain NT events fulfilled in Jesus, demonstrating that they practiced the hermeneutic taught and modeled by Jesus. Thus Jesus, John, and Peter collectively call attention to typology as a significant hermeneutic in understanding the NT's use of the OT, particularly Psalms, in connection to Jesus.

The fourth implication of this research is that it supports and clarifies the initial arguments offered by Moo in his study of the lament psalms in John and by Miura in his study of the psalms quoted in Acts (see chapter 1). The basic premise of both Moo and Miura is correct: prophetic David typology best explains John's and Luke's appropriation of psalms of David to Jesus.

The fifth implication of this study is Christological. Collectively, the repeat application of Davidic psalms to Jesus in John and Acts presents a specific and thoroughgoing portrait of who Jesus is in God's redemptive plan (see the summary sections in chapters 4–5). Put simply, David typology identifies Jesus as the future, new and greater David of OT expectation. The David typology reaches its fulfillment in Jesus and the events of his passion, as the goal of salvation history. Jesus not only repeats but fulfills what David's experiences were anticipating. Jesus is Israel's suffering king (like David before him), yet his death, resurrection, and exaltation show that his kingship surpasses David's. Thus, Jesus is the promised descendent of David, the divine Messiah-King of David's line, who fulfills God's eternal covenant promise to David.

Suggestions for Further Research

Additional research may build upon the findings of this study. First, the Psalms quotations in the other Gospels and in the epistles could be examined to see if prophetic David typology or some other prophetic typology best explains their uses. If a typological hermeneutic is present in those contexts, it would be helpful to identify what correspondences the NT writers highlight, how they reach fulfillment in Christ and his gospel, and how they signal the prophetic thrust of those typologies. Second, additional research on how to identify cases of OT and NT typology would be beneficial to the study of typology in general. Such work would help further to define the criteria for discerning OT types and delineate biblical principles for detecting the NT's typological understanding of OT texts.

Bibliography

Ahn, Sanghee Michael. "Old Testament Characters as Christological Witnesses in the Fourth Gospel." Ph.D. diss., Southern Baptist Theological Seminary, 2006.

Aland, Barbara, Kurt Aland, J. Karavidopoulos, C. M. Martini, and B. M. Metzger, eds. *The Greek New Testament* [UBS4]. 4th rev. ed. Stuttgart: Deutsche Bibelgesellschaft/United Bible Societies, 2001.

Aland, Kurt, Barbara Aland, Erwin Nestle, and Ebherhard Nestle, eds. *Novum Testamentum Graece* [NA27]. Nestle-Aland 27th ed. Stutgart: Deutsch Bibelgesellschaft, 1993. BibleWorks 9.

Albl, Martin C. *"And Scripture Cannot Be Broken": The Form and Function of the Early Christian Testimonia Collections*. NovTSup 96. Leiden: Brill, 1999.

Alexander, Jospeh A. *Commentary on the Acts of the Apostles: Two Volumes in One*. New York: Scribner, Armstrong & Co., 1875. Repr., Minneapolis: Klock & Klock Christian Publishing, 1980.

———. *The Psalms Translated and Explained*. Vol. 1. New York: Baker and Scribner, 1850. Repr., Forgotten Books, 2012.

Allen, David L. *Hebrews*. NAC 35. Nashville: B&H Publishing, 2010.

Allen, Leslie C. *Psalms*. WBC 21. Waco, TX: Word Books, 1983.

Amsler, Samuel. *L'Ancien Testament Dans L'Église: Essai d'herméneutique chrétienne*. Bibliothèque Thèlogique. Neuchatel: Delachaux et Niestlé, 1960.

Anderson, A. A. *The Book of Psalms*. 2 vols. NCBC. Grand Rapids: Eerdmans, 1972.

Archer, Gleason, Jr. *A Survey of Old Testament Introduction*. Rev. and exp. ed. Chicago: Moody Publishers, 2007.

Arnold, Bill T., and John H. Choi. *A Guide to Biblical Hebrew Syntax*. Cambridge: Cambridge University Press, 2003.

Arrington, French L. *The Acts of the Apostels: An Introduction and Commentary*. Peabody: Hendrickson, 1988.

Auffret, Pierre. "'Dieu sauvera Sion': Étude structurelle du Psaume LXIX." *VT* 46 (1996): 1–29.

Aune, David E. "Early Christian Biblical Interpretation." *EvQ* 41 (1969).

Baker, David L. *Two Testaments, One Bible: A Study of the Theological Relationships Between the Old & New Testaments*. Rev. ed. Downers Grove: InterVarsity Press, 1991.

Balla, Peter. "Does Acts 2:36 Represent an Adoptionist Christology." *EJT* 5 (1996): 137–142.

Bampfylde, G. "John 19:28: A Case for a Different Translation." *NovT* 11 (1969): 247–160.

Barr, James. *Old and New in Interpretation: A Study of the Two Testaments*. New York: Harper & Row, 1966.

Barrett, C. K. *A Critical and Exegetical Commentary on the Acts of the Apostles*. Vol. 1. ICC. Edinburgh: Clark, 1994.

———. *The Gospel According to St. John: An Introduction with Commentary and Notes on the Greek Text*. 2nd ed. Philadelphia: The Westminster Press, 1978.

———. "Luke/Acts." Pages 231–244 in *It is Written: Scripture Citing Scripture. Essays in Honour of Barnabas Lindars*. Edited by D. A. Carson and H. G. M. Williamson. Cambridge: Cambridge University Press, 1988.

Barrois, Georges A. *The Face of Christ in the Old Testament.* Crestwood, NY: St. Vladimir's Seminary Press, 1974.

Bassler, Jouette M. "A Man for All Seasons: David in Rabbinic and New Testament Literature." *Int* 40 (1986): 156–69.

Bateman, Herbert W., IV. "Psalm 110:1 and the New Testament." *BSac* 149 (1992): 438–53.

Bauer, David R. *The Book of Acts as Story: A Narrative-Critical Study.* Grand Rapids: Baker Academic, 2021.

Bauer, Walter, Frederick W. Danker, William F. Arndt, and F. Wilbur Gingrich. *Greek-Englich Lexicon of the New Testament and other Early Christian Literature* [BDAG]. 3rd ed. Universtiy of Chicago Press, 2000. BibleWorks 9.

Beale, G. K. "Finding Christ in the Old Testament." *JETS* 63.1 (2020): 25-50.

———. *Handbook on the New Testament Use of the Old Testament: Exegesis and Interpretation.* Grand Rapids: Baker Academic, 2012.

———. *A New Testament Biblical Theology: The Unfolding off the Old Testament in the New.* Grand Rapids: Baker Academic, 2011.

———. "Positive Answer to the Question: Did Jesus and His Followers Preach the Right Doctrine from the Wrong Texts? An Examination of the Presuppositions of Jesus' and the Apostles' Exegetical Method." Pages 387–404 in *The Right Doctrine from the Wrong Texts? Essays on the Use of the Old Testament in the New.* Edited by G. K. Beale. Grand Rapids: Baker Books, 1994.

———, ed. *The Right Doctrine from the Wrong Texts? Essays on the Use of the Old Testament in the New.* Grand Rapids: Baker Books, 1994.

Beale, G. K., and D. A. Carson, eds. *Commentary on the New Testament Use of the Old Testament.* Grand Rapids: Baker, 2007.

Beasely-Murray, George R. *John.* WBC 36. 2nd ed. Nashville: Thomas Nelson, 2000.

Belcher, Richard P., Jr. *The Messiah and the Psalms: Preaching Christ from All the Psalms.* Fearn, Scotland: Mentor, 2006.

Berding, Kenneth, and Jonathan Lunde, eds. *Three Views on the New Testament Use of the Old Testament.* Counterpoints Series. Bible & Theology. Grand Rapids: Zondervan, 2008.

Bernard, J. H. *A Critical Exegetical Commentary on the Gospel According to St. John.* Vol. 2. Edited by A. H. McNeile. Edinburgh: T. & T. Clark, 1928; reprint 1958.

Blackman, Edwin Cyril. *Biblical Interpretation.* Philadelphia: The Westminster Press, 1957.

Blass, F., A. Debrunner, and R. W. Funk. *A Greek Grammar of the New Testament and Other Early Christian Literature* [BDF]. Chicago: The University of Chicago Press, 1961.

Blomberg, Craig L. *A New Testament Theology.* Waco, TX: Baylor University Press, 2018.

Bock, Darrell L. *Acts.* BECNT. Grand Rapids: Baker Academic, 2007.

———. *Jesus according to Scripture: Restoring the Portrait from the Gospels.* Grand Rapids: Baker Academic, 2002.

———. "Luke, Gospel of." Pages 495–510 in *DJG.* Edited by Joel B. Green and Scot McKnight. Downers Grove: InterVarsity, 1992.

———. *Proclamation from Prophecy and Pattern: Lucan Old Testament Christology.* JSNTSup 12. Sheffield: JSOT Press, 1987.

———. "Proclamation from Prophecy and Pattern: Luke's Use of the Old Testament for Christology and Mission." Pages 280–307 in *The Gospels and the Scriptures of Israel*. Edited by Craig A. Evans and W. Richard Stegner. JSNTSup 104. SSEJC 3. Sheffield, Eng: Sheffield Academic Press, 1994.

———. *A Theology of Luke and Acts: God's Promised Program, Realized for All Nations*. BTNT. Grand Rapids: Zondervan, 2012.

———. "Use of the Old Testament in the New." Pages 97–114 in *Foundations for Biblical Interpretation: A Complete Library of Tools and Resources*. Edited by D. S. Dockery, K. A. Mathews and R. B. Sloan. Nashville: Broadman & Holman, 1994.

Borchert, Gerald L. *John*. NAC 25B. Nashville: B&H Publishing Group, 2002.

Bornkamm, Heinrich. *Luther and the Old Testament*. Translated by Eric W. Gritsch and Ruth C. Gritsch. Philadelphia: Fortress Press, 1969.

Bowling, Andrew. "לֵב." Pages 466–467 in *TWOT*. Vol. 1. Edited by R. Laird Harris, Gleason L. Archer, Jr., and Bruce K. Waltke. Chicago: Moody Press, 1980.

Brawley, Robert L. "An Absent Complement and Intertextuality in John 19:28–29." *JBL* 112 (1993): 427–443.

Bray, Gerald. "Allegory." Pages 34–36 in *DTIB*. Edited by Kevin J. Vanhoozer. Grand Rapids: Baker Academics, 2005.

———. *Biblical Interpretation: Past & Present*. Downers Grove: InterVarsity Press, 1996.

Briggs, Charles A., and Emilie G. Briggs. *A Critical and Exegetical Commentary on The Book of Psalms*. Vol. 1. ICC. Edinburgh: T. & T. Clark, 1906. Repr., Nabu Press.

———. *A Critical and Exegetical Commentary on the Book of Psalms*. Vol. 2. ICC. Edinburgh: T. & T. Clark, 1907.

Brooks, James A. *Mark*. NAC 23. Nashville: B&H Publishing Group, 1991.

Brown, Raymond E. *The Gospel According to John (1–12)*. AB 29. Garden City, NY: Doubleday, 1966.

———. *The Gospel According to John (13–21)*. AB 29A. Garden City, NY: Doubleday, 1970.

Broyles, Craig C. *Psalms*. NIBC. Edited by Robert L. Hubbard Jr. and Robert K. Johnston. Peabody: Hendrickson, 1999.

Bruce, F. F. *The Acts of the Apostles: The Greek Text with Introduction and Commentary*. 3rd rev. and enl. ed. Grand Rapids: Eerdmans, 1990.

———. *The Book of Acts*. NICNT. Rev. ed. Grand Rapids: Eerdmans, 1988.

———. *The Gospel of John: Introduction, Exposition, and Notes*. Grand Rapids: Eerdmans, 1983.

Brueggemann, Dale A. "The Evangelists and the Psalms." Pages 263–278 in *Interpreting the Psalms: Issues and Approaches*. Edited by David Firth and Philip S. Johnston. Downers Grove: IVP Academic, 2005.

Brueggemann, Walter. "Psalm 109: Three Times 'Steadfast Love'." *WW* 5 (1985): 144–154.

Bullock, C. Hassell. *Encountering the Book of Psalms: A Literary and Theological Introduction*. Grand Rapids: Baker Academic, 2001.

Bultmann, Rudolph. *The Gospel of John: A Commentary*. Edited by R. W. N. Hoare and J. K. Riches. Translated by G. R. Beasely-Murray. Oxford: Basil Blackwell, 1971.

———. "Ursprung und Sinn Der Typologie als hermeneutische Methode." *TLZ* (1950): 205–212.

Burge, Gary M. *John*. NIVAC. Grand Rapids: Zondervan, 2000.

Calvin, John. *Acts 1–13*. CNTC 6. Grand Rapids: Eerdmans, 1995.

———. *Commentary on the Book of Psalms*. Translated by James Anderson. Vols. 4–6 of *Calvin's Commentaries*. Grand Rapids: Baker Book House, 1981.

———. *Commentary on the Gospel according to John*. Translated by William Pringle. Vol. 2. Grand Rapids: Eerdmans, 1949.

———. *The Four Last Books of Moses*. Vol. 4 of *Calvin's Commentaries*. Translated by Charles W. Bingham. Grand Rapids: Baker Book House, 1981.

Carson, D. A. *The Gospel According to John*. PNTC. Grand Rapids: Eerdmans, 1991.

———. "John and the Johannine Epistles." Pages 245–264 in *It is Written: Scripture Citing Scripture. Essays in Honour of Barnabas Lindars*. Edited by D. A. Carson and H. G. M. Williamson. Cambridge: Cambridge University Press, 1988.

———. "Matthew." Pages 3–599 in EBC 8. Edited by Frank E. Gaebelein. Grand Rapids: Zondervan, 1984.

Carson, D. A., and Douglas J. Moo. *An Introduction to the New Testament*. 2nd ed. Grand Rapids: Zondervan, 2005.

Carson, D. A., and H. G. M. Williamson, eds. *It is Written: Scripture Citing Scripture. Essays in Honour of Barnabas Lindars*. Cambridge: Cambridge University Press, 1988.

Casey, Michael. *Sacred Reading: The Ancient Art of Lectio Divina*. Liguori, MO: Triumph Books, 1995.

Cho, Youngmo, and Hyung Dae Park. *Acts, Part One: Introduction and Chapters 1-12*. NCCS. Eugene, OR: Cascade Books, 2019.

Conzelmann, Hans. *Acts of the Apostles*. Translated by James Limburg, A. Thomas Kraabel and Donald H. Juel. Hermeneia—A Critical and Historical Commentary on the Bible. Philadelphia: Fortress, 1987.

Cosgrove, Charles H. "The Divine ΔΕΙ in Luke-Acts: Investigations into the Lukan Understanding of God's Providence." *NovT* 26 (1984): 168–190.

Craigie, Peter C. *Psalms 1–50*. WBC 19. Waco, TX: Word Books, 1983.

Cullmann, Oscar. *Salvation in History*. Translated by Sidney G. Sowers. Tübingen: J. C. B. (Paul Siebeck), 1965.

Currid, John D. "Recognition and Use of Typology in Preaching." *RTR* 53 (1994): 113–129.

Dahood, Mitchell. *Psalms I*. AB 16. Garden City, NY: Doubleday, 1965.

———. *Psalms II*. AB 17. Garden City, NY: Doubleday, 1968.

———. *Psalms III*. AB 17A. Garden City, NY: Doubleday, 1970.

Daly-Denton, Margaret. *David in the Fourth Gospel: The Johannine Reception of the Psalms*. AGJU 47. Leiden: Brill, 2000.

Daniélou, Jean. *From Shadows to Reality: Studies in Biblical Typology of the Fathers*. London: Burns & Oates, 1960.

Davidson, Richard M. *Typology in Scripture: A study of hermeneutical τύπος structures*. AUSDDS 2. Berrien Springs, MI: Andrews University Press, 1981.

Davis, Barry C. "Is Psalm 110 A Messianic Psalm?" *BSac* 157 (2000): 160–173.

Davis, Ellen F. "Exploding the Limits: Form and Function in Psalm 22." *JSOT* 53 (1992): 93–105.

Delitzsch, F. *Psalms*. Translated by Francis Bolton. 3 vols. Commentary on the Old Testament 5. Repr., Grand Rapids: Eerdmans, 1976.

Delling, G. "τέλος κτλ." Pages 49-87 in *TDNT*. Vol. 8. Edited by Gerhard Kittel and Gerhard Friedrich. Translated by Geoffrey W. Bromiley. Grand Rapids: Eerdmans, 1972.

Dietzfelbinger, Christian. *Das Evangelium nach Johannes*. Vol. 2. Zürcher Bibelkommentare. Zürich: Theologischer Verlag, 2001.

Doble, Peter. "The Psalms in Luke-Acts." Pages 83–117 in *The Psalms in the New Testament*. Edited by Steve Moyise and Maarten J. J. Menken. London: T & T Clark, 2004.

Dockery, David S. "Martin Luther's Christological Hermeneutics." *GTJ* 4 (1983): 189–203.

Dodd, C. H. *According to the Scriptures: The Sub-Structure of New Testament Theology*. London: Harper Collins, 1953. Repr., Eugene, OR: Wipf & Stock.

———. *The Interpretation of the Fourth Gospel*. Cambridge: Cambridge University Press, 1970.

Dormeyer, Detlev, and Florinzio Galindo. *Die Apostelgeschichte: Ein Kommentar für die Praxis*. Stuttgart: Katholisches Bibelwerk, 2003.

Drobner, Hubertus R. *The Fathers of the Church: A Comprehensive Introduction*. Translated by Siegfried S. Schatzmann. Peabody: Hendrickson Publishers, 2007.

Dunn, James D. G. *Unity and Diversity in the New Testament: An Inquiry into the Character of Earliest Christianity*. 3rd ed. London: SCM Press, 2006.

Dupont, Jacques. "'Assis à la droite de Dieu': l'interprétation du Ps 110, 1 dans le Nouveau Testament." Pages 210–295 in *Nouvelles Études sur Les Actes Des Apôtres*. LD 118. Paris: Éditions du Cerf, 1984.

———. "L'interpretation des Psaumes dans les Actes des Apôtres." Pages 283–307 in Études sur les Actes des Apôtres. LD 45. Paris: Éditions du Cerf, 1967.

———. "L'utilisation apologétique de l'Ancien Testament dans les discours des Actes." Pages 245–282 in Études sur les Actes des Apôtres. LD 45. Paris: Éditions du Cerf, 1967.

———. "La destinée de Judas prophétisée par David." Pages 309–320 in Études sur les Actes des Apôtres. LD 45. Paris: Éditions du Cerf, 1967.

Durham, John I. "*Psalms*." Pages 153–464 in BBC 8. Edited by Clifton J. Allen. Nashville: Broadman Press, 1971.

Efird, James M., ed. *The Use of the Old Testament in the New and Other Essays: Studies in Honor of William Franklin Stinespring*. Durham: Duke University Press, 1972.

Eichrodt, Walther. "Is Typological Exegesis an Appropriate Method?" Pages 224–245 in *Essays on Old Testament Hermeneutics*. Edited by Claus Westermann. Richmond: John Knox 1963.

Elliger, E. and W. Rudolph, eds. *Biblia Hebraica Stuttgartensia*. 4th rev. ed. Stuttgart: Deutsche Bibelgesellschaft, 1990. BibleWorks 9.

Ellis, E. Earle. Foreword to *Typos: The Typological Interpretation of the Old Testament in the New*, by Leonhard Goppelt, ix–xx. Translated by Donald H. Madvig. Eugene, OR: Wipf and Stock, 2002.

———. *The Old Testament in Early Christianity: Canon and Interpretation in the Light of Modern Research*. Grand Rapids: Baker Book House, 1992.

———. *Paul's Use of the Old Testament*. Eugene: Wipf and Stock, 1981.

Evans, Craig A. "Obduracy and the Lord's Servant: Some Observations on the Use of the Old Testament in the Fourth Gospel." Pages 221–236 in *Early Jewish and Christian Exegesis: Studies in Memory of William Hugh Brownlee*. Edited by Craig A. Evans and William F. Stinespring. SPHS 10. Atlanta: Scholars Press, 1987.

———. "Old Testament in the Gospels." Pages 579–590 in *DJG*. Edited by Joel B. Green and Scot McKnight. Downers Grove: InterVarsity Press, 1992.

———. "The Old Testament in the New." Pages 130–145 in *The Face of New Testament Studies: A Survey of Recent Research*. Edited by Scot McKnight and Grant R. Osborne,. Grand Rapids: Baker Academic, 2004.

———. "Prophecy and Polemic: Jews in Luke's Scriptural Apologetic." Pages 171–211 in *Luke and Scripture: The Function of Sacred Tradition in Luke-Acts*. Edited by Craig A. Evans and James A. Sanders. Minneapolis: Fortress, 1993.

Evans, Craig A., and W. Richard Stegner, eds. *The Gospels and the Scriptures of Israel*, JSNTSup 104. SSEJC 3. Sheffield, England: Sheffield Academic Press, 1994.

Fairbairn, Patrick. *Typology of Scripture: Two Volumes in One*. 2 vols. New York: Funk & Wagnalls, 1900. Repr., Grand Rapids: Kregel, 1989.

Farrer, Austin. "Important Hypothesis Reconsidered." *ExpTim* 67 (May 1956): 228–231.

Fitzmeyer, Joseph A. "David, 'Being Therefore A Prophet . . .'." *CBQ* 34 (1972): 332–339.

Foulkes, Francis. *The Acts of God: A Study of the Basis of Typology in the Old Testament*. London: The Tyndale Press, 1958.

Fowler, Arthur B. "Hand." Pages 333–334 in *ZPBD*. Edited by Merrill C. Tenney. Grand Rapids: Zondervan, 1964.

France, R. T. *Jesus and the Old Testament: His Application of the Old Testament Passages to Himself and His Mission*. Vancouver, British Columbia: Regent College Publishing, 1998.

———. "Relationship between the Testaments." Pages 666–672 in *DTIB*. Edited by Kevin J. Vanhoozer. Grand Rapids: Baker Academic, 2005.

Freed, Edwin D. *Old Testament Quotations in the Gospel of John*. Leiden: E. J. Brill, 1965.

Frei, Hans W. *The Eclipse of the Biblical Narrative: A Study in Eighteenth and Nineteenth Century Hermeneutics*. New Haven: Yale University Press, 1974.

Friedrich, Gerhard. "προφήτης κτλ." Pages 828–861 in *TDNT*. Vol 6. Edited by Gerhard Kittel and Gerhard Friedrich. Translated by Geoffrey W. Bromiley. Grand Rapids: Eerdmans, 1968.

———. "προφήτης κτλ." Page 835 in *TWNT*. Vol 6. Edited by Gerhard Kittel and Gerhard Friedrich. Stuttgart: Kohlhammer, 1965.

Fritsch, Charles T. "Biblical Typology." *BSac* 103 (Oct–Dec 1946): 293–305; 418–430.

———. "Biblical Typology." *BSac* 104 (Jan–Mar 1947): 87–100; 214–222.

Futato, Mark D. *Interpreting the Psalms: An Exegetical Handbook*. Handbooks for Old Testament Exegesis. Edited by David M. Howard Jr. Grand Rapids: Kregel Publications, 2007.

Garland, David E. *1 Corinthians*. BECNT. Grand Rapids: Baker Academic, 2003.

———. "John 18–19: Life through Jesus' Death." *RevExp* 85 (1988): 485–499.

———. "The Fulfillment Quotations in John's Account of the Crucifixion." Pages 229–250 in *Perspectives on John: Method and Interpretation in the Fourth Gospel*. Edited by R. B. Sloan and Mikeal C. Parson. Lewiston, NY: Edwin Mellen Press, 1993.

Gaventa, Beverly R. *The Acts of the Apostles*. ANTC. Nashville: Abingdon, 2003.

Gesenius, Wilhelm. *Gesenius' Hebrew Grammar*. Edited and enlarged by E. Kautzsch. Translated by A. E. Cowley. 2nd ed. Oxford: Clarendon Press, 1910; Repr., Mineola, NY: Dover Publication, 2006.

Gibbs, J. G. "Hour." Page 769 in *ISBE*. Vol. 2. Edited by Geoffrey W. Bromiley. Rev. ed. Grand Rapids: Eerdmans, 1982.

Glenny, W. Edward. "Typology: A Summary of the Present Evangelical Discussion." *JETS* 40 (1997): 627–638.

Godet, Frederic Louis. *Commentary on John's Gospel*. Grand Rapids: Kregel Publications, 1978.

Goldingay, John. *Psalms 1–41*. Vol. 1. BCOTWP. Grand Rapids: Baker Academic, 2006.

Goldsworthy, Graeme. *Preaching the Whole Bible as Christian Scripture: The Application of Biblical Theology to Expository Preaching*. Grand Rapids: Eerdmans, 2000.

Goppelt, Leonhard. "τύπος κτλ." Pages 246–259 in *TDNT*. Vol 8. Edited by Gerhard Kittel and Gerhard Friedrich. Translated by Geoffrey W. Bromiley. Grand Rapids: Eerdmans, 1972.

———. *Typos: The Typological Interpretation of the Old Testament in the New*. Translated by Donald H. Madvig. Eugene, OR: Wipf and Stock, 2002.

Goulder, M. D. *Type and History in Acts*. London: S. P. C. K., 1964.

Grant, Robert M., and David Tracy. *A Short History of the Interpretation of the Bible*. Rev. 2nd ed. Philadelphia: Fortress Press, 1984.

Greef, Wulfert de. "Calvin as Commentator on the Psalms." Pages 85–106 in *Calvin and the Bible*. Edited by Donald K. McKim. Cambridge: Cambridge University Press, 2006.

Green, J. B. "Death of Jesus." Pages 146–163 in *DJG*. Edited by Joel B. Green and Scot McKnight. Downers Grove: InterVarsity, 1992.

Green, Joel B. *The Gospel of Luke*. NICNT. Grand Rapids: Eerdmans, 1997.

Greidanus, Sidney. *Preaching Christ from the Old Testament: A Contemporary Hermeneutical Method*. Grand Rapids: Eerdmans, 1999.

Gren, Conrad R. "Piercing the Ambiguities of Psalm 22:16 and the Messiah's Mission." *JETS* 48 (2005): 283–299.

Grogan, Geoffrey W. *Psalms*. THOTC. Grand Rapids: Eerdmans, 2008.

Grundmann, Walter. "δεῖ." Pages 21–25 in *TDNT*. Vol 2. Edited by Gerhard Kittel. Translated by Geoffrey W. Bromiley. Grand Rapids: Eerdmans, 1964.

Guillet, Jacques. "Les Exégèsis d'Alexandrie et d'Antioch. Conflit ou malentendu?" *RevScRel* 34 (1947): 257–302.

Guinot, Jean-Noël. "La typologie comme technique herméneutique." Pages 1–34 in *Figures de l'Ancien Testament chez les Pères*. Edited by Pierre Maraval. Cahiers de Biblia Patristica 2. Strasbourg: Centre d'Analyse et de Documentation Patristiques, 1989.

Gundry, Stanley M. "Typology as a Means of Interpretation: Past and Present." *JETS* 12 (1969): 233–240.

Gunkel, Herman. *The Psalms: A Form-Critical Introduction.* Translated by Thomas M. Horner. Facet Books. BS 19. Philadelphia: Fortress 1967.

Guthrie, Donald. *New Testament Theology.* Downers Grove: Inter-Varsity, 1981.

Haenchen, Ernst. *The Acts of the Apostles: A Commentary.* Translated by B. Noble and G. Shinn. Revised by R. Wilson. Philadelphia: The Westminster Press, 1971.

———. *John: A Commentary on the Gospel of John Chapters 7–21.* Vol. 2. Hermeneia—A Critical and Historical Commentary on the Bible. Philadelphia: Fortress Press, 1984.

Hall, Christopher. *Reading Scripture with the Church Fathers.* Downers Grove, IL: InterVarsity, 1998.

Hamid-Khani, Saeed. *Revelation and Concealment of Christ: A Theological Inquiry into the Elusive Language of the Fourth Gospel.* WUNT 2. Reihe 120. Tübingen: Mohr Siebeck, 2000.

Hamilton, Victor P. "māshîaḥ." Pages 530–532 in *TWOT*. Vol. 1. Edited by R. Laird Harris, Gleason L. Archer, Jr., and Bruce K. Waltke. Chicago: Moody Press, 1980.

Hanse, H. "λαγχάνω." Pages 1–2 in *TDNT*. Vol. 4. Edited by Gerhard Kittel. Translated by Geoffrey W. Bromiley. Grand Rapids: Eerdmans, 1967.

Harris, M. J. "Resurrection, General." Pages 581–582 in *NDT*. Edited by Sinclair B. Ferguson, David F. Wright, and J. I. Packer. Downers Grove, IL: IVP Academic, 1988.

Harris, R. Laird. "she'ôl." Pages 892–893 in *TWOT*. Vol. 2. Edited by R. Laird Harris, Gleason L. Archer, Jr., and Bruce K. Waltke. Chicago: Moody Press, 1980.

Harrison, Roland K. "Gall." Pages 392–393 in *ISBE*. Vol. 2. Edited by Geoffrey W. Bromiley. Rev. ed. Grand Rapids: Eerdmans, 1982.

———. "Vinegar." Page 1225 in *New Bible Dictionary.* Edited by I. Howard Marshall, A. R. Millard, J. I. Packer, and D. J. Wiseman. 3rd ed. (Leicester: Inter-Varsity, 1996).

Hasel, Gerhard F. *New Testament Theology: Basic Issues in the Current Debate.* Grand Rapids: Eerdmans, 1978.

Heckert, Jakob K. *Discourse Functions of Conjoiners in the Pastor Epistles.* Dallas: SIL International, 1991.

Heidland, H. W. "ὄξος." Pages 288–289 in *TDNT*. Vol. 5. Edited by Gerhard Kittel. Translated by Geoffrey W. Bromiley. Grand Rapids: Eerdmans, 1967.

Heine, Ronald E. *Reading the Old Testament with the Ancient Church: Exploring the Formation of Early Christian Thought.* Grand Rapids: Baker Academic, 2007.

Heinemann, Mark H. "An Exposition of Psalm 22." *BSac* 147 (1990): 286–308.

Hengel, Martin. "The Old Testament in the Fourth Gospel." Pages 380–395 in *The Gospels and the Scriptures of Israel.* Edited by Craig A. Evans and W. Richard Stegner. JSNTSup 104. SSEJC 3. Sheffield, Eng: Sheffield Academic Press, 1994.

Hengstenberg, E. W. *Commentary on the Gospel of St. John.* Vol. 2. Edunburg: T&T Clark, 1865. Repr., Minneapolis: Klock & Klock Christian Publishers, Inc., 1980.

Hoffman, Mark George Vitalis. "Psalm 22 (LXX 21) and the Crucifixion of Jesus." Ph.D. diss., Yale University, 1996.

Hofmann, J. C. K. von. *Interpreting the Bible.* Translated by Christian Preus. Minneapolis: Augsburg Publishing House, 1959.

Holmgren, Fredrick C. *The Old Testament and the Significance of Jesus: Embracing Change—Maintaining Christian Identity*. Grand Rapids: Eerdmans, 1999.

Hoskins, Paul M. *Jesus as the Fulfillment of the Temple in the Gospel of John*. Eugene, OR: Wipf & Stock, 2006.

———. *That Scripture Might Be Fulfilled: Typology and the Death of Christ*. Longwood, FL: Xulon 2009.

Hoskyns, Edwyn Clement. *The Fourth Gospel*. 2nd rev. ed. London: Faber and Faber Limited, 1947.

Hubbard, David Allan. "John 19:17–30." *Int* 43 (1989): 397–401.

Hugenberger, G. P. "Introductory Notes on Typology." Pages 331–341 in *The Right Doctrine from the Wrong Texts? Essays on the Use of the Old Testament in the New*. Edited by G. K. Beale. Grand Rapids: Baker Books, 1994.

Hughes, H. Dale. "Salvation-History as Hermeneutic." *EvQ* 48 (1976): 79–89.

Hummel, Horace D. "The Old Testament Basis of Typological Interpretation." *BR* 9 (1964): 38–50.

Isbell, Barbara Ann. "The Past is Yet to Come: Typology in the Apocalypse." Ph.D. diss., Southwestern Baptist Theological Seminary, 2013.

Jervell, Jacob. *The Theology of the Acts of the Apostles*. New Testament Theology. Cambridge: Cambridge University Press, 1996.

Jipp, Joshua W. "Luke's Scriptural Suffering Messiah: A Search for Precedent, a Search for Identity." *CBQ* 72 (2010): 255–274.

Johnson, Elliott E. "Hermeneutical Principles and the Interpretation of Psalm 110." *BSac* 149 (1992): 428–437.

Johnson, Luke T. *The Acts of the Apostles*. SP 5. Collegeville, MN: Liturgical Press, 1992.

Johnston, P. S. "Afterlife." Pages 1–5 in *DOTP*. Edited by Mark J. Boda and J. Gordon McConville. Downers Grove, IL: IVP Academic, 2012.

Joüon, P., and T. Muraoka. *A Grammar of Biblical Hebrew: Third Reprint of the Second Addition, with Corrections*. SubBi 27. Rome: Gregorian & Biblical Press, 2011.

Juel, Donald. *Messianic Exegesis: Christological Interpretation of the Old Testament in Early Christianity*. Philadelphia: Fortress Press, 1988.

Justin Martyr. *Dialogue with Trypho*. Vol 6 of *The Fathers of the Church*. Translated by Thomas B. Falls. New York: Christian Heritage, 1948.

Kaiser, Walter C. *The Uses of the Old Testament in the New*. Chicago: Moody Press, 1985.

———. "יָשַׁב (yāshab) sit, remain, dwell." Pages 411–413 in *TWOT*. Vol. 1. Edited by R. Laird Harris, Gleason L. Archer, Jr., and Bruce K. Waltke. Chicago: Moody Press, 1980.

Kannengiesser, Charles. *Handbook of Patristic Exegesis: The Bible in Ancient Christianity*. Vol. 1. Edited by D. Jeffrey Bingham. Leiden: Brill, 2004.

Keener, Craig S. *Acts*. New Cambridge Bible Commentary. New York: Cambridge University Press, 2020.

———. *The Gospel of John: A Commentary*. Vol. 2. Peabody: Hendrickson, 2003.

———. *The IVP Bible Background Commentary: New Testament*. Downers Grove: InterVarsity, 1993.

Keil, C. F. *Minor Prophets*. 2 Vols. Translated by James Martin. *Commentary on the Old Testament* 10. Repr., Grand Rapids: Eerdmans, 1977.

Kellum, L. Scott. *Exegetical Guide to the Greek New Testament: Acts*. Nashville: B&H Academic, 2020.

Kidner, Derek. *Psalms 1–72: An Introduction and Commentary*. TOTC 15. Edited by Donald J. Wiseman. London: Inter-Varsity 1973. Repr., Downers Grove, IL: Inter-Varsity, 2008.

———. *Psalms 73–150: A Commentary on Books III–V of the Psalms*. TOTC. Leicester, England: Inter-Varsity, 1975.

Kilpatrick, G. D. "Some Quotations in Acts." Pages 81–97 in *Les Actes des Apôtres: Traditions, rédaction, théologie*. Edited by Jacob Kremer. BETL 48. Gembloux: J. Duculot; Louvain: Leuven University Press, 1979.

Kirk, J. R. Daniel. "Conceptualising Fulfilment in Matthew." *TynBul* 59 (2008): 77–98.

Koehler, Ludwig, Walter Baumgartner, and Johann J. Stamm. *The Hebrew and Aramaic Lexicon of the Old Testament [HALOT]*. Translated and edited by Mervyn E. J. Richardson. 5 vols. Leiden: Brill, 1994–2000. BibleWorks 9.

Kollmann, Bernd. "Der Priesterkönig zur Rechten Gottes (Ps 110)." Pages 157–170 in *Die Verheißung des Neuen Bundes: Wie alttestamentliche Texte im Neuen Testament fortwirken*. Edited by Bernd Kollmann. Biblisch-theologische Schwerpunkte 35. Göttingen: Vandenhoeck & Ruprecht, 2010.

Koskenniemi, Erkki, Kirsi Nisula, and Jorma Toppari. "Wine Mixed with Myrrh (Mark 15.23) and Crurifragium (John 19.31–32): Two Details of the Passion Narratives." *JSNT* 27 (2005): 379–391.

Köstenberger, Andreas J. *John*. BECNT. Grand Rapids: Baker Academic, 2004.

Köstenberger, Andreas J. "John." Pages 415-512 in *CNTUOT*. Edited by G. K. Beale and D. A. Carson. Grand Rapids: Baker Academic, 2007.

———. *A Theology of John's Gospel and Letters: Biblical Theology of the New Testament*. Grand Rapids: Zondervan, 2009.

———. *A Theology of John's Gospel and Letters: The Word, the Christ, the Son of God*. BTNT. Grand Rapids: Zondervan, 2009.

Krodel, Gerhard A. *Acts*. ACNT. Minneapolis Augsburg, 1986.

Kugel, James L., and Rowan A. Greer. *Early Biblical Interpretation*. Philadelphia: Westminster, 1986.

Labuschagne, C. J. "נתן ntn to give." Pages 774–791 in *TLOT*. Vol. 2. Edited by Ernst Jenni and Claus Westermann. Translated by Mark E. Biddle. Peabody, MA: Hendrickson, 1997.

Ladd, George Eldon. *A Theology of the New Testament*. Edited by Donald A. Hagner. Rev. ed. Grand Rapids: Eerdmans, 1974. Repr., 1993.

Lagrange, M.-J. *Évangile selon Saint Jean*. 5th ed. Paris: J. Gabalda, 1936.

Lampe, G. W. H. "The Reasonableness of Typology." Pages 9–38 in *Essays on Typology*. SBT. Naperville, IL: Alec R. Allenson 1957.

Lange, Harvey D. "The Relationship Between Psalm 22 and the Passion Narrative." *CTM* 43 (1972): 610–621.

Larkin, William J., Jr. *Acts*. IVPNTCS. Downers Grove: InterVarsity, 1995.

Le Donne, Anthony. *The Historiographical Jesus: Memory, Typology, and the Son of David*. Waco, TX: Baylor University Press, 2009.

Lee, Gary A. "Vinegar." Page 987 in *ISBE*. Vol. 4. Edited by Geoffrey W. Bromiley. Rev. ed. Grand Rapids: Eerdmans, 1982.

Legarth, Peter V. "Typology and its Theological Basis." *EuroJTh* 5 (1996): 143–154.

Lenski, R. C. H. *The Interpretation of St. John's Gospel*. Columbus, OH: Lutheran Book Concern, 1942.

Leupold, H. C. *Exposition of the Psalms*. Columbus, OH: The Wartburg Press, 1959. Repr., Grand Rapids: Baker Book House, 1969.

Levinsohn, Stephen H. *Discourse Feathers of New Testament Greek: A Coursebook on the Information Structure of New Testament Greek*. 2nd ed. Dallas: SIL International, 2000.

Lincoln, Andrew T. *The Gospel According to Saint John*. BNTC. New York: Hendrickson, 2005.

Lindars, Barnabas. *The Gospel of John*. NCBC. London: Oliphants, 1972.

―――. *New Testament Apologetic: The Doctrinal Significance of the Old Testament Quotations*. Philadelphia: The Westminster Press, 1961.

Lindblom, Johannes. "Erwägungen zu Psalm 16." *VT* 24 (1974): 187–195.

Longenecker, Richard N. "The Acts of the Apostles." Pages 207–573 in EBC 9. Edited by Frank E. Gaebelein. Grand Rapids: Zondervan, 1981.

―――. *Biblical Exegesis in the Apostolic Period*. 2nd ed. Grand Rapids: Eerdmans, 1999.

―――. "Negative Answer to the Question 'Who is the Prophet Talking About?' Some Reflections on the New Testament's Use of the Old." Pages 375–386 in *The Right Doctrine from the Wrong Texts: Essays on the Use of the Old Testament in the New*. Edited by G. K. Beale. Grand Rapids: Baker Books, 1994.

Longmann, Tremper, III. *How to Read the Psalms*. Grand Rapids: InterVarsity 1988.

Losie, L. A. "Triumphal Entry." Pages 854–859 in *DJG*. Edited by Joel B. Green and Scot McKnight. Downers Grove: InterVarsity 1992.

Louw, Johannes P., and Eugene A. Nida, eds. *Greek-English Lexicon of the New Testament* [Louw-Nida]. 2nd ed. New York: United Bible Societies, 1988. BibleWorks 9.

Luther, Martin. *Lectures on Titus, Philemon, and Hebrews*. Vol. 29 of *Luther's Works*. Edited by Jaroslav Pelikan. Translated by Walter A. Hansen. Saint Louis: Concordia Publishing House, 1968.

―――. *Sermons on the Gospel of St. John: Chapters 1–4*. Vol. 22 of *Luther's Works*. Edited by Jaroslav Pelikan. Translated by Martin H. Bertram. Saint Louis: Concordia Publishing House, 1957.

MacGregor, G. H. C. *The Gospel of John*. MNTC. New York: Harper and Brothers, 1928.

Maclaren, Alexander. *The Psalms*. Vol. 1. The Expositor's Bible. London: Hodder & Stoughton, 1898.

MacRae, George W. "The Fourth Gospel and Religionsgeschichte." *CBQ* 32 (1970): 13–24.

Maier, Gerhard. *Biblical Hermeneutics*. Translated by Robert W. Yarbrough. Wheaton, IL: Crossway Books, 1994.

Markus, R. A. "Presuppositions to the Typological Approach to Scripture." *Church Quarterly Review* 158 (October–December 1957): 442–451.

Marshall, I. Howard. "Acts." Pages 513–606 in *CNTUOT*. Edited by G. K. Beale and D. A. Carson. Grand Rapids: Baker Academic, 2007.

———. *Acts: An Introduction and Commentary*. TNTC 5. Inter-Varsity: Downers Grove, 1980.

———. "An Assessment of Recent Developments." Pages 1–21 in *It is Written: Scripture Citing Scripture. Essays in Honour of Barnabas Lindars*. Edited by D. A. Carson and H. G. M. Williamson. Cambridge: Cambridge University Press, 1988.

Mays, James L. "Prayer and Christology: Psalm 22 as Perspective on the Passion." *ThTo* 42 (1985): 322–331.

McCracken, Victor. "The Interpretation of Scripture in Luke-Acts." *ResQ* 41 (1999): 193–210.

McKown, Edgar Monroe. "The Influence of the Psalms upon the Ideas of the New Testament." Ph.D. diss., Boston University, 1932.

Menken, Maarten J. J. *Old Testament Quotations in the Fourth Gospel: Studies in Textual Form*. CBET 15. Kampen, the Netherlands: Kok Pharos, 1996.

Merrill, Eugene H. "Royal Priesthood: An Old Testament Messianic Motif." *BSac* 150 (1993): 50–61.

Metzger, Bruce M. *A Textual Commentary on the Greek New Testament: A Companion Volume to the United Bible Societies' Greek New Testament (Fourth Revised Edition)*. 2nd ed. Stuttgart: United Bible Societies, 1994.

———. "The Formulas Introducing Quotations of Scripture in the NT and the Mishnah." *JBL* 70 (1951): 297–307.

Michaelis, W. "ὁράω κτλ." Pages 315–382 in *TDNT*. Vol. 5. Edited by Gerhard Kittel and Gerhard Friedrich. Translated by Geoffrey W. Bromiley. Grand Rapids: Eerdmans, 1967.

Michaels, J. Ramsey. *The Gospel of John*. NICNT. Grand Rapids: Eerdmans, 2010.

Mickelsen, A. Berkeley. *Interpreting the Bible*. Grand Rapids: Eerdmans, 1963.

Millard, Matthias. *Die Komposition des Psalters: Ein formgeschichtlicher Ansatz*. FAT 9. Tubigen: J. C. B. Mohr (Paul Siebeck), 1994.

Miller, Patrick D., Jr. *Interpreting the Psalms*. Philadelphia: Fortress Press, 1986.

Miura, Yuzuru. *David in Luke-Acts: His Portrayal in the Light of Early Judaism*. WUNT 2. Reihe 232. Tübingen: Mohr Siebeck, 2007.

Moloney, Francis J. *The Gospel of John*. SP 4. Collegeville, MN: The Liturgical Press, 1998.

Moo, Douglas J. *The Old Testament in the Gospel Passion Narratives*. Sheffield, Eng.: The Almond Press, 1983.

———. "The Problem of *Sensus Plenior*." Pages 175–212 in *Hermeneutics, Authority, and Canon*. Edited by D. A. Carson and John D. Woodbridge. Grand Rapids: Zondervan, 1986.

Morgan, Richard. "Fufillment in the Fourth Gospel: The Old Testament Foundations." *Int* 11 (1957): 155–165.

Morris, Leon. *The Gospel according to Matthew*. PNTC. Grand Rapids: Eerdmans, 1992.

———. *The Gospel according to John*. NICNT. Rev. ed. Grand Rapids: Eerdmans, 1995.

———. *New Testament Theology*. Grand Rapids: Zondervan, 1986.

Motyer, J. A. "The Psalms." Pages in *New Bible Commentary: 21st Century Edition*. Edited by D. A. Carson, R. T. France, J. A. Motyer, and G. J. Wenham. Downers Grove: InterVarsity, 1994.

Moule, C. F. D. "Fulfillment-Words in the New Testament: Use and Abuse." *NTS* 14 (1967–68): 293–320.

———. *An Idiom Book of New Testament Greek*. 2nd ed. Cambridge: Cambridge University Press, 1959.

Mowinckel, Sigmund. *The Psalms in Israel's Worship*. 2 vols. Translated by D. R. Ap-Thomas. Rev. ed. Grand Rapids: Eerdmans; Dearborn, MI: Dove Booksellers, 2004.

Moyise, Steve. *The Old Testament in the New: An Introduction*. London: T&T Clark International, 2001.

Müller, H. "Type, Pattern." Pages 903–907 in *NIDNTT*. Vol. 3. Edited by Colin Brown. Grand Rapids: Zondervan, 1978.

Müller, Mogens. "The Reception of the Old Testament in Matthew and Luke-Acts: From Interpretation to Proof from Scripture." *NovT* 43 (2001): 315–330.

Nash, Steven Boyd. "Kingship and the Psalms in the Fourth Gospel." Ph.D. diss., Westminster Theological Seminary, 2000.

Newman, Barclay M., and Eugene A. Nida. *A Handbook on the Acts of the Apostles*. Helps for Translators. New York: United Bible Societies, 1972.

———. *A Handbook on the Gospel of John*. Helps for Translators. London: United Bible Societies, 1980.

Nicole, Roger. "The New Testament Use of the Old Testament." Pages 13–28 in *The Right Doctrine from the Wrong Texts? Essays on the Use of the Old Testament in the New*. Edited by G. K. Beale. Grand Rapids: Baker Books, 1994.

Novick, Tzvi. "Succeeding Judas: Exegesis in Acts 1:15–26." *JBL* 129 (2010): 795–799.

O'Keefe, John J., and R. R. Reno. *Sanctified Vision: An Introduction to Early Christian Interpretation of the Bible*. Baltimore: The John Hopkins University Press, 2005.

Obermann, A. *Die christologische Erfüllung der Schrift im Johannesevangelium: Eine Untersuchung zur johanneischen Hermeneutik anhand der Schriftzitate*. Tubingen: J. C. B. Mohr, 1995.

Orchard, Helen C. *Courting Betrayal: Jesus as Victim in the Gospel of John*. JSNTSup 161. Gender, Culture, Theory 5. Sheffield: Sheffield Academic Press, 1998.

Oropeza, B. J. "Judas' Death and Final Destiny in the Gospels and Earliest Christian Writings." *Neotestamenica* 44.2 (2010): 342–361.

Osborne, G. R. "Type; Typology." Pages 930–931 in *ISBE*. Vol. 4. Edited by Geoffrey W. Bromiley. Grand Rapids: Eerdmans, 1988.

Ostmeyer, Karl-Heinrich. *Taufe und Typos: Elemente und Theologie der Tauftypologien in 1. Korinther 10 und 1. Petrus 3*. WUNT 2. Reihe 118. Tübingen: Mohr Siebeck, 2000.

Oswalt, John N. "בָּשָׂר." Pages 135–136 in *TWOT*. Vol. 1. Edited by R. Laird Harris, Gleason L. Archer, Jr., and Bruce K. Waltke. Chicago: Moody Press, 1980.

Palmer, D. W. "The Literary Background of Acts 1:1–14." *NTS* 33 (1987): 427–438.

Patterson, Richard D. "Psalm 22: From Trial to Triumph." *JETS* 47 (2004): 213–233.

Paulien, Jon. "Elusive Allusions: The Problematic Use of the Old Testament in Revelation." *BR* 33 (1988): 37–53.

Pesch, Rudolf. *Die Apostelgeschichte*. 2 vols. EKKNT. Zurich: Benziger; Neukirchen-Vluyn: Neukirchener Verlag, 1986.

Peterson, David G. *The Acts of the Apostles*. PNTC. Eerdmans: Grand Rapids, 2009.

Polhill, John B. *Acts: An Exegetical and Theological Exposition of Holy Scripture*. NAC 26. Nashville: Broadman, 1992.

Popkes, Enno Edzard. *Die Theologie der Liebe Gottes in den johanneischen Schriften: Zur Semantik der Liebe und zum Motivkreis des Dualismus*. WUNT 2. Reihe 197. Tübingen: Mohr Siebeck, 2005.

Porter, Stanley E. "Can Traditional Exegesis Enlighten Literary Analysis of the Fourth Gospel? An Examination of the Old Testament Fulfilment Motif and the Passover Theme." Pages 396–428 in *The Gospels and the Scriptures of Israel*, edited by Craig A. Evans and W. Richard Stegner. JSNTSup 104. SSEJC 3. Sheffield, Eng: Sheffield Academic Press, 1994.

———., ed. *Hearing the Old Testament in the New Testament*. Grand Rapids: Eerdmans, 2006.

———. *Idioms of the Greek New Testament*. 2nd ed. Biblical Languages: Greek 2. London: Sheffield Academic Press, 1999.

———. "The Use of the Old Testament in the New Testament: A Brief Comment on Method and Terminology." Pages 79–96 in *Early Christian Interpretation of the Scriptures of Israel: Investigations and Proposals*. Edited by Craig A. Evans and James A. Sanders. JSNTSup 148. SSEJC 5. Sheffield: Sheffield Academic Press, 1997.

Poythress, Vern S. *The Shadow of Christ in the Law of Moses*. New Jersey: P&R Publishing, 1991.

———. "The Use of the Intersentence Conjunctions *De, Oun, Kai,* and Asyndeton in the Gospel of John " *NovT* 26 (1984): 312–340.

Preuschen, Erwin. *Die Apostelgeschichte*. HNT 4:1. Tübingen: Mohr [Siebeck], 1912.

Puckett, David L. *John Calvin's Exegesis*. Columbia Series in Reformed Theology. Louisville: Westminster John Knox Press, 1995.

Rad, Gerhard von. "Typological Interpretation of the Old Testament." Pages 17–39 in *Essays on Old Testament Hermeneutics*. Edited by Claus Westermann. Richmond: John Knox, 1963.

Rahlfs, Alfred, ed. *Septuaginta*. Stuttgart: Württembergische Bibelanstalt/Deutsche Bibelgesellschaft, 1935 in BibleWorks 9.

Ramaroson, Léonard. "Immortalité et Résurrection dans les Psaumes." *ScEs* 36 (1984): 287–295.

Ramm, Bernard. *Protestant Biblical Interpretation: A Textbook of Hermeneutics* 3rd rev. ed. Grand Rapids: Baker Book House, 1970.

Reinbold, Wolfgang. "Die Klage des Gerechten (Ps 22)." Pages 143–156 in *Die Verheißung des Neuen Bundes: Wie alttestanmentliche Texte im Neuen Testament forwirken*. Edited by Bernd Kollmann. Biblisch-theologische Schwerpunkte 35. Göttingen: Vandenhoeck & Ruprecht, 2010.

Rese, Martin. "Die Funktion der alttestamentlichen Zitate und Anspielungen in den Reden der Apostelgeschichte." Pages 61–79 in *Les Actes des Apôtres: Traditions, rédaction, théologie*. Edited by J. Kremer. BETL, no. 48. Leuven: Leuven University Press, 1979.

Ridderbos, Herman N. *The Gospel according to John: A Theological Commentary*. Grand Rapids: Eerdmans, 1992.

Rogerson, J. W., and J. W. McKay. *Psalms*. 3 vols. CBC. London: Cambridge University Press, 1977.

Roloff, Jürgen. *Die Apostelgeschichte*. NTD 5. Göttingen and Zürich: Vandenhoeck & Ruprecht, 1988.

Ross, Allen P. *A Commentary on the Psalms*. 2 vols. KEL. Grand Rapids: Kregel, 2011–2013.

Runge, Steven E. *Discourse Grammar of the Greek New Testament: A Practical Introduction for Teaching and Exegesis*. Peabody: Hendrickson Publishers, 2010.

Ryken, Leland, James C. Wilhoit, and Tremper Longmann III, eds. "Scepter." Page 764 in *DBI*. Downers Grove, IL: InterVarsity Press, 1998.

Sanders, J. N. *A Commentary on the Gospel according to St. John*. BNTC. London: Adam & Charles Black, 1968.

Sanders, Jack T. "The Prophetic Use of the Scriptures in Luke-Acts." Pages 191–198 in *Early Jewsih and Christian Exegesis: Studies in Memory of William Hugh Brownlee*. Edited by Craig A. Evans and William F. Stinespring. SPHS. Atlanta: Scholars Press, 1987.

Scacewater, Todd A. "The Predictive Nature of Typology in John 12:37-43." *WTJ* 75 (2013): 129-143.

Schlatter, Adolf. "Atheistische Methoden in der Theologie." Pages 134–150 in *Zur Theologie des Neuen Testaments und zur Dogmatik*. Edited by Ulrich Luck. Munich: C. Kaiser, 1969.

———. *Der Evangelist Johannes, Wie er spricht, denkt und glaubt: Ein Kommentar zum vierten Evangelium*. 3rd ed. Stuttgart: Calwer Verlag, 1960.

Schmitt, A. "Ps 16, 8–11 als Zeugnis der Auferstehung in der Apg." *BZ* 17 (1973): 229–248.

Schnackenburg, Rudolf. *The Gospel according to St. John*. Vol. 3. Translated by Kevin Smyth and Cecily Hastings et al. New York: Crossroad, 1982.

Schreiner, Thomas R. *New Testament Theology: Magnifying God in Christ*. Grand Rapids: Baker Academic, 2008.

Schrenk, Gottlob. "γράφω κτλ." Pages 743–773 in *TDNT*. Vol. 1. Edited by Gerhard Kittel. Translated by Geoffrey W. Bromiley. Grand Rapids: Eerdmans, 1964.

Schuchard, Bruce G. *Scripture Within Scripture: The Interrelationship of Form and Function in the Explicit Old Testament Citations in the Gospel of John*. SBLDS 133. Atlanta: Scholars Press, 1992.

Schunack, G. "τύπος." Pages 372-376 in *EDNT*. Vol. 3. Edited by Horst Balz and Gerhard Schneider. Grand Rapids: Eerdmans, 1993.

Schweizer, Eduard. "The Concept of the Davidic 'Son of God' in Acts and Its Old Testament Background." Pages 186–193 in *Studies in Luke-Acts: Essays presented in honor of Paul Schubert Buckingham Professor of New Testament Criticism and*

Intepretation at Yale University. Edited by Leander E. Keck and J. Louis Martyn. London: S.P.C.K., 1966.

Shepherd, Jerrry Eugene. "The Book of Psalms as the Book of Christ: A Christo-Canonical Approach to the Book of Psalms." Ph.D. diss., Westminster Theological Seminary, 1995.

Smith, D. Moody. "The Setting and Shape of a Johannine Narrative Source." *JBL* 95 (1976): 231–241.

Soards, Marion L. *The Speeches in Acts: Their Content, Context, and Concerns*. Louisville: Westminster John Knox Press, 1994.

Spicq, Ceslas. "παραδίδωμι." Pages 13–23 in *TLNT*. Vol. 3. Edited and translated by James D. Ernest. Peabody: Hendrickson, 1994.

Stählin, Gustav. *Die Apostelgeschichte*. NTD 5. Göttingen: Vandenhoeck & Ruprecht, 1980.

Stauffer, E. "ἵνα." Pages 323–333 in *TDNT*. Vol. 3. Edited by Gerhard Kittel and Gerhard Friedrich. Translated by Geoffrey W. Bromiley. Grand Rapids: Eerdmans, 1965.

Steinmetz, David C. "John Calvin as an Interpreter of the Bible." Pages 282–291 in *Calvin and the Bible*. Edited by Donald K. McKim. Cambridge: Cambridge University Press, 2006.

Stek, John H. "Biblical Typology Yesterday and Today." *CTJ* 5 (1970): 133–162.

Stevick, Daniel B. *Jesus and His Own: A Commentary on John 13–17*. Grand Rapids: Eerdmans, 2011.

Steyn, G. J. "LXX-Sitate in die Petrus- en Paulusredes van Handelinge." *SK* 16 (1995): 125–141.

Stolz, F. "צִיּוֹן ṣiyyôn Zion." Pages 1071–1076 in *TLOT*. Vol. 2. Edited by Ernst Jenni and Claus Westermann. Translated by Mark E. Biddle. Peabody: Hendrickson, 1997.

Stuart, D. K. "Sheol." Page 472 in *ISBE*. Vol. 4. Edited by Geoffrey W. Bromiley. Fully Revised. Grand Rapids: Eerdmans, 1988.

Stuhlmacher, Peter. *Vom Verstehen des Neuen Testament: Eine Hermeneutik*. 2nd ed. GNT 6. Göttingen: Vandenhoeck & Ruprecht, 1986.

Tannehill, Robert C. *The Narrative Unity of Luke-Acts: A Literary Interpretation*. Volume 2: *The Acts of the Apostles*. Minneapolis: Fortress, 1990.

———. *The Narrative Unity of Luke-Acts: A Literary Interpretation*. Volume One: *The Gospel according to Luke*. Minneapolis: Fortress Press, 1986.

Tate, Marvin E. *Psalms 51–100*. WBC 20. Dallas: Word Books, 1990.

Tenney, Merril C. "John." Pages 3–203 in EBC 9. Edited by Frank E. Gaebelein. Grand Rapids: Zondervan, 1981.

Tenney, Merrill C. *Interpreting Revelation: A Reasonable Guide to Understanding the Last Book in the Bible*. Peabody, MA: Hendrickson, 1957.

Terry, Milton S. *Biblical Hermeneutics: A Treatise on the Interpretation of the Old and New Testaments*. Hunt & Eaton, 1890. Repr., Eugene, OR: Wipf & Stock, 1999.

Thayer, Joseph H. *A Greek-English Lexicon of the New Testament* [Thayer's]. Translated and rev. and enl. by Joseph H. Thayer. 1889. Repr., International Bible Translators, 1998–2000. BibleWorks 9.

Tholuck, Augustus. *Commentary on the Gospel of John*. Translated by Charles P. Krauth. New York: Sheldon and Company, 1867.

Thomas, John Christopher. *Footwashing in John 13 and the Johannine Community.* JSNTSup 61. Sheffield: JSOT Press, 1991.

Torm, F. *Hermeneutik des Neuen Testaments.* Göttingen: Vandenhoek and Ruprecht, 1930.

Tostengard, Sheldon. "Psalm 22." *Int* 46 (1992): 167–170.

Tournay, Raymond J. "Note sur le Psaume 22.17." *VT* 23 (1973): 111–112.

Toy, Crawford Howell. *Quotations in the New Testament.* New York: Charles Scribner's Sons, 1884.

Trotter, Andrew W., Jr. *Interpreting the Epistle to the Hebrews.* GNTE. Grand Rapids: Baker Books, 1997.

Trull, Gregory V. "An Exegesis of Psalm 16:10." *BSac* 161 (2004): 304–321.

———. "Peter's Interpretation of Psalm 16:8–11 in Acts 2:25–32." *BSac* 161 (2004): 432–448.

Turner, George Allen, and Julius R. Mantey. *The Gospel According to John.* ECB 4. Grand Rapids: Eerdmans, 1964.

VanGemeren, Willem A. "Psalms." Pages in 3–880. EBC 5. Edited by Frank E. Gaebelein. Grand Rapids: Zondervan, 1991.

Virkler, Henry A., and Karelynne Gerber Ayayo. *Hermeneutics: Principles and Processes of Biblical Interpretation.* 2nd ed. Grand Rapids: Baker Academic, 1981.

Vos, Geerhardus. *The Teaching of the Epistle to the Hebrews.* Grand Rapids: Eerdmans, 1956.

Wallace, Daniel B. *Greek Grammar Beyond the Basics: An Exegetical Syntax of the New Testament.* Grand Rapids: Zondervan, 1996.

Waltke, Bruce K. "A Canonical Process Approach to the Psalms." Pages 3–18 in *Tradition and Testament: Essays in Honor of Charles Lee Feinberg.* Edited by John S. Feinberg and Paul D. Feinberg. Chicago: Moody Press, 1981.

———. "נֶפֶשׁ." Pages 587–591 in *TWOT*. Vol. 2. Edited by R. Laird Harris, Gleason L. Archer, Jr., and Bruce K. Waltke. Chicago: Moody Press, 1980.

Waltke, Bruce K., James M. Houston, and Erika Moore. *The Psalms as Christian Worship: A Historical Commentary.* Grand Rapids: Eerdmans, 2010.

Waltke, Bruce K., and M. O'Connor. *An Introduction to Biblical Hebrew Syntax.* Winona Lake, IN: Eisenbrauns, 1990.

Walton, John H., Victor H. Matthews, and Mark W. Chavalas. *The IVP Bible Background Commentary: Old Testament.* Downers Grove: InterVarsity, 2000.

Weiser, Alfons. *Die Apostelgeschichte: Kapitel 1–12.* Ökumenischer Taschenbuchkommentar zum Neuen Testament 5.1. Gütersloh: Gütersloher Verlagshaus Mohn, 1981.

Weiss, D. Bernhard. *Das Johannes-Evangelium.* 9th ed. KEK 2. Göttingen: Vandenhoeck und Ruprecht, 1902.

———. *Das Johannesevangelium: als einheitliches Werk.* Berlin: Trowitzsch & Sohn, 1912.

Wengst, Klaus. *Das Johannesevangelium.* Vol. 2. TKNT 4. Stuttgart: Verlag W. Kohlammer, 2001.

Wenham, John. *Christ and the Bible.* Eugene, OR: Wipf & Stock, 1994.

Westcott, B. F. *The Gospel According to St. John: The Authorized Version with Introduction and Notes.* Grand Rapids: Eerdmans, 1950.

Westermann, Claus. *The Psalms: Structure, Content, and Message.* Translated by Ralph D. Gehrke. Minneapolis: Augsburg Publishing House, 1980.

Wilcox, Max. "The Judas-Tradition in Acts 1.15–26." *NTS* 19 (1972–73): 438–452.

Williams, David J. *Acts.* NIBC 5. Grand Rapids: Baker Books, 1990.

Wilson, Gerald H. *Psalms Volume 1.* NIVAC. Grand Rapids: Zondervan, 2002.

Witherington, Ben, III. *John's Wisdom: A Commentary on the Fourth Gospel.* Louisville: Westminster John Knox Press, 1995.

Witkamp, L. T. "Jesus' Thirst in John 19:28–30: Literal or Figurative?" *JBL* 115 (1996): 489–510.

Wolff, Hans Walter. "The Hermeneutics of the Old Testament." *Int* 15 (1961): 439–472.

Woollcombe, K. J. "The Biblical Origins and Patristic Development of Typology." Pages 39–75 in *Essays on Typology.* SBT. Naperville, IL: Alec R. Allenson, 1957.

Wright, Christopher J. H. *Knowing Jesus Through the Old Testament.* Downers Grove: InterVarsity Press, 1992.

Wright, David P. "Ritual Anaology in Psalm 109." *JBL* 113 (1994): 385–404.

Young, Frances M. "Patristic Biblical Interpretation." Pages 566–571 in *DTIB*. Edited by Kevin J. Vanhoozer. Grand Rapids: Baker Academic, 2005.

Zahn, Theodor. *Das Evangelium des Johannes.* Kommentar zum Neuen Testament 4. Leipzig: Deichert, 1908.

Zwiep, Arie W. *Judas and the Choice of Matthias: A Study on Context and Concern of Acts 1:15–26.* WUNT 2. Reihe 187. Tübingen: Mohr Siebeck, 2004.

Index

Genesis
    28:12   42

Exodus
    4:22–23   49
    12:40–41   49
    12:46   50
    16:4   42
    16:15   42

Numbers
    9:12   50
    21:6–9   27, 42

Deuteronomy
    18:15   42
    18:15–19   54

2 Samuel
    7:5–16   153
    7:12–16   146
    7:13–16   143
    7:14   143
    23:2   140

1 Kings
    1:48   146
    5:5   146
    8:20   146

1 Chronicles
    28:5–6   146
    29:1   146
    29:23   146

2 Chronicles
    6:10   146

Psalms
    2   61, 153, 155, 156, 160
    2:1   158
    2:1–2 (LXX)   152
    2:1–2   151–163, 167–168
    2:1–3   153, 155
    2:2   154, 157, 158
    2:3   155
    2:7   143
    15:8–11 (LXX)   124–125
    16   5, 6, 126, 134, 162
    16:1–4   126

16:1–7	126	41:5–8	65
16:5–7	126	41:5–9	65
16:8	127	41:11–12	65, 70
16:8–11	124–140, 161–162, 167–168	41:9	63-77, 106, 167–168
		41:10 (MT)	64
16:9	127	68	5
16:9–11	127	68:5 (LXX)	77, 78
16:10	127–140	68:22 (LXX)	97, 98, 101
16:11	125, 131	68:26	110
21:19 (LXX)	84–85	69	5, 8, 66, 77, 78–79, 97, 98, 100, 101, 111, 162
22	5, 7, 8, 61, 62, 66, 85, 86, 88, 89, 98		
22:1–5	86	69:1–2	79
22:1–10	86	69:1–4	79
22:1–21	85	69:1–28	79
22:6–10	86	69:3	79
22:11	86, 92	69:4	77–84, 98, 99, 101, 106, 111, 116, 167–168
22:11–21	86		
22:12–17	87	69:5 (MT)	78
22:12–21	86	69:14	101
22:15	97	69:16–21	116
22:18	61, 84-96, 106, 167–168	69:18–19	101
		69:19	116
22:19 (MT)	84, 85	69:20	99
22:19–21	87	69:21	97–106, 167–168
22:20	91	69:22 (MT)	97, 98
22:21	87	69:22–28	101, 111
22:22–31	85	69:25	109–124, 159, 162, 167–168
22:24	92		
31	5	69:26	80, 116
34	5, 8	69:26 (MT)	110
34:19 (LXX)	77	69:29	116
35	77	69:29–36	79
35:19	77	80:17	148
40:10 (LXX)	64	89:20–24	148
41	5, 8, 65, 66, 67	108:8 (LXX)	110
41:1–3	65	109	5, 162
41:4	65	109:1 (LXX)	141
41:4–10	65	109:1	112

Index

109:1–5	112
109:2–4	113
109:2–5	113
109:4–5	113, 116
109:6–8	113
109:6–19	113
109:6–20	112, 113
109:8	109–124, 159, 162
109:9–10	113
109:11	113
109:12–13	113
109:19	113
109:20	113
109:21–29	112
109:30–31	112
110	5, 6, 141, 144, 152
110:1	133, 140–151, 162, 167–168
110:1–3	149
110:2	146
110:4	142
110:5–6	149
132:11	139

Isaiah
9:6–7	54
40–55	54
66	134

Jeremiah
23:5–6	54
30:9	54
33:14–26	54

Ezekiel
34:23–24	54
37:24–25	54
40–48	54

Daniel
12:1–2	134

Hosea
11:1	48

Joel
2:28–32	132

Zechariah
12:10	50
13:7	

Matthew
1:22	48
2:13–23	49
2:15	48
2:17	49
4:14	48
8:17	48
12:17	48
12:42	147
21:4–5	48
22:43–45	140
27:9	49

Mark
12:36	150
12:36–37	140

Luke
11:31	147
20:42–44	140
24	41
24:25–27	40
24:44	107, 115, 163, 169
24:44–47	4, 40, 115, 170

John

1:21	42
1:29	92
1:41	67
1:49	67
1:51	42
2:17	66, 77, 97
2:24–25	69
3:14–15	26, 42, 59
4:19	42
5:39	41
5:39–47	41
5:45	41
5:46	41
5:47	42
6:14	42
6:32	42
6:64	69, 73
6:70–71	69, 70, 73
7:26	67
7:41–42	67
7:40	42
9:22	67
10:17–18	92
10:24–25	67
10:34	84
11:27	67
12:13–15	67, 75
12:23	74
12:25	81
12:27	74, 75
12:37–38	74
12:38–40	75, 105
13	4, 9, 11–12, 63, 66, 67, 69
13–21	83
13:1	67, 69, 74, 83
13:2	70
13:3	69
13:9	71
13:10–11	69
13:18	2, 3, 63-77, 79, 84, 87, 93, 94, 100, 103, 105–107, 165–170
13:18–20	169
13:19	76–77
13:21	70
13:27	70
15	4, 9, 11–12, 63
15:18–19	80
15:20	81
15:22–24	81
15:23–24	81
15:24–25	82
15:25	2, 3, 63, 66, 75, 77-84, 87, 93, 94, 97, 98, 100, 103, 105–107, 111, 165–170
15:26–27	81
16:4	81
17:12	75
18–19	88, 100
18:4	88
18:19–24	88
18:33	88
18:33–19:22	67
18:36	88
18:37	88
18:38	92
18:39	88
19	4, 9, 11–12, 63, 102
19:1–3	88
19:4	92
19:6	92
19:7	89
19:10–11	89
19:12	88
19:14	66

Index

19:14–15	88	2:14–26	148
19:15	88	2:17–31	132
19:19	88	2:21	148, 149, 169
19:21	88	2:22	137
19:23–24	93	2:22–24	137
19:24	2, 3, 63, 75, 84–96, 97, 100, 103, 106–107, 165–170	2:23	136, 161, 169
		2:23–31	150
		2:24	137, 146
19:25	94–95	2:24–36	147
19:28	2, 3, 63, 66, 75, 77, 96, 97–107, 111, 165–170	2:25	133, 137, 168, 169
		2:25–28	2, 3, 109, 124–140, 162, 165–170
19:28–30	97, 101	2:25–32	169
19:29–30	98	2:25–36	133
19:30	91	2:27	133, 160, 161
19:31–35	49	2:27–28	160
19:33–38	88	2:29	134, 138, 168
19:36	49, 50, 75	2:29–31	134
19:36–37	49, 74, 96, 105	2:29–32	133, 138
19:37	50, 75, 88	2:30	135, 139, 140, 146
20:30	94, 105	2:30–31	124, 133, 138, 146, 150, 168, 169
20:30–31	95		
		2:30–32	135
Acts		2:31	132, 133, 136, 138, 139, 140, 148, 151
1	4, 10–12, 115, 163		
1:15–20	115	2:31–32	146
1:15–26	119	2:31–33	146
1:16	115, 116, 117, 119, 122, 123, 124, 140, 151, 159, 168, 169	2:32	140
		2:32–33	150
		2:33	145, 149
1:16–20	115	2:33–34	133, 146
1:16–22	120	2:33–36	145
1:18	118	2:33–38	148, 169
1:18–19	117	2:34	140, 145, 149, 150, 168, 169
1:20	2, 3, 109–124, 151, 159, 162, 165–170		
		2:34–35	2, 3, 109, 140–151, 162, 165–170
1:21	116, 119, 122, 169		
1:21–26	119	2:35	148, 149
2	4, 6, 10–12, 163	2:36	133, 150

2:38–39	149	2:9–10	148
4	4, 6, 10–12, 163	Hebrews	
4:24	151	1:1–2	23
4:25	140, 151, 153, 155, 158, 159, 168	1:5–13	148
4:25–26	2, 3, 109, 151–163, 165–170	2:5–8	149
		2:13	44
4:25–28	155, 162	3:7–4:13	44
4:26	156, 157, 159	5:6	44
4:27	155, 156, 157, 159, 169	5:10	44
4:27–28	152, 155, 169	6:20	44
4:28	136, 159, 161	7:1–28	44
13:33–37	140	8:5	51
13:35–37	138	9:1–10	44
13:36	136	9:8	44
20:27	136	9:9	44
		9:10–11	44
Romans		9:24	51
1:1–4	147	10:1	43
5:12–21	51	10:13	149
5:14	18, 50–52		
		1 Peter	
1 Corinthians		3:18–22	51
5:7	50	3:21	18, 50–52
10:1–13	51	3:22	149
10:6	18, 50–52		
10:11	50–52	2 Peter	
15:25	149	3:22	148
2 Corinthians		1 John	
3:14–16	23	2:23	81
Ephesians		Revelation	
1:20–21	148	1:7	50
1:22	149		
		2 Maccabees	
Colossians		7	134
1:15–20	148		
1:15–26	148		

www.ingramcontent.com/pod-product-compliance
Lightning Source LLC
Chambersburg PA
CBHW072006110526
44592CB00012B/1222